Niles'

Florida

The First War

"Such a man is a true patriot, and as long as the United States shall preserve its independence, so long shall the name of Hezekiah Niles…be revered, and his character quoted as an example for imitation, by all who desire to obtain that highest and noblest title: a good and honest man, in private life; in public; a pure disinterested patriot."

- Quote from *The Baltimore Sun*, upon the death of Hezekiah Niles.

Compiled and Edited by

David D. Fowler

—•⟫⊖◉ ⊖⟪⟪•—

Chez Ndeko Publishing / Panama City, Florida

Niles' Florida: The First War, is volume 1 of a five-volume set of books that highlight the history of Florida as outlined in the Niles' Weekly Register. Inquiries for purchases may be addressed to *Chez Ndeko Publishing*, 4019 Torino Way, Panama City, FL 32405, or visit http://www.fowlerlibrary.com

[Note: *Niles' Florida: Acquiring the New Territory* (ISBN-13: 978-1490592923) is superceded by *Niles' Florida: The First War* (Volume 1) and *Niles' Florida: Defending Our Actions* (Volume 2).]

Front Cover: Designed by David Fowler.

Includes image inset of *Andrew Jackson* by Charles Willson Peale (15 Apr 1741 - 22 Feb 1827); Oil on canvas, 1819, in the Masonic Library and Museum of Pennsylvania, Philadelphia. On display in National Portrait Gallery exhibition, "1812: A Nation Emerges," June 15 through Jan. 27, 2013. Digital image on the Smithsonian Institute web site.

Inset of *Map of Florida* compiled and drawn from various actual surveys and observations by Charles Vignoles, 1823, from the Map Division of the Library of Congress.

Reading Level:
- *Flesch-Kincaid Grade Level*: 19
- *Flesch Reading Ease*: 26
- Recommended for mature audience

Fowler, David D.
  Niles' Florida: The First War.

ISBN: 0988923130 (Volume 1)
ISBN: 0988923181 (5 Volume Set)
ISBN-13: 978-0-9889231-3-3 (Volume 1)
ISBN-13: 978-0-9889231-8-8 (5 Volume Set)

Library of Congress Control Number: 2015901424

[Chez Ndeko Publishing, Panama City, Florida]

—•》》ⓔ🌐ⓔ《《《•—

Niles' Florida:
The First War

Reflections of Florida

The attention of his majesty's government has of late been called to the measures pursued by the United States for the military occupation of West Florida.

— British Ambassador Foster,
July 2, 1811.

The President is desirous of availing the public of your services, in a concern of much delicacy and of high importance to the United States.

— Secretary of State to Georgia Governor Mitchell,
April 10, 1812

The storm which has been so long gathering, and so often predicted by honest, respectable citizens, has at length fallen on our infant and defenceless settlements.

— Letter, Fort Mimms massacre, along the West Florida frontier,
September 4, 1813.

The Lower Creeks have lately manifested a very unquiet disposition. They have already forgotten that we refused to exterminate them, as we might, when they exterminate our people, as they could. They have again listened to the seducer, and are acting in a way that will go far to reconcile their best friends to their extermination, which, I fervently say, may heaven forbid!

— Commentary on British influence over Southern Indians,
May 31, 1817.

I have seen in the newspapers, with equal surprize and indignation, the attempts that have been made to lull the public mind into a belief, that the hostile Indians desire peace, and are willing to lay down their arms! Sir, there will be no peace until those Indians are severely chastised.

— Major General Edmund P. Gaines,
January 23, 1818.

━─»»❂◉❂«««─

Introduction

September 7, 1811 through August 22, 1818

Early 19th century in America was a time of turmoil. Issues that propelled the ultimate destiny of the nation into the future included the plight of the American Indian, pressure to end slavery, concern over foreign intervention by Great Britain, and last, but not least, the insatiable quest by Americans for new territories.

The catalyst for expansion was largely ignited on May 2, 1803, with the sale of Louisiana by the French to the United States. Although comprising nearly one-fourth of modern-day America, the U.S. government in the early 19th century had little idea of what the vast Louisiana territory contained. Indeed, only a few weeks after the purchase, the U.S. Congress appropriated funds to send an expedition, led by Meriwether Lewis and William Clark, to learn more about the vast geography, its resources, and inhabitants.

It was no coincidence that in less than a generation, the U.S. government selected the nearly barren Oklahoma territory as the final stop in the forced removal of American Indians from east of the Mississippi River. By 1829, President Andrew Jackson called for the removal of the native inhabitants in his annual State of the Union address. The Indian Removal Act was passed by Congress on May 26, 1830 in spite of sharp controversy. It led to the reluctant, and at times forced, emigration of tens of thousands of America's original inhabitants to the West.

The Seminole Indians in Florida, and their African allies, did not willingly accept the deceitful policies enacted by the Great White Father. Spanish Florida was seen as a land of golden opportunity with land grabbers using every conceivable ploy to remove the native inhabitants from their lands. As European immigrants discovered the favorable climate of Florida, they began maneuvering to push the Seminole Indians out of the peninsula.

On August 24, 1814, British forces occupied Washington, DC, and burned the White House and the Capitol. Now they were attempting to break the supply lines coming out of the newly acquired American port of New Orleans. In preparation, British troops established operational bases in Spanish Florida at Pensacola and Apalachicola, where they recruited and trained Indians and Africans.

Since the arrival of the first African slaves in America, escape to Florida was, and continued to be, a primary means of gaining freedom from the imposed rigors of the Anglo-Saxons in the New World. Between the late 18th century to early 19th century, a large African population inhabited the banks of the Apalachicola River, the Suwanee River, and the St. John's River, cultivating the land, raising livestock, and living in relative freedom. These people were unconstrained, as long as they lived under the flag of His Catholic Majesty, the king of Spain. The unique servitude relationship they developed with the Seminole Indians reinforced their safety from the slave grabbers that tried to enter the Spanish territory.

When the time came, African warriors joined forces with the Seminole Indians in self defense of the American attacks. The early forays (1817-1818) into the Spanish territory of Florida by the Americans were nothing more than retaliatory expeditions to suppress the often violent defiance by the Indians and Africans living along the frontier. Andrew Jackson's military actions in Florida put an end to the Seminole uprisings along the frontier.

The Indians and their African allies escaped and evaded across the St. Juan (Suwanee) River into the desolate swamps and lands further south. Jackson saw no need to pursue them, essentially calling the end of the campaign and sending most of the military forces under his command back to their homes.

Niles Weekly Register

Hezekiah Niles was the quintessential news publisher of his day. The *Niles Weekly Register* had a broad circulation around the country, including a large number of prominent political leaders. No other weekly news organization covered the birth of the state of Florida quite like Niles. This was essentially an encyclopedic resource on Florida's birth as a state of our Union. The *Niles Weekly Register* was published between September 1811 through June 1849, under three different titles with four different editors.

Niles' reporting on events, first, in Spanish East and West Florida, and, subsequently, the Florida territory was comprehensive and indepth. His weekly newspaper was in essence a time capsule, replete with documentation on Florida, much of which has largely been neglected in our schools during the ensuing two hundred year period.

A few words about this book would be useful to the casual reader. The collection of articles is placed in chronological order, as shown by the *Volume Number, Date of Publication*, and *Page Number.* Topic headings have been added to facilitate the flow of the ongoing story. You can read the book entries much as you would read a newspaper. You will soon discover the articles that are of interest to you and will desire to find more related articles. Trust me, its there.

For the serious researcher (or if you are looking for specific information), the *epub* version is an essential tool that allows you to search for virtually anything in the book. You can easily cross-reference the volume, date, and page number to locate the same information in this hard-copy version.

You will observe that the grammar and style of the early 19th century was somewhat different from our modern day authors. Don't let this lull you into the belief that these people from our past were any less intelligent. Indeed, if anything, it is quite the opposite. The reading level of the *Niles Weekly Register* surpasses much of the contemporary national news reporting.

It is interesting to note that, while modern day publications are printed and distributed as quickly as you can type on a computer keyboard, the process was not so simple in Niles' day. Each letter was meticulously placed on a printing board, one at a time, backwards, and errors did occur.

Dates were often described in terms of *instant, ultimo,* or *proximo,* or their abbreviations. These originate from Latin, and are shortened forms of *instante mense* (in the current month), *ultimo mense* (in the previous month), and *proximo mense* (in the next month).

I can fairly state that most of what is included in this book is taken exactly as it was published in Niles. Any variation from Niles that is grammatically incorrect by today's standard is by my doing. Compiling more than a million words on Florida's history is, quite frankly, a challenge.

As a final note, I should tell you that *Niles' Florida* is for a mature audience. In addition to a high reading level, it contains detailed, and often times very gruesome, accounts of events that took place just down the road from many of us. After reading about the things that occurred in Florida's past, a walk through the woods will give you a new perspective about who came here before you.

Map of Early 19th Century Florida

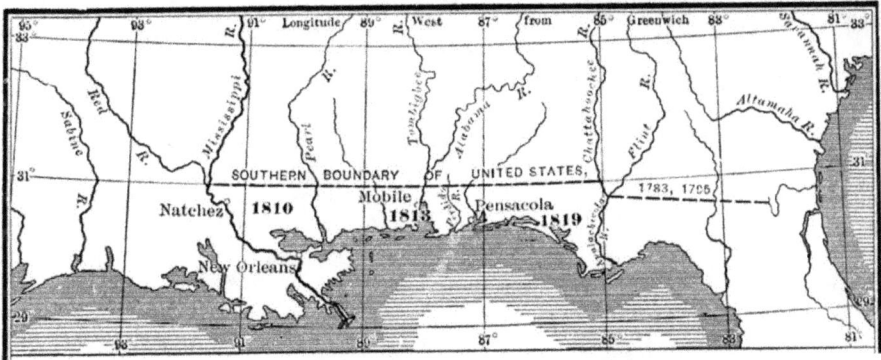

In 1810 Madison by proclamation annexed West Florida to the Perdido; but it was occupied only to the Pearl. In 1812 this part of West Florida was admitted to the Union as a portion of Louisiana. In 1813 Mobile and the country to the Perdido was occupied. In 1819 by treaty Spain ceded all territory claimed by her, east of the Mississippi, to the United States. [Map Source: Albert Bushnell Hart, LL.D., *The American Nation: A History*, Volume 12, (New York, NY: Harper and Brothers, 1906), page 142]

—»»)Ə◉Ə«««—

Let's begin the story of Florida in the year 1811.

Along the eastern seaboard of the United States, the British government has harassed the Americans by blockading our sea ports, capturing American vessels and impressing our merchant sailors into the Royal Navy against their will. In both the north, on the Canadian border, and in the south, along the coastal area of Spanish Florida, British military forces have attempted to incite American Indian tribes to counter American operations. African exiles, particularly in Spanish Florida, are encouraged to join in the grand scheme of countering American incursion in the Spanish territories.

Diplomatic communications begin to flow between the United States and Britain over the issue of the Floridas. The British purportedly have a diplomatic interest in the Spanish territories along the southern border of the United States. Alleging a special relationship with Spain, Augustus Foster, the British Minister Plenipotentiary to the United States, addresses a formal inquiry to James Monroe, the United States Secretary of State.

As we will soon see, however, things are not what they may appear on either side. Both the Americans and the British are surreptitious in their aims regarding the Spanish Florida territories.

NILES' WEEKLY REGISTER.

THE PAST — THE PRESENT — FOR THE FUTURE.

EDITED, PRINTED AND PUBLISHED BY H. NILES, AT $5 PER ANNUM, PAYABLE IN ADVANCE.

Volume 1

(September 7, 1811 - February 29, 1812)

British Interests in the Floridas

Volume 1, November 9, 1811, pages 153-154

The President's Message.

The President communicated to both houses by Mr. Edward Coles, his private secretary, the following *Message*.

[Excerpt] Among the occurrences produced by the conduct of British ships of war hovering on our coasts, was an encounter between one of them and the American frigate commanded by captain Rodgers, rendered unavoidable on the part of the latter, by a fire, commenced without cause, by the former; whose commander is, therefore, alone chargeable with the blood unfortunately shed in maintaining the honor of the American flag. The proceedings of a court of enquiry, requested by captain Rodgers, are communicated— together with the correspondence relating to the occurrence between the secretary of state and his Britannic majesty's envoy. To these are added the several correspondences which have passed on the subject of the British orders in council— and to both the correspondence relating to the Floridas, in which congress will be made acquainted with the interposition which the government of Great Britain has thought proper to make against the proceedings of the United States.

(Signed)   JAMES MADISON.
Washington, Nov. 5, 1811.

Occupation of West Florida

Volume 1, November 16, 1811, pages 187-190

Mr. Foster, [British Plenipotentiary] to Mr. Monroe, [U. S. Secretary of State].

Washington, July 2d, 1811.

Sir— The attention of his majesty's government has of late been called to the measures pursued by the United States for the military occupation of West Florida. The language held by the president at the opening of the late session of congress, the hostile demonstrations made by the American forces under captain Gaines, the actual summoning of the fort of Mobile, and the bill submitted to the approbation of the American legislature for the interior administration of the province, are so many direct and positive proofs that the government of America is prepared to subject the province of West Florida to the authority of the United States.

The Spanish minister in London addressed a note in the month of March last to his majesty's secretary of state for foreign affairs, expressing in sufficient detail the feelings of the government of Spain respecting this unprovoked aggression on the integrity of that monarchy.

Mr. Morier in his note to Mr. Smith of December 15, 1810, has already reminded the American government of the intimate alliance subsisting between his majesty and Spain, and he has desired such explanations on the subject as might convince his majesty of the pacific disposition of the United States towards Spain. Mr. Smith in his reply has stated that it was evident that no hostile or unfriendly purpose was entertained by America towards Spain; and that the

American minister at his majesty's court had been enabled to make whatever explanations might comport with the frank and conciliatory spirit which had been unvariably manifested on the part of the United States.

Since the date of this correspondence Mr. Pinkney has offered no explanation whatever of the motives which have actuated the conduct of the United States in this transaction; a bill has been introduced into congress for the establishment, government and protection of the territory of Mobile, and the fortress of that name has been summoned without effect.

His royal highness the prince regent in the name on the behalf of his majesty, is still willing to hope that the American government has not been urged to this step by ambitious motives or by a desire of foreign conquest, and territorial aggrandizement. It would be satisfactory however to be enabled to ascertain that no consideration connected with the present state of Spain has induced America to despoil that monarchy of a valuable foreign colony.

The government of the United States contends that the right to the possession of a certain part of West Florida will not be less open to discussion in the occupation of America than under the government of Spain.

But the government of the United States, under this pretext, cannot expect to avoid the reproach, which must attend the ungenerous and unprovoked seizure of a foreign colony, while the parent state is engaged in a noble contest for independence, against a most unjustifiable and violent invasion of the right both of the monarch and people of Spain.

While I wait, therefore, for an explanation from you, sir, as to the motives which led to this unjust aggression by the United States on the territories of his majesty's ally, I must consider it as my duty to lose no time in fulfilling the orders of his royal highness the prince regent by which I am commanded in the event of its appearing on my arrival in this city that the United States still persevere by menaces and active demonstration to claim the military occupation of West Florida, notwithstanding the remonstrances of his majesty's charge d'affairs and the manifest injustice of the act, to present to you the solemn protest of his royal highness in the name and on behalf of his majesty against an attempt so contrary to every principle of justice, good faith, and national honor, and so injurious to the alliance subsisting between his majesty and the Spanish nation.

I have the honor to be, with the highest consideration, sir, your most obedient humble servant.

AUG. J. FOSTER.

To the hon. James Monroe,
&c. &c. &c.

————

Mr. Monroe to Mr. Foster.

Department of State,
July 8, 1811.

Sir—I have had the honor to receive the note which you have presented, by the order of his royal highness the prince regent, to protest, in behalf of the regency of Spain, against the possession lately taken by the United States of certain parts of West Florida.

Although the president cannot admit the right of Great Britain to interfere in any question relating to that province, he is willing to explain, in a friendly manner, the considerations which induced the United States to take the step against which you have ordered to protest.

It is to be inferred from your view of the subject, that the British government has been taught to believe that the United States seized a moment of national embarrassment to wrest from Spain a province to which they had no right, and that they were prompted to it by their interest alone, and a knowledge that Spain could not defend it. Nothing, however, is more remote from the fact, than the presumption on which your government appears to have acted. Examples of so unworthy a conduct are unfortunately too frequent in the history of nations, but the United States have not followed them. The president had pursuaded himself that the unequivocal proofs which the United States have given in all their transactions with foreign powers, and particularly with Spain, of an upright and liberal policy, would have shielded them from such an unmerited a suspicion. He is satisfied that nothing is wanting but a correct knowledge of facts completely to dissipate it.

I might bring to your view a long catalogue of injuries which the United States have received from Spain since the conclusion of their revolutionary war, any one of which would most probably have been considered cause of war, and resented as such by other powers. I will mention two of these only; the spoliations that were committed on their commerce to a great amount in the last war, and the suppression of their deposit at New-Orleans just before the commencement of the present war, in violation of a solemn treaty; for neither of which injuries has any reparation or atonement been made. For injuries like those of the first class, it is known to you that Great Britain and France made indemnity. The United States, however, do not rely on these injuries for a justification of their conduct in this transaction, although their claims to reparation for them are by no means relinquished, and it is to be presumed, will not always be neglected.

When I inform you that the province of West Florida to the Perdido was a part of Louisiana, while the whole province formerly belonged to France, that although it was afterwards separated from the other part, yet that both parts were again reunited in the hands of Spain, and by her reconveyed to France in which state the entire province of Louisiana was ceded to the United States in 1803, that in accepting the cession and paying for the territory ceded, the United States understood and believed that they paid for the country as far as the Perdido, as part of Louisiana; and that on a conviction of their rights they included in their laws provisions adapted to the cession in that extent— it cannot fail to be a cause of surprise to the prince regent, that they did not proceed to take possession of the territory in question as soon as the treaty was ratified. There was nothing in the circumstances of Spain at that time, that could have forbidden the measure. In denying the right of the United States to this territory, her government invited negociation on that and every other point in contestation between the parties. The United States accepted the invitation, in the hope that it would secure an adjustment and reparation for every injury which had been received, and lead to the restoration of perfect harmony between the two countries, but in that hope they were disappointed.

Since the year 1805, the period of the last negociation with Spain, the province of West-Florida has remained in a situation altogether incompatible with the welfare of these states. The government of Spain has scarcely been felt there; in consequence of which the affairs of that province had fallen into disorder. Of that circumstance, however, the United States took no advantage. It was not until the last year, when the inhabitants, perceiving that all authority over them had ceased, rose in a body with intention to take the country in their own hands, that the American government interposed. It was impossible for the United States to behold with indifference a movement in which they were so deeply interested. The president would have incurred the censure of the nation, if he suffered that province to be wrested from the United States, under a pretext of wresting it from Spain. In taking possession of it in their name, and under their authority, except in the part which was occupied by the Spanish troops, who have not been disturbed, he defended the rights and secured the peace of the nation, and even consulted the honor of Spain herself. By this event the United States have acquired no new title to West Florida. They wanted none. In adjusting hereafter all the other points which remain to be adjusted with Spain, and which it is proposed to make the subject of amicable negociation as soon as the government of Spain shall be settled, her claim to this territory may also be brought into view, and receive all the attention which is due to it.

Aware that this transaction might be misconceived and misrepresented, the President deemed it a proper subject of instruction to the ministers of the United States at foreign courts to place it in a true light before them. Such an instruction was forwarded to Mr. Pinkney, their late Minister Plenipotentiary at London, who would have executed it, had not the termination of his mission prevented it. The president cannot doubt that the frank and candid explanation which I have now given, by his order, of the considerations which induced the United States to take possession of this country, will be perfectly satisfactory to his royal highness the Prince Regent.

With great respect and consideration, I have the honor to be, sir, your most obedient servant,

(Signed)   JAS. MONROE.

Augustus J. Foster,
Esq. &c. &c. &c.

———

Mr. Foster to Mr. Monroe.

Philadelphia, Sept. 5, 1811.

Sir—The Chevalier d'Onis, who has been appointed minister from his Catholic majesty to the United States, has written to inform me that he understands by letters from the governor of East Florida, under the date of the 14th ult. that governor Matthews, of the state of Georgia, was at that time at Newtown, St. Mary's, on the frontiers of Florida, for the purpose of treating with the inhabitants of that province for its being delivered up to the United States' government, that he was with this view using every method of seduction to effect his purpose, offering to each white inhabitant who would side with him fifty acres of land and the guarantee of his religion and property; stipulating also that the American government would pay the debts of the Spanish government, whether due in pensions or otherwise, and that he would cause the officers and soldiers of the garrisons to be conveyed to such place as should be indicated, provided they did not rather choose to enter into the service of the United States.

M. D'Onis has done me the honor to communicate to me a note which he purposes transmitting to you, sir, in consequence of this detached and most extraordinary intelligence, and considering the intimate alliance subsisting between Spain and Great Britain, as well as the circumstances under which he is placed in this country, he has urgently requested that I would accompany his representation with a letter on my part in support of it.

After the solemn asseverations which you gave me in the month of July, that no intentions hostile to the Spanish interests in Florida existed on the part of your government, I am wholly unable to suppose that governor Matthews can have had orders from the President for the conduct which he is stated to be pursuing; but the measure he is stated to be taking in corresponding with traitors, and is endeavoring by bribery and every act of seduction to infuse a spirit of rebellion into the subjects of the king of Spain in those quarters, are such as to create the liveliest inquietude, and to call for the most early interference on the part of the government of the United States.

The government of the United States are well aware of the deep interest which his royal highness the prince regent takes in the security of Florida; for any attempt to occupy the Eastern part of which by the United States not even the slightest pretext could be alleged, such as were brought forward in the endeavor to justify the aggression on West Florida.

I conceive it therefore to be my duty, sir, in consideration of the alliance subsisting between Spain and Great Britain, and the interest of his majesty's subjects in the West India Islands, so deeply involved in the security of East Florida, as well as in pursuance of the orders of my government in case of any attempt against that country, to lose no time in calling upon you for an explanation of the alarming steps which governor Matthews is stated to be taking for subverting the Spanish authority in that country, requesting to be informed by you upon what authority he can be acting and what measures have been taken to put a stop to his proceedings. I have the honor to be, &c.

(Signed)   AUG. J. FOSTER.

To the hon. James Monroe,
&c. &c. &c.

———

Mr. Monroe to Mr. Foster.

November 2, 1811.

Sir—I have had the honor to receive your letter of September 5th, and to submit it to the view of the president.

The principles which have governed the United States in their measures relative to West Florida, have already been explained to you. With equal frankness I shall now communicate the part they have acted with respect to East Florida.

In the letter which I had the honor to address to you on the 8th of July, I stated the injuries which the United States had received from Spain, since their revolutionary war, and particularly by spoliations on their commerce in the last war, to a great amount, and of the suppression of their right of deposit at New-Orleans, just before the commencement of the present war, for neither of which had reparation been made. A claim to indemnity for these injuries, is altogether unconnected with the question relating to West Florida, which was acquired by cession from France in 1803.

The government of Spain has never denied the right of the United States to a just indemnity for spoliations on their commerce. In 1802, it explicitly admitted this right by entering into a convention, the object of which was to adjust the amount of the claim, with a view to indemnity. The subsequent injury by the suppression of the deposit at New-Orleans produced an important change in the relations between the parties, which has never been accommodated. The United States saw in that measure eminent cause of war, and that war did not immediately follow, cannot be considered in any other light than as a proof of their moderation and pacific policy. The executive could not believe that the government of Spain would refuse to the United States the justice due to these accumulated injuries, when the subject should be brought solemnly before it, by a special mission. It is known that an envoy extraordinary was sent to Madrid in 1805, on this subject, and that the mission did not accomplish the object intended by it.

It is proper to observe, that in the negociation, with Spain in 1805, the injuries complained of by the United States of the first class were again substantially admitted to a certain extent, as was that also occasioned by the suppression of the deposit at New-Orleans, although the Spanish government, by disclaiming the act, and imputing it to the intendant, sought to avoid the responsibility due from it; that to make indemnity to the United States for injuries of every kind, a cession of the whole territory claimed by Spain, eastward of the Mississippi was made the subject of negociation, and that the

amount of the sum demanded for it was the sole cause that a treaty was not then formed, and the territory added.

The United States have considered the government of Spain indebted to them a greater sum for the injuries above stated, than the province of East Florida can by any fair standard between the parties be estimated at. They have looked to this province for their indemnity, and with the greater reason, because the government of Spain itself has countenanced it. That they have suffered their just claims so long unsatisfied, is a new and strong proof of the moderation, as it is of their respect for the disordered condition of that power. There is, however, a period beyond which those claims ought not to be neglected. It would be highly improper for the United States, in their respect for Spain, to forget what they owe to their own character, and to the rights of their injured citizens.

Under these circumstances it would be equally unjust and dishonorable in the United States to suffer East Florida to pass into the possession of any other power. Unjust, because they would thereby lose the only indemnity within their reach, for injuries which ought long since to have been redressed. Dishonorable, because in permitting another power to wrest from them that indemnity, their inactivity and acquiescence could only be imputed to unworthy motives. Situated as East Florida is, cut off from the other possessions of Spain, and surrounded in a great measure by the territory of the United States; and having also an important bearing on their commerce, no other power could think of taking possession of it, with other than hostile views to them. Nor could any other power take possession of it without endangering their prosperity and best interests.

The United States have not been ignorant or inattentive to what has been agitated in Europe, at different periods, since the commencement of the present war, in regard to the Spanish provinces in this hemisphere; nor have they been unmindful of the consequences into which the disorder of Spain might lead in regard to the province in question, without due care to prevent it. They have been persuaded that remissness on their part might invite the danger, if it had not already done it, which it is so much their interest and desire to prevent.—Deeply impressed with these considerations, and anxious, while they acquitted themselves to the just claims of their constituents, to preserve friendship with other powers, the subject was brought before the congress at its last session, when an act was passed authorising the executive to accept possession of East Florida from the local authorities or to take it against the attempt of a foreign power to occupy it, holding it in either case subject to future and friendly negociation. This act therefore evinces the just and amicable views by which the United States have been governed, towards Spain, in the measure authorised by it. Our ministers at London and Paris were immediately apprised of the act and instructed to communicate the purport of it, to both governments, and to explain at the same time, in the most friendly manner, the motives which let to it. The president could not doubt that such an explanation would give all the satisfaction that was intended by it. By a late letter from the American charge d'affaires at London, I observe, that this explanation was made to your government in the month of _____ last. That it was not sooner made was owing to the departure of the minister plenipotentiary of the United States before the instruction was received.

I am persuaded, sir, that you will see, in this view of the subject, very strong proof of the just and amicable disposition of the United States towards Spain, of which I treated, in the conference, to which you have alluded. The same disposition still exists; but it must be understood that it cannot be indulged longer than may comport with the safety, as well as with the rights and honor of the nation. I have the honor to be, &c. &c.

JAMES MONROE.

Augustus J. Foster,
Esq. &c. &c. &c.

Volume 1, December 29, 1811, page 307

Congress—House of Representatives
West Florida

December 24.—Mr. *Poindexter* moved that the house do come to the following resolution:

Resolved, That the president of the United States, be requested to inform the house whether any negociation is now pending between the United States and Spain, or any other power, respecting the claim of the United States to that tract of country of which possession was taken by virtue of the president's proclamation, bearing date the 27th day of October, 1810; and also whether he is possessed of any information which in his opinion requires that the legislative authority of congress over said country should be suspended with a view to future negociation on that subject.

This resolution was ordered to lie on the table.

Volume 1, January 5, 1812, page 335

The Chronicle.
From the Orleans Gazette
of Nov. 28

Extract of a letter from a Gentleman at Mobile dated November 18.—"The court of Spain has given orders to the governor of Pensacola, to give up the Floridas as far as the river Perdido. This news I received to-day from my correspondent at Pensacola, dated the 14th instant. I have also seen several other letters mentioning the same."

—»»⊖ ◎ ⊖««—

NILES' WEEKLY REGISTER.

THE PAST — THE PRESENT — FOR THE FUTURE.

EDITED, PRINTED AND PUBLISHED BY H. NILES, AT $5 PER ANNUM, PAYABLE IN ADVANCE.

Volume 2

(March 7, 1812 - August 29, 1812)

Volume 2, March 14, 1812, page 19

Twelfth Congress
House of Representatives.

Friday, March 6. — West Florida.
— Mr. Johnson submitted the following
resolution:

Resolved, that a committee be
appointed to enquire into the situation
of that part of West Florida west of the
Perdido river, the possession of which
was taken under the proclamation of the
president of the United States on the 27th
October 1810, and the committee have
leave to report by bill or otherwise.

Mr. Pitkin enquiring the particular
object of this motion,

Mr. Johnson replied that by the
proclamation of the president of the
United States, the territory embraced by
the resolution was attached to the Orleans
territory. It is well known that the
constitution of that territory in conformity
to the laws of congress had arrived and
was now before the house. The territory
in question, not being included within
the limits prescribed for the new state,
must either be attached to some other
government or included in a separate
administration. In addition to this
circumstance, there were many grievances
of which the people of that territory
complained, which required investigation.
He had a number of memorials in his
possession, and reference of which at
a proper time he would move to that
committee.

The resolution was adopted.

Volume 2, March 28, 1812, page 71

Chronicle, &c.

The bill for the admission of
Louisiana into the union, has passed the
house of representatives, with a provision
to include within the limits of that state so
much of the West Florida territory as lies
west of the Pearl river.

A bill with the same title, also passed
its third reading in the senate.

(*National Intelligencer.*

Volume 2, April 4, 1812, page 86

Chronicle.

East Florida, it is stated, has declared
itself independent of Spain.

Volume 2, April 11, 1812, page 93

Amelia Island.
Savannah, March 26.

*Extract of a letter from St. Mary's
dated March 20th.*

"The insurgents or patriots, formed
a camp on Roses's Bluff, opposite
St. Mary's, at the same time the gun-
boats, were ordered to proceed down
to the sound, when they were moored,
their guns loaded, and every man to
his station — several signal guns were
fired by the commodore; the insurgents
then embarked in boats from Rose's
Bluff, and proceeded to Amelia Island,
where they landed, colonel Lodowick
Ashley at their head, and demanded
the surrender of the island, which was
refused by the commandant, but who
requested a parly until he could send a
deputation to commodore Campbell,
who was then sailing up and down the
harbor, to ascertain whether he would
assist the insurgents in case they were
resisted — the commodore's reply was,
that he would assist the insurgents. The
island was then surrendered to colonel
Ashley, and the flag of the patriots was
immediately displayed on the ramparts
of the fort, which was soon succeeded by
the flag of the United States. The United
States troops are now in possession of
the island of Amelia — the country of

East Florida in possession of the patriots, and the town of Augustine and the garrison in possession of the soldiers of Ferdinand the 7th. The governor of that place is determined to hold out to the last extremity."

———

*Extract of a letter
from Fernandina, March 21.*

"In my last I gave you a hint of what was going on here, I have now to inform you, that a large party of men crossed the river St. Mary's, about 20 miles above this place, and succeeded in revolutionising all the country between St. Mary's and St. John's. Amelia is the only place that showed any resistance, but from the threats of the American gun-boats, under the command of commodore Campbell, and the formidable appearance of the revolutionists, the commandant of Amelia surrendered the town and garrison of Fernandina without firing a shot, on the following terms that the commandant and troops would be allowed to march out with the honors of war, and upon delivering their arms would receive their parole, not to take up arms against the revolutionists during their present contest. That all individual property, whether lands or otherwise shall be considered sacred, and neither be examined or touched, but remain and to be used to the same manner as before the capitulation; the island 24 hours after the capitulation shall be ceded to the United States of America under the express conditions, that the port of Fernandina shall not be subject to any of the restrictions of commerce which at present exist in the United States, but shall be open as heretofore to British and other vessels and produce, on paying the lawful duties and tonnage, and in case of a war between the United States and Great Britain, the port of Fernandina shall be open to British merchandize and merchant vessels, and considered a free port until 1st May, 1813.

The inhabitants who had grants to cut lumber shall have the same continued until 1st May, 1813.

All vessels of every description shall be protected and clearances given to any port as before, excepting to the coast of Africa, as well as all vessels arriving before the 1st May, 1813.

All British or other merchandize, which have been regularly entered according to the laws and regulations of the Spanish government shall be exported from here and admitted in the ports of the United States free of duties until the 1st May, 1813. And all vessels owned by Spanish subjects of this island, shall be entitled to regular American registers.

All inhabitants of this place, who do not choose to remain under the American government, are allowed one year to settle their business, and should a war take place between the United States and Spain, they will be allowed to appoint agents to settle their business.

The above is as near the substance of the terms or capitulation, as I can at present recollect. I have only to add that general George Mathews, agent for the United States; has confirmed the same, on account of his government.

P. S. — On the morning of the 18th, the gun-boats came and anchored before the town, immediately put springs on their cables, loaded their guns with cannister shot, and levelled them at this defenceless place, when they were ordered by the commandant not to pass the garrison, they answered that they did not come in a hostile manner, but that they would aid and assist the *patriots*, and was it not for their interference we could have defeated any force the revolutionists could bring before us.

You will observed that goods are not allowed to enter from here until the president approves of this measure.

———

Charleston, March 27. — We had the pleasure of conversing with a gentleman, who left Amelia Island on Sunday last, and who arrived this morning in the stage from Savannah. He states, that a day or two previous to the 16th inst. Amelia Island was summoned to surrender by the revolutionists at St. Mary's who accompanied their summons with a declaration, that the United States troops stationed there would assist them in taking possession of it, should they refuse. The commandant of Amelia having requested and obtained a short time to return an answer, wrote immediately to major Laval and commodore Campbell, to know whether it was their intention to co-operate with them. The major returned for answer, that having had no instructions from his government to that effect, he should not. In the mean time, major Laval was superceded in the command by colonel Smythe. The commodore did not answer until the next morning, when he stated, that he had no instructions, to render such assistance but that he should act with them on his own responsibility; and accordingly, on the 16th or 17th proceeded to drop the gun-boats down the river. Some signal guns having been fired by the commodore, Amelia was taken possession of, without opposition, on Wednesday the 18th by the Spanish revolutionaists, conjointly with the United States troops. One company of riflemen was sent from colonel Smythe's command. The gentleman mentioned above on whose information we rely with confidence, entertains no doubt of their having proceeded immediately to St. Augustine, where, we understand, there is some considerable force. — *Times.*

———

Additional. — A company of riflemen, belonging to the United States army, proceeded from the American side of the St. Mary's, under the command of a lieutenant and accompanied by general Matthews, of Virginia, to Amelia: when the patriotic forces, who had been increased by reinforcements to about 130 men, were drawn up to receive them; and the place was formally surrendered to the American arms. The patriot flag was now, in its turn, pulled down, and the American standard hoisted in its place. By the articles of capitulation entered into between the commander of the patriotic forces, and Don Lopez, the Spanish commandant, it was stipulated that Amelia Island should remain a free port until the first of May, 1813, that it should not be subject to our restrictive laws until that time; that British and other vessels by paying proper duties, should, with their cargoes, have free admission, to sell, &c. that private property should be respected, &c. &c. It is said that all the rest of East Florida is in possession of the revolutionists, except St. Augustine.

Volume 2, May 2, 1812, page 151

Twelfth Congress.
House of Resprespentatives.

Tuesday, April 28. — On motion of Mr. Poindexter,

Resolved, that a committee be appointed to enquire into the expediency of annexing that part of West Florida lying east of Pearl river, and west of the Perdido, to the Mississippi territory; and that the committee have leave to report by bill or otherwise.

[The remainder of this territory, it will be recollected, has been already annexed to the state of Louisiana; and as Mr. Poindexter stated, this portion will in a few day be destitute of any government.]

Messrs. Poindexter, New, Goldsborough, Earle, and Alston, were appointed the committee.

Volume 2, May 9, 1812, pages 166-167

Twelfth Congress.
House of Representatives.

Friday, May 1. — Mr. Poindexter from the select committee appointed on the subject, reported a bill to annex a portion of West Florida to the Mississippi territory; which was twice read.

[The bill proposes the annexation to the territory of Mississippi of all that part of West Florida which lies west of the Perdido and east of the Pearl river.]

And the bill was ordered to be engrossed for a third reading to-morrow.

Monday, May 4. — [After some minor business was disposed of] —

The engrossed bill to annex to the Mississippi territory that part of West Florida east of the Pearl river, was read a third time.

Mr. Pitkin asked for information as to the intention in relation to the future state of this territory; whether it was to be held subject to future negociation, &c. and in what light that part of the territory near Mobile, now in the occupation of a Spanish garrison, was to be considered, &c.

The bill was ordered to lie on the table.

—••»⊖◉⊖«««•—

East Florida

Volume 2, May 30, 1812, pages 201-202

Mr. Pickering's Letters.
From the Boston Repertory.

*To the citizens of the
commonwealth of Massachusetts.*

Embargo, — and War with Great Britain.

Fellow-citizens,— In my last letter I gave the history of president Jefferson's embargo in 1807. By undertaking to state his reasons for recommending that destructive measure, he has exposed himself to detection; and I presume that every fair-minded reader will be convinced from his own documents, which I recited, of his hypocrisy, duplicity, falsehood and treachery. President Madison has been more cautious in his embargo, assigning no specific reasons for recommending it. But we have Mr. Jefferson's assurance (in his answer to the Baltimore Tammuany Society, when he went out of office) that Mr. Madison, when secretary of state, had cordially co-operated with him in his measures: which he considered as a pledge, that, now become president, he would pursue the same system. But this testimony of his patron was not necessary to induce full expectation and belief in those who are acquainted with Mr. Madison's political character, that he would go on in the same course. That he should therefore recommend an embargo at *this juncture*, is perfectly consistent. Having joined with the French emperor "in twisting a knot about our necks," his further co-operation was naturally to be expected. And nothing could so effectually promote the emperor's views, at this time, as an embargo— to be followed by a war with Great Britain. Such a war, however, I think Mr. Madison must be a littel apprehensive, would not be sufficiently popular for him to venture upon, unless Great Britain can, by some cunning management, be induced to commence it; and in some way that may enable him to persuade the people that he had taken every possible precaution to avoid a war. The proceedings in West Florida may lead to this result. The basis of these proceedings was the act of congress secretly passed during the last session of congress, authorising the president *to take possession of that Spanish province, in case an arrangement had been or should be made with the local authority thereof, for delivering possession of it, or of any part of it, to the United States; or in any foreign government.* And one hundred thousand dollars were appropriated and placed at the president's disposal, "to defray such expenses as the president might deem necessary for *obtaining* as aforesaid, and the security of that territory."

The provisions of this act, and subsequent events, deserve consideration—, And first — How was the president to obtain possession of East Florida? "By an arrangement with the local authority thereof." And what constituted that "local authority?" The Spanish governor and other officers. And why attempt an "arrangement" with those Spanish officers? The president and congress knew that the *sovereign power of Spain alone* could lawfully make an "arrangement" for transferring the possession of the province to the United States. What sort of an "arrangement," then, could be made with the governor and other officers of East Florida? There could be but one— and that one could be accomplished only by the voluntary *treason* of those officers, of which the president was to take advantage — or by his employing our agent to *reduce* them from their *allegiance*, and by *corruption* tempt them to become *traitors* to their country. And from the statement I am now making, such will appear to have been the deliberate plan of the "virtuous and amiable Madison!" Of the same man who, in his late message to congress, communicating the papers delivered him by John Henry, affected to be deeply wounded by an act of general Craig, the British governor of Canada, in sendin Henry to Boston, to learn, if there be any truth in his story, what was the situation of public affairs, with the strength and plans of parties, at a time when this country was groaning under the oppression of Mr. Jefferson's treacherous and ruinous embargo. — Mr. Madison, then, could warmly declaim on this intermeddling of a British governor, insinuating too, that Henry was the "secret agent" of the *British government* — although it does not appear, by the papers themselves, that Henry was employed by governor Craig, with the knowledge of his *government*. — With the like baseness and with the absolute want of truth, Mr. Madison says, that Henry was "employed in fomenting disaffection to the constituted authorities of the nation, and in intrigues with the disaffected, for the purpose of bringing about resistance to the laws, and eventually, in concert with a British force, of destroying the union." But there is nothing in Henry's apapers to warrant this accusation. Henry says he did not open his lips to a single person on the subject of his mission. Of course he did not "foment disaffection to the constituted authorities of the nation," or form any intrigues with the disaffected." It is a vile slander on the respectable *federal* inhabitants of Boston, whom Mr. Madison meant to designate by the term "disaffected." And why should Mr. Madison, in a formal communication to congress, utter this base slander? — The important elections in Massachusetts were approaching. His message was *short* and would be read by *thousands*; while Henry's documents were *long* and would be read by *few*. And still fewer were likely to read them with the attention requisite to detect Mr. Madison's misrepresentations.

But to return to East Florida. The British minister at Washington, Mr. Foster, on the 5th of September last [1811], stated to Mr. Monroe, secretary of state, his information received from the Spanish minister in Philadelphia, that governor Matthews, of Georgia, was on the frontiers of East Florida, "for the purpose of treating with the inhabitants of that province, for its being delivered up to the United States' government; that he was with this view using every method of seduction to effect his purpose; offering to each white inhabitant who would side with him, 50 acres of land and the guarantee of his religion and property; stipulating also that the American government would pay the debts of the Spanish government whether due in pensions or otherwise; and that he would cause the officers and soldiers of the garrisons to be conveyed to such places as should be indicated, provided they did not rather choose to enter into

the service of the United States." These terms held out to the Spanish subjects of Florida, have on the face of them the stamp of public authority. A private individual, for his own private purposes, would never have dreamed of making such overtures. Mr. Foster adds—"After the solemn asseverations which you gave me in the month of July, that no intentions hostile to the Spanish interests in Florida existed on the part of your government, I am wholly unable to suppose that general Matthews can have had orders from the president for the conduct he is stated to be pursuing; but the measure he is said to be taking in corresponding with traitors, and endeavoring by bribery and every art of seduction to infuse a spirit of rebellion into the subjects of the king of Spain in those quarters, are such as to create the liveliest inquietude, and to call for the most early interference on the part of the government of the United States." And then Mr. Foster earnestly asks of Mr. Monroe an explanation of those alarming steps of governor Matthews for subverting the Spanish authority in Florida.

Nearly two months are suffered to elapse before *Mr. Monroe* gives an answer to Mr. Foster.— At length, on the 2d of November, 1811, he sends him one, drawn up with all the act with which Mr. Madison is capable. Instead of the requested explanation, it gives a long tale of grievances for injuries received from the Spanish government in the course of the last fifteen years; all of which Madison had reason to believe, and which when time permits, I will show to have originated with the French government, while Spain was absolutely under her control. And Mr. Foster's request to be informed "upon what authority governor Matthews was acting, and what measures had been taken to up a stop to his proceedings," was altogether evaded. These were the only important points in Mr. Foster's letter; and to them he obtains no answer. This amounts to an admission that governor Matthews was president Madison's agent in this nefarious, faithless transaction!!—I know governor George Matthews very well. I regret that he has not a more honorable employment. He was an intrepid officer in our revolutionary war. Brave and enterprising, no man could be better qualified to execute Mr. Madison's designs on East Florida. This no one will doubt when I add, that governor Matthews was the governor of Georgia, when the Legislature of that state made grants to some companies of speculators of *forty millions of acres of land* with the claimed boundaries of that state; and the governor's agency was necessary to the completion of those grants. But the succeeding legislature declared they had been obtained by gross bribery and corruption; corruption so atrocious, that the laws by virtue of which those grants had been made, were expunged from their records, and stamped with all the ignominy which a public burning before the assembled people could inflict.

We have just now received advices, by the newspapers, of the effects of governor Matthews' agency. A party of the Spanish subjects exited to an insurrection, have seized upon the Spanish post in Amelia Island; the commander of the United States gun boats there giving countenance and support to the insurgents, and the commander of the American troops on the neighboring shore of Georgia, detaching a company of riflemen, who accompanies by general Matthews, received the surrender of the place to the American arms!—Now let Mr. Madison again petulantly clamour and vilify general Craig and the British government for employing John Henry; and henceforward let him and his adherents reproach Great Britain for her attack on Copenhagen!— An attack the sole object of which was to get possession of the Danish fleet of ships of war, to prevent their falling into the hands of her formidable and implacable enemy, the emperor of France. As to Mr. Monroe's details of Spanish wrongs, and the pretended title of the United States to West Florida—they are so full of errors and misrepresentations as greatly mislead the public mind. It is of public importance to correct them; and when I can spare the time I will correct them. At present I must content myself with affirming, that when the bargain was made in Paris for the purchase of Louisiana, West Florida was not in contemplation as a part of it.—That the United States never paid for it: And they have no title to it.

The history I have given of the East Florida business, concurs with other acts to show the true character of our government; by which the United States are dishonored; and by which we may be drawn into a war with Great Britain and Spain. This last consideration was the direct object of these details. If we are plunged into a destructive war, it behooves Mr. Madison to have it so brought in as that Great Britain may appear to be the aggressor in commencing it— Great Britain is the faithful ally of Spain. She has more than once interposed remonstrance against the acts of our government concerning the Florida. She alone in the present condition of the Spanish monarchy, could be expected to send troops to retake and defend East Florida. Should she do it, the American and British arms will come in collision— the projected war will commence. Mr. Madison setting up a claim to East Florida, as the means of indemnity for the injuries the United States have received from Spain (all of which is already intimated, may be shown to have originated with France) will say of *East* as he has already said of *West* Florida, that "the president cannot admit the right of Great Britain to interfere in any question relating to that province."* And if the people of the United States shall be satisfied (and from their past astonishing confidence in him and Mr. Jefferson, we feel authorised to expect it) the war, of consequence, will be a popular one.—On the principles and course of conduct of our rulers, *war is to them indispensible. Without war they cannot raise money.* I will explain this in my next letter.

TIMOTHY PICKERING.

April 17, 1812.

[* Monroe's letter to Foster, July 8, 1811.]

Volume 2, Supplement to May 30, 1812, page 220

Extract of Letter from Mr. Monroe to Mr. Barlow.

Department of State, Nov. 21, 1811

Sir—I have the honor to transmit to you a copy of the president's message to congress at the commencement of the session, and of the documents which accompanied it.

[Extract] You will also find among the printed documents, a correspondence with Mr. Foster [British Minister] respecting the Floridas. To his remonstrance against the occupation of West Florida by the troops of the United States, he was told that it belonged to them by a title which could not he improved. And to that relative to East Florida, he was informed that Spain owed the United States for spoliations on their commerce, and for the suppression of the deposit of New Orleans, more than it was worth; that the United States looked to East Florida for their indemnity; that they would suffer no power to take it, and would take it themselves, either at the invitation of the inhabitants, or to prevent its falling into the hands of another power. With so just a claim on it, and without any adverse claim, which, under existing circumstances, is any wise sustainable, more especially, as the necessary severance of the Spanish colonies from Old Spain is admitted, and the known disposition and interest of the inhabitants are in favor of the United States, the idea of purchasing the territory, otherwise than as it has been already more than paid for, in the property wrongfully taken from the citizens of the United States, does not merit, and has not received a moment's consideration here. You will therefore, discountenance the idea every where, and in every shape.

Volume 2, June 6, 1812, pages 236-237

Extract of Letter from Mr. Monroe to Mr. Russell.

Sir—This letter will be delivered to you by Mr. Barlow, who is appointed to represent the United States at Paris, as their minister plenipotentiary. You will deliver to him the papers in your possession, and give him all the information in your power, relative to our affairs with the French government.

The president has instructed me to communicate to you his approbation of your conduct in the discharge of the duties which devolved on you as charge d'affaires at Paris, after the departure of general Armstrong, which I execute with pleasure. As an evidence of this confidence and favorable disposition, he has appointed you to the same trust in London, for which I enclose you a commission. It is hoped, that it may suit your convenience to repair to that court, and to remain there till a minister shall be appointed, which will be done as soon as the congress convenes. The frigate which takes Mr. Barlow to France will pass on to some port in Holland, to execute a particular instruction from the secretary of the treasury relative to our debt in that country. She will the a return to France, and take you to such English port as may be most convenient to you.

You will receive a copy of the notes of Mr. Foster on several important topics, and my answers to them, particularly on the British orders in council, the possession taken by the United States of certain parts of West Florida, and the late encounter between the United States' frigate the *President* and the British sloop of war the *Little Belt*. It is hoped that the British government will proceed to revoke its orders in council, and thus restore in all respects, the friendly relation which would be so advantageous to both countries.

The papers relative to West Florida shew the ground on which that question rests. The affair of the Little Belt cannot excite much feeling, it is presumed, in England: The chase was begun by the British captain he fired the first shot and the first broad side; to which it may be added, that the occurrence took place near our coast, which is sometimes infested by vessels from the West Indies, without commission, and even for piratical purposes. It seems to be a right inseparable from the sovereignty of the United States to ascertain the character and nation of the vessels which hang on their coast. An inquiry is ordered into commodore Rodgers' conduct, at his request, for the purpose of establishing all the facts appertaining to this occurrence.

JAMES MONROE.

Jonathan Russell,
Esq. &c. &c.

Extract from Military Notices.

An attack was contemplated to be made upon St. Augustine, in East Florida on the 4th of July, by the United States troops (200) patriots (400) and militia volunteers from Savannah, (90) all under the command of colonel Smith. The force of the garrison is not stated.

Extract from Military Notices.

Fourteen hundred United States troops were expected at St. Johns (East Florida) on the 9th of July. A few Spanish troops had arrived in that country from Havana, and others were expected. Considerable bodies of volunteers from Georgia were marching to assist in terminating the controversy.

Extract from Military Notices.

The following is an extract of a letter from an officer in the detachment to East Florida, the bearer of despatches to governor Mitchell, in St. Mary's, to his friend in Savannah dated,

"ST. MARY'S, July 10.

"We have received intelligence that the new governor of Florida (Kinderland) has sent a flag to governor Mitchell, by one Arredondo, with a message to this effect— "That if the United States were determined to take the fortress of Augustine, it should be surrendered but if they demanded it for the patriots only, that he would hold out to the last extremity." We are in hourly expectation of the result of this interview, and the governor's message to colonel Smith, our commander, predicated thereon. It is expected, however, that the troops will be ordered to take the place immediately."

The above is confirmed by another letter.

NILES' WEEKLY REGISTER.

THE PAST—THE PRESENT—FOR THE FUTURE.

EDITED, PRINTED AND PUBLISHED BY H. NILES, AT $5 PER ANNUM, PAYABLE IN ADVANCE.

Volume 3

(September 5, 1812 - February 27, 1813)

Volume 3, September 5, 1812, page 16

Extract from The Chronicle.

The revolutionists in East Florida have formed a convention, consisting of 15 members to draft a constitution, and make such other municipal regulations as may be deemed expedient. The convention was to have met on the 27th ult. for the purpose of choosing a director or governor general. They intend, immediately after their government is organized, to make a vigorous effort to possess themselves of the province and deliver it up to the United States. [*Washington (Georgia) Monitor.*

Volume 3, September 5, 1812, page 16

Extract from The Chronicle.

We understand by a gentleman from East Florida, that the patriots had a convention, and have appointed John Houston McIntosh, governor, and elected members of the legislature.

This looks like men determined to be free, and in all their *laudable* exertions, we most heartily wish them success.— We trust that under the guidance of that Omnipotent Power, whose darling attribute is liberty, they will be able to burst the fetters which have enchained them under a despot, and assume their proper rank among the people as freemen. [*Georgia Argus.*

Volume 3, September 12, 1812, pages 19-20

East Florida.

The following documents were confidentially communicated to Congress on the first of July last. The injunction of secrecy was afterwards taken off.— They have not yet been generally published, and afford much information as to the late events in those countries.

*From the Secretary of State
to general George Matthews
and colonel John McKee, dated*

Department of State,
January 26, 1811.

The president of the United States having appointed you jointly and severally commissioners for carrying into effect certain provisions of an act of congress (a copy of which is enclosed) relative to the portion of the Floridas situated to the east of the river Perdido, you will repair to that quarter with all possible expedition, concealing from general observation the trust committed to you with that discretion which the delicacy and importance of the undertaking require.

Should you find governor Folk, or the local authority existing there, inclined to surrender in an amicable manner the possession of the remaining portion or portions of West Florida now held by him in the name of the Spanish monarchy, you are to accept, in behalf of the United States, the abdication of his, or of the other existing authority, and the jurisdiction of the country over which it extends. And should a stipulation be insisted on for the re-delivery of the country, at a future period, you may engage for such re-delivery to the lawful sovereign.

The debts clearly due from the Spanish government to the people of the territory surrendered may, if insisted on, be assumed within reasonable limits and under specified descriptions to be settled hereafter as a claim against Spain in an adjustment of our affairs with her. You may also guarantee in the name of the United States, the confirmation of all such titles to land as are clearly sanctioned by Spanish laws: and Spanish civil functionaries, where no special reasons may require changes, are to be permitted to remain in office, with the assurance of a continuation of the prevailing laws, with such alterations only as may be necessarily required in the new situation of the country.

If it should be required, and be found necessary, you may agree to advance as above a reasonable sum for the transportation of the Spanish troops.

These directions are adapted to one of the contingencies specified in the act of congress, namely, the amicable surrender of the possession of the possession of the territory by the local ruling authority.— But should the arrangement, contemplated by the statute, not be made, and should there be room to entertain a suspicion of an existing design in any foreign power to occupy the country in question, you are to keep yourselves on the alert, and on the first undoubted manifestation of the approach of a force for that purpose, you will exercise the promptness and vigor the powers with which you are invested by the president to preoccupy by force the territory, to the entire exclusion of any armament that may be advancing to take the possession of it. In this event you will exercise a sound discretion in applying the powers given with respect to debts, titles to land, civil officers and the continuation of the Spanish laws; taking care to commit the government on no point further than may be necessary. And should any Spanish military force remain within the country, after the occupancy by the troops of the United States, you may, in such case, aid in their removal from the same.

The universal toleration which the laws of the United States assures to every religious persuasion, will not escape you as an argument for quieting the minds of uninformed individuals, who may entertain fears on that head.

The conduct you are to pursue in regard to East Florida, must be regulated by the dictates of your own judgments, on a close view and accurate knowledge of the precise state of things there, and of the Spanish government, always recurring to the present instruction as the paramount rule of your proceedings.— Should you discover an inclination in the governor of East Florida, or in the existing local authority, amicably to surrender that province into the possession of the United States, you are to accept it on the same terms that are prescribed by these

instructions in relation to West Florida. And in case of the actual appearance of any attempt to take possession by a foreign power, you will pursue the same effective measures for the occupation of the territory and for the exclusion of the foreign force, as you are directed to pursue with respect to the country of the Perdido, forming, at this time, the extent of governor Folk's jurisdiction.

If you should, under these instructions obtain possession of Mobile, you will lose no time in informing governor Claiborne thereof, with a request that he will without delay, take the necessary steps for the occupation of the same.

All ordnance and military stores that may be found in the territory must be held as the property of the Spanish government, to be accounted for hereafter to the proper authority; and you will not fail to transmit an inventory thereof to this department.

If in the execution of any part of these instructions you should need the aid of a military force, the same will be afforded you upon your application to the commanding officer of the troops of the United States on that station, or to the commanding officer of the nearest port, in virtue of orders which have been issued from the war department.— And in case you should moreover need naval assistance, you will receive the same upon your application to the naval commander in pursuance of orders from the navy department.

From the treasury department will be issued the necessary instructions in relation to imposts and duties, and to the slave ships whose arrival is apprehended.

The president, relying upon your discretion, authorises you to draw upon the collectors of Orleans and Savannah for such sums as may be necessary to defray unavoidable expenses that may be incurred in the executions, not exceeding in your drafts on New Orleans eight thousand dollars, and in your drafts on Savannah two thousand dollars, without further authority, of which expenses you will hereafter exhibit a detailed account duly supported by satisfactory vouchers.

Postscript.— If governor Folk should unexpectedly require and pertinaciously insist that the stipulation for the re-delivery of the territory, should also include that portion of the country which is situated west of the river Perdido, you are, in yielding to such demand, only to use general words that may by implication comprehend that portion of country;— but, at the same time, your are expressly to provide, that such stipulation shall not in any way impair or affect the right or title of the United States to the same.

Volume 3, September 12, 1812, pages 20-21

The Secretary of State
to General Matthews.

Department of State,
April 4, 1812.

Sir—I have had the honor to receive your letter of the 14th of March, and have now to communicate to you the sentiments of the President, on the very interesting subject to which it relates.

I am sorry to have to state that the measures which you appear to have adopted for obtaining possession of Amelia Island and other parts of East Florida, are not authorised by the law of the United States, or the instructions founded on it, under which you have acted.

You are authorised by the law, a copy of which was communicated to you, and by your instructions which are strictly conformable to it, to take possession of East Florida, only in case one of the following contingencies should happen: either that the governor or other existing local authority should be disposed to place it amicably in the hands of the United States, or that an attempt should be made to take possession of it by a foreign power. Should the first contingency happen, it would follow that the arrangement being amicable, would require no force on the part of the United States to carry it into effect. It was only in case of an attempt to take it by a foreign power that force could be necessary, in which event only were you authorised to avail yourself of it.

In neither of these contingencies was it the policy of the law, or purpose of the executive, to wrest the province forcibly from Spain; but only to occupy it with a view to prevent its falling into the hands of any foreign power, and to hold that

pledge under the existing peculiarity of the circumstances of the Spanish monarchy, for a just result in an amicable negociation with Spain.

Had the United States been disposed to proceed otherwise, that intention would have been manifested by a change in the law, and suitable measures to carry it into effect. And as it was in their power to take possession whenever they might think that circumstances authorised and required it, it would be the more to be regretted, if possession should be effected by any means irregular in themselves, and subjecting the government of the United States to unmerited censure.

The views of the executive respecting East Florida, are further illustrated by your instructions as to West Florida. Although the United States have thought that they had a good title to the latter province, they did not take possession until after the Spanish authority had been subverted by a revolutionary proceeding, and the contingency of the country being thrown into foreign hands, had forced itself into view. Nor did they then, nor have they since dispossessed the Spanish troops of the post which they occupied. If they did not think proper to take possession by force, of a province, to which they thought they were justly entitled, it could not be presumed that they should intend to act differently, in respect to one to which they had not such a claim.

I may add, that although due sensibility has been always felt for the injuries which were received from the Spanish government in the last war, the present situation of Spain has been a motive for a moderate and pacific policy towards her.

In communicating to you these sentiments of the executive on the measures you have lately adopted for taking possession of East Florida, I add with pleasure that the utmost confidence is reposed in your integrity and zeal to promote the welfare of your country. To that zeal the error into which you have fallen, is imputed. But in consideration of the part which you have taken, which differs so essentially from that contemplated and authorised by the government, and contradicts so entirely the principles on which it has uniformly and sincerely acted, you will be sensible of the necessity of discontinuing the service in which you have been employed.

You will, therefore, consider your powers as revoked on the receipt of this letter. The new duties to be performed will be transferred to the governor of Georgia, to whom instructions will be given on all the circumstances to which it may be proper, at the present juncture, to call his attention.

I have the honor to be, very respectfully, sir, your obedient servant.

General Matthews, &c.

Volume 3, September 12, 1812, pages 21-22

The Secretary of State to
D. B. Mitchell, the governor of Georgia.

Department of State,
April 10, 1812.

Sir—The President is desirous of availing the public of your services, in a concern of much delicacy and of high importance to the United States. Circumstances with which you are in some degree acquainted, but which will be fully explained by the enclosed papers, have made it necessary to revoke the powers heretofore committed to general Matthews, and to commit them to you. The president is persuaded that you will not hesitate to undertake a trust so important to the nation and peculiarly to the state of Georgia. He is the more confident on this belief, from the consideration that these new duties may be discharged without interfering, as he presumes, with those of the station which you now hold.

By the act of the 15th of January, one thousand eight hundred and eleven, you will observe that it was not contemplated to take possession of East Florida, or of any part thereof, unless it should be surrendered to the United States, amicably, by the governor or other local authority of the province, or against an attempt to take possession of it by a foreign power; and you will also see that general Matthews' instructions, of which a copy is likewise enclosed, correspond fully with the law.

By the documents in possession of the government it appears that neither of these contingencies have happened, that instead of an amicable surrender by the governor or the local authority, the troops of the United States have been used to dispossess the Spanish authority by force. I forbear to dwell on the details of this transaction, because it is painful to recite them. By the letter to general Matthews, which is enclosed open for your perusal, you will fully comprehend the views of the government respecting the late transaction, and by the law, the former instructions to general and the letter now forwarded, you will be made acquainted with the course of conduct which it is expected of you to pursue in future, in discharging the duties heretofore enjoined on him.

It is the desire of the president that you should turn your attention and direct your efforts, in the first instance, to a restoration of that state of things in the province, which existed before the late transactions. The executive considers it proper to restore back to the Spanish authorities Amelia island, and such other parts, if any, of East Florida, as may have been taken from them. With this view, it will be necessary for you to communicate *directly* with the governor or principal officer of Spain in that province, and to act in harmony with him in the attainment of it. It is presumed that the arrangement will be easily and amicably made between you. I enclose you an order from the secretary of war to the commander of the troops of the United States to evacuate the country, when requested so to do by you, and to pay the same respect to your orders, as he had been instructed to do to that of general Matthews.

In restoring to the Spanish authorities Amelia island and such other parts of East Florida as may have been taken possession of in the name of the United States, there is another object to which your particular attention will be due. In the measures lately adopted by general Matthews to take possession of that territory, it is probable that much reliance has been placed by the people who acted in it, on the countenance and support of the United States. It will be improper to expose these people, to the resentment of the Spanish authorities. It is not to be presumed that those authorities, in regaining possession of the territory in this amicable mode from the United States, will be disposed to indulge any such feeling towards them. You will, however, come to a full understanding with the Spanish governor on this subject, and not fail to obtain from him the most explicit and satisfactory assurance respecting it.—Of this assurance you will duly apprise the parties interested, and of the confidence which you repose in it. It is hoped on this delicate and very interesting point, the Spanish governor will avail himself of the opportunity it presents to evince the friendly disposition of his government towards the United States.

There is one other remaining circumstance, only, to which I wish to call your attention, and that relates to general Matthews himself. His gallant and meritorious services in our revolution, and patriotic conduct since, have always been held in high estimation by our government. His errors in this instance are imputed altogether to his zeal, to promote the welfare of his country; but they are of a nature to impose on the government the necessity of the measures now taken, in giving effect to which, you will doubtless feel a disposition to consult, as far as may be, his personal sensibility.

I have the honor to be, &c.

(Signed)   JAMES MONROE.

P. S.—Should you find it impracticable to execute the duties designated in the above requests, you will be so good as to employ some respectable character to represent you in it, to whom you are authorised to allow a similar compensation. It is hoped, however, that you may be able to attend to it in person, for reasons which I need not enter into. The expence to which you may be exposed, will be promptly paid to your draft on this department.

Volume 3, September 12, 1812, page 22

The Secretary of State
to D. B. Mitchell, governor of Georgia.

Department of State,
May 27, 1812.

Sir,—I have had the honor to receive your letter of the 2d instant, from St. Mary's, where you had arrived in discharge of the trust reposed in you by the president, in relation to East Florida.

My letter by Mr. Isaacs, has, I presume, substantially answered the most important of the queries submitted in your letter; but I will give to each a more distinct answer.

By the law, of which a copy was forwarded to you, it is made the duty of the president to prevent the occupation of East Florida, by any foreign power.— It follows that you are authorised to consider the entrance, or attempt to enter, especially under existing circumstances, of British troops of any description, as the case contemplated by law, and to use the proper means to defeat it.

An instruction will be immediately forwarded to the commander of the naval force of the United States, in the neighborhood of East Florida, to give you any assistance, in case of emergency, which you may think necessary, and require.

It is not expected, if you find it proper to withdraw the troops, that you should interfere to compel the patriots to surrender the country, or any part of it, to the Spanish authorities. The United States are responsible for their own conduct only, not for that of the inhabitants of East Florida. Indeed, in consequence of the compromitant, of the United States to the inhabitants, you have already been instructed not to withdraw the troops, unless you find that it may be done consistently with their safety, and to report to the government the result of your conferences with the Spanish authorities, with your opinion of their views, holding in the mean time the ground occupied.

In the present state of our affairs with Great Britain, the course above pointed out is the more justifiable and proper.

I have the honor to be, &c.

(Signed)   JAMES MONROE.

Volume 3, September 26, 1812, pages 49-50

Secret Journal of the
House of Representatives—
So Far as Relates to Floridian Affairs.

Friday, June 19, 1812.—On motion of Mr. Troup,

Resolved, That the committee to whom was referred so much of the President's message at the

33

commencement of the session, as relates to Spanish American colonies, be instructed to inquire into the expediency of authorising the president of the United States to occupy East and West Florida, without delay.

And then the doors were opened.

Monday, June 22.—On motion made and leave given,

Mr. Mitchill, from the committee appointed on the part of the President's message at the commencement of the session, which relates to the Spanish American colonies, presented a bill authorising the President of the United States to take possession of a tract of country lying south of the Mississippi territory and of the state of Georgia, and for other purposes, which was read the first time—When

A question was taken, whether the subject matter of the said bill required secrecy,

And passed in the affirmative—Yeas 71, nays 44.

The said bill was then read the second time, and committed to a committee of the whole house to-morrow.

And the doors were then opened.

Thursday, June 25.—The house resolved itself into a committee of the whole house, on the bill authorising the President to take possession of a tract of country lying south of the Mississippi territory and the state of Georgia, and for other purposes; and after some time spent therein, Mr. Speaker resumed the chair, and Mr. Lewis reported, that the committee had, according to order, had the said bill under consideration, and made an amendment thereto, which he delivered in at the clerk's table, where it was again read, and concurred in by the house.

The question was then taken that the said bill be engrossed and read the third time,

And passed in the affirmative—yeas 70, nays 48.

Ordered, That the said bill be read the third time to-day.

The said bill was engrossed and read the third time accordingly—When

A motion was made by Mr. Ridgely,

that the same be postponed until Monday next.

And the question being taken,

It was determined in the negative.

The question was then taken, that the said bill do pass?

And resolved in the affirmative.

Ordered, That the title be "An act authorising the President to take possession of a tract of country lying south of the Mississippi territory and of the state of Georgia, and for other purposes."

Mr. Mitchill and Mr. Troup were appointed a committee to carry the said bill to the senate, and inform them that this house have passed the same in confidence, and request their concurrence therein.

The doors were then opened.

Friday, June 26. A motion was made by Mr. Randolph, that the injunction of secrecy imposed by this house on the bill, entitled

"An act authorising the President to take possession of a tract of country lying south of the Mississippi territory and of the state of Georgia, and for other purposes," together with the injunction of secrecy imposed upon the proceedings on the said bill, be taken off."

And on the question that the house do now proceed to the consideration of the said motion.

It was determined in the negative.

A motion was then made by Mr. Ridgely, that the house do come to the following resolution:

"Resolved, That the President of the United States be requested, if in his opinion it be compatible with the public interest, to lay before this house, confidentially or otherwise, full information of all of the proceedings that have been had under and by virtue of the act of congress, entitled "An act to enable the President of the United States, under certain contingencies, to take possession of the country lying east of the river Perdido, and south of the state of Georgia and the Mississippi territory, and for other purposes," and also copies of all instructions that may have been issued by the executive branch of this government under the said act.

And on the question, that the house do now proceed to the consideration of the said resolution,

It passed in the affirmative—yeas 78, nays 38.

The question was then taken, that the said resolution do pass?

And was resolved in the affirmative—yeas 58, nays 51.

Mr. Ridgely and Mr. Ringgold were appointed a committee to present the said resolution to the president.

The doors were then opened.

Wednesday, July 1, 1812.— Mr. Ridgely from the committee appointed on the 26th ultimo, to present a resolution to the President of the United States, reported, that the committee had performed that service, and that the President answered that a due attention should be paid to the subject.

A message, in writing, was then received from the President of the United States, by Mr. Coles, his secretary, who delivered in the same and withdrew.

Friday, July 3, 1812.—A message was received from the senate by Mr. Smith, of Maryland, and Mr. Leib, a committee appointed for the purpose of notifying the house that the senate had rejected the bill, entitled "an act authorising the president to take possession of a tract of country lying south of the Mississippi territory and of the state of Georgia, and for other purposes."

A motion was then made by Mr. Randolph, that the injunction of secrecy be removed from the bill sent from this house and rejected by the senate, entitled "an act authorising the president to take possession of a tract of country lying south of the Mississippi territory and of the state of Georgia, and for other purposes."

And on the question, that the house do now proceed to the consideration of the said motion.

It was determined in the negative— Yeas 22, Nays 58.

Monday, July 6, 1812. On motion of Mr. Bibb,

Resolved, That the injunction of secrecy so far as concerns "an act to enable the president of the United States, under certain contingencies, to take possession of the country lying east of the river Perdido, and south of the state of Georgia and the Mississippi territory, and for other purposes," passed on the 26th of June last, and the proceedings thereon, respectively, be removed: and also so far as relates to the following letters: two from the secretary of state to general G. Matthews, one dated the 26th of January, one thousand eight hundred and eleven, and the other the fourth of April, one thousand eight hundred and twelve; and two, from Mr. Monroe to general D. B. Mitchill, one dated the tenth of April, the other the twenty-seventh of May, one thousand eight hundred and twelve.

The doors were then opened.

Volume 3, September 26, 1812, page 52

The Floridas. [Extract]

For the following sketch, containing much interesting matter, we are indebted to the Nashville (Ten.) "Clarion."

In the year 1803, when the violation of our right of deposit at New-Orleans had fixed the attention of the general government upon the interest of the western country, a committee of the house of representatives, of whom Dr. Dickson was one, were directed to report upon the propriety and practicability of annexing the Floridas to the United States. The report submitted on that occasion presents some views extremely interesting at the present moment, when the union of these provinces with the American states is on the point of being realized, and when necessity of a water communication between Tennessee and bay of Mobile, is felt and acknowledged by all the friends of their country.

The report describes the rivers which rising in the country of the Cherokees, and traversing the country inhabited by the Creek confederacy, discharge themselves into the Mobile bay. "In these rivers, says the report, the eastern parts of Tennessee are deeply interested; as some of the great branches of the Mobile approach very near to some of those branches of the Tennessee river which lie above the Muscle Shoals. Even if it should be difficult to connect them, yet the land carriage will be shorter, and the route to the sea more direct, than the river Tennessee furnishes. These rivers possess likewise an advantage which is denied to the Mississippi. As their sources are not in the mountain, and their course is through a level country, their currents are gentle, and the tide flows considerably above our boundary. This circumstance, together with the depth of water which many of them afford, render them accessible to sea vessels; and ships of two hundred tons burthen may ascend several hundred miles into the heart of our own territory. These rivers, however, which run almost exclusively within our own limits, and which it would seem as if nature had intended for our own benefit, we must be indebted to others for the beneficial use of, so long as the province of West Florida shall continue in the possession of a foreign nation. If the province of West Florida were still an independent empire it would be the interest of it government to promote the freedom of trade, by laying open the mouths of rivers to all nations; this having been the policy of those nations who possess the mouths of the Rhine, the Danube, the Po, the Tagus, with some others. But the jealousy of the colonial spirit will not admit of this policy, so liberal in itself, and so reciprocally advantageous to the citizens of the United States and of West Florida."

The report then speaks of East Florida. "Though not so important to the United States, the committee nevertheless deem its acquisition very desirable. From its junction with the State of Georgia at the river St. Mary's it stretches nearly four hundred miles into the sea, forming a large peninsula and has some very fine harbors. The southern point, Cape Florida, is not more than one hundred miles from the *Havana*, and the possession of it may be beneficial to us in relation to our trade with the West Indies. It would likewise make our whole territory compact, would add considerably to our sea coast, and by giving us the Gulf of Mexico, for our southern boundary, would render us less liable to attack in what is deemed the most vulnerable part of the union." The report concludes with stating: "If we look forward to the free use of the Mississippi, the Mobile,

the Apalachicola, and the other rivers of the west, by ourselves and our posterity, New-Orleans and the Floridas must become a part of the United States, *either by purchase or by conquest.*"

To this valuable report we are indebted for the acquisition of New-Orleans and the free navigation of the Mississippi. The congress of 1803 made a great stride towards securing the happiness and prosperity of the western country, and the congress of 1812 has undertaken to follow up their steps and complete their work.

Volume 3, October 17, 1812, page 107

The Southern Frontier.
From the Tennessee Herald
of September 5.

It has been expected for a long time that an English force would be thrown into Pensacola; it is now ascertained that black troops, under the command of British officers, have arrived from Cuba, and taken possession of that place; and are reconstructing the works for its defence.

The policy of stationing troops of that description upon our frontiers cannot be mistaken. The same band which has incited against us the scalping knife and the tomahawk of the Indians, will not stop to renew upon the Mobile and lower Mississippi the tragedy of St. Domingo.

The alarms of the people on the Mobile, are not without a foundation. On the north, and north-west six thousand Creeks and two thousand Choctaws divide them from the settled parts of the United States. On the south they are exposed to the incursion of the British and their black and Spanish allies: in their own bosom they contain a population which, if excited to insurrection, will require their whole force to keep it down.

Georgia and South Carolina cannot be supposed to be in a situation to afford them assistance; from Tennessee alone can they expect to receive aid; and Tennessee is three hundred miles from them. Remote from assistance, incapable of self protection, and surrounded by danger, this flourishing settlement is liable to become the theatre of great distresses.

No doubt can be entertained but that the troops from this state are destined by the general government to succour the settlements on the Mobile, to expel the British from West Florida, and to extend the boundaries of the republic to the gulf of Mexico. Nor will the president be disappointed in his expectation of finding in this state of force competent to the accomplishment of these objects. Forty thousand men, brave, robust and burning with impatience to emulate the fame of the young state of Ohio, present the materials from which a respectable army may be organised at the shortest notice.

There are still living among us many of those veterans whose courage triumphed over the British discipline at the battle of King's mountain; and of the early settlers of this country hardly one can be found who has not acquired the reputation of a soldier in the wars with the Indians.

Our local position places us at a distance from the ravages of the war. The arms of the English cannot reach us; the Indians she will excite will become the victims of their perfidious policy; the first effort of Tennessee will crush the whole of these savages that dare to lift their arms against us.

Our forces will therefore be at liberty to act upon any part of the continent where the public service shall require them; and the ardor of our young men impatient to receive the signal which shall call them from an inglorious repose to the field of honor and of danger.

Volume 3, October 24, 1812, pages 125-126

Events of the War—Military.
[Extracts]

Colonel Newman [*Newnan*], with 117 Georgia volunteers, had the last of September, an engagement with an equal number of Indians, near the Lochaway town. The latter were defeated with thirty killed, among whom was their king *Pain*. The Americans had one killed and ten wounded.

———

There have been several smart skirmishes between some small bodies of our troops and certain tribes of the southern Indians. But from the exertions now making we believe the war in that quarter will pretty soon terminate— if the *British* are expelled from Florida. The safety of the southern sates demands it, *and it must be done.* There are most important reasons for it. And the bill which passed the house of representatives of the United States, authorising the President to take possession of the country under certain circumstances, (which have now happened) but which was rejected by the senate, we hope, will become a law immediately on the meeting of congress.

———

Naval

It is confidently said the *British* are establishing a navy yard at Pensacola, in *East Florida.*

Volume 3, November 7, 1812, pages 154-155

Events of the War—Military.
[Extracts]

"Your solicitude, no doubt, is awakened, with regard to the *Southern* as well as the Northern frontier of the United States. *Here,* our citizens are alive with apprehension, as to those events which burthen the womb of futurity. The *ally* of Britain is our near neighbor. She admits into her ports, the property captured from our brethren. She becomes a medium of intelligence to the enemy cruising on our coast, and *professes friendship*, but is evidently making every preparation for war. Already has nearly three hundred *Negro* troops arrived from the Havanna; part of whom, with a few days past, reached Fort Conde at the *town of Mobile*, which, by an act of congress of the 14th May last, was declared to be within the territory of Mississippi, subject to the laws of the United States and the benefit of its institutions.

"The passage from Orleans to this, even for coasting vessels from the *Bayou St. John's*, through Lake Pontchartrain, is rendered extremely dangerous. Considerable supplies of military stores, particularly cannon, have been on the way, more than a month, and have not yet arrived, although the voyage is frequently performed in 5 and 6 days. A small schooner was taken a few days since by a British armed boat, which lay concealed near one of the numerous islands which line the coast.

"The Spaniards appear elated with the new constitution of the Cortez, and have even elected *deputies* under it, *at our town of Mobile*, to choose members for the provincial assembly at the Havanna— the American inhabitants are in the most awful situation, and their persons and property, are subject to the despotic control of a petty Spanish commandant. When they saw the act of congress annexing the country west of the *Perdido* and southward of the *old line* of demarkation, to the Mississippi territory—and the proclamation of governor Holmes, including them within the county of Mobile, and extending to them the privileges of our blessed constitution, they began to feel like *freemen*, and to believe and act as if they were Americans, indeed; but, how sadly have they been disappointed! How lamentable has been the change within a few days! The judge of this district was applied to for a writ of habeas corpus, in behalf of a prisoner confined within the walls of the Spanish fort, at *our town of Mobile*.—He hastened down and had the writ regularly served on the *commandant*, who refused to deliver up the prisoner, and referred the judge to the *governor at Pensacola*, for an answer; and possibly, before this time, the prisoner has been shipped off for the decision of the governor.

"Nothing indeed can be more perplexing than the situation of a civil magistrate in this country—he is told by congress, that American laws are to extend from *Pearl river to the Perdido*; he is bound to act as an American magistrate; but when he attempts to exercise the power vested in him by law—he is referred to the fiat of a foreign governor, stationed without our limits, by a little tyrant, executing with a rod of iron, the laws of Spain within our acknowledged jurisdiction.

"All those evils would have been happily arrested, had the senate of the United States, but concurred in taking possession of the Floridas—it will now require the loss of much blood to conquer even *our own town of Mobile*. General Wilkinson, I believe, is in momentary expectation of orders in relation to the Floridas—and every preparation is made to act at a minute's warning."

Volume 3, November 7, 1812, page 155

Extract of a letter from Benjamin Hawkins, Esq., Agent of the United States in the Creek nation of Indians, dated "Creek Agency, 13th October.

"The chiefs of some of our larger towns of the Lower Creeks, have been recently with me on affairs of their own. They say they are unanimously determined to preserve the friendship of the United States; that if the British should make an offer of arms, they will endeavor to restrain their young men from accepting of them; or, if they should accept them from using them against their friends the United States— that they depended for safety, not on arms and ammunition, but on the friendship of the president; that they are surrounded and have no back country to fly to, and if they had, they would not change their present situation of any prospects founded on uncertainty. The annual meeting of the nation will be on the 22d.— Travelling appears to be quite safe. We have had no complaints on the road of improper conduct from Indians, since the execution of the murderers."

Volume 3, November 7, 1812, page 156

Events of the War—Military
[Extract]

We are much gratified to hear (says the Milledgeville Journal) that his excellency the governor intends raising, as early as possible, several hundred mounted riflemen, for the purpose of punishing the aggressions of the Seminole Indians. Such a step has become indispensable; or we shall soon see our frontier settlers flying before the uplifted tomahawk, and the murderous scalping knife reeking with the blood of our women and children.

[Spanish] Governor Kinderland has recently augmented his premium for American scalps. He now offers eight dollars and a bottle of rum for each. We have not words to express our abhorrence of such infamous conduct, equally repugnant to humanity and every principle of honorable warfare. [*Milledgeville (Georgia) Journal, Oct 14.*

Volume 3, November 7, 1812, page 156

Savannah,
Oct. 24.

The following is extracted from a letter from a gentleman at the southward to another in this city, dated St. Mary's (Georgia) Oct. 17:—

"The only authentic news we have from Florida, since my last, is a few lines from colonel Newman to general Floyd, (which I have seen) dated last Sunday, from the plantation of Mr. Kingsly, on the river St. John's, where he had just arrived from near the Lotchway town. He does not give any account of his engagements with the Indians further than their ambuscading him on his return when they killed two of his advanced guard. The main body immediately charged and killed four Indians; the others broke, and many left their arms behind.

"Newman has preserved all his sick and wounded, and begs general Floyd to join him with 100 men, which, with him, will be sufficient to destroy the Lotchway towns.

"General Floyd started from this place at one o'clock to-day, to Colerain, with colonel Scott and major Clark; and to-morrow morning crosses the river, with from 80 to 100 men, well armed and equipped, to join Newman. I regret much my business would not admit of being of the party.

"I have conversed with the express sent by Newman, who declares that Newman lost eight men in the different battles, and killed fifty Indians; and a note from major Smith to his wife, in this town, says, Kingsly's house is handsomely decorated with Indian scalps; but does not say the number."

Volume 3, November 7, 1812, page 160

The Chronicle [Extract]

A collection of people at Savannah have destroyed a vessel at that place, loaded with supplies for St. Augustine;

and at a meeting of the citizens, resolutions have been entered into expressing their detestation of all who engage in furnishing supplies to those who have proved themselves so inimical to the United States. In the affair first mentioned, one or two persons were unfortunately killed.

Volume 3, November 14, 1812, page 170

Events of the War—Military
[Extract]

It is stated that 700 troops have arrived at Pensacola. The condition of the southern frontier becomes more and more interesting. But its defence is committed to an able officer, major general Pinkney, and he appears to be well supported.

Volume 3, November 14, 1812, page 171

Extract of a letter from an officer of rank in the southern army, dated

Hollingsworth's,
October 7, 1812.

"Contrary to my expectation, colonel Newman left Picolatta on the 24th ult. for the Lotchway Towns, with seventy-five of his own men (the remainder of the detachment refusing to prolong their service—eighteen men of Neiley's volunteers and twelve patriots.) I was not informed of his movement until some days after he commenced his march. He had proceeded within seven miles of the first town, when, on the 27th, he met a party of Indians upwards of one hundred, all mounted. They appeared much surprised at seeing him and immediately dismounted, forming the line of battle, and advancing a few paces. Newman ordered the charge; and the Indians remained firm until the volunteers were within fifty paces of them, when they broke off for the swamps, which were on three sides of the battle ground. The fire of the Georgians did great execution. King Paine fell in this action, but his body was rescued by his warriors. This engagement lasted from 11 A. M. to 3 P. M.; the Indians lost 20 or 30 killed and wounded, with all their baggage, including provisions. Just before night of the same day, the action was renewed with great obstinacy on the part of the Indians, who had received a large reinforcement from their town, but were again repulsed with great loss. Newman finding his situation extremely hazardous from the increasing number of the enemy, who begun to surround him on all sides, and unable from his wounded, either to advance or retreat, threw up a small breastwork, in which he defended himself until the 4th inst. The Indians continued to harrass him day and night, and finding they could make no impression upon him, shot his horses. Soon after the first engagement, a messenger was dispatched to me for aid. Unfortunately his guide was not good, which protracted the journey some days. From my helpless condition, I could not give him that aid which was required; however 25 horsemen were raised, and instantly dispatched to his relief with provisions; unfortunately on the arrival (which was on the night of the 4th) the camp was evacuated, nor could they tell where Newman had gone to. They returned without accomplishing the object of their expedition. An express again arrived on the 5th, who informed that the Indians had continued daily their fire, but without effect; that on the 4th, from the perfect silence which had reigned in Newman's camp for one or two days previous, the Indians believed the work deserted, and approached within fifty paces of it, when they were so roughly handled as occasioned them to retreat with precipitation, having sustained considerable loss. Newman then decamped without molestation and retired ten miles on the Picolatta road, where he awaits the arrival of provisions and horses, of which he stands much in need. Fifteen men, being all that could procure horses able to perform the service, were dispatched to his relief. We have heard of his having lost five killed and seven wounded. The Indians in the different engagements could not have lost less than sixty killed and wounded.—Too much praise cannot be bestowed on this detachment for their intrepid conduct. I flatter myself the severe check which they have received will keep them quiet awhile; if not, it will be absolutely necessary to send a sufficient force to destroy all their towns in the province for the security of our frontier."

Extract from a Message
of the governor of Georgia
(D. B. Mitchell)

In March last a revolution commenced in East-Florida, and from the part taken by the commissioner of the United States, and the movement of their troops, I flattered myself that they had determined on the immediate occupation of the whole province.

The progress of this revolution became extremely interesting to Georgia, and I am indebted to the vigilance and attention of brigadier-general Floyd, for the first and a regular continuance of information upon the subject; from which I soon began to suspect that the course pursued would not only fail of success, but that our frontier in that quarter might soon be involved in much difficulty and distress. Under these impressions, and conceiving that if the general government had determined upon the occupancy of the province, they would have communicated the fact to the government of Georgia, and placed the state on her guard against a failure of the enterprize, since in that event she would be the immediate sufferer, I wrote a letter to the secretary of war, stating my apprehensions of the evil consequences that were likely to result to Georgia from the manner in which the proceedings in Florida were conducted, and requested that the contents of my letter might be communicated to the President. Before that letter had reached its destination, I received one from the secretary of state, by order of the President, in which he declares, that the proceedings of the agent in the transactions in Florida were unauthorised, and calling upon me, as governor of the state, to act for the general government, inasmuch as the interests of Georgia were implicated as well as those of the United States; and also containing instructions as to the course which it was expected I would pursue in so delicate and important a transaction. It required but a few days to dispatch such public business as was then in the executive office, and to prepare every thing necessary to admit of my absence. This being accomplished I proceeded without delay to St. Mary's, as the most convenient spot where I could, by mail, have a free communication with any part of the union, and with the governor of East Florida, and colonel Smith, the commander of the American troops, at the same time. On my arrival at that place, I found the progress of the revolution stopped before St. Augustine, the patriots being unable alone to attack that formidable post, and the American troops not permitted to act on the offensive. In a short time I sent to Augustine, in compliance with the instructions I had received, and a correspondence between the person then acting as governor and myself commenced, which however soon terminated, in consequence of the Spaniard preferring the application of force to remove the American troops, which he actually tried on the 16th May, to the more tedious operation of having it done by negociation in a peaceful manner. The experiment, however, did not succeed, and the troops kept their ground. The letters of the secretary of state to me of the 2d and 27th of May last, will explain the reason why the troops were not withdrawn; they are reasons founded on the soundest principles of policy as well as justice and humanity, and they apply to our present situation and the present situation of East Florida with double force.

The confidence with which I anticipated the declaration of war against Great Britain, led me with equal confidence to anticipate an enlargement of the powers of the President, by congress, as the necessary consequence, having for its object the entire occupancy of East and West Florida. That this should have been the course pursued, I was extremely solicitous; knowing as I did, and still do, that the interests of Georgia would be effectually promoted by that event, and the views and wishes of the general government at the same time accomplished.—The senate of the United States, however, in their wisdom had different views of the subject, and the matter was permitted to remain as before the war.—It is nevertheless my sincere and candid opinion, that the peace and safety of this state will be hazarded, if the occupancy of East Florida, by our government, is relinquished, or much longer delayed. The present force in Augustine is of a description which we cannot tolerate, and the mode of

warfare which the governor of that place has commenced, is so savage and barbarous, that it is impossible for an American to hear it without feeling the utmost indignation and resentment against the power who commands or even permits it. I recommend this subject in an especial manner to your most serious consideration, as involving, not only your immediate interest, but your future peace and happiness. It is with real pleasure that I assure you of my entire confidence in the disposition of the president to proceed in the business with the utmost decision, if he is authorised by congress. Copies of such documents as are calculated to give you a clear view of the subject and enable you to form correct conclusions, will accompany this communication: And should any additional information be desired during the session, if in the power of the executive, it will be furnished with pleasure. I have been the more particular upon this head because I feel its importance, and because too, the agency which I have had in it, has been grossly misrepresented, and conduct and motives attributed to me as malicious as they are unfounded. That agency will now be committed to another person.

The Spanish officers in Augustine, St. Marks and Pensacola are using every effort to stimulate the Creek Indians to commence hostilities against us.—As yet those within the United States' line, as I have before observed, profess peace and friendship; but, those of the Seminoles, whose towns are in Florida, have been guilty of such outrages as leave no doubt of their intention, and ought to satisfy us that no time is to be lost in applying that chastisement which their crimes deserve. In August last some parties of them made their appearance upon the frontier of Camden county, and killed and scalped a young man about seventeen years of age, the son of Mr. Thomas Wilder, who resided near Trader's hill on St. Mary's river; and, at the same time, shot another lad, and wounded him severely, but who had the good fortune to make his escape. As soon as I received information of these facts, and numerous others of less atrocity, I sent an order to brigadier general Floyd, to cause a block house to be erected on Trader's hill, and to put a small garrison in it for the protection of that part of the frontier, and if the Indians should again make their appearance, in a hostile manner, to collect a force, and pursue and punish them. I also wrote a letter to colonel Hawkins, demanding that the murderers would be apprehended and delivered up to the civil authority of Camden county, there to take their trial. Colonel Hawkins' answer, with subsequent information which I have received, fully convinces me that we have no satisfaction to expect from these Indians, and consequently that we ought to look to our own safety. With this view, I have given orders to have a stock of provender and provision contracted for and deposited at Trader's hill, for five hundred cavalry, and intended as soon as those supplies were procured, to order that number to take the field. This subject claims the immediate attention of the legislature. Copies of all papers in the executive office, relating thereto, from which you can derive any information, as well as those relating to the deceased Mr. Meredith and Mr. Arthur Lott, who were murdered while peaceably travelling through the Creek nation, accompany this communication.

Volume 3, December 5, 1812 , page 215

Events of the War

To the *South* we have also looked with great anxiety; but we have no particulars—further than that the legislature of Georgia considering that state as in "imminent danger," were about to adopt measures, having, perhaps, for their *ulterior* object, the seizure of Florida—or at least the dispersion of the *hostile* force.

Volume 3, December 5, 1812 , page 216

A letter from colonel Edward P. Gaines, of the U. S. Army, dated at Knoxville, Ten. Nov 16, says "a war with the Lower Creeks seems now inevitable"—but the colonel is inclined to believe that the Upper Creeks, being further removed from foreign influence, will remain at peace, if the "Siminoles do not obtain a few partial victories," and if "a strong British force does not make its appearance in West Florida." We trust all these apprehensions, as well as those of the people of Georgia, may be allayed by

a law of the United States, authorising, at least, a temporary possession of the whole country.

A letter from Natchez says, that colonel Claiborne, at the head of 500 or 600 men of the militia of the Mississippi territory, had marched for Baton Rouge, with a supposed ulterior destination of *Pensacola*.

Volume 3, December 5, 1812 , page 223

Indian Retaliation

Savannah,
October 20.

A letter has been received by a gentleman in this city from his friend in the Creek nation, giving assurances that eight Creek Indians have been executed, and seven cropped and whipped, under the sentence of the chiefs of that nation, for the murders and thefts committed on the frontiers of Tennessee. To this is added, that there is as much safety in travelling among them at this time, (the Seminola tribes excepted) as there is through Georgia. The promptness with which the chiefs have complied with the wishes of colonel Hawkins on this occasion, gives new evidence of his indefatigable zeal and usefulness, as well as the pleasing hope that he will succeed in keeping them at peace with the United States.

The heated imaginations of many silly writers, have been employed in vain efforts, without taking truth for their guide, to stain the character of colonel Hawkins. It is not necessary, nor would it be correct for him to silence these scribblers by giving publicity to his motives for all his actions. It is enough that he has passed sixteen years in the constant employment of his country, without any other desire relative to his political life, than that of standing well with himself. The birth he holds he was asked to receive: It cannot be desirable to a man of his mental qualifications; and was it not for the great purposes of civilization which he has in view, there is no doubt but he would long since have retired from it. It is ardently hoped that the general government will justly appreciate his usefulness, and that he will be encourage to persevere in the laudable plans which he has commence until the

42

experiment is fairly tested.

——»»ΘⒼΘ«««—

Newnan's Expedition Against the Florida Indians

Volume 3, December 12, 1812 , pages 235-237

Newnan's Expedition.

Detailed account of colonel Newnan's late expedition against the Florida Indians.

In the House of Representatives of Georgia.

Thursday, 5th Nov. 1812—On motion,

Resolved, that his excellency the governor be requested to lay before this house any information, which may be in his possession, relative to an expedition lately conducted by the adjutant-general of this state, against the Seminolie Indians in East Florida. Read and agreed to.

Attest, HINES HOLT, Clerk.

Executive Department, Georgia,

Milledgeville, 7th Nov. 1812.

Mr. Speaker, and gentlemen of the house of representatives!

In compliance with your resolution of the 4th inst. Calling for information relative to an expedition lately conducted by the adjutant-general of this state, against the Seminolie Indians in East Florida, you will herewith receive a copy of a letter recently received at this department from colonel Daniel Newnan, which contains all the official information I possess. It is proper to remark that, as far as my knowledge extends, the expedition referred to was a voluntary act of the officers and men who were engaged in it.

D. B. MITCHELL.

New-Hope, St. John's, Oct. 19, 1812.

Dear Sir—I have now the honor of transmitting to your excellency an account of the several engagements which have taken place between the Lotchaway and Alligator Indians, and the detachment of Georgia volunteers under my command. As the object of this expedition, and the views of the persons engaged in it, have been misconstrued, and misstatements, relative to its protraction circulated, I ask the indulgence of your excellency to detail every transaction from its commencement to its termination.

I arrived upon St. John's, in obedience to your orders, about the 15th of August, with the whole of my detachment, consisting [including officers] of about 250 men, and with few on the sick report. I immediately waited on colonel Smith, before Augustine, and received orders dated the 21st of August, to proceed immediately against the hostile Indians within the province of East Florida, and destroy their towns, provisions and settlements. I then returned to the detachment upon the St. John's, and made every preparation to comply with my orders, by dispatching parties to procure horses from the few inhabitants that had not fled from the province, in preparing packs and provisions, and taking every step Which I deemed necessary to insure success to the enterprize. In consequence of the sickness of myself and nearly one half of the detachment, the period of our marching was delayed until the 24th of September; and when just upon the eve of departing, and express arrived from colonel Smith informing me that his provision waggons and the escort was attacked by a body of Negroes and Indians, and ordering me to join him immediately with 90 men, and bring all the horses and carriages I could command, for the removal of his baggage, field-pieces, and sick, he having only 70 men fit for duty. I marched to the relief of the colonel with 130 men and 25 horses, and assisted him in removing to the Block-house upon Davis's creek. This service delayed for a few days our expedition to the nation; and when the detachment again assembled upon the St. John's, and were about to commence their march, the men had but six or seven days to serve. About this time I received a letter from colonel Smith, advising me to propose to the detachment an extension of their service for 15 or 20 days longer, as the time for which they were engaged was deemed insufficient to accomplish any object of the expedition. This measure I had contemplated, and its sanction by the colonel met with my most hearty approbation; for I was unwilling to proceed to an enemy's country with a single man, who would declare, that, in any event, he would not serve a day longer than the time for which he had originally volunteered. I accordingly assembled the detachment, and after stating the necessity of a tender of further service, proposed that the men should volunteer for three weeks longer; when 84 men, including officers, stepped out and were enrolled, which, with the addition of 23 volunteer militia sent to my aid by colonel Smith, and 9 patriots under the command of captain Cone, made my whole force amount to 117. With this small body, provided with four days provisions and 12 horses, I was determined to proceed to the nation and give those merciless savages at least one battle; and I was emboldened in this determination by the strong expectation of being succored by a body of cavalry from St. Mary's, and which it has since appeared did assemble at Colerain, but proceeded no farther. On the evening of the 24th of September, we left the St. John's marching in Indian file, captain Humphrey's company of riflemen in front, captain Ford's company, under the command of lieutenant Fannin, in the centre, and captain Coleman's company, with Cone's detachment, under the command of lieutenant Broadnax, in the rear. A small party marched in front of the main body, and another in the rear, the openness of the country (except in particular places) rendered it unnecessary to employ men upon the right and left. Our encampment of nights (there being three companies) was in the form of a triangle, with the baggage in the centre, the men with their clothes on, lying with their feet pointing outwards, and their firelocks in their arms. In case of an attack, the officers were instructed to bring up their companies upon the right and left of the company fronting the enemy, and attend to the Indian mode of fighting until ordered to charge. In case of meeting the enemy upon our march, Humphrey's company was instructed to file off to the right, Fort's company to advance and form to the front in single rank, and Coleman's company to file off to the left; the whole then to advance in the form of a crescent, and endeavor to encircle the enemy. On the morning of the fourth day of our march, when within six or seven miles of the Lotchaway towns, our advance party discovered a body of Indians marching along the path meeting us, and at the same moment they appeared to have discovered us. As soon as I was informed of it, I lost no time in giving the necessary directions for the companies to advance, and obey the instructions which had been previously given to them, and which appeared exactly suited to the situation in which we found the enemy. As soon as Fort's company (at the head of which I had placed myself) had advanced to its proper ground, I discovered the Indians falling back, and making every preparation for battle, by unslinging their packs, trimming their rifles, and each man taking his place. We continued to advance, taking advantage of the trees in our progress, until we were within 130 yards of the Indians, when many of them fired, and I instantly ordered the charge, which drove them from behind the trees, and caused them to retire with the greatest precipitation; our men all the while firing at them slew several, and by repeated charges, drove them half a mile, when they took shelter in the swamp. It unfortunately happened (I presume through inadvertence) that Humphrey's company in filing to the right took too great a circuit, got a small swamp between them and the enemy, and thereby rendered the victory less decisive than it would have been, had the whole charged together, and before the Indians had dispersed themselves, and extended their force (which they soon did) near half a mile up and down the swamp. The company, however, was of service afterwards in preventing the enemy, after their dispersion, from entering our camp, retaking their baggage and provision (all of which fell into our hands) or falling upon the wounded, that had been sent to the rear. The action, including the skirmishing upon the flanks, lasted two hours and a half, the Indians frequently attempting to outflank us and get in our rear, but were repulsed by the companies extending to the right and left. We had one man killed and nine wounded, two of which have since died of their wounds.

The loss of the enemy must have been considerable. I saw seven fall to the ground with my own eyes, among whom was their king, Payne, two of them fell near the swamp, the rest our men had the curiosity to scalp. The rifle company on the right and Broadnax's on the left, speak of killing several near the swamp, who were borne off by their comrades, it being a principle among the savages to carry off their dead at the risk of their lives. We remained on the battle ground watching the movements of the Indians, who were near the swamp painting themselves, and appeared to be in consultation, all of which indicated an intention to renew the combat. Accordingly a half an hour before sunset, having obtained a considerable reinforcement of negroes and Indians, from their towns, they commenced the most horrid yells imaginable, imitating the cries and noise of almost every animal of the forest, their chiefs advancing in front in a stooping serpentine manner, and making the most wild and frantic gestures, until they approached within two hundred yards of us, when they halted and commenced firing. Our men were not to be alarmed by their noise and yells, but as instructed, remained perfectly still and steady behind logs and trees until the enemy by this forbearance had approached somewhat nearer, when a brisk and well directed fire from our line soon drove them back to their original ground. I would now have ordered the charge, but being under the necessity, from the extension of the enemy's line, of detaching nearly one-half of my force to protect our camp and wounded (the assailing of which is a great object with Indians) I was left to contend with a force three times as numerous as my own. The action lasted until eight o'clock, when the enemy were completely repulsed in every attempt whether made upon our centre or flanks. We had two men killed and one wounded; the enemy carried off several of their men before it was dark—after which all firing (of course random) was at the spot from whence the flash arose. After fighting and fasting the whole day, we had to work throughout the night, and at day light had a tolerable breast work of logs and earth, with port holes on the ground on which the battle was fought. We were reduced to this necessity, for in dispatching captain Whitaker about dark to St. John's

for a reinforcement, six more men took the liberty to accompany him, taking with them our best horses; our pilot and surgeon (who was sick) was among the number. The two days succeeding the battle, we neither saw nor heard any thing of the enemy, but on the evening of the third day they commenced firing at our work at a long distance, and renewed it every day for five or six days, but without killing or wounding any of our men.— After killing two or three of them through our port holes they seldom came within gun-shot. Seven or eight day had now elapsed since our express had left us, hunger was staring us in the face, and we were now reduced to the necessity of eating one of our horses; we had no surgeon to dress the wounded, and apprehensions were entertained that the enemy would receive reinforcements from Augustine or the Makasukie Indians. Expecting relief every hour, I was unwilling to leave our breast works while we had a horse left to eat, but I understood from some of my officers that a certain captain was determined to leave us with his company, and that many of the men giving up all hopes of relief, talked of deserting in the night rather than perish, or fall a sacrifice to the merciless negroes and Indians, whom they were taught to believe would surround us in great numbers in a few days. In this trying situation, which our few remaining horses were shot down by them, and the number of our sick daily increasing, I reluctantly assented to leave our works that night, and directed the litters to be prepared to carry the wounded. About nine o'clock we commence our distressing march, carrying five wounded men in litters and supporting two or three more. We had not proceeded more than eight miles, when the men became perfectly exhausted from hunger and fatigue and were unable to carry the wounded any farther. About two hours after we left our breast works, 25 horsemen, with provisions, arrived to our relief, on a different road from the one we had taken, but, from motives best known to themselves, instead of following us, returned to St. John's, and we were left to encounter new difficulties, two men that I had dispatched on the path the horsemen came, by some means or other missing them. We again constructed a place of defence, and I dispatched serjeant-major

Rees with one private to Picolata, to learn what had occasioned the delay of our expected supplies, and told him I should remain where I was until I could hear from him, and endeavored to procure cattle, as we discovered signs of their being near us.

The evil genius of captain _____ again prevailed, and I have since learned from captain Cone, that this person instigated not only him, but many of the privates to urge a departure from our works even in the day time, when I was convinced that the Indians knowing our weak situation would endeavor to ambuscade. This gentleman if innocent will have an opportunity of proving himself so before a court martial. With a burning fever on me, and scarcely able to walk, the march was ordered about three o'clock in the afternoon. I had directed the adjutant, captain Hardin, to march in front, to avoid all places where there could be an ambuscade, and the litters should be distributed among the different companies. Being extremely weak I marched in the rear with captain _____ (who carried my firelock) lieutenant Fannin and about fifteen or twenty privates. We had scarcely marched five miles before the front of the detachment discovered the heads of several Indians on both sides of the path, from among several pine trees that were laid prostrate by the hurricane; the same instant, the enemy fired upon our advanced party, and shot down four of them, one a Spaniard, died on the spot, and two survived a few days; my negro boy was one of them. The moment I heard the firing I ordered the detachment to charge, and the Indians were completely defeated in fifteen minutes, many of them dropping their guns, and the whole running off without ever attempting to rally. Four were left dead on the field, and I am convinced from the constant fire we kept up, that many more must have been slain, but were hid from our view by the thick and high Palmetto bushes. We lay on the battle ground all night, and started next day at 10 o'clock, marched five miles and again threw up breast works between two ponds, living upon gophers, alligators and palmetto stocks, until serjeant-major Reese arrived with provisions, and 14 horses when we were enabled to proceed to St. John's with all our sick and wounded, where a gun-boat by the direction of colonel Smith was in waiting for us, which conveyed us to his camp, where we met with every attention that humanity or benevolence could bestow. I cannot refrain from here expressing the high sense I have of the care and anxiety which colonel Smith has manifested for the detachment under my command, and his promptitude in affording every aid in his power, when apprized of our situation. My pen can scarcely do justice to the merits of the brave officers and men under my command, their fortitude under all their privations and distresses never forsaking them. Captain Hamilton, (who volunteered as a private, his company having left him at the expiration of their time,) lieutenant Fannin, ensign Hamilton and adjutant Harden distinguished themselves in a particular manner, being always among the first to charge, and first in pursuit; serjeants Holt and Attaway likewise acted very bravely, and Fort's company in general (being always near me, and under my immediate view) advanced to the charge with the steadiness of veterans. Lieutenant Broadnax shewed a great deal of courage and presence of mind, and ensign Mann who was wounded in the first action fought well. Captain Cone who was wounded in the head early in the action behaved well, and lieutenant Williams did himself great honor in every action, but particularly in the bold and manly stand he made in the night engagement. Serjeant Hawkins and corporal Neil of Coleman's company acted like soldiers, and serjeant-major Reese's activity was only surpassed by his courage; he was every where and always brave. Captain Humphreys' company acted bravely, particularly lieutenant Reed, serjeant Fields, serjeant Cowan, serjeant Denmark and many of the privates. I can only speak of captain Humphreys from the report of some of his men, who say he acted well; it so happening he never met my eye during either of the engagements, while the conduct of every other person that I have mentioned (except one or two) came under my personal observation. The number of Indians in the first engagement, from every circumstance that appeared, must have been from seventy-five to an hundred—in the second engagement, their number [including negroes, who are their best soldiers] was double ours, and in the third engagement there appeared to be fifty which was nearly equal to our force, after deducting the sick and wounded.—From every circumstance, I am induced to believe that the number of killed and wounded among the Indians must be at least fifty.

I have the honor to be, with great respect, your most obedient servant,

DANIEL NEWNAN.

His excellency David B. Mitchell.

Volume 3, December 12, 1812 , page 240

Valuable Information.

The writer of this is informed by general Twiggs, that there is in this state a large quantity of *flint rock*, of an excellent quality for gun flints; it lies about 35 miles below Augusta, near a place called Mobley's pond, in Burke county, and not more than four or five miles from the river Savannah. The quarry contains both the opaque or black, and the transparent or oil flint; and the general often supplied himself from it during the American war. [*Augusta Chronicle.*

Volume 3, December 19, 1812, page 249

Extract of a letter to the editor of the Augusta Chronicle from a volunteer in the United States requisition from Georgia, dated at colonel Smith's camp, on the St. Johns, thirty-two miles from Augustine, on the 10th of November.

"The first detachment of two hundred and ten men landed here in perfect health and safety last evening, having halted one night on our way at the village of Fernandino on Amelia Island—the boat that conveyed us here will return immediately to Point-Petre to bring on the remainder of the requisition. Colonel Smith remained at Fernandino, but is expected here daily. We are yet ignorant how we shall be employed, whether against Augustine or the Indians."

Volume 3, December 26, 1812, page 263

Events of the War—Military.

Accounts from Georgia mention that major-general Pinckney had set off to take command of the troops destined for Florida, with a view to occupy it for the United States.

Volume 3, December 26, 1812, page 272

Extract from The Chronicle

The legislature of Georgia have authorised the governor of that state to direct colonel Hawkins to demand of the chiefs of the Upper Creek nation to deliver up all of their warriors who, it was ascertained were engaged with the Seminoles in the late battles against the Americans under colonel Newnan, in order that retributive justice should be awarded them.

Volume 3, January 2, 1813, page 282

Events of the War—Military.

Appointment— James Gadsden, second lieutenant of engineers, December 2, 1812.

Volume 3, January 9, 1813, page 300

Events of the War—Military.

Two hundred and forty mounted volunteers from East Tennessee arrived at Washington, Georgia, under the command of colonel *John Williams*, about the 20th ult.; as hardy, robust and brave a body of men, perhaps, as ever trod the "tented field." They were raised in a few weeks, in consequence of a spirited proposition from colonel *Williams*, and major-general *John Cocke*, who is himself a soldier in the ranks.—Their first destination is St. Johns, to co-operate with the United States troops and Georgia militia, in East Florida, to cut up the Indians. They offered their services to the president, but marched without an acceptance of them, requesting it might be sent after them. They are uniformed and completely equipped, and will march to any post or place where they may be thought useful.

A Raleigh (N.C.) paper says that about 500 United States' troops stationed at Salisbury, have been ordered to proceed *towards* the *Floridas*.

About 100 regulars embarked at Savannah on the 23d ult. for Point Petre—the same day a considerable detachment arrived there from Augusta.

General Jackson, (says a

Milledgeville, Georgia, paper) we understand, has been ordered to Mobile with 1,500 militia from West Tennessee. A part of the United States' troops at Fort Hawkins are likewise in motion, destined we believe for the same place. From these movements and other concomitant circumstances, it would seem that an attack is meditated by our government upon East and West Florida at the same time; the two armies will probably form a junction at or near Pensacola.

We learn from an unquestionable source, that propositions have been made to colonel Hawkins, and through him to the secretary at war, by the Indian chiefs of East Florida, requesting that he will intercede with the United States in procuring peace for them; which he has promised to do, if they will immediately lay down their arms, make full and ample reparation for all the injuries we complain of, and give satisfactory pledges to our government of their friendly disposition in future. To these terms they will doubtless accede, as they are much alarmed, and will do any thing to avert the storm which impends over them.

Volume 3, January 16, 1813, pages 311-312

East Florida.

*Copy of a letter from
the governor of St. Augustine to
the governor of the state of Georgia.*

St. Augustine,
12th Dec. 1812.

Sir—It is only lately that your speech to the legislature of Georgia reached this place, otherwise your misrepresentations respecting the province of East-Florida, and the part you have acted in that infamous aggression on a friendly power, would not have remained unanswered until now. It has been a prominent feature in the conduct of all, who, like yourself, have taken an active part in this scene of iniquity, to deprive us of the means of undeceiving the American people, by interrupting our communication with Georgia; but truth will force its way in spite of all your arts, and however you may attempt to disguise your feelings, it is evident from your speech, that you are now tortured with the conviction that your infamous conduct is fully disclosed, even to the president, and that the world will

soon know how very unworthy he deems you of filling the station of commissioner.

Your discourse, sir, commences by an explicit declaration of your hopes, that the general government had demurred on the immediate occupation of the whole province, as soon as the news of the revolution reached you: this declaration is of more moment than you are aware, as it gives us a key to many of your subsequent acts, when named the United States' commissioner. For the present, all argument on the subject of your fears, for the difficulty and distress that might result to the state of Georgia, in case of the rebels failing to gain their point, I beg to ask you, sir, if you yourself could seriously believe, what you were gravely stating to your legislature? Wherein had the province of East-Florida ever given the smallest cause of alarm, or what means did she possess of annoying the state of Georgia, to whom she had been a peaceable neighbor for twenty-eight years? No, sir, you dreaded nothing of this, but you had pre-determined the occupancy of the province in your own mind, and it was indifferent to you by what means it was brought about; truth or falsehood was the same to you, provided your end was attained.

On the same principles, your conduct as commissioner was predicated. "You sent," you say, "to St. Augustine, in compliance with the instructions you had received"—You sent what? I will tell you: You sent a letter, dated the 4th day of May, which was delivered by colonel Cuthbert, on the 9th, and answered the same day: as you have not published your letter or the answer, I have communicated copies to one who will gratify the American people with a perusal of them, and enable them to judge betwixt you and the Spanish commander. "And a correspondence between the person then acting as governor and myself commenced, which, however, soon terminated in consequence," &c. Sir, there was no further correspondence with that person, than the letter mentioned and its answer, to which you never gave a reply, because it was unanswerable, unless you had dropped the mask. Colonel Cuthbert promised, on his word of honor, to bring an answer in six days, and did not come; in the mean time the rebels were permitted, by the American troops, to distress the city, by capturing the fishermen and wood-cutters, within two miles of our walls : two days after the period colonel Cuthbert was to have returned, these marauders were dislodged, and the American officer finding that some of the balls reached his camp, moved it back two miles; this you call keeping the ground; this purely defensive act, on the part of the Spaniards, with your usual regard to veracity, you are pleased to call "an experiment to remove the Americans, by force of arms, in preference to the slow mode of negociation;" but, sir, unless you can show that colonel Cuthbert was already on his return to St. Augustine, when this event took place, your subterfuge will not avail you, and had he been even at the camp, at the time it happened, the explanation given you by governor Kindelan, in your subsequent correspondence, would have satisfied any man, who was not pre-determined, as you were, to avoid all measures of accommodation. Your excellency must be aware, from what has been said, that I have seen your correspondence with that gentleman, I am therefore entitled to ask you, how you have ventured to assert to your legislature, that they would find, in the letters of the secretary of state to you, dated the 2d and 27th of May, the reason why the troops were not withdrawn, when you are conscious, that you never once mentioned the subject to governor Kindelan? That a governor may deceive his legislature, if they are credulous enough to take his *ipse dixit*, may be perfectly fair, for aught I know; but for an officer to state officially, what he knows to be unfounded, for the purpose of imposing upon his superiors, and prejudicing them against a foreign power, I know of no epithet in the English language, sufficiently strong to express the abhorrence we must feel for such a person. In the same class of rank and unprincipled imposition, I place, without hesitation, the picture you are pleased to draw of the situation of this garrison, and the mode of warfare carried on, for the purpose of alarming your fellow-citizens. At the moment I write, sir, there is more sobriety, and more subordination to legal authorities in St. Augustine, than in the town of Savannah; and, whatever alderman Charlton, and his town-meetings, may say to the contrary,

we feel ourselves very superior to him and his mob of incendiaries. Our mode of warfare was forced upon us, for we did not seek it; you threatened to starve us, and you allowed your allies, the banditti, whom you unblushingly call patriots, to proscribe, by proclamation, the free people of color, who, you ought to know, form part of the militia in all Spanish colonies: after such conduct you have no right to prescribe to us, what arms we are to make use of; as well might the mid-night ruffian insist upon your laying aside your blunderbuss, and meeting him on a footing of equality with pistols; retrace your steps, withdraw from our country, and you have nothing to fear from our ***** troops; but the Indians you say—well, sir, why wantonly provoke the Indians, if you dislike their rifle and tomahawk? General Matthews told Paine, in the square of Latchuo, that he intended to drive him from his land. M'Intosh sent a message to Bowlegs, another Indian chief, that he intended to make him as a waiting man; the Florida convention partitioned their lands amongst their volunteers, as appears by a certificate in my possession, signed by director M'Intosh; the Indian trade was destroyed by you and your friends, and they found that, from the same cause, they were to be deprived of their annual presents. These, sir, are the provocations about which you are silent. What are the outrages introduced into your speech with so much solemnity of diction? The murder of a youth, whose father was engaged in the Florida rebellion. The province of East-Florida may be invaded in time of profound peace, the planters ruined, and the population of the capital starved, and, according to your doctrine, all is fair; they are a set of out-laws if they resist, with such means as they have in their power. The Indians are to be insulted, threatened, and driven from their lands; if they resist, nothing less than extermination is to be their fate; but you deceive yourself, sir, if you think the world is blind to your motives; it is not long since the state of Georgia had a slice of Indian lands, and the fever is again at its height. Is your excellency altogether pure—does not the name of *Gunby* bring a blush upon your cheek? Does it not remind you that your character is in the power of all the persons privy to the bargain?

Governor, I now take my leave of you; what I have said is more for the purpose of unmasking your apparent patriotism, than from any expectation of its influencing the determination of Congress.—Whatever assurances you may have received from the president, of his solicitude to "act with decision," if authorised by that body, we flatter ourselves, that it possesses too much virtue, to permit an act of injustice, which must stamp the American name with infamy. The nomination of general Pinckney is an assurrance to the contrary, as we are convinced, that he never will lend his name to authorise an action that might disgrace his fair character.

I remain, your excellency's, very obedient servant,

BENIGNO GARZIA.

Governor Mitchell,
State of Georgia.

———

Copy of a letter from Governor Mitchell to the Governor of St. Augustine.

St. Mary's,
4th May, 1812.

Sir—The President of the United States has commissioned me to communicate with you on the transactions which have recently taken place in East-Florida, and in which the forces of the United States have been used, and I am authorised to assure you, that these transactions were not authorised by the government.

I hasten to make this communication under the fullest confidence that it will be received as evidence of the friendly disposition of the government of the United States to that of Spain, and of their desire to maintain and preserve, uninterrupted, that harmony which has so long subsisted between the two nations.

I send my aid de camp, colonel Cuthbert, to you with this letter, who will, if you desire it, wait for, and bring me your answer, which I have to request in writing. In the mean time, if you are disposed to make any verbal communications to him, with the view of conveying to me your sentiments [in that way,] on any point regarding the business upon which he is sent, you may have reliance upon his honor in executing your

wishes in that respect.

I am, sir, with high consideration, your very obedient servant,

(Signed)   D. B. MITCHELL.

To the governor of East-Florida,
in St. Augustine.

———

Translation of the Governor
of St. Augustine's
answer to the foregoing.

Most Excellent Sir—This day I received by your aid de camp, colonel Cathbert, your letter dated in St. Mary's, Georgia, 4th instant, by which you are pleased to inform me, that you are commissioned by the president of the United States to communicate with me on the subject of the transactions that are taking place in this country, in consequence of the active part taken by the regulars of the United States, which proceedings have been disapproved by the government, as it is desirous of maintaining the good understanding that has subsisted so long between the two nations.

Spain has always endeavored to give proofs of her good faith by a scrupulous fulfilment of her treaties; she therefore never could have imagined that her province of East Florida, under my charge, would have been exposed to the insults she has suffered. The public papers of the United States having announced the disapprobation of the hostile conduct of general Mathews and commodore Campbell, I flattered myself that the United States troops would have been withdrawn ere now:—until that take place, I can hold no treaty, and in the mean time, protest, as I have verbally informed colonel Cuthbert, against whatever may happen, as I do not acknowledge any other authority on this side of the dividing line, marked out by both nations, in their treaty of friendship, limits and navigation, dated 27th Oct. 1795.

God preserve you many years.

9th May, 1812.

JUAN JOSE DE ESTRADA.

Governor Mitchell,
State of Georgia.

Volume 3, January 16, 1813, page 316

Events of the War—Military.

The various movements towards and about the capital of *East-Florida* indicate decisive measures.— Our forces in the neighborhood of *St. Augustine* is constantly augmenting, and the army is very respectable.

Volume 3, January 23, 1813, page 330

Events of the War—Military.

The Spanish force in St. Augustine is said to consist of 400 white and 500 black troops. An attack upon it is anticipated.

Volume 3, February 20, 1813, page 396

Events of the War—Military.

It is stated in an *Augusta* paper, that general *Flournoy* has determined to employ the *Tennessee* volunteers with captain *Saunder's* rifle company, in an expedition against the Seminole Indians; and adds "if so, the fate of that nation is sealed."

Volume 3, February 27, 1813, page 410

Extract of a letter to the editor of the Weekly Register, dated Fort Stoddert, Feb. 3, 1813.

"The legislature of the Mississippi Territory, have appointed commissioners to select a place within the *country of Mobile* for the holding of courts, and it is said, they very *happily* have designated the *city of Mobile* as the most eligible situation. In April next, the superior court commences its first session there, *nearly under the walls of the Spanish fort*, and there is no doubt but what the Dons will *forcibly* resist the exercise of our authority.—We cannot of course, avoid giving the *retort courteous*, and must *oust* them of their *strong holds, to preserve the peace.* Judge Toulmin, who presides, is peculiarly calculated to meet the difficulties which are the consequence of our embarrassing situation, and will act with *becoming energy*, should he be opposed in the execution of his duty.

"When I passed Mobile on the 21st ultimo, I had occasion to purchase a small quantity of bread, which could only be got out of the town, by *secreting* it under the garments of one of my men—the sale being prohibited because of its scarcity; the same want of flour prevails at Pensacola, said to be occasioned by a *vacuum* in Ferdinand the VII's *strong chest*, and a consequent loss of credit— but, I presume, by the high prices in the Orleans market, where flour was selling by the cargo, at 20 to 21 dollars per barrel.

"We have from 500 to 600 volunteers enrolled at New-Orleans, and in ten or twelve days shall have upwards of 300 performing duty at this post. At Baton Rouge, there are betwixt 600 and 700 militia embodied, of the Mississippi Territory, and I presume *at least* 600 volunteers are now raised in the counties west of Pearl River—all for the defence of Louisiana—Yet, Claiborne has not the power to call out a single *militia man*, and perhaps the *legislature* may not invest him with it.

"General Wilkinson is concentrating his force at Orleans, by order of government, to repel an invasion which it is presumed is meditated against that island.

"Colonel Hawkins, the U. S. Agent for the *Creeks*, informs us by the last mail but one, that a deputation of those Indians had lately been to visit *their friends* at Nassau (New Providence) and that the nation generally were solicitous for the arrival of the British at St. Marks and St. Augustine, to obtain presents; but, he believes, they would not engage in the war."

❧━━≫⊖⊛⊖≪━━❧

NILES' WEEKLY REGISTER.

THE PAST—THE PRESENT—FOR THE FUTURE.

EDITED, PRINTED AND PUBLISHED BY H. NILES, AT $5 PER ANNUM, PAYABLE IN ADVANCE.

Volume 4

(March 6, 1813 - August 28, 1813)

Volume 4, March 13, 1813, page 29

Events of the War—Military.

Milledgeville, Feb. 24.—A gentleman of respectability in St. Mary's, writes to his friend in this place under date of the 6th inst. As follows:

"Two hundred and fifty horsemen, including the Tennessee volunteers, and two hundred infantry from St. John's, commanded by colonel Smith, started last Wednesday for the Aulotcheewans. They will form a junction this day within six miles of the first town. God send them success!"

Volume 4, March 20, 1813, page 48

Events of the War—Military.

The volunteers from *Tennessee*, whose arrival in *Georgia* was noticed sometimes since, with some additional corps under colonel *Smith*, have entered the Indian country, destroyed several towns, containing in the whole 350 houses, among which were Payne's town and Bowlegs' town, killed from 50 to 60 Indians, seized 300 horses, &c. with the loss of only one man killed and 7 wounded. We expect particulars for our next paper.

The destruction of the *Seminoles* appears sealed. They are the most barbarous of all the Southern Indians.

Volume 4, March 27, 1813, page 67

Events of the War—Defeat of the Indians.

Savannah, March 4—We have been politely favored with an extract of a letter from a gentleman in St. Mary's to his friend in this city, dated Feb. 27, 1813, from which we extract the following:

"On the evening of the 22d ult. Brigadier-general Flournoy received an express from captain Pinkney stating, that the volunteers sent against the Lotchway and Seminole Indians had returned, and had completely defeated them. Since then, I have conversed with several of the volunteers—they state, that they had three engagements, killed thirty-eight Indians, wounded many, and took seven prisoners— burnt three hundred and eighty-six houses, destroyed several thousand bushels of corn, took four hundred horses, and about the same number of cattle. The Indians disappeared entirely before the detachment left the settlement. Mr. Wildcar, who had a son murdered and scalped some months ago by these savages, went on the expedition and found his son's scalp in one of their houses. These wretches had also taken up the bodies of Newnan's men, cut off their heads and pinned them to the trees.— One of the Tennessee volunteers, under the command of colonel Williams, was killed, and 7 wounded. This is the only loss the whole detachment met with in the three engagements.

Volume 4, April 17, 1813, page 116

Events of the War—Military.

The war against the southern Indians appears to be finished. The late excursion to the *Seminole* towns have reduced the deluded people to the most calamitous condition. The survivors are literally starving.

Great distress prevails in *St. Augustine* for want of provisions. The inhabitants are deserting it for want of bread. The crops of corn, &c. in Florida were last year very short, and the war has prevented their usual supplies from the United States.

East Florida.

*St. Augustine,
March* 18, 1813.

Proclamation.

Don Sebastian Kindelan y Oregon, knight of the order of St. James, brigadier-general of the national armies, civil and military governor of the city of St. Augustine, East Florida, and of said province, for his majesty, &c.

I make known to the inhabitants of the province, that his excellency, the captain-general of it and the island of Cuba, under the date of 11th Feb. last, writes me as follows.

His excellency, the secretary of state for the affairs of grace and justice, under date of 16th Dec. last, writes me the annexed decree.

Decree.—"Don Fernando VII, by the grace of God, and by the constitution of the Spanish monarchy, king of Spain, and during his absence and captivity, the regency of the kingdom specially authorised by the general and extraordinary cortes, to grant an amnesty to the insurgents, who have co-operated in the invasion of the Spanish territory in East and West Florida, acting in conformity with the beneficent and conciliatory principles of the said cortes, and wishing to give a new proof of their clemency in favor of the Spanish subjects, who, unfortunately forgetful of their duties, have added to the distress of the mother country, during a most critical epoch; has determined to grant them a general pardon with oblivion of the past, on condition that, in future and after the proclamation of this amnesty, they shall demean themselves as good and faithful Spaniards, yielding due obedience to the legitimately constituted authorities of the national government of Spain, established in the peninsula.

"Wherefore you will take notice thereof and cause the same to be fulfilled in conformity."

By order of their highness, I transmit the same to your excellency for your information and its fulfillment on your part. And I transcribe the same to your excellency, that it may be put in execution in the district of your command. And

that the same may come to the knowledge of all persons whatsoever, I order the publication thereof, by proclamation, and that the notarial copies be exhibited in the usual places of this city, assigning the term of four months, calculated from the date of these presents, for all persons interested to make their appearance to avail themselves of this royal amnesty.

*St. Augustine, East Florida,
15th March*, 1813.

SEBASTIAN KINDELAN.

By order of his excellency, as actuating witnesses for want of a notary.

JOHN DE ENTRALGO,
BERNARD JOSEPH SEQUI.

———

Counterpart.—A Proclamation.

Resolved unanimously, That the legislative council view with disdain and abhorrence the proffer of pardon by the corrupt government of St. Augustine; that they will, and do, pledge their reputation and property, to support the glorious cause in which they are engaged, and persist until they secure the safety, independence and liberty of themselves and constituents.

Patriots of East Florida!— At last the corrupt government of St. Augustine has come forward with a proclamation offering "amnesty to the insurgents who have co-operated in the invasion (falsely so called) of the Spanish territory in East and West Florida." Weak must be the mind that can have the least dependence upon a promise so hollow and deceitful. Can any one believe, that such a corrupt, jealous and arbitrary government will adhere to promises however sacredly made? Will they not screw every title of your property from you, under the pretext of making retribution for damages done to individuals who have adhered to their oppressors? Aided by a venal judge, supported by a cruel government, your enemies will harrass you as long as a cent remains with you. But, it is needless to dwell upon the subject; The pardon no doubt has been manufactured in St. Augustine— the government of Spain knows nothing of it. It is designed to entrap the unwary; thinking that you are depressed by the rumor (however false) that the troops are to be removed.

Can you! Will you! In poverty become the sport of slaves and the abhorred army in St. Augustine? It has been unanimously resolved by the legislative council, that they, in their representative and individual capacity, will not receive the pardon so treacherously offered; but will proceed, and act to the utmost of their power, until their liberty and independence are secured. We call upon you all to unite, and by our joint exertions secure our safety, property, liberty and independence. There can be but two parties, friends and enemies— those that are not with us will be treated as foes. Measures are now, and will be taken to punish rigorously those who basely desert. Spies and emissaries will meet their just punishment.

Done in council, 30th March, 1813.

B. HARRIS,
President of the legislative council.
Attest,   DANIEL S. DELAMIG,
Secretary of state.
Approved, JOHN H. M'INTOSH,
Director Ter. East-Florida.

—•»»☻◉☻«««—

General Wilkinson Takes Control of Mobile

Volume 4, April 24, 1813, page 132

Extract of a letter
from Fort Stoddart, to the editor
of the Weekly Register,
dated 1st April, 1813.

"On or about the 10th inst. general Wilkinson will take, either peaceably or forcibly, possession of the town and citadel of Mobile, and the American standard will at last wave victorious over the venerable ramparts of Fort Conde. The great strength of this fortress (erected during the reign of Louis XIV.) may be deduced from the circumstance of its having been defended several weeks by 80 men, against the united attack of 2000 under Don Galvez, in 1780, and finally capitulated honorably. One hundred and fifty rations are said to be the daily issues to the Spanish garrison, but I scarce think that the number of troops can justify it.

Be assured, the disasters of the North will never be repeated in our South Western army; for its commander prefers death to defeat, and all his officers are equally emulous of distinction."

Volume 4, May 8, 1813, page 159

Events of the War—Miscellaneous.

We have it in report that appears worthy of credit, that *East Florida* is to be immediately evacuated by the United States' troops. It is stated that only to the 28th ult. was allowed the patriots to make their submission to the *Spanish* government, or retire. This regulation, it is said, will produce great distress among the people — they cannot, in safety, submit — nor remove without ruin. *Amelia* island will, of course be given up, and a might scene of smuggling and treasonable intercourse must be expected. Nor are the black troops in *Florida*, very pleasant neighbors to the people of the South. We may soon expect more particular intelligence from that country in respect to which (considering the subserviency of the *Spanish* government to the views of Great Britain) we are unpleasantly fixed.

Volume 4, May 8, 1813, page 160

Copy of a letter from
brigadier-general Thomas Flournoy
to his excellency governor Mitchell,
dated Creek Agency, 15th April, 1813.

Sir— I find on my arrival at this place that many of the reports, respecting Indian hostility, are totally unfounded, and those founded in truth, much exaggerated.

The chiefs of the tribes are in council on the subject of the late outrages, and it is expected that the offenders will be brought to justice.

Colonel Hawkins is decidedly of opinion that there is no danger to be apprehended in passing to Fort Stoddart, to which place I shall proceed in the morning.

I have the honor to be, your excellency's obedient servant,

THO. FLOURNOY.
His excellency D. B. Mitchell.

Volume 4, May 29, 1813, page 209

Events of the War—Military.

Letter to the Editor of the Weekly
Register, dated

"Fort Charlotte,
Town of Mobile,
April 18.

"Sir—On the 15th inst. Don
Cayetano Perez and the Spanish garrison,
surrendered to the United States troops
under general Wilkinson, and were
immediately shipped to Pensacola
in public transports. The fort was
well supplied with munitions of war
and military stores—and presented a
formidable battery of sixty-two pieces of
ordnance.

"In a few days we march with a
considerable detachment to the Perdido
river— the extreme eastern boundary
of the Mississippi territory, to awe the
Indians, who are said be encouraged to
acts of hostility by the Spaniards. An
express arrived a few moments since,
advising, the governor of Pensacola had
sent *runners* to the Creeks and Seminoles,
with an offer of arms, ammunition,
and *presente*, if they would attack our
frontier settlements on the Alabama
and Tombigby. General Wilkinson,
anticipating such measures, has deposited
a number of muskets in the hands of
the colonels of militia, for defensive
operations; and the citizens, very much
alarmed, are erecting block-houses, to
retire to in case of necessity."

Volume 4, June 12, 1813, page 239

Events of the War—Military.

Augusta, May 28— Mr. Fromentin,
a senator in Congress from Louisiana,
arrived here last evening on his way to
Washington. Mr. Fromentin travelled
here through the Creek nation without
interruption. On his way he fell in with
a party of warriors under the direction of
M'Queen, king of the upper towns, who
had been in Pensacola for the purpose
of obtaining arms, &c. from the Spanish
governor of West Florida; the governor
informed the deputation that he had
instructions to arm the nation generally,
but not partially, and provided a majority
of the nation would make application he

would furnish them with arms— and Mr.
Fromentin understood that a meeting of
the Indians was to be held immediately
in the different towns to determine on
the propriety of the application. At the
house of Manac, a chief of considerable
property and influence, a number of
runners from the North Western Indians
were constantly assembled, and were
daily going and returning from the seat
of war, and they have much earlier
information of events in that quarter than
their white neighbors.

Mobile, May 4—By a gentleman
on whose veracity we can rely, and who
has just returned from Pensacola, we are
informed that the former governor of that
place has departed for Havanna; and
that Gonzales Manrique, has arrived at
Pensacola, as governor of West Florida.
The former governor had favored the
assembling at Pensacola, of about
400 Indians in the course of last week
and the week before, supposed to be
Seminoles and disaffected Creeks. Our
informant saw about 60 chiefs there last
week. The new governor had dismissed
them, with his pointed disapprobation
of their assembling and of their object.
He appears to recommend a peaceable
deportment of the Indians towards the
people of the United States.

Volume 4, June 26, 1813, page 271

Events of the War—Military.

Those of the *Creek* Indians who
lately murdered certain white persons,
were first outlawed by the nation, and
afterwards put to death. The murderers
with a few adherents made battle, but
were every one destroyed by the warriors
of the tribes, headed by Mr. M'Intosh. A
British officer at *Pensacola* "has arms
and ammunition for the red people"—
this kind of neutrality that will not be
permitted, though there is every reason
to believe the Creeks will inviolably
preserve the peace.

56

Volume 4, August 28, 1813, pages 417-418

Events of the War—Military.

The Creek Indians.—No longer considering the deluded *Creeks* as separated from the general allied war against us, we shall hereafter notice events transpiring among them as belonging to the common enemy. They have received from *Canada* an order upon the *English* store at *Pensacola* for arms and ammunition, and one account says they have actually received therefrom "100 pack-horse loads" of supplies. The *Big Warrior* (a friendly Indian) reports that the hostile Creeks had killed two white men— that some skirmishes had taken place between the opposite parties, in which the *British* allies rather had the advantage. From every appearance an active and bloody war, a "war of extermination," perhaps, has commenced.

Volume 4, August 28, 1813, page 424

The Chronicle.

East Florida.— A battle took place between the patriots and royalists of *East Florida*, on the 7th inst. in sight of *St. Marys*. The latter proceeded from Amelia Island. The royalists were completely defeated; and had 6 men killed and 12 or 14 wounded. It is thought that *Amelia* will soon be attacked by the patriots.

—※»☻◉☻«※—

NILES' WEEKLY REGISTER.

THE PAST—THE PRESENT—FOR THE FUTURE.

EDITED, PRINTED AND PUBLISHED BY H. NILES, AT $5 PER ANNUM, PAYABLE IN ADVANCE.

Volume 5

(September 4, 1813 - February 26, 1814)

Volume 5, September 4, 1813, page 7

Events of the War—Military.

The Creeks.—The war party is reported to be 3000 strong—the peace party at 1000. The governor of Georgia has went on to the frontiers to prepare for the reception of the military force he had called out; which has marched under the command of brigadier general *Stewart.*

Volume 5, September 25, 1813, page 56

Events of the War—Miscellaneous.

A report prevailed at *Milledgeville,* Georgia, on the 26th ult. that the Spaniards had demanded the repossession of Mobile, and the territory west of the *Perdido.* And certain accounts had been received that the *Creeks* had obtained arms and ammunition from *Pensacola.* It was understood they were fortifying themselves on the *Alabama.*

Volume 5, October 2, 1813, page 77

Events of War—Military.

The Creek Indians.—The friends of humanity have manifold cause to regret the horrid tale that follows, communicated in a letter from *St. Stephens,* M. T. dated the 4th ult. and confirmed in substance by several other accounts. They will not only lament the butchery at *Tensaio,* but see in that affair the annihilation of the pleasing prospect they had of the amelioration of the Creeks, and their final settlement in civilized life. To effect this, the government of the United States, under every administration, had treated them with parental tenderness. Surrounded as they are by the white people and without a back country to fly to, they have many years existed by the

justice of the United States; who have restrained all attempts to infringe on their territory or violate their rights—though the luxuriance of the land they hold has excited the avarice of many; and, remote as they were rendered it no easy task to secure to them "peace, liberty and safety." Many of the chiefs had fully fallen into the plan of civilization; cultivating their lands in regular order; and, in their domestic or household affairs, approaching us so nearly that the difference could hardly be discovered. A gentleman of great respectability who passed through their country some months ago, informed the editor of the Register, that he had dined at one of the chief's houses where the whole business of eating and drinking was done in a style and manner that might be compared with that of any private gentleman in the best settled states. All the pleasant prospects we had are clouded by blood, and forever blasted by that treacherous people, for whom we have done so much; so that *mercy* itself seems to demand their extermination, to prevent greater clamity. This is one of the horrible fruits of the *"ever watchful influence of England,"*— and destruction follows wherever her consels lead, in *America* as well as in *Europe.* But what cares she for the annihilation of the *Creeks?* What is it to her, that humanity must lament the destruction of these *Aborigines?* But the cruelty of exciting them to a war in which she knows they must perish, shall be registered to her infamy, and add a little to the fullness of the cup of her abominations—and the world shall rejoice when she herself becomes the prey of that desolation, which the hardness of her heart and serpent-blooded feeling of her rulers, has spread through all nations and people that listened to her voice or felt the power of her arms.—

"The storm which has been so long gathering, and so often predicted by honest, respectable citizens, has a length fallen on our infant and defenceless settlements. On Monday last [Aug.

8, 1813] the Creek Indians commence hostilities against us, and on that day reduced one fort at Tensaio, about 15 miles from Stoddert; in which there were between three and four hundred persons of every description. Of these, about one hundred and thirty-five were volunteers in the service of the United States and local militia. 'Tis said the fort was surprised; and that the Indians entered at one of the gates and set fire to an old frame house in the centre of the pickets. All was done that could be effected by cool determined bravery; but overpowered by numbers, they were literally *butchered*, the house set on fire, and the old men, women and children (who were in an upper room) burnt to death. Our little Spartan band sold their lives well, having killed (as stated by the few who escaped) about two hundred, and wounded many more. Of all that were in the fort, eight only have got in, and they escaped by cutting down the pickets. Under the double influence of British gold and furious fanaticism, the savages fought in a manner scarcely to be credited. The fight was obstinately maintained for a long time; and the opponents, overcome by fatigue and exertion, loaded their pieces deliberately and shot each other down, or were mutually dispatched by the bayonet and tomahawk.

"The brave and much lamented major Beaseley commanded, and was killed at the gate, very early in the action; at this place sixty-three of the savages were killed. Not an officer of the fort survived—they fell bravely discharging their duty to their country. This disastrous event has stricken a panic into many citizens east of Tombigbee, and they are flying in every direction. At this place we have made a stand, and must either repulse the enemy or share the fate of those who fell in the fort at Tensaio."

—•»»·❂·◉·❂·«««·—

Fort Mims Massacre

Volume 5, October 16, 1813, pages 105-107

Indian Warfare.

The following letter from Judge Toulmin to the editor of the Raleigh Register, gives a particular account of the late shocking massacre at Tensaw:

"Mobile,
September 7.

"Dear Sir—The dreadful catastrophe which we have been some time anticipating has at length taken place. The Indians have broken in upon us, in numbers and fury unexampled. Our settlement is overrun, and our country, I fear, is on the eve of being depopulated. The accounts which we received led us to expect an attack about the full moon of August; and it was known at Pensacola, when the ammunition was given to the Indians who were to be the leaders of the respective parties destined to attack the different parts of our settlement. The attempt was made to deprive them of their ammunition (issued by the Spaniards on the recommendation of a British general) on the way from Pensacola (and in which it was said the Indians lost more than 20 men, although only one third of our people stood their ground) it is highly probable in some measure retarded their operations; and the steady succession of rain contributed to produce the same effect. Had their attempt been conducted with more judgment and supported with more vigor, there would have been an end, for a time of Indian warfare. In consequence of the delay, our citizens began to grow careless and confident; and several families who had removed from Tensaw to Fort Stoddert, returned again and fell a sacrifice to the merciless savages.

Our whole plan of defence was erroneous. It was adopted by the citizens under an imperfect view of their danger. From the best accounts with I can obtain, I suppose that there must have been twenty forts erected on the two sides of the river between Fort Stoddert and the upper settlements, a distance of about 70 miles, which in a country so thinly settled as ours, could not be maintained, even if they had been better constructed. About the 20th of August, intelligence was communicated to us by the Choctaw Indians, that in eight or ten days, that an attack would be made by distinct bodies of Creeks on Mims's Fort, in the Tensaw settlement, which is on the east side of Alabama, nearly opposite to Fort Stoddert—on the forts in the forks of Tombigby and Alabama—on Easely's fort, near the Choctaw line on the Tombigby—and finally on the Fort and United States' trading house at Ft. Hopkins. A very valuable officer, major Beasely of Mississippi Territory volunteers, commanded at Fort Mims. About a mile or two from it was another fort at Pierce's mills; and a few miles below that place, at another mill a small party of soldiers was also stationed. Mims, however, where were the greatest number of families and property collected, seems to have been the sole object of attack in that quarter.

A few days before the attack, some negroes of Mr. M'Girt's who live in that part of the Creek territory which is inhabited by half breeds, had been sent up the Alabama to his plantation for corn; three of them were taken by a party of Indians. One escaped and brought down news of the approach of the Indians. The officer gave but little credit to him; but they made some further preparation to receive the enemy. On the next day Mr. James Cornes, a half-breed, and some white men, who had been out on the late battle ground, and discovered the trail of a considerable body of Indians going towards Mr. M'Girt's, came to the fort and informed the commanding officer, of the discovery. Though their report did not appear to receive full credit, it occasioned greater exertions; and Saturday and Sunday, considerable work was done to put the fort in a state of defence. Sunday morning three negroes were sent out to attend the cattle, who soon returned with an account that they had seen 20 Indians.—Scouts were sent out to ascertain the truth of the report. They returned and declared that they could see no signs of Indians. One of the negroes belonging to Mr. Handon was whipped for bringing what they deemed a false report.—He was sent out

again on Monday, and saw a body of Indians approaching; but afraid of being whipped he did not return to Mims's, but to Pierce's fort; but before his story could be communicated, the attack was made. The commanding officer called upon Mr. Fletcher, who owned another of the negroes, to whip him also.—He believed the boy and resisted two or three applications; but at length they had him actually brought out for the purpose, when the Indians appeared in view of the fort. The gate was open. The Indians had to come through an open field 150 yards wide, before they could reach the fort, and yet they were within thirty steps of the fort, at 11 in the morning, before they were noticed. The sentry then gave the cry of 'Indians!' and they immediately set up a most terrible war-whoop and rushed into the gate with inconceivable rapidity, and got within it before the people of the fort had any opportunity of shutting it. This decided their fate. Major Beasely was shot through the belly near the gate. He called to the men to take care of the ammunition and to retreat to the house. He went himself to a kitchen where it is supposed he must have been burnt.

The fort was originally square. Major Beasely had it enlarged, by extending the lines of two side about 50 feet, and putting up a new side into which the gate was removed. The old line of pickets stood, and the Indians upon rushing into the gate, obtained possession of this additional part, and through the port holes of the old line of pickets fired on the people who held the interior. On the opposite side of the fort, an offset or bastion was made round the back gate, which being open on the outside was also taken possession of by the Indians, who with the axes which lay scattered about immediately began to cut down the gate. There was a large body of Indians, though they probably did not exceed 400. Our people seemed to sustain the attack with undaunted spirit. They took possession of the port holes in the other lines of the fort and fired on the Indians who remained in the field. Some of the Indians got on the block house, at one of the corners; but after firing a good deal down upon the people they were dislodged. They succeeded however in setting fire to a house near the pickets from which it was communicated to the kitchen and from thence to the main dwelling house. They attempted to do it by burning arrows, but failed. When the people in the fort saw the Indians retained full possession of the outer court, that the gate continued open, that their men fell very fast, and that their houses were in flames, they began to despond. Some determined to cut their way through the pickets and escape.— Of the whole number of white men and half-breeds in the fort, is supposed that not more than 25 or 30 escaped and of these many were wounded. The rest and almost all of the women and children fell a sacrifice either to the arms of the Indians or to the flames. The battle terminated about an hour or an hour and a half before sunset.

The information thus far, was given to me by a person of character and credibility, who was present during the whole scene, and who escaped through the opening made in the pickets: The women and children took refuge in an upper story of the dwelling house: and it is said that the Indians when the building were in flames, danced round them with savage delight. The helpless victims perished in the flames. It is also reported, that when the buildings were burning and the few who remained were exposed to the heavy fire of enemy, they collected as many as they could of the guns of the deceased, and threw both them and the remaining stock of ammunition into the flames, to prevent their becoming subservient in the hands of the Indians, to the destruction of their fellow citizens. Surely this was an instance of determined resolution and benevolent foresight of which there are not many examples.

But notwithstanding the bravery of our fellow-citizens, the Indians carried all before them, and murdered the armed and the helpless without discrimination. Our loss is 7 commissioned officers and about 100 non-commissioned officers and privates, of the first regiment of Mississippi Territory volunteers. There were about 24 families of men, women and children in the fort, of whom almost all have perished, amounting to about 160 souls. I reckon, however, among them about six families of half breeds, and seven Indians. There were also about 100 negroes, of whom a large proportion were killed. The half-breeds have uniformly done themselves honor, and those who

survive will afford great assistance in the prosecution of the war. Some of the most respectable among them were at Pierce's fort, and are ready with all their dexterity and all their courage, to avenge the death of their friends, and the destruction of their property. It was principally through them that we learnt that the real object of the Indians, in obtaining ammunition at Pensacola, was to make immediate war on the white people, and that the idea entertained in the eastern part of the Creek Nation, that this was only a secondary and remote object, was not founded in fact, and was probably suggested for the purpose of putting us off our guard, and keeping out of sight the real intention of their revolt against the constituted authorities of their nation.

The mournful tale of the disaster at Mims' reached the cantonment near Fort Stoddert, a distance of 16 miles, not until about 10 o'clock on Tuesday night. This cantonment (called Mount Vernon) was very ill calculated for defence, and was like the fort on Tensaw, wonderfully encumbered by helpless families. It had been suggested in the morning of that day, that the removal of the helpless to a place of security, would be highly expedient; but the difficulties of removal and of support when removed, presented themselves more forcibly to the minds of many, than the danger of delay; and even those who saw the propriety of the measure, could not reconcile themselves to the idea of abandoning their fellow citizens.

When, however, the news of the massacre at Fort Mims arrived, there was no longer any hesitation; and such was the hurry of a flight conducted almost at midnight, that few took any thing with them, even to support themselves on their way to Mobile. Some pushed off by water, others fled by land in the darkness of the night, and the whole face of the country exhibited a scene of consternation and distress.—Widows fled for the preservation of their own lives, whilst tortured by a belief in the direful death of their husbands or friends—and some escaped from fort Stoddert, lamenting in the bitterness of agonized grief the murder of mothers, fathers, sisters and brothers.— The river was strewed with boats from fort Stoddert to Mobile; and here many have no shelter and no means of support, unless the commanding officer of the troops, impressed by a view of the distressing urgency of their situation, should afford them assistance out of the public stores.

What attacks have been made on the upper forts at St. Stephens, and in the forks, which are now reduced to two, I do not know.—I fear however the same result was at Mims; and all which the survivors can hope for, is that some little respite may be afforded to the straggling inhabitants, and to the town of Mobile, after the forts are demolished, and that the necessity of taking care of their wounded and carrying home their plunder may induce the Indians to delay for a few weeks an attack on the town of Mobile, and on the military station near fort Stoddert.

But at all events, I think it probable that by the first quarter of the next moon, they will return in greater force; and as the Spaniards unquestionably encourage them, it is possible that they may then be ready to support them.—Should no assistance come from the Mississippi, from Tennessee and from Georgia, the whole country from the Choctaws to the sea will be a desolate waste and a white man will not dare to raise his head out of the limits of a military garrison. As it is we have abandoned our houses, our crops and our herds, and wherever the Indians have appeared, they have involved the whole within their reach in one scene of desolation.

It is said that they have left their wives and children at a western frontier settlement of the Creeks on a branch of the Tom Bigby, called the Black Warrior, and should they be closely pressed, (of which however I see no probability.) they will decamp with the whole and join the western tribes.

Had the Choctaws been engaged in our service, they would have given them a check; but as it is, our only hope for aid, or rather for revenge at some distant day, rests on the energy of our fellow citizens of the United States.

I am dear sir, yours very sincerely and respectfully.

HENRY TOULMIN.

Sept. 14—A British armed schooner has arrived at Pensacola with ammunition, clothing and blankets from the Bahamas, for the hostile Indians.

Volume 5, October 16, 1813, page 117

Events of the War—Military.

Many letters from the Creek country confirm the horrid account of the fight and massacre at Tensio, or Tensaw, as notice on page 77, with additional particulars. There were 308 souls, in all, in the fort, of whom only 17 or 18 escaped. The Indian force was about 700 warriors; who, after the massacre, ravaged all the adjacent country, burnt the houses, and killed or carried off the negroes and stock. It is thought they lost nearly 200, for our people, seeing no hope of escape, fought desperately. There appears a disposition to blame colonel *Hawkins* for giving a false security; and for restraining the military movements for the defence of the country. A considerable number of general *Jackson's* mounted volunteers were to have rendezvoused near Nashville on the 26th ult. to go against the savages.— For some interesting particulars, see page 105-6.

The garrison at Norfolk is kept up by fresh troops from the interior. Among them is a company of riflemen, completely equipped, of whom it is said every one can bring down his man at the distance of 200 yards.

Volume 5, November 6, 1813, page 172

Events of the War—Miscellaneous.

Facts are developing themselves to show that the *Spaniards* at Pensacola are deeply engaged in the late proceedings of the *Creeks*.

Volume 5, November 6, 1813, page 173

Events of the War—Military.

A letter from Pass Christian, dated September 17, states that information had been received there of the arrival of a British vessel at *Pensacola*, having on board a large quantity of ammunition, and two *Seminole Indians*, who have the rank of *Brigadier generals* in the British service.

Americans Respond to Creek Indian Aggression

Volume 5, November 27, 1813, page 210

Extract from Governor Mitchell's Message to the Georgia Legislature.

Milledgeville,
Nov. 1, 1813.

The hostility of the Creeks being unexpected by the government, they were in no state of preparation in this quarter for the equipment and supply of such a body of troops, which laid me under the necessity of providing for them, until the United States could have time to do so. For this purpose I advanced from the state funds appropriated for military disbursements, the sums necessary for the contractor and quarter-master's department, every cent of which has been returned and is now in the treasury. This advance was indispensable, and occasioned by the necessity that existed for immediately marching the troops to the frontier, to quiet the fears of the people, and keep them from breaking up and leaving their homes; and their stay at their rendezvous has been occasioned by the difficulty of procuring the equipments necessary to supply the various wants of so numerous a detachment. In this respect, however, they are exclusively under the control of the general government and their movements regulated by their order. They have now entered the enemy's country, and I trust under Divine Providence they will aided by the co-operation of other detachments ordered upon the same service, soon subdue the faithless savages and compel them to unconditional submission. The supplies of ammunition which these hostile savages have received from the Spanish governor at Pensacola, for the avowed purpose of making war upon us, is a subject, the cognizance of which belongs to the United States; and it is to be hoped, that this secret enemy will no longer be permitted with impunity under his pretended neutrality, to put into the hands of our enemy the means of destroying us.

In addition to the detachment now in the field, other cautionary measures for the safety of the frontier have been resorted to. Some small forts and block-houses have been built, and spies and scouts have been, and are at this time kept out; And although we have occasionally had false reports which have produced temporary alarm, the savages have not dared to approach our settlements; that they have not, has been occasioned, I have no doubt, by our attitude and readiness to punish them on the very first aggression.

Volume 5, November 27, 1813, page 217

Events of the War—Military.

The Creeks.— It will be seen by the official statements below, that the war against the Creeks has commenced with a signal victory; a victory, that will, unquestionably, be followed with an entire overthrow of the faithless and ungrateful barbarians. A very considerable force was collected at fort *Stoddert*, on the first of the present month, under brigadier-general *Flournoy*. The Creeks, beholding the storm they had raised, were reported to have retired, or being about to retire into Florida, for protection from the Spaniards; who, to speak of them in the most favorable terms, have been the agents of the British in the horrid murders of these Indians. It is positively stated, that general *Flournoy* will pursue them, go where they may; and, if the Spaniards are impolitic enough to shelter them, that he will make a common cause against both. A case similar to this is alluded to in the speech of *Tecumseh* (see Niles, vol. 5, page 174). The British had excited the Indians to the former war; they were defeated by *Wayne*, at the *Rapids of the Miami* and expected to have found shelter in the British fort— and they would have been protected, but for the energy of the general; who solemnly declared, if the *British* received them that he would storm the fort and put every man to death. The British believed *Wayne* would do what he promised, and suffered their *then* secret allies to perish in the *tornado** they had excited. [*Note: Tornado, or *Jug Wind*, the Indians' name for *Wayne*.] Of this *Tecumseh* complains. Fort Stoddert is only 110 miles distant from *Pensacola*, and general *Flournoy's* force is represented as strong enough for any possible opposition that all *Florida* can offer to the chastisement of the savages; and we hope and trust that it will be prosecuted to an extent that shall forever secure the frontier** from the intrigues of the inhuman *English*, who have sacrificed this people—a people from when we had done more than justice, as well as all that *humanity* required, and who had not the semblance of a complaint to prefer against us. [**Note: A party of the Creeks have lately entered Morgan county, Georgia, murdered several persons, and burnt two or three houses.]

It is stated that brigadier-general *Williams* has proceeded to the army at fort *Stoddart*. The energy of his character may be very useful in the course to be pursued.

Volume 5, December 4, 1813, page 240

Glorious Postscript.

The editor has just received a letter from his friend at Nashville, Tennessee, communicating many particulars of an action between general Jackson and the British allies, the Creek Indians, fought on the 7th ult. in which the enemy was completely defeated with the loss of two hundred and seventy eight killed.—It was supposed many more were slain that had not been found, on account of the high grass that covered the field of battle. The Indians were 1100 strong and engaged in besieging a fort of Friendly Indians, who on being released were ready to join their forces with ours. We had 15 men killed and 84 wounded, generally slightly. The battle was fought at Talladega, about 30 miles from the Hickory ground. Among the trophies of victory was a standard bearing the Spanish cross! Particulars hereafter.

Volume 5, December 11, 1813, pages 251-252

Events of the War—Military.

The Creeks. We have not yet received general *Jackson's* account of his splendid victory over the Creeks at Talledaga, as noticed in the postscript to our last. But are satisfied that such a victory has been gained, and wait

contented for a regular detail of the battle. We may soon expect news of the operations of the troops from *Georgia*, on the other side of the Indian country.

Major general *Pinkney* has proceeded to Milledgeville, Georgia, to have a general charge of the expeditions against the Creeks. A detachment of 100 U. S. Dragoons left Savannah on the 20th ult. for fort *Hawkins*.

The *Georgia* militia, under general *Floyd*, in the Creek country, have been delayed in their movements by the default of the contractor. The general having made his case known to the governor, he communicated it to the legislature, and $20,000 were instantly appropriated by that patriotic state to forward the expedition.

Volume 5, December 18, 1813, page 265

Events of the War—Military.

Third victory over the allies in the south.—General *White*, of the Tennessee volunteers, was detached on the 12th ult. with 1200 mounted men, (including upwards of 300 *Cherokees*) to the [Creek] *Hillabee* towns. On the 17th, at one o'clock at night, being within 8 miles of the upper town, he received information from a half-breed, that his family and property would be sacrificed the next morning, if general White did not relieve them; on which he pushed forward with 300 troops and a part of the Indians, and at sun-rise on the 18th completely surrounded and surprized the enemy. They fired several guns, but the bayonet, in 10 or 15 minutes, settled the business. *They held up a flag and were spared:* 65 had been killed, and 251 were taken prisoners. We had not one man even wounded. The Cherokees behaved in the best possible manner.

Of this affair, we shall have the pleasure to record the official details. The wretched and deluded *Creeks* by this time must see (*as all people* will see) the worse than *madness* that tempted them into alliance with the *pest of the world—blood-stained England*. But we trust the gallant spirits of the south and west will not believe their work done, until they teach fear and trembling to the base Spaniards who made themselves the "*go-between*" of the barbarian *British*, to place the tomahawk and scalping knife in the hands of this people, for whom, in the true spirit of justice and humanity, we had done so much. *The massacre at Fort Mims demands this*. How cruel was it in the *British* to excite this war; which they must have seen would begin in murder and end in the destruction of the Indians? If this thing be weighted in the mind, connected with the fact, that the *Creeks* have not even the semblance of the complaint to prefer against us,—we shall discover the bloody turpitude, and savage disposition of the foe, in its true colors. A disposition that would ally itself to any thing, in any way, for a temporary purpose, careless of the issue.

Volume 5, December 18, 1813, pages 267-268

Events of the War—Military
Second Victory Over the Creeks.

Nashville, Nov. 23—*Official papers—Communicate on Thursday last.*

Senators and Representatives of Tennessee.

I have the honor to transmit an extract of a letter received yesterday from general Jackson now in the service of the United States, acting against the Creek Indians; containing all the details of the late engagement between the detachment from West Tennessee and the Creeks; and informing of the favorable result of that important achievement—they deserve well of their country for their gallant conduct.

––––––

(Extract.)

*Camp Strother,
near Ten Islands of Coosa,
Nov. 11.*

Sir—I am just returned from an excursion which I took a few days ago, and hasten to acquaint you with the result.

Late on the evening of the 7th inst. a runner arrived from the friendly party in Lashley's fort, (Talledega) distant about thirty miles below us, with the information that the hostile Creeks in great force had encamped near the place, and were preparing to destroy it; and earnestly entreated that I would lose no

time in affording relief. Urged by their situation as well as by a wish to meet the enemy so soon as an opportunity would offer, I determined upon commencing my march thither with all my disposable force, in the course of the night; and immediately dispatched an express to general White, advising him of my intended movement, and urging him to hasten to this encampment by a forced march, in order to protect it in my absence. I had repeatedly written to the general to form a junction with me as speedily as practicable, and a few days before had received his assurance, that on the 7th he would join me. I commenced crossing the river at the Ten Islands, leaving behind me my baggage waggons and whatever might retard my progress; and we encamped that night within six miles of the fort I had set out to relieve. At midnight I received by an Indian runner, a letter from general White, informing me that he had received my order, but that he had altered his course; and was on his march backwards to join major-general Cocke, near the mouth of Chatuga. I will not now remark upon the strangeness of this maneuver; but it was now too late to change my plan, or make any new arrangement; and between three or four o'clock I recommenced my march to meet the enemy, who were encamped within a quarter of a mile of the fort. At sunrise we came within half a mile of them, and having formed my men, I moved on in battle order. The infantry were in three lines—the militia on the left and the volunteers on the right. The cavalry formed the extreme wings; and were ordered to advance in a *curve*, keeping their rear connected with the advance of their infantry lines, and enclose the enemy in a circle. The advanced guard whom I sent forward to bring on the engagement, met the attack of the enemy with great intrepidity; and having poured upon them four or five very gallant rounds, fell back as they had been previously ordered, to the main army. The enemy pursued, and the front line was now ordered to advance and meet him; but owing to some misunderstanding a few companies of militia, who composed a part of it, commenced a retreat. At this moment a corps of cavalry commanded by lieutenant colonel Dyer, which I had kept as a reserve, was ordered to dismount

66

and fill up the vacancy occasioned by the retreat.—This order was executed with a great deal of promptitude and effect.

The militia, seeing this, speedily rallied; and the fire became general along the first line, and on that part of the wings which were contiguous. The enemy, unable to stand it, began to retreat; but were met at every turn, and pursued in every direction. The right wing chased them with a most destructive fire to the mountains, a distance of about three miles; and had I not been compelled by the *faux pas* of the militia in the onset of the battle, to dismount my reserve, I believe not a man of them would have escaped. The victory however was very decisive—two hundred and ninety of the enemy were left dead; and there can be no doubt but many more were killed who were not found. Wherever they ran, they left behind traces of blood; and it is believed, that very few will return to their villages in as sound a condition as they left them. I was compelled to return to this place to protect the sick and wounded, and get my baggage. In the engagement we lost 15 killed and 15 wounded, two of whom have since died. All the officers acted with the utmost bravery, and so did all the privates, except that part of the militia who retreated, at the commencement of the battle; and they hastened to atone for their error. Taking the whole together, they have realized the high expectations I had formed of them, and have fairly entitled themselves to the gratitude of their country.

In haste, I have the honor to be,

(Signed,) ANDREW JACKSON

His excellency,
William Blount,
Nashville.

The foregoing is an extract from the general's letter to me—other parts of it give no other details of the engagement, or the order of battle—the general had not received information that the president had accepted into the public service the 3,500 men, authorised by the act of the 27th September, to be raised; or the foregoing would no doubt have been addressed to the secretary of war; a copy of his letter will be transmitted to that department; and the foregoing is

transmitted to the general assembly for their information of the good conduct of the troops; their act in part authorized the raising of the said troops; and from a desire that the citizens of Tennessee may know it. As the Tennessee, Georgia and regular troops ordered on the campaign against the Creeks, are by the government, expected to act in concert, it is not improbable that general Cocke has thought it advisable, from the information he may have received from the regular or Georgia detachments, respecting possibly their exposed situation, to go on to them, and after uniting with them, to join general Jackson; this may account for general White's not proceeding to the Ten Islands—he never will do an act to injure the service; neither will general Jackson or Cocke injure it by any act of theirs; they are all acting in support of one cause, and no doubt they will do their duty well, as will the detachments generally upon any and every proper occasion.

WILLIE BLOUNT

Volume 5, December 18, 1813, pages 270-271

The Destiny of the Creeks.

The unwarrantable attack upon fort *Mims*, and subsequent slaughter of the garrison, with all the women and children, in the whole about 300 persons, only *seventeen* of whom made their escape, has already been *registered*. A letter to the editor, dated at *Tombigbe*, contains many particulars of that horrible massacre by the *Creeks*, as well as some pointed remarks on the character of the savages—both which, as they belong to the enquiry, shall be noticed.

The letter says—the fort was attacked by 725 Indians, with great fury, at 12 o'clock in the day; they were entirely *naked*, except a flap; they rushed up to the *port holes*, and disputed the possession with those within, and finally prevailed; the women were butchered, then stripped and subjected to every brutal indignity that the savages could think of. Indeed there was a refinement of horror that ought to be mentioned: pregnant women were cut open; and the unborn infant taken out of them and tomahawked!—Many of the women had *two* scalps taken from them; and numerous instances were afforded that *several* savages had assisted in the murder of an individual. The report of the party that returned from burying the dead, rivals any that the history of the Indian affords; but *delicacy* forbids a full statement of what they beheld. It is a tale of terror.

The writer then goes on to describe the ravages of the *Creeks*, through a great extent of country, lately flourishing and happy, and filling with an industrious population. *"To those who never beheld people flying from the savages, it would be useless to attempt to convey the picture."* A solitary farm house did not remain in the possession of the owner; every thing was abandoned; and the few persons that remained were cooped up in two small forts, surrounded by the blood-thirsty allies of the *"defender of the faith!"* The *tomahawk* of the *savage* and *torch* of [Sir George] *Cockburn*, in "Holy League," finished the work of death and desolation. All the settlements are laid waste. *The savages received their ammunition from the governor of* Pensacola, *in consequence of an order from the* British *in Canada*.

These facts are notorious and indisputable—*Such were the doings of the Creeks, and such the agency of the British government in their murders*.

Our indignant correspondent adds—

"This account will be read as the many we have received from the *west*, and the sensation on the mass of men produced by the recital will be only the same— but a *most important*— an awfully important question or two flashes on the mind of *every reflecting man*. *Is this the nation of Indians with whom the government has been, through colonel Benjamin Hawkins, now about sixteen years engaged in the work of civilization?* Is this the nation of savages on whom thousands have been expended, produced by the labor and sweat of our citizens? And, good God! Is this the point at which they have arrived? Even *gratitude* to a benefactor has not yet been infused into their breasts? Even *regard for the female character* is unknown amongst them. Without a single provocation, in the moment while they are receiving the benevolence of our government, they fly to the assistance of our enemies. They take advantage of the moment of our distress to plunder, murder, burn and destroy, our country. Since the commencement of our government to the present day, there has always been a number of persons, well and *practically* acquainted with the savage character, who have smiled at the benevolent but weak attempt of our system for the civilization of savages. They viewed it as the production of the closet, generated with brains of speculative theorists. *If the subject is not now at rest it never can be decided.* If after *sixteen* years we cannot secure even the *friendship* of a nation of savages, if we cannot give existence to the *most common effects of the slightest degree of civilization*, when are we to expect to make any impression on them? Or is the whole attempt a farce?

"Among the party who committed the before-mentioned massacre, were a number of Indians, *nay, hundreds*, who spoke the English language, had a constant intercourse with the whites, and many of them were raised among the white people.

"At this moment a medal chief of the *Choctaw* nation is soliciting to be employed with his nation by the white people; for he says his warriors cannot be restrained; and if we do not employ them they must fight for somebody. This is another nation we are engaged in civilizing!"

We sincerely lament that these remarks appear too strongly buttressed by truth, in the facts that have happened, to have their force weakened by philanthropy; but we cannot regret that the attempt was made to render this people happy. The scheme of humanity, that began with *Washington*, that was patronized by *Adams*, and zealously extended and encouraged by *Jefferson* and *Madison*, has *completely failed*, through the native propensity of the *Indians* to rapine, and the universal disposition of Britain to encourage it. Colonel *Hawkins* had persuaded himself; (and I apprehend sincerely believed) that the *Creeks* had made great progress in civilization, as well in their *sentiments* as in their manner of life. Many of them were regular *farmers*; the men labored in the field, the women plied the wheel and the shuttle at home. Schools, apparently well attended, had been established; one half of the various tribes known by the general name of *Creeks*, spoke the English language; and very few of them had altogether refused to adopt the habits of civilized man. Much time, labor and money had been spent upon them—their lands and rights had been carefully guarded—they are without excuse, for they had nothing to complain of. *They listened to the serpent*, and became the murderers of the *benefactors*—the horrible assassins of *women* and *children*. The vile nation that contrived the partition of *France*, and that inveigled or bullied *Holland, Switzerland, Sardina, Tuscany*, the Pope, *Naples*, many states of *Germany*; and indeed, that has been in alliance and at war with every nation of *Europe, protestant, Catholic* or *Mahometan*, no matter what, within a few years, *France* only excepted—that has brought about the utter extinction of many, and deluged the whole with rivers of blood, *for her commerce*—has also machinated the destruction of the *Creeks*; and with it annihilated the hope of humanity, that, through justice and benevolence, they might be civilized.— Let the *British "bible societies,"* the *"societies for propagating the gospel among the heathens,"* and other like institutions, examine this matter!

From the three victories obtained over the *Creeks*, (where the unresisting were spared) and the powerful body of troops that are in their country, we consider the war as finished; for the wretches have no back country to fly to, to escape the vengeance due them. If they are received by the *Spaniards in Florida*, they will be pursued; if they are protected, a common cause will be made against both—for it is impossible that the *Spaniards* can be permitted to proceed in the diabolical course *Great Britain* has directed. What shall be done with them? We cannot reconcile ourselves to the extermination of them, however just the *retaliation* might be; nor should we banish them from the land of their ancestors to the wilds of the *Mississippi*, where they might hereafter perplex us— or become extinct through their wars with the tribes in possession, for the right of soil. We should be "angry with them but sin not;" and carry our resentment no further than our safety requires.

Their country is ours by every principle of the natural or civil law, and we have a right to prescribe the terms on which they shall reside in it.—Let these be as lenient as possible, so that *power* shall finally destroy the savage spirit that *humanity* vainly strove to subdue. Their *whole* population, before the war, did not, perhaps, exceed 25,000 souls—but their territory, among which is large tracts of the finest land in the world, would support *millions* of civilized men. Suppose small tracts, slips of land, not more than 10 or 15 miles wide, were reserved for them, with intervals 20 or 30 miles wide, to be settled by the whites? The spaces allotted would be more than an hundred times sufficient for them as *agriculturalists*, but not enough as *hunters*; and they would be *compelled*, more or less, to attend to husbandry. This, in time, would ameliorate their manners; and though they might commit some petty depredations on their neighbors, they never could do extensive mischief; and they might, generally, govern themselves by their own laws with a few simple regulations to secure good order between them and the people of the vicinity. Some provision should be made for the ultimate right of the reserved land, by prescribing on what conditions the Indian title may become extinct; but forbidding that they themselves should dispose of it, without the consent of the United States. The hourly intercourse they would have with the white people, and their detached situation, might, in a few years, totally eradicate their savage propensities, and finally incorporate them with the body of the people. As *indians*, they would decrease; and, if scattered in society, could have no effect upon it.

This project I think reasonable and rightful—and may, at least, afford some idea to the many persons enquiring, *"what shall be done with the Creeks."*

Volume 5, December 25, 1813, page 280

Events of the War—Miscellaneous.

Florida.—Two British sloops of war, having under convoy a very valuable ship laden with dry goods, &c. passed Havana, November 1, from New-Providence bound to *Pensacola*.

Volume 5, December 25, 1813, pages 282-283

Events of the War—Military.
Third Victory Over the Creeks.

*Copy of a letter from
major-general Cocke,
to the secretary of war, dated*

Head Quarters, Fort Armstrong,
Nov. 28th, 1813.

Sir—I have the honor to enclose you a copy of brigadier-general James White's detailed report of his excursion of the Hillibee Towns.

I am, with sentiments of esteem, your most obedient servant,

JOHN COCKE,
Major-general.

———

Fort Armstrong,
Nov. 24th, 1813.

Dear General—In mine of the 19th instant by major Outlaw, I promised you a detailed report, respecting the detachment ordered by you to the Hillibee Towns, in the Creek nation. In compliance with that promise, I have now the honor to state— That under your order of the 11th inst., I immediately marched with the mounted infantry, under the immediate command of colonel Burch. The cavalry under the command of major Porter, and a few of the Cherokee Indians under the command of colonel Morgan, with very short rations for four days only. We continued our march to Little Oakfuskie, when we fell in with and captured five hostile Creek warriors, supposed to be spies. Finding no other Indians at that place, we burned the town, which consisted of 30 houses. We then proceeded to a town, called Genalga, and burned the same, consisting of 93 houses; thence we proceeded to Nitty Chaptoa, consisting of about 25 houses, which I considered it most prudent not to destroy, as it might possibly be of use at some future period. From thence we marched to the Hillibee town, consisting of about 20 houses, adjoining which was Grayson's farm.— Previous to our arrival at that place, I was advised that a part of the hostile Creeks was assembled there. Having marched within six or seven miles of it on the 17th, I dismounted a part of the force under my command, and sent them under the command of colonel Burch, with the Cherokees under the command of colonel Morgan, in advance, to surround the town in the night, and make the attack at daylight on the 18th. Owing to the darkness of the night, the town was not reached until after daylight— but so complete was the surprise, that we succeeded in surrounding the town, and killing and capturing almost (if not entirely) the whole of the hostile Creeks assembled there, consisting of about 316, of which number about 60 warriors were killed on the spot, and the remainder made prisoners. Before the close of the engagement, my whole force was up and ready for action, had it become necessary; but owing to the want of knowledge on the part of the Indians of our approach, they were entirely killed and taken before they could prepare for any effectual defence. We lost not one drop of blood in accomplishing this enterprize. We destroyed this village; and, in obedience to your orders, commenced our march for this post, which we were unable to reach until yesterday. I estimate the distance from this to Grayson's farm, at about 100 miles. The ground over which we travelled, is so rough and hilly as to render a passage very difficult. Many defiles it was impossible to pass in safety, without the greatest precaution. For a part of the time, the weather was so very wet, being encumbered with prisoners, and the troops, and their horses having to subsist in a very great degree upon such supplies as we could procure in the nation, rendered our march more tardy than it otherwise would have been.

The troops under my command have visited the heart of that section of the Creek nation where the Red Sticks were first distributed.

In justice to this gallant band, I am proud to state, that the whole of the officers and men under the command of colonel Burch performed their duty cheerfully and without complaint— that from the cool, orderly and prompt manner in which major Porter and the cavalry under his command, formed and conducted themselves in every case of alarm, I had the highest confidence in them. Colonel Morgan and the Cherokees under his command, gave undeniable evidence that they merit the employ of their government. In short, sir, the whole detachment under my command, conducted in such a manner as to enable me to assure you that they are capable of performing any thing to which the same number of me are equal.

It gives me pleasure to add, that Mr. M'Corry, who acted as my aid in this expedition, rendered services that to me were indispensable, to his country very useful, and to himself highly honorable.

I have the honor to be, most respectfully, your obedient servant,

JAMES WHITE,
Brig. Gen.

Major-general John Cocke.

———

Copy of a letter from colonel R. J. Meigs to the secretary of war, dated

Highwasse Garrison,
28th Nov. 1813.

Sir—I received a letter last evening from major general Cocke, commanding one of the divisions of the Tennessee volunteers acting against the hostile Creeks, a copy of which I do myself the honor to transmit to you. The repeated defeats of these barbarous allies of Britain has opened their eyes;—though late, they are already convinced that friendship with the British is the direct road to ruin, and their resentment will probably recoil on their seducers.

RETURN J. MEIGS.

*The honorable
the Secretary of War.*

———

Head-Quarters,
Fort Armstrong,
November 22d, 1813.

Sir—On the 11th instant I detached general White with the mounted men and such of the cavalry as had horses fit for duty, accompanied by a few Cherokees, headed by colonel Gideon Morgan, to the Hillebee towns, with a hope that he would fall in with and punish the hostile Creeks in that quarter. On his march he killed three warriors and took six prisoners, supposed to be spies. On the 18th, the general reached Graysons, one of the Hillebee towns, one hundred miles

from this place, where he found a party of hostile Creeks. They were attacked and defeated. He killed at that place sixty-one warriors and took two hundred and fifty prisoners, a part of whom are warriors, the residue women and children, without any loss on our part, either killed or wounded. My aid, major Outlaw, who was with the general, arrived yesterday morning, with a report from him. The general speaks in the highest terms of the officers and men under his command, and adds, that the Cherokees behaved in the best manner. I expect the arrival of the detachment tomorrow. I have the honor to be, &c.

JOHN COCKE.

Colonel Meigs.

Volume 5, December 25, 1813, pages 283-284

Fourth Victory Over the Creeks.

*Milledgeville, Georgia,
December 8.*

The massacre at Tensaw is avenged!—and hundreds of savages atone for the murder of our citizens in Morgan county. Captain Barton arrived here express from our army with despatches for general Pinckney, giving the official details of a brilliant victory over the Indians.

———

[OFFICIAL.]

Head-Quarters,
sixth and seventh districts,
Milledgeville,
7th December, 1813.

Sir—I have the honor of enclosing to you a copy of the official account which I have just received from brigadier-general Floyd, of an attack made by him on the hostile Indians, and sincerely congratulate your excellency on the good conduct and bravery displayed on this occasion by the officers and troops of the state in which you preside.

I have the honor to be, very respectfully, your excellency's most obedient servant.

THOMAS PINCKNEY.

His excellency Peter Early.

Camp, west of Catahouchie,
Dec. 4, 1813.

Major-General Pinckney,

Sir—I have the honor to communicate to your excellency, an account of an action fought the 29th ult. on the Talapoosie river, between part of the force under my command and a large body of the Creek Indians.

Having received information that numbers of the hostile Indians were assembled at Autossee, a town on the southern bank of the Talapoosie, about eighteen miles from the Hickory ground, and twenty above the junction of that river with the Coosa, I proceeded to it with 950 of the Georgia militia, accompanied by between 300 and 400 friendly Indians. Having encamped within nine or ten miles of the point of destination the preceding evening, we resumed the march a few minutes before 1 on the morning of the 29th, and at half past 6, were formed for action in front of the town.

Booth's battalion composed the right column, and marched from its centre. Watson's battalion composed the left, and marched from its right; Adams' rifle company, and Merriwether's under lieutenant Hendon, were on the flanks; captain Thomas' artillery, marched in front of the right column in the road.

It was my intention to have completely surrounded the enemy, by *appuying* the right wing of my force on Canlehee creek, at the mouth of which I was informed the town stood; and resting the left on the river bank below the town; but to our surprise, as day dawned we perceived a second town, about five hundred yards below that which we had first viewed, and were preparing to attack. The plan was immediately changed—three companies of infantry on the left were wheeled to the left into *echellon*, and were advance to the low town, accompanied by Meriwether's rifle company, and two troops of light dragoons under the command of captains Irwin and Steele.

The residue of the force approached the upper town, and the battle soon became general. The Indians presented themselves at every point, and fought with the desperate bravery of real fanatics.— The well directed fire,
however, of the artillery, added to the charge of the bayonet, soon forced them to take refuge in the out houses, thickets and copses in the rear of the town; many it is believed concealed themselves in caves, previously formed for the purpose of secure retreat, in the high bluff of the river, which was thickly covered with reed and brush-wood. The Indians of the friendly party who accompanied us on the expedition, were divided into four companies and placed under the command of leaders of their own selection. They were by engagement entered into the day previous, to have crossed the river above the town and been posted on the opposite shore during the action, for the purpose of firing upon such of the enemy as might attempt to escape, or keep in check any reinforcements which might probably be thrown in from the neighboring towns, but owing to the difficulty of the ford, and coldness of the weather, and the lateness of the hour, this arrangement failed, and their leaders were directed to cross Canleebee creek and occupy that flank, to prevent escapes from the Tallisee town. Some time after the action commence our red friends thronged in disorder in the rear of our lines. The Cowetaws, under M'Intosh, and the Tookabatchians under Mad Dog's Son, fell in our flanks, and fought with an intrepidity worthy of any troops.

At 9 o'clock the enemy was completely driven from the plain, and the houses of both towns wrapped in flames. As we were then 60 miles from any depot of provisions, and our five days rations pretty much reduced, in the heart of the enemy's country, which in a few moments could have poured from its numerous towns hosts of the fiercest warriors. As soon as the dead and wounded were disposed of, I ordered the place to be abandoned, and the troops to commence their march to Chatahouche.

It is difficult to determine the strength of the enemy, but from the information of some of the chiefs, which it is said can be relied on, there were assembled at Autosse, warriors from eight towns for its defence, it being their beloved ground, on which they proclaimed no white man could approach without inevitable destruction. It is difficult to give a precise account of the loss of the enemy; but from the number which were lying scattered over the field together with those destroyed in the towns, and the many slain on the banks of the river, which respectable officers affirm they saw lying in heaps at the water's edge where they had been precipitated by their surviving friends, their loss in killed independent of their wounded, must have been at least, 200, (among whom are the Autosse and Tallissee kings) and from the circumstance of their making no efforts to molest our return, probably greater.— The number of buildings burnt, some of a superior order for the dwelling of savages, and filled with valuable articles, is supposed to be 400.

Adjutant-general Newman rendered important services during the action, by his cool and deliberate courage. My aid, major Crawford, discharged with promptitude the duties of a brave and meritorious officer. Major Pace, who acted as field-aid also distinguished himself; both these gentlemen had their horses shot under them, and the latter lost his. Dr. Williamson, hospital surgeon, and Dr. Clopton were prompt and attentive in discharge of their duty towards the wounded during the action.

Major Freeman at the head of Irwin's troop of cavalry and part of Steele's made a furious and successful charge upon a body of Indians, sabred several and completely defeated them—captain Thomas and his company, captain Adams, and lieutenant Hendon's rifle companies killed a great many Indians, and deserve particular praise. Captain Batton's company were in the hottest of the battle, and fought like soldiers. Captain Myrick, captain Little, captain King, captain Broadnax, captain Cleveland, captain Joseph T. Cunningham and captain Lee with their companies distinguished themselves.— Brigade-major Sharkleford was of great service in bringing the troops into action, and adjutant Broadnax and major Montgomery, who acted as assistant adjutant, shewed great activity and courage.— Major Booth used his best endeavors in bringing his battalion to action, and major Watson's battalion acted with considerable spirit.— Irwin's, Patterson's and Steele's troops of cavalry, whenever an opportunity presented, charged with success. Lieutenant Strong had his horse shot and narrowly escaped, and quarter-master Tennal displayed

the greatest heroism, and miraculously escaped, though badly wounded, after having his horse shot from under him. The topographical engineer was vigilant in his endeavors to render service.

The troops deserve the highest praise for their fortitude in enduring hunger, cold and fatigue without a murmur, having marched a hundred and twenty miles in seven days.

The friendly Indians lost several killed and wounded, the number not exactly known. Captain Barton, an active and intelligent officer (the bearer of these despatches) can more particular explain to your excellency the conduct, movements and operations of the army.

I have the honor to be with high regard, your most obedient servant,

JOHN FLOYD, B. G.

—⟫⊖◉⊖⟪—

Subtle Incursions into Florida by British Forces

Volume 5, January 1, 1814, page 300

Events of the War—Miscellaneous.

Pensacola.—A writer in a Tennessee paper says, Pensacola "is the hot-bed of corruption, the *Halifax* (for the British fleet) and the *Malden* (for the savages) of the southern part of our country."

Volume 5, January 15, 1814, page 330

Events of the War—Miscellaneous.

South Western Frontier. The accounts from *Mobile* are contradictory. While some say that a large British [land] force has arrived at *Pensacola*, and united itself to the savages; others report, the enemy have no troops at all, and that their vessels are badly manned. The latter is by far the most probable. The whole coast is closely blockaded.

Volume 5, January 15, 1814, page 331

Events of the War—Military.

The Creeks. We have no late important particulars of the war with the Creeks. We apprehend that the pursuit of them has been retarded from the expiration of the term of service of a considerable part of the *Tennessee* militia. It appears, however, that some volunteers had marched to join Jackson, and that active operations might soon recommence. General *Floyd*, recovering of his wounds, was expected to resume the command of the *Georgians*. One account says, that 3000 warriors of the friendly Creeks had rendezvoused at *Cowetaw*, to act as directed.

It is stated that brigadier-general *Parker*, of the U. S. Army, is to have the command at *Norfolk*.

Certain British vessels lying off *Pensacola* have undertaken to interdict all intercourse with that port and every place to the westward of it. They capture every thing—*Spanish* vessels, as well as others. It is stated they have proposed to send two regiments of black troops to help in the defence of that place. It is also said that the Big Warrior has defeated the rebels [Indians] in a general engagement, many of whom have fled to Pensacola for refuge. The Big Warrior is a friendly Creek.

Volume 5, January 29, 1814, page 365

Events of the War—Military.

The Creeks.— We are without distinct intelligence of the state of things in the Creek country; but we presume that nothing important has latterly happened.

One thousand men, of the North Carolina militia, have been called for by major-general *Pinkney*, to march to Fort Stoddert, to relieve the Georgia troops.

Volume 5, January 29, 1814, page 365

Events of the War—Military.

Extract of a letter from brigadier-general Floyd, to major-general Pinkney, dated

"Fort Mitchell,
Jan 2d, 1814.

"By the indians it is reported, that the army from Mobile, on the 30th ult. destroyed Chootsaputka, an indian town of *seven hundred* inhabitants, situated about thirty or thirty-five miles below the fork of the Coosau and Tallapoosa, and that a heavy firing of cannon and small arms has been since heard in the neighborhood of Tustigee, still higher up.

"They also state, that the British had arrived at Pensacola, and are holding out inducement to the war party of indians to persist in their designs, by abundant presents of goods and ammunition; and that M'Queen has sent a party to procure the latter article.

"I give this information as I received it."

Volume 5, February 5, 1814, pages 383-384

Events of the War—Military.

The Creeks.—The first army from *Tennessee* has been nearly disbanded. Major-general Jackson however held his position, soon expecting to be reinforced. A letter to the editor of the *Register* from Nashville, dated the 14th inst. says that a brigade of volunteers, for sixty days, had marched, who were supposed have reached him some time before that date.—2500 militia were raising to march in a few days from West Tennessee, to join general *Jackson*. Colonel Williams' regiment of twelve months regulars, is ordered into the Creek country. General *Blount*, of Tennessee, on calling out the requisition of militia says—

"Tennesseeans have done much by their valor, but much remains to be done to effect the object of government in this campaign in a desirable manner, and as is contemplated by the general government for the general good, and for the immediate and special benefit of the state. Let it be the pleasure of Tennesseeans, as it ever has been, to aid in an accomplishment of the views of the government of our choice, which is found to be actively engaged in securing and protecting us against the rude attacks of savages, who have heretofore drenched our frontier with the blood of innocent women and children. *Now is the accepted time—act all-act promptly and vigorously*—such conduct will soon put an end to the campaign against the enemies of our peace, and will secure to Tennesseeans the important benefits which they have sought for years, with the best efforts of government in their favor in time of peace. And above all, they should afford to the world an additional unequivocal evidence of their attachment to our government—this the president most confidently relies on."

The Cherokees and Choctaws, with a considerable number of the Creeks remain faithful. They have, of themselves, lately conducted several active enterprizes against the hostile indians. A letter from Savannah has the following paragraph—

"It is reported from good authority, that colonel Hawkins, who has been endeavoring for many years to keep peace with the indians, now says that half of the "Creek warriors must be exterminated, in order to prevent their killing the other half, who are friendly to the United States"—and the work of death, I believe, is progressing regularly and certainly— probably 4000 or 5000 will be the number sacrificed to British arts and policy.

Volume 5, February 19, 1814, page 409

Events of the War—Military.

Heroism. The following extraordinary instance of heroism is noticed in a *Georgia* paper:— "The signal bravery displayed by the detachment of our army in the battle of Autossee, is the theme of general admiration. In this affair our troops acted more like veterans than militia, and the feats of many officers and privates would do honor to Spartan valor. We shall particularly notice the conduct of one man, whose sufferings have been equal to his intrepidity. Quarter-master William A. Tennille, the worthy son of an excellent revolutionary soldier, had his horse shot under him while charging the indians. The horse falling on him, Mr. Tennille with some difficulty extricated himself—he was alone surrounded by enemies, and had scarcely recovered his feet before his *right arm* was broken by a musket ball, and he received a wound in this thigh—the indians rushed forward to tomahawk him— but presenting his pistol, they recoiled until they discovered it had missed fire— the savages again advanced— by this time he had drawn his sword, and wielding it in the left hand, kept his assailants at bay until our troops made a second charge, cut the indians to pieces and rescued this admirable young soldier, who for extraordinary bravery and presence of mind deserves to be ranked with the best heroes of ancient Rome.

We are sorry to mention that Mr. Tennille's arm has been amputated near the shoulder. He is said to be on the recovery."

Volume 5, February 19, 1814, pages 411-412

Events of the War—Military.

Milledgeville,
January 31.

An express from general Pinckney to the governor arrived here last night with the following important intelligence.

———

Head-quarters,
fort Hawkins,
Jan. 30, 1814.

Sir—I have the honor of enclosing for your information, copies of despatches received early this morning from general Floyd: This additional proof of the good conduct and gallantry of the troops of the state in which you preside must be highly gratifying to your excellency. Be pleased to accept my sincere congratulations thereon.

Colonel Milton and a detachment of regulars, will speedily reinforce the arm.

I have the honor to be very respectfully, your excellency's most obedient servant.

TH. PINKNEY.

His excellency gov. Early.

———

Camp Defiance,
(48 miles west of Chatahoochie)
January 27, 1814.

Major general Pinkney,

Sir—I have the honor to acquaint your excellency that this morning at 20 minutes past 5 o'clock, a very large body of hostile Indians made a desperate attack upon the army under my command.

They stole upon the centinels, fired on them, and with great impetuosity rushed upon our line: In 20 minutes the action became general, and our front, right and left flanks were closely pressed, but the brave and gallant conduct of the field and line officers, and the firmness of the men, repelled them at every point.

The steady firmness, and incessant fire of captain Thomas's artillery, and captain Adams' riflemen, preserved our front lines; both of these companies suffered greatly. The enemy rushed within thirty yards of the artillery, and captain Broadnax, who commanded one of the picquet guards, maintained his post with great bravery, until the enemy gained his rear, and then cut his way through them to the army—on this occasion, Timpooche Barnard, a half breed, at the head of the Uchies, distinguished himself, and contributed to the retreat of the picquet guard; the other friendly Indians took refuge within our lines, and remained inactive with the exception of a few who joined our ranks—as soon as it became light enough to distinguish objects, I ordered majors Watson's and Freeman's battalions to wheel up at right angles with major Booth's and Cleveland's battalions [who formed the right wing] to prepare for the charge. Captain Duke Hamilton's cavalry [who had reached me but the day before] was ordered to form in the rear of the right wing, to act as circumstances should dictate. The order for the charge was promptly obeyed, and the enemy fled in every direction before the bayonet. The signal was given for the charge of the cavalry, who pursued and sabred fifteen of the enemy, who left thirty seven dead on the field—from the effusion of blood, and the number of head-dresses and war-clubs found in various directions, their loss must have been considerable, independent of their wounded.

I directed the friendly Indians, with Merriwether's and Ford's rifle companies, accompanied by captain Hamilton's troop, to pursue them through Caulaebee swamp, where they were trailed by their blood, but they succeeded in overtaking but one of the wounded.

Colonel Newman received three balls in the commencement of the action, which deprived me of the services of that gallant and useful officer. The assistant adjutant general Hardin was indefatigable in the discharge of his duty, and rendered important services; his horse was wounded under him. The whole of the staff were prompt, and discharged their duty with courage and fidelity. Their vigilance, the intrepidity of the officers, and the firmness of the men, meet my approbation, and deserve the praise of their country.

I have to regret the death of many of my brave fellows, who have found honorable graves, in the voluntary support of their country.

My aid-de-camp, in executing my orders, had his horse killed under him; general Lee and major Pace, who acted as additional aids, rendered me essential services, with honor to themselves, and usefulness to the cause in which they have embarked. Four waggon and several other horses were killed, and two of the artillery horses wounded. While I deplore the loss sustained on this occasion, I have the consolation to know, that the men whom I have the honor to command have done their duty. I herewith transmit you a list of the killed and wounded, and have the honor to be most respectfully your obedient servant.

JOHN FLOYD, B. G.

Total killed, 17; *total wounded* 132.

N. B. One of the wounded since dead—5 of the friendly Indians killed, 15 wounded.

———

Copy of a letter from
brigadier general Claiborne,
of the volunteers,
to the secretary of war, dated

Fort Claiborne,
east bank of Alabama,
85 miles above Fort Stoddart,
January 1st, 1814.

Sir—On the 13th ult, I marched a detachment from this post with a view of destroying the towns of the inimical Creek Indians, on the Alabama, above the mouth of the Cahaba. After having marched about eighty miles, from the best information I could obtain, I was within thirty miles of a town newly erected on a ground called Holy, occupied by a large body of the enemy, under the command

76

of Witherford, the half breed chief, who was one of those who commanded the Indians that destroyed the garrison at Mims in August last, and who has committed many depredations on the frontier inhabitants. I immediately caused a stockade to be erected for the security of the heavy baggage and sick. On the morning of the 22d the troops resumed their line of march, chiefly through woods without a track to guide them. When near the town on the morning of the 23d, my disposition for attack was made.— The troops advanced in three columns. With the centre column I advanced myself, ordering Lester's guards and Wells' troop of dragoons to act as a corps of reserve. About noon the right column, composed of twelve months' volunteers, commanded by colonel Joseph Carson, came in view of the town called Eccanachaca (or Holy Ground) and was immediately vigorously attacked by the enemy, who were apprized of our approach, and had chosen their field of action.

Before the centre, commanded by lieutenant colonel Russell, with a part of the 3d regiment of United States' infantry and mounted militia riflemen, or the left column, which was composed of militia and a party of Choctaws under Pushamuttaha, commanded by major Smoot of militia, who were ordered to charge, could come generally into action, the enemy were repulsed and were flying in all directions, many of them were casting away their arms.

Thirty of the enemy were killed, and judging from every appearance many were wounded. The loss on our part was one corporal killed, and one ensign, two sergeants, one corporal and two privates wounded.

A pursuit was immediately ordered; but from the nature of the country, nothing was effected. The town was nearly surrounded by swamps and deep ravines, which rendered our approach difficult, and facilitated the escape of the enemy. In the town we found a large quantity of provisions and immense property of various kinds, which the enemy, flying precipitately, were obliged to leave behind, and which, together with two hundred houses were destroyed. They had barely time to remove their women and children across the Alabama, which runs near where the town stood. The next day was occupied in destroying a town consisting of sixty houses, eight miles higher up the river, and in taking and destroying the enemy's boats. At the town last destroyed was killed three Indians of some distinction. The town first destroyed was built since the commencement of hostilities, and was established as a place of security for the inhabitants of several villages. The leader, Witherford, Francis, and the Choctaw Sinquistur's son, who were principal prophets, resided here. Three Shawnese were among the slain.

Colonel Carson of the volunteers. Lieutenant colonel Russell of the 3d regiment United States infantry, and major Smoot of the militia, greatly distinguished themselves. The activity and zeal of the assistant deputy quarter master general, captain Wert, and of my brigade major, Kennedy, merit the approbation of government. I was much indebted to my aid de camp lieutenant Calvit of volunteers, to lieutenant Robeson of the 3d regiment, and major Caller of militia, who acted as my aids on that day, for the promptness and ability with which they performed their several duties. The officers of the different corps behaved handsomely, and are entitled to distinction.— Courage animated every countenance, and each vied with the other in rendering service. I have taken the liberty of communicating to you directly, in consequence of the distant station of the general commanding the district, and also for the purpose of forwarding to you the enclosed original document which was found in the house of Wetherford. It shews partially the conduct of the Spaniards towards the American government.

The third regiment has returned to this place, and volunteers are on their march to Mount Vernon near fort Stoddart for the purpose of being paid off and discharged, their terms of service having generally expired.

I have the honor to be, with great respect, your excellency's most obedient servant,

FERD. L. CLAIBORNE,
Brig. Gen. of vols.

His excellency John Armstrong.

Events of the War—Military.

The Spaniards.— The following letter from the governor of *Pensacola* to the Creek indians, was found by general *Claiborne*, of the volunteers, and forwarded to governor *Blount*:

Pensacola, 29th Sept. 1814.— *Gentlemen*, I received the letter that you wrote me in the month of August, by which, and with great satisfaction, I was informed of the advantages which your brave warriors obtained over your enemies.

I represented, as I promised you, to the captain general in Havanna, the request (which the last time I took you by the hand) ye made me, of arms and munitions—but until now I cannot yet have an answer. But I am in hopes, that he will send me the effects which I requested; and as soon as I receive them, I shall inform you.

I am very thankful for your generous offers to procure me the provisions and warriors necessary, in order to re-take the post of Mobile;— and you ask me at the same time, if we have given up the post of Mobile to the Americans? To which I answer, for the present, I cannot profit of your generous offer—not being at war with the Americans; who did not take Mobile by force—since they purchased it from the miserable officer, destitute of honor, who commanded there, and delivered it without authority:— by which reason, the sale and delivery of that place is totally void and null— and I hope that the Americans will restore it again to us, because nobody can dispose of a thing that is not his own property:— in consequence of which, the Spaniards have not lost their right to it: and I hope that you will not put in execution the project which you tell me of, *to burn the town*; since those houses and properties do not belong to Americans, but to true Spaniards.

To the bearers of your letter, I have ordered some small presents to be given. And I remain, forever, your good father and friend.

(Signed)   MANXIQUE.

—•))⊖ⓞ⊖((•—

Battle of Horseshoe Bend

Volume 5, February 26, 1814, pages 427-429

Copy of a letter from general Jackson, of the Tennessee volunteers to general Pinckney.

Head-Quarters,
Fort Strother,
Jan. 29.

Major General Thos. Pinckney,

Sir, I had the honor of informing you in a letter of the 31st ult. forwarded by Mr. M'Candles [express] of an excursion I contemplated making still further into the enemy's country, with the new raised volunteers from Tennessee. I had ordered those troops to form a junction with me on the 10th inst. but they did not arrive until the 14th. Their number, including officers, was about 800; and on the 15th I marched them across the river to graze their horses. On the next day I followed with the remainder of my force, consisting of the artillery company, with one 6 pounder, one company of infantry of 48 men, two companies of spies, commanded by captains Gordon and Russel, of about 30 men each, and a company of volunteer officers, headed by general Coffee, who had been abandoned by his men, and who still remained in the field awaiting the order of the government; making my force exclusive of indians, 930.

The motives which influenced me to penetrate still further into the enemy's country, with this force, were many and urgent. The term of service of the new raised volunteers was short, and a considerable part of it was expired; they were expensive to the government, and were full of ardor to meet the enemy. The ill effects of keeping soldiers of this description long stationary and idle, I had been made to feel but too sensible already—other causes concurred to make such a movement not only justifiable but absolutely necessary. I had received a letter from captain M'Alpin of the 5th instant, who commanded at Fort Armstrong in the absence of colonel Snodgrass, informing me that 14 or

15 towns of the enemy, situated on the waters of the Tallapoosa, were about uniting their forces and attacking that place, which had been left in a very feeble state of defence. You had in your letter of the 24th ult. informed me that general Floyd was about to make a movement to the Tallapoosa near its junction with the Coosee; and in the same letter had recommended temporary excursions against such of the enemy's towns or settlements as might be within striking distance, as well to prevent my men from becoming discontented as to harrass the enemy. Your ideas corresponded exactly with my own, and I was happy in the opportunity of keeping my men engaged, distressing the enemy, and at the same time making a diversion to facilitate the operations of general Floyd.

Determined by these and other considerations, I took up the line of march on the 17th inst. and on the night of the 18th encamped at Talledega Fort, where I was joined by between 200 and 300 friendly indians: 65 of whom were Cherokees, the balance Creeks. Here I received your letter of the 9th inst. stating that general Floyd was expected to make a movement from Cowetau the next day, and that in 18 days thereafter he would establish a firm position at Tuckabotchee; and also a letter from colonel Snodgrass, who had returned to Fort Armstrong, informing me that an attack was intended soon to be made on that Fort by 900 of the enemy. If I could have hesitated before, I could now hesitate no longer. I resolved to lose not time in meeting this force, which was understood to have been collected from New Yorcau, Oakfuskee and Ufauley towns, and were concentrated in the bend of the Tallapoosa, near the mouth of the creek called Emucfau, on an island below New Yorcau.

On the morning of the 29th your letter of the 10th inst. forwarded by Mr. M'Candles, reached me at the Hillabee Creek, and that night I encamped at Entochapco, a small Hillabee village about twelve miles from Emuckfau. Here I began to perceive very plainly how little knowledge my spies had of the country, of the situation of the enemy, or of the distance I was from them. The insubordination of the new troops and the want of skill in most of their officers;

also became more and more apparent. But their ardor to meet the enemy was not diminished; and I had a sure reliance upon the guards; and a company of old volunteer officers, and upon the spies, in all about 125. My wishes and my duty remained united, and I was determined to effect, if possible, the objects for which the excursion had been principally undertaken.

On the morning of the 21st, I marched from Enotachopco, as direct as I could for the bend of the Tallapoosa, and about 2 o'clock, P. M., my spies having discovered two of the enemy, endeavored to catch them but failed. In the evening I fell in upon a large trail, which led to a new road, much beaten and lately travelled. Knowing that I must have arrived within the neighborhood of a strong force, and it being late in the day, I determined to encamp, and reconnoitre the country in the night. I chose the best site the country would admit, encamped in a hollow square, sent out my spies and picquets, doubled my centinels and made the necessary arrangements before dark, for a night attack. About 10 o'clock at night, one of the pickets fired at three of the enemy and killed one, but he was not found until the next day. At 11 o'clock, the spies whom I had sent out returned with the information, that there were a large encampment of indians at the distance of about three miles, who from their whooping and dancing seemed to be apprized of our approach. One of these spies, an Indian in whom I had great confidence, assured me that they were carrying off their women and children, and that the warriors would either make their escape or attack me before day. Being prepared at all points, nothing remained to be done but await their approach, if they meditated an attack, or to be in readiness, if they did not, to pursue and attack them at day light. While we were in this state of readiness, the enemy about 6 o'clock in the morning commenced a vigorous attack on my left flank, which was vigorously met; the action continued to rage on my left flank, and on the left of my rear for about half an hour. The brave general Coffee, with colonel Sittler, the adjutant-general, and colonel Carroll, the inspector-general, the moment the firing commenced, mounted their horses and repaired to the line, encouraging and animating the men to the performance of their duty. So soon as it became light enough to pursue, the left wing having sustained the heat of the action and being somewhat weakened, was reinforced by captain Ferrill's company of infantry, and was ordered and led on to the charge by general Coffee, who was well supported by colonel Higgins and the inspector-general, and by all the officers and privates who composed that line. The enemy was completely routed at every point, and the friendly indians joining in the pursuit, they were chased about two miles with great slaughter.

The chase being over, I immediately detached general Coffee with 400 men and all the indian force to burn their encampment; but it was said by some to be fortified. I ordered him, in that event, not to attack it, until the artillery could be sent forward to reduce it. On viewing the encampment and its strength, the general thought it most prudent to return to my encampment and guard the artillery thither. The wisdom of this step was soon discovered—in half an hour after his return to camp, a considerable force of the enemy made its appearance on my right flank, and commenced a brisk fire on a party of men who had been on picket guard the night before, and were then in search of the indians they had fired upon, some of whom they believe had been killed. General Coffee immediately requested me to let him take 200 men and turn their left flank, which I accordingly ordered; but, through some mistake, which I did not then observe, not more than fifty-four followed him, among whom were the old volunteer officers. With these, however, he immediately commenced an attack on the left flank of the enemy; at which time I ordered 200 of the friendly indians to fall in upon the right flank of the enemy, and co-operate with the general. This order was promptly obeyed, and in the moment of its execution, what I expected was realized. The enemy had intended the attack on the right as a feint, and, expecting to direct all my attention thither, meant to attack me again and with their main force on the left flank, which they had hoped to find weakened and in disorder—they were disappointed. I had ordered the left flank to remain firm to its place, and the moment the alarm gun was heard in that quarter, I repaired

thither, and ordered captain Ferrill, part of my reserve, to support. The whole line met the approach of the enemy with astonishing intrepidity, and having given a few fires, they forthwith charged with great vigor. — The effect was immediate and inevitable. The enemy fled with precipitation, and were pursued to a considerable distance, by the left flank and the friendly indians, with a galling and destructive fire. Colonel Carroll, who ordered the charge, led on the pursuit, and colonel Higgins and his regiment again distinguished themselves.

In the mean time general Coffee was contending with a superior force of the enemy. The indians who I had ordered to his support, and who had set out for the purpose, hearing the firing on the left had returned to that quarter, and when the enemy were routed there entered into the chase. That being now over, I forthwith ordered Jim Fife, who was one of the principal commanders of the friendly Creeks, with one hundred of his warriors, to execute my first order; so soon as he reached general Coffee, the charge was made and the enemy routed: they were pursued about three miles, and forty-five of them slain, who were found. General Coffee was wounded in the body, and his aid-de-camp, A. Donaldson, killed, together with three others. Having brought in and buried the dead, and dressed the wounded, I ordered my camp to be fortified, to be the better prepared to repel any attack which might be made in the night; determined to commence a return march to fort Strother the following day. Many causes concurred to make such a measure necessary, as I had not set out prepared or with a view to make a permanent establishment, I considered it worse than useless to advance and destroy an empty encampment.

I had indeed, hoped to have met the enemy there, but having met and beaten them a little sooner, I did not think it necessary or prudent to proceed any further: not necessary, because I had accomplished all I could expect to effect by marching to their encampment; and because if it was proper to contend with and weaken their forces still farther, this object would be more certainly attained by commencing a return, which, having to them the appearance of a retreat, would inspire them to pursue me. Not prudent, because of the number of my wounded; of the reinforcements from below, which the enemy might be expected to receive; of the starving condition of my horses, they having had neither corn nor cane for two days and nights; of the scarcity of supplies for my men, the indians who joined me at Talladega having drawn none, and being wholly destitute; and because, if the enemy pursued me, as it was likely they would, the diversion in favor of general Floyd would be the more complete and effectual. Influenced by these considerations, I commenced my return march at half after ten on the 23d, and was fortunate enough to reach Enotachopco before night, having passed without interruption a dangerous defile, occasioned by a hurricane. I again fortified my camp, and having another defile to pass in the morning, across a deep creek, and between two hills, which I had viewed with attention as I passed on, and where I expected I might be attacked, I determined to pass it at another point, and gave directions to my guide and fatigue men accordingly. My expectation of an attack in the morning was increased by the signs of the night, and with it my caution. Before I moved the wounded from the interior of my camp, I had my front and rear guards formed, as well as my right and left columns, and moved off my centre in regular order, leading down a handsome ridge to Enotachopco creek, at a point where it was clear of reed, except immediately on its margin. I had previously issued a general order, pointing out the manner in which the men should be formed in the event of an attack on the front or rear, or on the flanks, and had particularly cautioned the officers to halt and form accordingly, the instant the word should be given.

The front guard had crossed with part of the flank columns, the wounded were over, and the artillery in the act of entering the creek, when an alarm gun was heard in the rear. I heard it without surprise, and even with pleasure, calculating with the utmost confidence on the firmness of my troops, from the manner in which I had seen them act on the 22d. I had placed colonel Carroll at the head of the centre column of the rear guard: its right column was commanded by colonel Perkins, and its left by colonel Stump. Having chosen the ground, I

expected there to have entirely cut off the enemy by wheeling the right and left columns on their pivots, recrossing the creek above and below, and falling in upon their flanks and rear. But to my astonishment and mortification, when the word was given by colonel Carrol to halt and form, and a few guns had been fired, I beheld the right and left columns of the rear guard precipitately give way. This shameful retreat was disastrous in the extreme: it drew along with it the greater part of the centre column, leaving not more than twenty-five men, who being formed by colonel Carrol, maintained their ground as long as it was possible to maintain it, and it brought consternation and confusion into the centre of the army, a consternation which was not easily removed, and a confusion which could not soon be restored to order. There was then left to repulse the enemy, the few who remained of the rear guard, the artillery company and captain Russell's company of spies. They however realized and exceeded my highest expectations. Lieutenant Armstrong, who commanded the artillery company in the absence of captain Deadrick, (confined by sickness) ordered them to form and advanced to the top of the hill, whilst he and a few others dragged up the six pounder. Never was more bravery displayed than on this occasion. Amidst the most galling fire from the enemy, more than ten times their number, they ascended the hill and maintained their position until their piece was hauled up, when, having levelled it, they poured upon the enemy a fire of grape, reloaded and fired again, charged and repulsed them.

The most deliberate bravery was displayed by Constantine Perkins and Craven Jackson of the artillery, acting as gunners. In the hurry of the moment, in separating the gun from the limbers, the rammer and picker of the cannon were left tied to the limber: No sooner was this discovered, than Jackson, amidst the galling fire of the enemy, pulled out the ramrod of his musket and used it as a picker; Primed with a cartridge and fired the cannon. Perkins having pulled off his bayonet, used his musket as a rammer, drove down the cartridge; and Jackson using his former plan, again discharged her. The brave lieutenant Armstrong, just after the first fire of the cannon, with captain Hamilton, of East Tennessee,

Bradford and M'Govock, all fell, the lieutenant exclaiming as he lay, "*my brave fellows, some of you may fall, but you must save the cannon.*" About this time, a number crossed the creek and entered into the chase. The brave captain Cordon of the spies, who had rushed from the front, endeavored to turn the left flank of the enemy, in which he partially succeeded, and colonel Carroll, colonel Higgins, and captains Elliot and Pipkins pursued the enemy for more than two miles, who fled in consternation throwing away their packs and leaving 26 of their warriors dead on the field. This last defeat was decisive, and we were no more disturbed by their yells. I should do injustice to my feelings if I omitted to mention that the venerable judge Cocke, at the age of 65, entered into the engagement, continued the pursuit of the enemy with youthful ardor, and saved the life of a fellow soldier by killing his savage antagonist.

Our loss in this affair was— killed and wounded; among the former was the brave captain Hamilton, from East Tennessee, who had with his aged father and two others of his company, after the period of his engagement had expired, volunteered his services for this excursion, and attached himself to the artillery company. No man ever fought more bravely or died more gloriously; and by his side fell with equal bravery and glory, Bird Evans, of the same company. Captain Quarles, who commanded the centre column of the rear guard, preferring death to the abandonment of his post, having taken a firm stand in which he was followed by 25 of his men, received a wound in his head of which he has since died.

In these several engagements our loss was 20 killed and 75 wounded, 4 of whom have since died.— The loss of the enemy cannot be accurately ascertained; 189 of their warriors were found dead; but this must fall considerably short of the number really killed. Their wounded can only be guessed at.

Had it not been for the unfortunate retreat of the rear guard in the affair of the 24 inst. I think I could safely have said that no army of militia ever acted with more cool and deliberate bravery; undisciplined and inexperienced as they were, their conduct in the several engagements of the 22d could not have been surpassed by regulars. No men ever met the approach of an enemy with more intrepidity, or repulsed them with more energy. On the 24th, after the retreat of the rear guard, they seemed to have lost all their collectedness, and were more difficult to be restored to order than any troops I have ever seen. But this was no doubt owing in a great measure or altogether to that very retreat, and ought rather to be ascribed to the want of conduct in many of their officers than to any cowardice in the men, who on every occasion have manifested a willingness to perform their duty so fit as they knew it.

All the effects which were designed to be produced by this excursion, it is believed have been produced. If an attack was meditated against fort Armstrong, that has been prevented. If general Floyd is operating on the east side of the Tallaposee, as I suppose him to be, a most fortunate diversion has been made in his favor. The number of the enemy has been diminished, and the confidence they may have derived from the delays I have been made to experience, has been destroyed. Discontent has been kept out of my army, while the troops who would have been exposed to it have been beneficially employed. The enemy's country has been explored, and a road cut to the point where their force will probably be concentrated when they shall be driven from the country below. But in a report of this kind, and to you who will immediately perceive them, it is not necessary to state the happy consequences which may be expected to result from this excursion. Unless I am greatly mistaken, it will be found to have hastened the termination of the Creek war, more than any measure I could have taken with the troops under my command.

I am, sir, with sentiments of high respect your obedient servant,

ANDREW JACKSON, maj. Gen.

Volume 5, February 26, 1814,
Supplement to Vol. 5, pages 63-68

The Floridas.

Confidential proceedings in congress.

In Senate.

Saturday, July 31st, 1812.—On motion, by Mr. Anderson,

Ordered, That the confidential proceedings of the senate at their last session, in relation to East Florida, be made public.

Thursday, December 10th.—Mr. Anderson submitted the following motion for consideration, which was read:

Resolved, That a committee be appointed to consider whether it be expedient to authorise the president of the United States to occupy and hold the whole or any part of East Florida, including Amelia Island, and also those parts of West Florida which are not now in possession and under the jurisdiction of the United States, with leave to report by bill or otherwise.

Tuesday, December 15th, 1812.— The senate proceeded to consider the motion submitted on the 10th inst. respecting the Floridas, and after debate,

Ordered, That the further consideration there be postponed to Monday next.

Wednesday, December 16th, 1812.— Mr. Leib submitted the following motion for consideration:

Resolved, That the president of the United States be requested to cause to be laid before the senate any information which he may have of the intention of the enemy to take possession of East Florida, and of the disposition of the people of that territory to be received under the protection of the government of the United States; the amount of the American force in that neighbourhood, and under the command of general Wilkinson; and the quantum of Spanish or other force in St. Augustine, Pensacola, and Mobile.

Friday, December 18th, 1812.—The senate proceeded to consider the motion submitted the 16th inst. calling upon the president of the United States for information respecting East Florida; and

On motion, by Mr. Goodrich,

To amend the motion so as to read as follows:

Resolved, That the president of the United States be requested to cause to be laid before the senate, any information

which he may have of the intention of the enemy to take possession of East Florida, and of the disposition of the people of the territory to be received under the protection of the government of the United States, the amount of the American force in that neighbourhood, and under the command of general Wilkinson, and the quantum of the Spanish or other force in St. Augustine, Pensacola, and Mobile, and respecting any negociation that may have been had for the payment of differences and claims, existing between the United States and Spain, not heretofore laid before the senate; respecting any proposal or negociation that may have been made, or had by or with any person or persons exercising the powers of the government of Spain, or claiming to exercise the powers of said government, or with their respective agents, for the cession of East Florida to the United States; respecting any proposal to or from the local authorities of East Florida (not heretofore communicated,) for the cession, surrender, or occupancy thereof, to or by the United States; and also any information respecting the relations of the United States with Spain or said territory of East Florida, which the president may deem proper the communicate.

On motion by Mr. Anderson,

Ordered, That the further consideration of the motion for amendment, be postponed to Monday next.

Tuesday, November 22d, 1812.— The senate resumed the motion made the 10th to appoint a committee to enquire into the expediency of taking possession of East Florida, and

On motion, by Mr. Smith of Maryland,

It was determined in the negative, yeas 15, nays 15.

On motion, by Mr. Leib,

To strike out the words "with leave to report by bill or otherwise."

It was determined in the negative.

On the question, to agree to the original motion.

It was determined in the affirmative, yeas 18, nays 12.

Ordered, That Mr. Anderson, Mr.

Goodrich, Mr. Smith of Maryland, Mr. Tait, and Mr. Varnum, be the committee.

The senate resumed the consideration of the motion made the 16th inst. calling upon the president of the United States for information respecting East Florida, together with the amendment proposed thereto on the 18th inst. and having agreed to the amendment;

Resolved, That the motion be agreed to as amended.

Ordered, That the secretary lay this resolution before the president of the United States.

Thursday, January 14th, 1813.— The following confidential message was received from the president of the United States, by Mr. Coles, his secretary

To the senate of the United States,

I transmit to the senate a report of the secretary of state, complying with the resolution of the 22d December.

JAMES MADISON.

January 14th, 1813.— The message and report were read; and

On motion, by Mr. Leib,

That they be printed confidentially for the use of the senate.

It was agreed that the motion be postponed until to-morrow.

Friday, January 15th, 1813.—The senate resumed the consideration of the motion made yesterday, "that the message and report, respecting East Florida, be printed confidentially for the use of the senate with the exception of the return of the number of troops and their respective stations, on their southern and western frontier;"

On the question, to agree thereto? It was determined in the negative, yeas 13, nays 18.

On motion, by Mr. Anderson,

Ordered, That the message and documents therein referred to, be referred to the committee appointed the 22d December, on the same subject, to consider and report thereon.

Mr. Bradley submitted the following motion for consideration:

Resolved, That the president of the United States be requested to cause to be laid before the senate, all letters and communications that have passed between the government of the United States and that of Spain, or the ministers thereof, since the 9th day January, 1804, on the subject of indemnities for spoliations committed on our commerce by her subjects before that time; and also in relation to French seizures and condemnation of our vessels in the ports of Spain, during the late war with France; together with such communications between this and the French government, as relate to the same subjects; with such instructions as have been given to the ministers of the United States in relation to the same. And any propositions or negociations that have been had or made with France or Spain, for ceding East Florida to the United States, previous to the 15th day of January, 1811, not heretofore communicated.

Saturday, January 16th, 1813.—The senate proceeded to consider the motion submitted yesterday, by Mr. Bradely; and

On motion, by Mr. Campbell of Ohio,

Ordered, That the further consideration thereof be postponed until Monday next.

Monday, January 18th, 1813.—The motion submitted by Mr. Bradley on the 15th inst. was resumed and agreed to without amendment.

Ordered, That the secretary lay the said resolution before the president of the United States.

Tuesday, January 19th, 1813.—Mr. Anderson, from the committee appointed the 22d December on the subject, reported the following bill:

A bill authorising the president of the United States to take possession of a tract of country lying south of Mississippi territory, and of the state of Georgia, and for other purposes.

BE it enacted by the Senate and House of Representatives of the United States of America, in Congress assembled, That the president be, and he is hereby authorised to occupy and hold all that tract of country called West Florida, which lies west of the river Perdido, not now in possession of the United States.

Sec. 2. *And be it further enacted,* That the president be, and he is hereby authorised to hold all that part of West Florida, east of the Perdido, and the whole or any part of East Florida, including Amelia Island.

Sec. 3. *And be it further enacted,* That for the purpose of occupying and holding the country aforesaid, and of affording protection to the inhabitants thereof, under the authority of the United States, the president may employ such parts of the military and naval force of the United States, as he may deem necessary.

Sec. 4. *And be it further enacted,* That for defraying the necessary expenses _____ dollars are hereby appropriated, to be paid out of any monies in the treasury not otherwise appropriated, and to be applied for the purposes aforesaid, under the direction of the president.

Sec. 5. *And be it further enacted,* That until further provision be made by congress, the president shall be and hereby is empowered to establish within the country he may acquire by this act, a temporary government, the civil and military authorities of which shall be vested in such person or persons as he may appoint; and be exercised in such manner as he may direct: *Provided,* That he shall take due care for the preservation of social order, and for securing to the inhabitants the enjoyments of their personal rights, their religion, and their property: *And provided also,* That the section of country herein designated, that is situated to the eastward of the river Perdido, may be the subject of future negociation.

The bill was read; and

Ordered, That it pass to the second reading.

Friday, January 22d, 1813.—The bill authorizing the president of the United States to take possession of a tract of country lying south of the Mississippi territory and of the state of Georgia, and for other purposes, was read the second time.

Mr. Leib submitted the following motion for consideration.

Resolved, That the documents which accompanied the president's message of the 14th inst. be confidentially printed for the use of the senate, excepting those papers which relate to the stations, and the amount of the military force of the United States and the letter of general Pinckney of the 27th December.

On motion of Mr. Leib,

That the bill be now taken up and considered:

It was determined in the negative.

Monday, January 25th, 1813.—On motion of Mr. Anderson,

That the bill authorising the president of the United States to take possession of a tract of country lying south of the Mississippi territory and of the state of Georgia, and for other purposes, be now considered;

It was determined in the negative.

The senate proceeded to consider the motion submitted the 22d inst by Mr. Leib; and

On motion, by Mr. Bayard,

That the further consideration thereof be postponed until to-morrow;

It was determined in the negative.

On the question to agree to the resolution?

On motion, by Mr. Reed,

It was agreed that it be taken by yeas and nays; and

On motion by Mr. Bayard, the senate adjourned.

Tuesday, January 26th, 1813.—On motion, by Mr. Anderson,

The senate resumed, as in committee of the whole, the consideration of the bill authorising the president of the United States to take possession of a tract of country lying south of the Mississippi territory and of the state of Georgia, and for other purposes; and

On motion, by Mr. Leib,

That the further consideration of the bill be postponed, in order to consider his motion, to have printed certain documents referred to in the message of the president of the United States of the 14th instant; and

It was determined in the negative.

Mr. Gaillard was requested to take the chair; and the consideration of the bill was recurred to.

A motion was made by Mr. Smith, of Maryland to strike out the second section of the bill; and

On his motion,

It was agreed to take the question by yeas and nays.

On motion, by Mr. Bradley,

Ordered, That the further consideration of the bill be postponed to, and be made the order of the day for to-morrow.

On motion, by Mr. Leib,

The senate resumed his motion submitted the 22d instant, that the document referred to in the message of the president of the United States of the 14th inst. be printed; and the motion was amended.

Resolved, That the documents which accompanied the president's message of the 14th instant, be confidentially printed for the use of the members of the senate, excepting those papers which relate to the stations and amount of the military force of the United States, the report of the secretary of state, and the letters of general Pinckney.

On the question, to agree to the motion as ammended?

It was determined in the affirmative, yeas 18, nays 12.

Mr. Tait presented the memorial of the legislature of the state of Georgia, recommending to, and soliciting congress to authorise the president of the United States to take immediate possession of the province of East Florida, and that portion of West Florida, purchased from France but still retained by Spain; for reasons stated at large in the memorial; which was read.

The following confidential message was received from the president of the United States, by Mr. Coles, his secretary.

To the Senate of the United States:

I transmit to the senate a report of the secretary of state, complying with their resolution of the 8th inst.

JAMES MADISON.

January 26th, 1813.

The message and report were read.

Wednesday, January 27th, 1813.— The following confidential message was received from the president of the United States by Mr. Coles, his secretary:

To the Senate of the United States:

I transmit to the senate a report of the secretary of war, complying with their resolution of the 7th inst.

JAMES MADISON.

January 27th, 1813.

The message and report were read.

Mr. Horsey submitted the following motion for consideration, which was read.

Resolved, That the injunction of secrecy in relation to the president's message of the 16th inst. communicating certain papers marked A and B, in compliance with the resolution of the senate of the 18th instant be, and the same is hereby removed.

Thursday, January 28th, 1813.— The senate resumed, as in committee of the whole, the consideration of the bill authorising the president of the United States to take possession of a tract of country lying south of the Mississippi territory and of the state of Georgia, and for other purposes; and

On motion, by Mr. Anderson,

Ordered, That the further consideration thereof be postponed to, and made the order of the day for to-morrow.

The senate proceeded to consider the motion submitted yesterday by Mr. Horsey, to remove the injunction of secrecy from certain papers; and

On motion,

Ordered, That the further consideration thereof be postponed until to-morrow.

Friday, January 29th, 1813.— Agreeably to the order of the day, the senate resumed, as in committee of the whole, the consideration of the bill authorising the president of the United States to take possession of a tract of

86

country lying south of the Mississippi territory and of the state of Georgia, and for other purposes; and Mr. Gaillard was requested to take the chair; and

The motion to strike out the second section of the bill was resumed; and after debate,

Adjourned.

Monday, February 1st, 1813.— Agreeably to the order of the day, the senate resumed, as in committee of the whole, the consideration of the bill authorising the president of the United States to take possession of a tract of country lying south of the Mississippi territory and of the state of Georgia, and for other purposes, together with the motion to strike out the second section thereof; and Mr. Gaillard was requested to take the chair; and after debate,

Ordered, That the consideration thereof be further postponed until to-morrow.

Tuesday, February 2d, 1813.— Agreeably to the order of the day, the senate resumed, as in committee of the whole, the consideration of the bill authorising the president of the United States to take possession of a tract of country lying south of the Mississippi territory and of the state of Georgia, and for other purposes, together with the motion to strike out the second section thereof; and Mr. Gaillard was requested to take the chair;

On the question, to strike out the second section as follows:

"Sec. 2. *And be it further enacted,* That the president be, and he is hereby authorised to occupy and hold all that part of West Florida east of the Perdido, and the whole or any part of East Florida, including Amelia Island;"

It was determined in the affirmative, yeas 19, nays 16.

A motion was made by Mr. Smith of Maryland, to strike out the fifth section of the bill; and

On motion,

The senate adjourned.

Wednesday, February 3d, 1813.—On motion, by Mr. Anderson,

The senate resumed, as in committee of the whole, the consideration of the bill authorising the president of the United States to take possession of a tract of country lying south of the Mississippi territory and of the state of Georgia, and for other purposes, together with the motion to strike out the fifth section; and Mr. Gaillard was requested to take the chair:

Whereupon,

Mr. Smith, of Maryland withdrew his motion to strike out the fifth section of the bill.

A motion was made by Mr. Campbell, of Ohio, to insert in lieu of the second section stricken out, the following:

"And be it further enacted, That if hostilities shall be committed by the Spanish nation, its colonies or dependencies against the United States, or if it shall be ascertained to the satisfaction of the president of the United States that the safety and security of the United States, or any part thereof, are in imminent danger from the Spanish authorities in East Florida, and in that part of West Florida lying east of the river Perdido, the president of the United States is hereby authorised to occupy the said provinces or any part thereof including Amelia Island."

Whereupon,

A motion was made by Mr. Bradley to amend the proposed section, by inserting, after the word "that," in the 1st line, the following words: *"upon the troops of the United States being withdrawn from the province of East Florida."*

And a motion was made by Mr. Pope, that the further consideration of the bill be postponed to the first Monday in June next; and

It was determined in the negative, yeas 16, nays 17.

On the question to agree to the motion for amendment to the amendment:

It was determined in the negative;

The senate being equally divided, yeas 17, nays 17.

On the question, to agree to the motion for amending the 2d section;

It was determined in the negative, yeas 14, nays 20.

On motion,

It was agreed to strike out the fifth section of the bill.

On the question "shall the bill be engrossed and read a third time as amended?"

It was determined in the affirmative.

Friday, February 5th, 1813.—The bill authorising the president of the United States to take possession of a tract of country lying south of the Mississippi territory and the state of Georgia, and for other purposes, was reported by the committee correctly engrossed; and the bill was read the third time.

On motion by Mr. Anderson,

It was agreed to fill the blank with the words "twenty thousand."

On the question, "Shall the bill pass?"

It was determined in the affirmative, yeas 22, nays 11.

So it was

Resolved, That the bill do pass; and

On motion,

It was agreed that the title thereof be "An act authorising the president of the United States to take possession of a tract of country lying south of the Mississippi territory and west of the river Perdido."

On motion, by Mr. Anderson,

Resolved, That a committee be appointed to consist of two members, to carry the said bill to the house of representatives, and ask their concurrence therein.

Ordered, That Mr. Anderson and Mr. Bradley be the committee.

The senate resumed the consideration of the motion submitted the 27th January, to print certain documents; and after debate,

On motion,

The senate adjourned.

Monday, February 8th, 1813.—On motion,

Ordered, That Mr. Dana be of the committee appointed the 5th instant to carry a confidential bill to the house of representatives, in place of Mr. Bradley,

absent.

Tuesday, February 9th, 1813.—A confidential message was received from the house of representatives by Mr. Troup and Mr. Robertson, two of their members—Mr. Troup, chairman:

Mr. President—The house of representatives have passed the bill sent from the senate, entitle "An act authorising the president of the United States to take possession of a tract of country lying south of the Mississippi territory and west of the river Perdido."

And they withdrew.

Thursday, Friday 11th, 1813.—Mr. Campbell of Ohio, from the committee, reported the bill, entitle "An act authorising the president of the United States to take possession of a tract of country lying south of the Mississippi territory and west of the river Perdido," duly enrolled.

A message from the house of representatives, by Mr. Crawford and Mr. Goodwin, two of their members—Mr. Crawford, chairman:

Mr. President—The speaker of the house of representatives having signed an enrolled bill, we are directed to bring it to the senate for the signature of their president. And they withdrew.

The president signed the enrolled bill last reported to have been examined, and it was delivered to the committee to be laid before the president of the United States.

Saturday, February 18th, 1813.—Mr. Campbell, of Ohio, from the committee, reported that they yesterday laid before the president of the United States the enrolled bill, entitle "An act authorising the president of the United States to take possession of a tract of country lying south of the Mississippi territory and west of the river Perdido."

A message from the president of the United States, by Mr. Coles, his secretary.

Mr. President—The president of the United States did, on the 12th instant, approve and sign, "An act authorising the president of the United States to take possession of a tract of country lying south of the Mississippi territory and west of the river Perdido."

Ordered, That the secretary communicate this information to the house of representatives.

Tuesday, February 16th, 1813.—The senate resumed the consideration of the motion submitted by Mr. Horsey on the 27th January, to remove the injunction of secrecy from certain papers; and

On motion,

It was agreed to amend the same to read as follows:

Resolved, That the injunction of secrecy in relation to the paper marked A communicated in the president's message of the 26th instant be, and same is hereby removed.

On the question to agree to the motion as amended?

The senate being equally divided, it was determined in the negative, yeas 16, nays 16.

Thursday, Feb. 18th, 1813.—The following written message was received from the president of the United States, by Mr. Coles, his secretary.

I transmit to the senate a report of the secretary of state, complying with their resolution of the 18th, of January, 1813.

JAMES MADISON.

February 18th, 1813.

The message and documents therein referred to, were read.

NILES' WEEKLY REGISTER.

THE PAST—THE PRESENT—FOR THE FUTURE.

EDITED, PRINTED AND PUBLISHED BY H. NILES, AT $5 PER ANNUM, PAYABLE IN ADVANCE.

Volume 6

(March 5, 1814 - August 27, 1814)

Volume 6, March 5, 1814, page 12

Events of the War—Military.

The Creeks.— A body of excellent men 1,020 strong, has marched from *South Carolina* against the Creeks. They are chiefly volunteers.

Volume 6, March 12, 1814, page 37

Events of the War—Southern Frontier.
From the Georgia Journal.

Extract of a letter from Colonel Benjamin Hawkins to Major General Pinckney,

dated, Camp near fort Mitchell, Feb. 16.

"A runner who is intelligent, and was sent by me to the chiefs low down this river, who are connected with the Seminolies, returned this evening. He heard a talk from the governor of Pensacola to the Seminolies, delivered in his presence to the chiefs of the villages. The purport was—

"That being an ignorant people, they should listen to their old chiefs, and aid them to crush the prophets, who had deceived them by their lies, As they had misapplied the powder he gave them to hunt provisions for their women and children, he should give them no more—they had deceived, divided, and ruined their nation. The British were not expected to possess the country bordering on the tide waters of the Floridas, and if they should come, they could not remain long, as the United States would drive them off. The Indians had once been deceived by them, and must take care how they trusted them again. It was expected peace would be made among the white people every where this year, and it would be right for the Seminolies to help their old chiefs to destroy the prophets. The deception played on him was through the fears of his officer under him and second in command, who urged him to let the prophet's party come and take him by the hand, and to give them some ammunition to hunt for their women and children. The chiefs he saw were friendly.

If any credit be due to the professions of the governor of Pensacola, we may calculate from this talk to the Seminolie chiefs, that no more ammunition will be obtained by the hostile Indians from him. Until further lights are shed on the subject, it may remain doubtful whether his acquiesence in their demands proceeded from fear of them or enmity to us. It is quite likely that our formidable force in the Creek nation may have intimidated the Spanish commandant more than the threats of the Indians, and that he finds it prudent to change his tone to them, and to offer the best apology he can to our government.

The following statement handed us by an officer of the patriots, directly from their camp, and on his way to Washington City, [for the purpose, we presume, of supplicating assistance from the general government,] contains, we believe, a correct view of the situation and prospects.

"On the tenth of January the patriots left the St. Mary's river, about seventy strong; their numbers increased in their march to about ninety, and on the sixteenth of the same month, they arrived at the Aulotohewan Indian settlement called Paine's town. On the eighteenth they commenced a blockhouse, twenty-five feet square, which they soon reared two stories high, and immediately proceeded to surveying the land. On the tenth of this month the force of the patriots had increased to one hundred and sixty men, and by this time, I have no doubt they muster more than two hundred, as recruits were daily arriving.

The Aulotchewan country exceeds any that I have seen. The cattle, of which there are large numbers in the range, and as fat as I ever saw killed in the woods. The land is equal in quality to any in America. Within seven miles of fort Mitchell is a large lake, about five miles over, and no doubt communicates with lake George or the river St. John's which is about twenty-two miles S. E. of fort Mitchell.

These waters bring an excellent navigation into the heart of the country. On the twenty-fifth of January a large water melon was found, which was quite round, and eat well. The wild vegetable poke was growing in abundance at the height of twelve or fourteen inches. The orange tree grows spontaneously, and is now ornamented with its yellow fruits. The fort stands on a prairie, which is seven or eight miles wide and twenty-three long. This district of country is admirably suited to the culture of the sugar cane.

The patriots are well supplied with ammunition and provision. They will raise a crop this season, and are determined to hold the country or lose their lives in defending it."

A letter, dated the 27th January, complaining of the conduct of the patriots, some of whom originally went from this state, has been received by governor Early from the governor Augustine. The letter intimates that unless effectual steps are taken to put a stop to their illegal proceedings, *it may lead to disagreeable consequences*. Our executive will doubtless disregard this empty threat, and leave the Spaniards and patriots to settle their differences in their own way.

Volume 6, March 19, 1814, page 44

Events of the War—Miscellaneous.

Floyd's victories over the allies of *England*, have been honorably noticed at *Savannah*, under direction of the city police.

Volume 6, March 19, 1814, page 46

Events of the War—Military.

Daniel Bissel, colonel of the 5th infantry, *Edmund P. Gaines*, colonel of the 25th infantry, and *Winfield Scott*, colonel of the 2nd artillery, have been respectively promoted by the president, with the advice and consent of the senate, to the rank of brigadier generals in the service of the United States.

Volume 6, April 16, 1814, page 115

Events of the War—Southern Indians.

Augusta, (Georgia)
March 25.

Hostilities will again commence from this frontier in a few days. Already the troops of the United States, consisting of part of the 8th regiment, one rifle company, and two of dragoons, with the Carolina militia, are at fort Hawkins, and in the different forts erected in the nation by general Floyd; and those from North Carolina in two divisions, amounting to 1200 men, command by colonel Pearson, passed through Washington in Wilkes county, on Saturday and Sunday last, on their way to the general rendezvous. This force, when united, will amount to about 3,500 effective men—an army sufficient to destroy or reduce to order and obedience, the hostile part of the Creek nation—but unless supplies, sufficient for the expedition, making the necessary advance for delay and accident, shall accompany the troops, no force, however brave or numerous, can perform any important service to their country in this war. Experience has taught us this lesson, and we sincerely hope, it will not be without its effects.

Volume 6, April 23, 1814, page 130

Events of the War—Military.

The Creek Indians.—The following gives us an account of the most decisive victory ever obtained over the indians of North America. When to its immediate effects, we take into consideration what may be accomplished by the *two* other bodies of troops in the country, *viz.* the *Carolinians* on one side, and the force under general *Claiborne* on the other, the war may be regarded as finished. It has thus far been a war of extermination, and perhaps, must close with destruction, to prevent a recurrence of the horrible massacres with which it began. The tragedy at fort *Mims*—where to the murder of women and children, was superadded deeds too savage record—cannot be obliterated; and it seems just, that they who, without provocation or cause for complaint, so conducted themselves, should be swept from the face of the earth. But this is a dreadful necessity.

The war with the *Creeks* was of pure *British* origin—got up by that unfeeling nation to make a "diversion" of our force, with a perfect knowledge that it would begin by massacre and finish in extermination; for the *Creeks* had no hope to escape the punishment of their ingratitude. But what does *England* care for ten or fifteen thousand lives? What is it her, that the scheme of humanity for the civilization of these great tribes of indians has failed?

There is very little doubt but that the same kind of war will have to be carried on against the north western indians. When beaten, they were spared; when hungry, we fed them; when naked, we clothed them—and now, existing through these extensions of charity, they are about to bury the tomahawk in the heads of their preservers, instigated by *magnanimous* Englishmen!—The lenient policy has been fairly tried, decisive measures alone remain to secure our frontiers from the ravages of a people that no sense of justice controuls, of mercy influences, or of gratitude confines.

Volume 6, April 23, 1814, pages 130-131

Events of the War—Military.

Milledgeville,
April 2, 1814.

The following very important despatch from general Jackson to general Pinckney, has this moment been received by governor Early—this last battle decides the fate of the Creek indians.

———

Head-quarters, 6th and 7th districts.

Fort Hawkins,
April 2, 1814.

Sir—I have the honor of enclosing to your excellency the official account of a decisive victory over the hostile Creek indians, achieved by the military talents and enterprize of general Jackson, supported by the distinguished valor and good conduct of the gallant troops under his command: While the sigh of humanity will escape for this profuse effusion of human blood, which results from the savage principle of our enemy, neither to give nor accept quarter—and while every American will deeply lament the loss of our meritorious fellow soldiers who have fallen in this contest, we have ample cause of gratitude to the Giver of all victory for thus continuing his protection of our women and children, who would otherwise be exposed to the indiscriminate havoc of the tomahawk and all the horrors of savage warfare.

I have the honor to be, very respectfully, your excellency's most obedient servant,

THOS. PINCKNEY,
Maj. Gen. U. S. Army.

His excellency governor Early.

———

On the battleground,
in the bend of the
Tallapoosie,
28th March, 1814.

Maj. Gen. Pinckney.

Sir—I feel peculiarly happy in being able to communicate to you the fortunate eventuation of my expedition to the Tallapoosie. I reached the bend near Emucfau (called by the whites the Horse

Shoe) about ten o'clock in the forenoon of yesterday, where I found the strength of the neighboring towns collected: expecting our approach, they had gathered in from Oakfuskee, Oakchaga, New Yaucan, Hillibees, the Fish Pond and Eufaulee towns, to the number it is said of 1000. It is difficult to conceive a situation more eligible for defence than they had chosen, or one rendered more secure by the skill with which they had erected their breastwork. It was from 5 to 8 feet high, and extended across the point in such a direction, as that a force approaching it would be exposed to a double fire while they lay in perfect security behind. A cannon planted at one extremity could have raked it to no advantage.

Determining to exterminate them, I detached general Coffee with the mounted men and nearly the whole of the indian force, early on the morning of yesterday to cross the river about two miles below their encampment, and to surround the bend in such a manner, as that none of them should escape by attempting to cross the river. With the infantry I proceeded slowly and in order, along the point of land which led to the front of their breastwork; having planted my cannon (one six and one three pounder) on an eminence at the distance of 150 to 200 yards from it, I opened a very brisk fire, playing upon the enemy with the muskets and rifles whenever they shewed themselves beyond it; this was kept up, with short interruptions, for about two hours, when a part of the indian force, and captain Russell's and lieutenant Bean's companies of spies, who had accompanied general Coffee, crossed over in canoes to the extremity of the bend, and set fire to a few of the buildings which were there situated; they then advanced with great gallantry towards the breastwork, and commenced a spirited fire upon the enemy behind it.

Finding that this force, notwithstanding the bravery they displayed, was wholly insufficient to dislodge them, and that general Coffee had entirely secured the opposite bank of the river, I now determined to take their works by storm. The men by whom this was to be effected had been waiting with impatience to receive their order, and hailed it with acclamation.

The spirit which animated them was a sure augury of the success which was to follow. The history of warfare furnishes few instances of a more brilliant attack— the regulars led on by their intrepid and skillful commander, colonel Williams, and by the gallant major Montgomery, soon gained possession of the works in the midst of a most tremendous fire from behind them, and the militia of the venerable general Doherty's brigade, accompanied them in the charge, with a vivacity and firmness that would have done honor to the regulars. The enemy were completely routed. Five hundred and fifty-seven were left dead on the peninsula, and a great number of them were killed by the horsemen in attempting to cross the river; it is believed that no more than ten had escaped.

The fighting continued with some severity about five hours, but we continued to destroy many of them who had concealed themselves under the banks of the river until we were prevented by the night. This morning we killed 16 which had been concealed.—We took 250 prisoners, all women and children except two or three. Our loss is 106 wounded and 26 killed. Major M'Intosh [the Cowetan] who joined my army with part of his tribe, greatly distinguished himself. When I get an hour's leisure I will send you a more detailed account.

According to my original purpose, I commenced my return march to fort Williams to-day, and shall, if I find supplies there, hasten to the Hickory ground. The power of the Creeks is, I think, forever broken.

I send you a hasty sketch, taken by the eye, of the situation on which the enemy were encamped, and of the manner in which I approached them.

I have the honor to be, with great respect, your obedient servant,

ANDW. JACKSON, Maj. Gen.
Major-general Pinckney.

*Extract of a letter from
major-general Pinckney,
to his excellency the
governor of Georgia, dated,*

Fort Hawkins,
20th Feb. 1814.

Since I had the honor of addressing
you on the 27th January—I have received
your excellency's letters of the 31st of
January and 9th of this month. Nothing
could exceed the zeal and alacrity of the
South-Carolina militia in volunteering
their services, and proceeding to this
place, without either tents or arms, and
furnished only with the scanty supply
of camp equippage, which colonel Earle
was enabled suddenly to collect.—By
the indefatigable activity and judicious
conduct of this officer in bringing the
troops forward so expeditiously, the
public service has been materially
benefitted; which you will be able
more justly to appreciate, when you are
informed that without this timely arrival
we should probably have been compelled
to abandon our advanced post at Fort
Hull, 130 miles from this frontier, and
to have fallen back to the Chatahouche,
thereby relinquishing a tract of country 45
miles in extent, and exposing the frontier
inhabitants to the depredations of the
savages, encouraged by this retreat.

I know the penury of our magazine
in Charleston, and was aware of the delay
which must attend the equipment of this
corp, resulting from the army regulation
which directs all requisitions to be
forwarded to the war office and approved
before executed, by the purchasing
department. I therefore requested your
excellency's aid in these equipments. It is
with pleasure I acknowledge your ready
compliance therewith, and the prompt
arrangement made for the march of the
troops, which I have represented in its
proper place as a patriotic exertion, and
consider it is a personal obligation.

Events of the War.
Jackson's Victory.

Fort Williams,
March 31, 1814.

His excellency Willie Blount,

Sir—I have just returned from the
expedition which I advised you in my last
I was about to make to the Tallapoosee;
and hasten to acquaint you with the good
fortune which attended it.

I took up the line of march from this
place on the morning of the 21st inst.
and having opened a passage of 52 1-2
miles over the ridges which divide the
waters of the two rivers, I reached the
bend of the Tallapoosa three miles beyond
where I had the engagement of the 22d of
January, and at the southern extremity of
New-Youka, on the morning of the 27th.
This bend resembles in its curvature that
of a horse shoe, and is then called by that
name among the whites. Nature furnishes
few situations so eligible for defence,
and barbarians have never rendered one
more secure by art. Across the neck of
the bend which leads into it from the
north they had erected a breastwork of the
greatest compactness and strength, from
five to eight feet high, and prepared with
double port holes very artfully arranged.
The figure of this wall manifested no
less skill in the projection of it, than its
construction; an army could not approach
it without being exposed to a double
and cross fire from the enemy, who lay
in perfect security behind it. The area
of this peninsula, thus bounded by the
breastwork, includes I conjecture, eighty
or hundred acres.

In this bend the warriors from
Oakfuska, Oakehagu, New Youka,
Hillabeea, the Fish ponds, and Eufaula
towns, apprised of our approach, had
collected their strength. Their exact
number cannot be ascertained; but it is
said by the prisoners we have taken to
have been a thousand. It is certain they
were very numerous, and that relying
with the utmost confidence upon their
strength, their situation and the assurances
of their prophets, they concluded on
repulsing us with great ease.

Early on the morning of the 27th,
having encamped the preceding night at
the distance of five miles from them—I

detailed general Coffee with the mounted men and nearly the whole of the indian force, to cross the river at a ford about three miles below their encampment, and to surround the bend in such a manner that none of them should escape by attempting to cross the river. With the remainder of the forces I proceeded along the point of land which leads to the front of their breast-work; and at half past ten o'clock A. M. I had planted my artillery on a small eminence, distant from its nearest point about 80 yards, and from its farthest about two hundred and fifty; from whence I immediately opened a brisk fire upon its centre. With the musketry and rifles I kept up a galling fire wherever the enemy shewed themselves behind their works, or ventured to approach them. This was continued with occasional intermissions for about two hours, when captain Russell's company of spies, and a part of the Cherokee force, headed by their gallant chieftain colonel Richard Brown, and conducted by the brave colonel Morgan, crossed over to the peninsula in canoes, and set fire to a few of their buildings there situated. They then advanced with great gallantry towards the breast-work, and commenced firing upon the enemy who lay behind it.

Finding that this force, notwithstanding the determination they displayed, was wholly insufficient to dislodge the enemy, and that general Coffee had secured the opposite banks of the river, I now determined upon taking possession of their works by storm. Never were men better disposed for such an undertaking than those by whom it was to be effected. They had entreated to be led to the charge with the most pressing importunity, and received the order which was now given with the strongest demonstrations of joy. The effect was such as this temper of mind foretold. The regular troops, led on by their intrepid and skillful commander, colonel Williams, and by the gallant major Montgomery, were presently in possession of the nearer side of the breast-work; and the militia accompanied them in the charge with a vivacity and firmness which could not have been exceeded, and has seldom been equalled by troops of any description. A few companies of general Doherty's brigade on the right, were led on with gallantry by colonel Russell—the advance guard, by the adjutant-general, colonel Sisler, and the left extremity of the line by captain Gordon of the spies, and captain M'Murry of general Johnson's brigade of West Tennessee militia.

Having maintained for a few minutes a very obstinate contest, musket to musket, through the port holes, in which many of the enemy's balls were welded to the bayonets of our muskets, our troops succeeded in gaining possession of the opposite side of the works. The event could no longer be doubtful. The enemy, although many of them fought to the last, with that kind of bravery which desperation inspires, were at length entirely routed and cut to pieces. The whole margin of the river which surrounds the peninsula was strewed with the slain. Five hundred and fifty-seven were found by officers of great respectability, whom I had ordered to count them; besides a great number who were thrown into the river by their surviving friends, and killed in attempting to pass it, by general Coffee's men, stationed on the opposite banks. Captain Hammonds, who with his company of spies occupied a favorable position opposite the upper extremity of the breast-work, did great execution—and so did lieutenant Bean, who had been ordered by general Coffee to take possession of a small island pointing to the lower extremity.

Both officers and men, who had the best opportunities on judging, believe the loss of the enemy in killed, not to fall short of eight hundred; and if their number was as great as it is represented to have been, by the prisoners, and as it is believed to have been by colonel Carroll and others, who had a fair view of them, as they advanced to the breast-works, their loss must even have been more considerable—as it is quite certain that not more than twenty can have escaped. Among the dead was found their famous prophet Monahell—shot in the mouth by a grape shot, as if heaven designed to chastise him impostures by an appropriate punishment. Two other prophets were also killed—leaving no others, as I can learn, on the Tallapoosa. I lament that two or three women and children were killed by accident. I do not know the exact number of prisoners taken, but it must exceed three hundred—all women and children except three.

The battle may be said to have continued with severity for about five hours; but the firing and slaughter continued until it was suspended by the darkness of the night. The next morning it was resumed, and sixteen of the enemy slain, who had concealed themselves under the banks. Our loss was twenty-six whitemen killed, and one hundred and seven wounded. Cherokees eighteen killed, and thirty-six wounded—friendly Creeks, five killed and eleven wounded.

The loss of colonel Williams' regiment of regulars, is seventeen killed, fifty-five wounded, three of whom have since died. Among the former were major Montgomery, lieutenant Sommerville and lieutenant Moulton, who fell in the charge which was made on the works. No men ever acted more gallantly or fell more gloriously.

Of the artillery commanded by captain Parish, 11 wounded; one of whom, Samuel Garner, has since died. Lieutenants Allen and Ridley were both wounded. The whole company acted with its usual gallantry. Captain Bradford of the 39th U. S. Infantry, who acted as chief engineer, and superintended the firing of the cannon, has entitled himself by his good conduct to my warmest thanks. To say all in a word, the whole army who has achieved this fortunate victory, have merited by their good conduct the gratitude of their country. So far as I can, or could learn, there was not an officer or soldier who did not perform his duty with the utmost fidelity. The conduct of the militia, on this occasion, has gone far towards redeeming the character of that description of troops. They have been as orderly in their encampment, and on their line of march, as they have been signally brave in the day of battle.

In a few days I shall take up the line of march for the Hickory ground, and have every thing to hope from such troops.

Enclosed I send you general Coffee's original report.

I have the honor to be, with great respect, your obedient humble servant,

ANDREW JACKSON,
Maj. Gen.

Volume 6, April 30, 1814, page 148

Report from general Coffee,
to general Jackson,
dated April 1.

Sir—Agreeably to your order of 27th ult. I took up the line of march at half past 6 o'clock, A. M. of the same day with a detachment of seven hundred cavalry and mounted gunmen, and about six hundred Indians, five hundred of which were Cherokees and the balance friendly Creeks. I crossed the Tallaposee river at the little island ford, about three miles below the bend, in which the enemy had concentrated, and then turned up the river bearing away from its cliffs—when within half a mile of the village the savage yell was raised by the enemy, and I supposed he had discovered and was about to attack me. I immediately drew up my forces in line of battle in an open hilly woodland, and in that position moved on towards the yelling of the enemy—previous to this had ordered the Indians, on our approach to the bend of the river, to advance secretly and take possession of the bank of the river, and prevent the enemy from crossing on the approach of your army in his front— when within a quarter of a mile of the river, the firing of your cannon commenced, when the Indian with me immediately rushed forward with great impetuosity to the river bank—my line was halted and put in order of battle, expecting an attack on our rear from Oakfuskee village, which lay down the river about eight miles below us—the firing of your cannon and small arms in a short time became general and heavy, which animated our Indians, and seeing about one hundred of the warriors and all the squaws and children of the enemy running about among the huts of the village, which was open to our view, they could no longer remain silent spectators, while some kept up a fire across the river (which is about 120 yards wide) to prevent the enemy's approach to the bank, others plunged into the water and swam the river for canoes that lay at the other shore in considerable numbers, and brought them over, in which crafts a number of them embarked, and landed on the bend with the enemy. Colonel Gideon Morgan who commanded the Cherokees, captain Keer, and captain William Russell with a part of his company of spies was among the first that crossed the river, they advanced into the village and very soon drove the enemy from the huts up the river bank to the fortified works from which they were fighting you—they pursued and continued to annoy during your whole action. This movement of my Indian forces left the river bank unguarded and made it necessary that I should send a part of my line to take possession of the river bank, I accordingly ordered about one third of the men to be posted around the bend on the river bank, whilst the balance remained in line to protect our rear.— Captain Hammond's company of rangers took post on the river bank on my right, and during the whole engagement kept up a continued and destructive fire on those of the enemy that attempted to escape into the river, and killed a very large proportion of those that were found dead under the bank as well as many others sunk under water.— I ordered lieutenant Bean to take possession of the island below with forty men, to prevent the enemy's taking refuge there, which was executed with promptitude and which had a very happy effect, as many of the enemy did attempt their escape to the island, but not one ever landed—they were sunk by lieutenant Bean's command ere they reached the bank. Attempts to cross the river at all points of the bend was made by the enemy, but not one ever escaped, very few ever reached the bank and that few was killed the instant they landed. From the report of my officers as well as from my own observation, I feel warranted in saying that from two hundred and fifty to three hundred of the enemy was buried under water and was not numbered with the dead that were found.

Volume 6, April 30, 1814, pages 148-149

*Copy of a letter from
colonel Gideon Morgan,
commander of the Cherokees,
to William G. Blount, esq. dated*

Fort Williams,
April 1, 1814.

You have been informed of our departure from fort Strother, and arrival at this place on the 21st March, on the 24th general Jackson took up his line of march for Tohopiska, or fortified town on the Tallapoosa, commonly called the Horse Shoe—on the evening of the 28th, he encamped abut six miles north-west of it—the army next morning was divided into two divisions. The horse and indians commanded by general Coffee, crossed the river two miles below the town, with directions to line the bank in the whole extent of the bend, by the Cherokees and friendly Creeks—while the horse acted as a guard upon the high ground, to defend our rear from an attack from the Oakfuskee indians, who were expected from below. This precaution was, however, unnecessary, as their whole force had been concentrated the day before. General Coffee had arrived on the opposite shore, about half a mile below the town, when general Jackson's approach before the fortification, was announced by the discharge of artillery, and in quick succession that of a brigade of infantry. The Cherokees immediately rushed to the point assigned them, which they did in regular order, and in a manner honorable to themselves, that is, the bank was in no place left vacant, and those fugitives who had taken to flight, fell an easy prey to their vengeance. The draft which lieutenant Rece encloses, will give you a better description of the place than I can, to which I refer. The breast-work was composed of 5 large logs, with two ranges of port holes well put together, artillery had no effect, more than to bore it wherever it struck; nature had done much, but when completed by art, the place was formidable indeed, the high ground which extended about mid way from the breast-work to the river, was in some manner open, but the declivity and flat which surrounded it, was filled with fallen timber, the growth of which was very heavy, and had been so arranged, that every tree afforded them a breast-work, forming a communication or cover to the next, and so on to the river bank, in which caverns had been dug for their security, and our annoyance. The breast-work in its whole extent was lined by savages, made desperate from their situation. The 39th was drawn up on the left, in a line extending from the centre to the river bank, the right was occupied by the militia. The artillery on an eminence two hundred yards in rear of the breast-work, on which it kept up a steady and well directed fire, though without effect. In this manner the battle became stationary for some time, say one hour, when the Cherokees crossed the river by swimming, and brought from the opposite shore a number of canoes, in which they crossed under cover of the town, and their own guns; they halted under cover of the bank, and the canoes were sent back for a reinforcement. Understanding general Jackson was about charging the breast-works in its whole extent, I rode with all possible dispatch to inform major Montgomery who commanded the left of the 39th, on the river above. On my return, about 150 or 200 Cherokees had crossed, and were then warmly engaged with the hostile Creeks. I then crossed with major Walker and 30 others, and ascended the high ground, which the Cherokees were then in possession of—we were warmly assailed on every quarter, except our rear, where we only kept open by the dint of hard fighting. The Cherokees were continually crossing, and our number increased in about the proportion in which the Creeks were diminished, who laid prostrate in every quarter—their numbers were vastly superior to ours, but were occupied in maintaining their breast-work, which they appeared determined never to surrender; about one hour after my arrival on the summit, I received a wound in the right side of my head, which had like to have terminated my existence—I however in a short time recovered, and heard the heavenly intelligence that the 39th had charged, and were then in possession of the breast-works—this was an arduous undertaking, and the cool deliberate manner in which it was effected, reflects the highest credit on this bulwark of our army. I shall not attempt a description— in the detailed official account justice no doubt will be done them. The fight commence 17 minutes after 10, and continued without intermission until dark; the next morning some were killed, who it appears were determined never to quit their enchanted ground. On counting their dead, 557 were found on the field, many I know perished in crossing, and numbers were sunk in the river—the whole loss in killed could not be less than 700 or 800. The loss of the 39th, 72 killed and wounded. Major Montgomery, lieutenant Sommerville, and lieutenant Moulton were among the former. The loss of the Cherokees, 18 killed and 35 wounded, many badly. The Cherokees have been permitted to return to their homes.

Volume 6, May 7, 1814, page 166

Events of the War—Military.

Pittsburg,
April 27, 1814.

Victory Over the Creek Indians. We have the pleasure this week of presenting our readers with the following official accounts of another and a signal victory gained by general Jackson, and his brave companions in arms over the savage foe. Language is inadequate to describe the brilliancy of this gallant achievement. The heroes who executed it, will long be held in the grateful remembrance of their countrymen. A friend has favored us with a draft of the scene of action, taken by an officer on the spot. We copy it into the Mercury, with as much accuracy as the nature of letter-press printing will admit. It will be found to throw considerable light on the official details. The bend of the river, at this place is circular, resembling the form of a horse shoe, and the breast-work was thrown across the mouth or entrance of the peninsula.

Our friend writes us that a second battle has, ere this, taken place at the Hickory Ground, and that they are hourly looking for expresses.

Volume 6, May 14, 1814, page 175

Events of the War-Miscellaneous.

Creek War.—It is positively stated, that the Creek indians have surrendered themselves and sued for peace. Several of the principal men and chief murderers of the white people had been delivered up.

Georgia.—*By his excellency, Peter Early, governor and commander in chief of the army and navy of this state and of the militia thereof.*

A Proclamation.—Whereas I have received repeated information that divers persons, citizens of this state, are making settlements on the indian lands contiguous to our frontier by clearing ground and preparing to raise a crop thereon. And whereas such trespasses in addition to the severe punishment annexed to them, are at this time peculiarly improper, I have therefore thought fit to issue this my *proclamation*, warning all persons against a perseverance in, or repetition of such unwarrantable procedures— And do hereby require all persons, citizens of this state, who have made any settlement, or cleared any ground on the Indian lands, forthwith to abandon the same—And do further require all person holding commissions as justices of the peace, or justices of the inferior courts who may have information of such offences to cause to be apprehended such individuals as may refuse obedience to this proclamation, and to bind them in sufficient recognizance to appear at the circuit court of the United States for the district of Georgia, to the end that they may be prosecuted as is directed by the act of congress.

Given under my hand and the great seal of the state, at the state-house in Milledgeville this twenty-fifth day of April in the year of our Lord one thousand eight hundred and fourteen, and in the thirty-eighth year of the independence of the United States of America.

PETER EARLY.

By the governor,

ABNER HAMMOND,
Sec'ry of the State.

April 27, 1814.

Volume 6, May 21, 1814, page 194

Events of the War—Miscellaneous.

The Creek War.—is finished, says report. We daily expect the details and particulars. They have submitted unconditionally. Several of the chiefs, and among them Wetherford, the leader of the butchery at fort Mims, have given themselves up. A chief of Cowetau, accompanied by Marshal, a half breed, is on his way to Washington city to consult the president (as is supposed) on the probable disposition of the Creek lands. General *Pinkney* was in command at the junction of the Coosa and Talapoosa, and general Jackson was on his return march to fort Williams. The deluded wretches

have suffered a dreadful penalty for their most horrible crimes. What they were and what they are, are fruitful themes for reflection and remark.

Volume 6, May 28, 1814, page 210

Events of the War—Miscellaneous.

Creek Eloquence.—The following (say the Nashville "Clarion,") is a specimen of that bold eloquence which nature seldom bestows, and still less seldom bursts forth from the uncultivated mind.

Wetherford, the speaker, has been, through this war, one of the most active and enterprising chiefs. As a partizan leader he has frequently opposed his enemy where he was little expected. Seeing that it was in vain any longer to resist, he voluntarily came in and delivered himself up; in a private interview with general Jackson, he made the following short, though forcible and bold address, which was forwarded by a person who was present:

"I fought at Fort Mimms—I fought the Georgia army—I did you all the injury I could—had I been supported as I was promised, I would have done you more. But my warriors are all killed—I can fight you no longer. I look back with sorrow, that I have brought destruction on my nation. I am now in your power, do with me as you please—I am a soldier."

Volume 6, May 28, 1814, pages 211-212

Events of the War—Military.

General *Floyd* who lately combatted the red indians of the interior, has come to meet the allies on the sea-board. He issued the following "brigade orders" at S. Mary's, May 7—

"IN consequence of the menacing appearance of the enemy, who have been for the last eight days hovering on the coast, with the intention, as it appears (from the promulgation of admiral *Cochrane's Proclamation,* at the town of *Fernandina,* in East Florida, and other information entitle to credit) of destroying this town, or committing depredations on some part of the sea coast of this state.—

The brigadier-general orders, and directs colonel Scott, of the third regiment of militia, to order out without a moment's delay, one hundred and twenty men from his command, properly armed, equipped, and officered, to be stationed at S. Mary's, for its protection until further orders.

The lieutenant-colonels of the respective regiments of the first brigade, are also required to hold the men, under their respective commands, in complete readiness to march at a moment's warning to any point where their services may become necessary; and to be vigilant in the mean time in causing a strict and faithful discharge of patrol duty.

Under the present aspect of affairs it becomes the duty of every citizen to be on the alert, and prepared to guard against impending danger.

And, whereas, the Spanish authority at Fernandina, has permitted an intercourse between some of the individuals of that place and the enemy, having a tendency to promote and encourage their designs, it is enjoined on every officer, both civil and military, to be vigilant in detecting and apprehending all suspicious characters—and it is strongly and seriously recommended to the respective town authorities, to cause all strangers to report themselves, in order that the object of their visit may be known, and thereby avoid unnecessary trouble.

The brigadier-general avails himself of this opportunity to recommend to the corporation of St. Mary's, the propriety of completing without delay the stockade, which has been begun for the defence of the town, and to exert all the means in their power to put the town in the best possible state of defence, until ample means are provided for its security.

JOHN FLOYD,
brig. gen.

Volume 6, May 28, 1814, page 212

Official despatch from general Jackson to his excellency governor Blount, dated

Camp at the junction of the Coosee and Talapoosee, April 18th, 1814.

Sir—I am happy to inform you that the campaign is at length drawing to a prosperous close. We have scoured the Coosee and Tallaposee, and the intervening country. A part of the enemy on the latter river made their escape across it just before our arrival, and are flying in consternation towards Pensacola. Many of those on the Coosee and the neighboring country, have come in and surrendered unconditionally; and others are on their way and hourly arriving to submit in the same day.

We will overtake those who have fled, and make them sensible there is no more safety in flight than in resistance. They must supplicate peace if they would enjoy it.

Many of the negroes who were taken at fort Mimms, have been delivered up, and one white woman (Polly Jones) with her two children. They will be properly taken care of. The Tallapoosee king has been arrested, and is here in confinement. The Tostahatchee king of the Hickory Ground tribe has delivered himself up. Weatherfield has been with me, and I did not confine him. He will be with me again in a few days. Peter M'Quin has been taken, but escaped; he must be taken again. Hillinhagee, their great prophet, has also absconded; but he will be found. They were the instigators of the war, and such is their situation.

The advance of the eastern division formed a junction with me at Hallawellee, on the 15th, and accompanied me to fort Decatur opposite Tuckabatchee, and the rest will arrive in a few days, except what will be left for the retention of the posts. Major-general Pinckney will join the army at this place to-morrow or the next day. The business of the campaign will not I presume require that I or my troops should remain here much longer.— General Pinckney, and colonel Hawkins who is now with me, have been appointed to make the treaty.

I am, sir, very respectfully, your most obedient humble servant,

AND. JACKSON, *Major General.*

His excellency Willie Blount, governor of Tennessee.

Events of the War—Miscellaneous.

Creek War.—All the forces of the United States have retired from the Creek country except a brigade of militia from the Carolinas, a part of the 39th U. S. infantry, 2 companies of artillery, and 1 of dragoons. The following extracts of a letter from colonel Hawkins, agent of the U. S. in the Creek nation, to governor Hawkins, of North Carolina, dated at fort Toulouse, at the confluence of the Tallapoosa and Coosa, are interesting:

"I believe you know this is the name of the old French fort at Tuskogee. We commenced to-day to build a permanent fort on the ruins of the old one. Lieutenant colonel Atkinson's division formed a part of the centre army which united with the army of Tennessee at Tooscehatchee. They, united, arrived here on the 27th. Colonel Pearson, with his division, arrived yesterday. My countrymen look well, and appear in good health. Being much occupied yesterday and to-day, I have not been able to get acquainted with them. The Tennessee army are on their way home—General Graham is in consequence second in command—he enjoys, apparently, fine health.

"The hostile Indians are retreating from us in various directions mostly towards Kone-cau a few miles above our line of limits. The terrible chastisement inflicted by the army of militia, regulars, Cherokees and Creeks, under general Jackson, at Newyou-cau, on the hostile Indians, has alarmed the whole party. Believing blood enough has been spilt to atone for past transgressions, General Pinckney on the 23d communicated through me to the enemy the terms upon which peace will be granted them.

"The United States will retain as much of the conquered territory as may appear to the government to be a just indemnity for the expences of the war, and as a retribution for the injuries sustained by its citizens and the friendly Creek Indians.

"The United States will retain the right to establish military posts and trading houses, and to make and use such roads as they may think necessary, and freely to navigate all the rivers and water courses in the Creek territory.

"The enemy must, on their part, surrender their Prophets, and such other instigators of the war as may be designated by the government of the United States, and they must agree to such restrictions upon their trade with foreign nations, as shall be established by the government of the United States.

"I have, and shall by various channels communicate these terms to those concerned. To the army of the friendly Indians with us I did it here. Some few have come in here, and many of those above us, to a place assigned them by general Jackson."

Fort Williams, April 25, at night.— Sir—General Pinckney joined me at fort Jackson, on the 20th. The enemy continuing to come in from every quarter, and supplicate peace; and it being now evident that the war was over, I received an order at 8 o'clock, P. M. on the 21st, to march my troops back to fort Williams, and after having dispersed any bodies of the enemy who may have assembled on the Cahawba, or within striking distance, and provided for the maintainance of the posts between Tennessee and fort Jackson, to discharge the remainder. Within two hours after receiving this order, I was on the line of march; and reached this place last evening, a distance of about sixty miles.

To brigadier-general Doherty, I shall assign the duty of keeping up the posts which from the time of communication between Tennessee and the confluence of the Coosa and Tallapoosa, making the necessary arrangements to enable him to do so. About 400 of the East Tennessee militia will be left at this place, 250 at for Strother, and 75 at fort Armstrong and New Deposit. Old Deposit will be maintained by captain Hammond's company of rangers.

To-morrow I detail 500 of the militia under the command of brigadier-general Johnston, to the Cahawba, with instructions, to unite with me at fort Deposit, after having dispersed any bodies of the enemy they may find assembled there.

The commissioners who have been appointed to make a treaty with the Creeks, need have nothing to do but assign them their proper limits.—Those of the friendly party who have associated with me will be easily satisfied; and as to those of the hostile party, they consider a favor that their lives have been spared them, and will look upon any space that may be allowed them for their future settlement, as a bounteous donation. I have taken the liberty to point out what I think ought to be the future lines of separation, with which I will hereafter make you acquainted. If they should be established, none of the Creeks will be left on the west of the Coosa.

I have the honor to be, very respectfully, your obedient servant,

ANDREW JACKSON,
maj. gen.

His excellency W. Blount.

Volume 6, June 4, 1814, page 220

Events of the War—Miscellaneous.

New Blockade! The following legitimate burlesque on the late outrageous proclamation of the enemy, issued by admiral *Cochrane*, for blockading the whole coast of the United States, well deserves preservation in the Register. It is copied from the *Lancaster Intelligencer*:

By the right valiant Paul Jones, knight of the deep, &c. &c. &c.—

A Proclamation.

WHEREAS, admiral the honorable sir Aleck Cochrane did, by virtue of the power and authority to him given, by his proclamation, dated at *Bermuda* the 25th day of April, 1814, declare all the ports, harbors, bays, creeks, rivers, inlets, outlets, islands and sea coasts, from the mouth of the river *Mississippi*, to the northern and eastern boundaries between the United States and New-Brunswick, in America, to be in a state of strict and rigorous blockade; and whereas I am as capable of enforcing so extensive a blockade as *Aleck Cochrane* is:

I do, therefore, by virtue of the power and authority in me inherent, and in retaliation for said strict and rigorous blockade, declare all the ports, harbors, bays, creeks, rivers, inlets, outlets, channels, firths, loughs, islands, and sea coasts of Great Britain and Ireland to be in a state of strict and rigorous blockade. And I do further declare, that I am determined to maintain the blockade of the places herein before mentioned in the most rigorous manner.

And I do hereby require all whom it may concern, to pay the strictest regard and attention to the execution of the proclamation. And I do caution and forbid the ships and vessels of all and every nation under the sun, from entering or attempting to enter, or from coming out or attempting to come out, of any of the hereby blockaded place, after due notification of said blockade, under any pretence whatever, under penalty of the consequences. And I do further declare, that I have given orders to all commanding officers under my jurisdiction, or to be employed on the British stations, to sink, burn and destroy every ship or vessel attempting to violate said blockade.

And that no person may plead ignorance of the proclamation, I have cause the same to be published.

Given under my fist, at Bunker's Hill, the 17th day of May, 1814.

PAUL JONES.

To all whom it may concern.

By command of his valiancy,

JONATHAN HORNET,
Sec'ry.

Volume 6, June 4, 1814, page 222

Events of the War—Military.

General *Jackson*, of the Tennessee militia, *the finisher of the wars of the Creeks*, has been appointed by the president, a major general in the army of the United States vice major general *Harrison* resigned.

Major general *Pinkney* arrived, at Charleston on the 18th inst. from the Creek country. Major general *Wilkinson* was at *Albany*. General *Winder* arrived at *Plattsburg* on the 20th ult.

A detachment of regulars, lately employed against the Creeks, passed through Milledgeville on the 6th ult. on their way to the sea-board; where warm work is expected.

Events of the War—Military.

The Creeks.—A letter to the editor of the Register says—the South Carolina volunteers, and North Carolina militia, chiefly remained at fort *Jackson* (on the site of old fort Toulouse)—the Tallissee king (reported to have been killed in one of general *Floyd's* battles with the Creeks) is with our army—he has been regarded as a great prophet; is more the 100 years old, from appearance; bent almost double; with a head as white as snow. The friendly Creeks want much to destroy this old man; but *Weatherford* moves among them unmolested and they tremble in his presence. The indians lately hostile were coming in daily. *M'Queen*, the half-breed, remained on the Kahabaw, or as thought near the Perdido.

Events of the War—Military.

The Creek Indians.—There is some reason to believe that there is no security but in the extermination of the war party of this silly people. How distressing is the alternative—how cold-hearted and callous to all the fine feelings of humanity must the be, that intrigue the destruction of the race, without any possible good or legitimate war object! Reduced and weakened as they are, with the "vantage ground" we at this time possess in the nation, even if it should be true as stated below, that 2000 British troops have recently landed in Florida, they must fall an easy prey to the incensed people of the south and west. The British, employing indians, may be fought and beaten with indians. They dare not complain of this, though they feel all the miseries that their *barbarisms* have caused to others.

Events of the War—Military.

Fort Stoddert, May 11, 1814.— After the last victory of general Jackson over the Creeks, they began to flock to the country lying between this place and Pensacola, where they have been constantly making depredations on our cattle, and have killed the few individuals that were exposed on the east side of the bay. It is supposed that there are from 1000 to 1,500 in this part of the country. The Choctaws are after them, and it is said that wounded Creek indians are daily going into Pensacola. Our own troops are on the point of marching into the nation; but the general opinion is, that no indians will be found there. Letters from Pensacola to persons in Mobile, state that the governor had received orders from the Havanna (which orders were made public on Friday last) to furnish the Creek indians with what arms, ammunition, &c. They might want. The vessel which brought the orders, brought the means; and there is no doubt but that on Saturday last the indians received every thing necessary for carrying on the war. So many were never known to be in Pensacola at one time. Our settlements are still in imminent danger.

[*National Intelligencer.*

Events of the War—Military.

From the Augusta Chronicle, June 3.—A gentleman straight from fort Hawkins, informs us, that an express from general Graham reached Milledgeville on Friday morning last, bringing the information, that the hostile indians, (*fifteen hundred* strong) had returned to the Alabama and Talapoosa from Pensacola, with a supply of arms and ammunition, and were determined to renew the war. The stragglers who had secreted themselves in the woods and swamps, were daily increasing their force, and fears were entertained lest they should attack the North Carolina militia, who, with a few from South Carolina, were the only force remaining in the nation.

Events of the War—Military.

Copy of a letter from colonel Hawkins to the governor, dated

Creek Agency, 25th May.

"Mr. M'Girth, express from colonel Milton at Alabama Heights, reports, that an express arrived there for general

Pinckney, which he is the bearer of, expecting to see the general at fort Jackson. The express stated that they had received certain accounts of an arrival from the *Havanna*, with the munitions of war for the "Red Clubs" and orders to supply them with provisions—that they were fully supplied with guns, ammunition and provisions, and that a great number were assembled at Pensacola, and further, that orders had been received from general Flournoy to evacuate Mobile point. It is eight days since he left the heights."

Volume 6, June 18, 1814, page 264

Events of the War—Military.

Milledgeville, June 1.—A letter dated Creek Agency, May 31st has been received in town from colonel Hawkins communicating the following *important intelligence*, transmitted to him by his assistant agent, who received the intelligence from John Steddom, residing on the Chotachoochie, a friendly half-breed chief, and one in whom confidence can be placed.

He states that the British had landed a body of 2000 men at the mouth of the Appalachicola (East Florida)—that they were actively engaged in erecting block-houses, and offering inducements to the indians to gain them—that the Eufaulees were solicited to aid them but had refused—and that all the lower towns had already gone. A trusty indian had been dispatched down the river to ascertain the truth of the above information.—*Argus*.

Volume 6, June 25, 1814, pages 280-281

Events of the War—Miscellaneous.
[Excerpts]

Depredations in Massachusetts.— In another place we have noticed the late great activity of the enemy [British] on the eastern coast in destroying the small vessels.

The enemy entered the harbor of *Scituate* (Mass.) some 10 or 13 days ago, and burnt nine small vessels lying there. They had burnt or destroyed 30 or 40 small vessels near Boston in the space of a few days.

The southern coast is also vexed

by the enemy's cruisers; several small vessels have lately been captured near *Savannah*.

Volume 6, July 2, 1814, page 297

Events of the War—Miscellaneous.

Creek Indians. From the Milledgeville Journal of June 17.—An express from colonel Hawkins to the executive has this moment arrived, and confirms the landing of the enemy in Florida. Several intelligent chiefs whose situation gave them any opportunity of knowing, state in a report of 7th, that "the British have taken possession of Pensacola, and given a large quantity of arms and ammunition to the Seminolies—that two British ships are at the mouth of the Appalatchicola, one of fifty guns the other a smaller vessel—that the enemy are stationed on Deer Island, and have built four houses, one of which is filled with ammunition—and that a number of indians, chiefly Seminolies and Red Clubs, have joined them, to whom a British officer delivered the following *talk*:

"I am sent to see whether the indians were destroyed in their war with the United States—if not, to afford them help. I have some supplies, and I will give to each town four large casks of powder and some short muskets. I am directed to hold talks with the Creeks, Cherokees, Chocktaws and Chickasaws. I have 2000 men. The red people who have been driven from the Tallapoosa must assemble [and were assembling it is said] between the bay of Pensacola and Appalatchicola. They will concentrate at Choctauhatchee, and remain ready for further orders. Our plan is to take Mobile, Perdido, Yellow-water, Choctauhatchee, an island near St. Mary's, an island near *Savannah, and that town* and an island near Charleston at the same time. One of my vessels will sail immediately for supplies for the red people, and I expect in 25 days to receive them, when this plan is to take effect. In the mean time the indians can be recruiting their strength, exhausted by recent wars and by famine, and be ready to co-operate with their friends the British, who will strike at and occupy all these places at the same time."

The prophets observed to the

Seminolies in the presence of the reporters—we have brought our difficulties on ourselves, without advice from any one—the old chiefs need not expect we will be given up. We have friends now, and if they attempt to follow us, we will spill their blood. We have lost our country and retreated to the sea side, where we will fight till we are all destroyed—we are collected, and find a few more than a *thousand* warriors left."

It is stated in another report, that the enemy's force does not exceed a thousand—that all the troops, with the exception of fifty, had left the island, but were to return in twenty days—and that only two towns had received ammunition, the rest refusing to take it.

Colonel Hawkins observes in a letter of the 15th to the governor, that lieutenant Lewis, who commands a company of spies and guards, informs, that "M'Queen and Francis had delivered themselves as prisoners to colonel Milton. Several hundred of the deluded followers of the prophets have also surrendered themselves at our military posts, and are fed by order of the government."

[A letter to the editor of the Register, from an intelligent friend in the south, whose means of information are most respectable, after noticing a variety of reports, assures me that the "*Creek* war is done." It seems the few stragglers that remain hostile, are of themselves, too weak to attempt any thing; and the country is too much exhausted to support a regular hostile force. The nation has suffered incredibly by the war. The chief part of those that exist are they that were friendly—and the *Cherokees* and other friendly tribes are in full force. It is probable that the U. S. might now have the services of at least 2000 warriors in that country, and perhaps more if required; and certainly we shall not neglect to employ them against the allies, and the authors of the controversy.

The letter above alluded to contains many interesting particulars of the country &c. which shall be communicated.]

—◦))⊖ ◉ ⊖((◦—

Americans Assume a War Attitude with British and Indians Opposing

Volume 6, July 2, 1814, pages 298-299

Events of the War—Military.

The whole eastern coast of the United States is assuming a military attitude.

Head-quarters, 2d division, Nashville, May 24, 1814.

Brave Tennesseans of the 2d division—The Creek war through the Divine aid of Providence, and the valor of those engaged in the campaign, in which you bore a conspicuous share, has been brought to a happy termination. Good policy requires that the territory conquered should be garrisoned, and possession retained until appropriated by the government of the United States. In pursuance of this policy, and to relieve the troops now stationed at forts Williams, Stother and Armstrong on the Coosa river, as well as Old and New Deposit, I am commanded by his excellency governor Blount, to call from my division one thousand men in the service of the United states, for the period of six months, unless sooner discharged by order of the president of the United States.

The brigadier-generals, or officers commanding the 4th, 5th, 6th, 7th and 9th brigades of the 21 division, will forthwith furnish from their brigade, respectively, by draft or voluntary enlistment, two hundred men, with two captains, two first, two second and two third lieutenants, and two ensigns, well armed and equipped for active service, to be rendezvoused at Fayetteville, Lincoln county, in the state of Tennessee, on the 20th of June next; and there be organized into a regiment, at which place the field officers and muster-master will be ordered to meet them.

Officers commanding the brigades composing the 2d division of Tennessee militia, are charged with the prompt and due execution of this order.

ANDREW JACKSON,
*Maj. Gen. , Commanding
2d division T. M.*

106

Adjutant-general's office,

Richmond, 22nd June, 1814.

General Orders.—The probability of an invasion from the enemy during the present summer, and the uncertainty at what moment it may be attempted, render it necessary that the most effectual precautionary measures be immediately taken to resist such attempt. The commandants of the 38, 102, 23, 39, 83, 62, 71, 40, 15, 74, 30, 16, 45, 25, 6, 33, 52, 87, 9 and 19th regiments will therefore parade their respective regiments in battalion for the purpose of inspecting the arms, accoutrements, ammunition, &c. in their possession. They will make to this office special reports, without delay, of the order and condition of the whole, the deficiency in any respect which may exist; and what articles are indispensably necessary to place them in the most respectable posture of defence. Should any delinquency exist, the law in relation thereto must be rigidly enforced. Every company will be immediately placed in requisition, and held in complete readiness to take the field at a moment's warning. The commandants of regiments contiguous to the probable theatre of invasion, will be vigilant in watching the movements of the enemy. Should he manifest an intention of making a descent upon any particular point, the commandants obtaining such information, will lose no time in communicating it to the commandants of regiments from which succour can be derived, with orders to proceed forthwith, with their commands en masse, to the places of general rendezvous hereafter detailed, to check his operations. The men will not wait to march in a body, but proceed, when ordered, by squads, to the place of general rendezvous.

Let every officer and private be *on the alert.* The war may probably in a short time assume a different character. In such an event, Virginia will doubtless engage no small portion of the enemy's attention. Inflated with the most splendid successes in Europe, he will omit no exertion or preparation to make us feel his strength. How disgraceful would it be, if slumbering in imagined security, we should be found *unprepared* at the hour of his coming!—But reasoning of this sort is unnecessary to rouse the martial spirit of freemen and soldiers. They must see the propriety and feel the importance of vigilance and activity. The danger of indulging a further hope of peace, without prompt and effectual measures to meet the most vigorous attempts of the enemy, must be obvious to all. The officers particularly, in whose fidelity, courage and activity, their country has placed implicit confidence, mindful of the sacred trust will use every exertion in preparing their respective commands to acquit themselves as becomes Americans.

By order,

CLAIBORNE W. GOOCH,
D. A. G.

For MOSES GREEN, *A. G.*

Note: To obviate any misconstruction, (says the *Enquirer*) which may arise upon the general order of the adjutant-general, we deem it necessary to state that it is not founded upon any new information in the possession of the government. It is the act of the state executive alone, founded upon the general aspect of the times.— And surely it is a wise and prudent precaution, to prepare for any danger which may be meditated against our repose. For reasons which will suggest themselves to every reader, we omit that part of the order which designates the points of rendezvous, &c. &c.

Volume 6, July 2, 1814, page 299

Events of the War—Naval.

We learn from *Bermuda* that admiral *Cochrane* was about to leave the station for our coast. One account says, he was coming with 10 sail of the line (besides transports) and 10,000 men; another, that he had only 2 ships of the line and 3,000—the latter is the probable story.

The enemy continues his depredations on the eastern coast, and destroys some small vessels. Some of his barges lately entered *Sheepscut* (or *Wiscassett*) river, but were beaten off by the militia. The people have been roused from their state of apathy, and appear determined to resist the foe to the utmost, in his attempts on the coast. A general alarm prevails, and means of defence are every where actively resorted to.

Volume 6, July 9, 1814, page 317

Events of the War—Miscellaneous.

The eastern coast of the United States is much vexed by the enemy. Having destroyed a great portion of the coasting craft whose owners were hardy enough to venture to sea, they seem determined to enter the little out ports and villages, and burn every thing that floats. Captain *Perry* is at *Wiscassett.* He was ably seconded by the people, and they succeeded in repulsing the enemy. The citizens are roused, and meet the enemy with great alacrity. They have also made some unsuccessful attacks upon other places; but a letter from G. Allen, esq., postmaster, Providence, R. I. to general Baily, P. M. New York, dated July 4, says, "we have this moment received the distressing news that the enemy have burnt the town of *Newbedford.*

This town was damaged by the same enemy to the amount of 96,000 [English pounds] in 1778. By the last census it contained 4361 inhabitants. It has a fine harbor, and was a place of considerable trade. These barbarians are horrible; but will have effect directly the reverse of what the enemy expects, and rouse the nation to every exertion.

Volume 6, July 9, 1814, page 319

Events of the War—Naval.

At our last accounts from *Bermuda*, admiral *Cochrane* still remained there, with 4 *74's,* 6 frigates, and several sloops of war—1400 marines had lately arrived from England.

Volume 6, July 9, 1814, page 320

Postscript.

A Milledgeville paper of June 22, states that colonel Pearson, with the North Carolina militia, had made prisoners of 450 of the hostile indians. They were overtaken and surrendered without opposition—300 of them had arrived at Fort Jackson. It was understood that M'Queen was about to send in his adhesion to the terms granted the other Creeks.

Volume 6, July 16, 1814, page 336

Events of the War—Miscellaneous.

From Bermuda we have a report that orders had been given for temporary barracks to be immediately built for the accommodation of *twenty-five thousand men.*

Volume 6, July 16, 1814, page 337

Events of the War—Naval.

The enemy force at *Bermuda*, on the 17th of June, has reported 9 sail of the line, 13 frigates, besides transports, and 15,000 troops—the greater part of which had recently arrived. It is also said that *Cochrane* would sail for our coast on the 1st inst.

Volume 6, July 26, 1814, page 353

Events of the War—Miscellaneous.

The Creeks.—We are without any certain intelligence from the Creek country since our last; but the arrival of a British force on the coast is confirmed—one account says they have brought many stand of arms, and that they are to bring from Cuba 10,000 brigands. The matter is, probably, greatly exaggerated.

Indian Affairs.—From the *Savannah Republican* of the 12th inst. The following extract of a letter, relative to our indian affairs, is from a gentleman at fort Hawkins to another in this city, dated the 30th ult.

"General Graham in a letter I got from him yesterday, states that a part (say 1200) of the troops will be in by the 12th July, and the residue about the 15th August.

"It is not true, as reported, that M'Queen and Francis have delivered themselves up to the militia.

"Report, and it is believed to be well founded, says, they are at Pensacola, at the head of 1500 *red people.*"

By a gentleman direct from New-Orleans we learn that a body of 300 British troops had landed at St. Mark's—

that they brought with them 2300 stand of arms, which they were distributing among the indians, and were actively engaged in the fortifying Deer Island, situated near the mouth of Apalatchicola. Our informant adds that the report of M'Queen's surrender is incorrect—on the contrary, it was stated he had sent word to our officers that he would soon be enabled to give them another trial of strength. Deluded fanatic! He would wind up the tragedy by exterminating his unhappy race rather than accept the mercy proffered to him.

Volume 6, July 26, 1814, page 354

Events of the War—Military.

It is stated that about 1000 Creeks were collected and encamped near Pensacola, well armed and supplied by the "religious" English—who had also 17,000 stand of arms to dispose of, for (as was thought) the *"humane"* purpose of enabling the slaves to destroy the white population—men, women and children. History will ascribe to the faction the baseness it deserves, for attributing to an enemy so unprincipled, the virtues that adorn society. The truth of these reports will soon be ascertained. Major-general *Jackson* has passed into the Creek country for certain information of the proceedings of the *Spaniards* and *British*; and, it seems, has power to act as the emergency may require. If this armament has been permitted at *Pensacola*, there can be no hesitation as to the course we should pursue.

Volume 6, July 30, 1814, page 368

Events of the War—Miscellaneous.

From Bermuda.—*Extract of a letter from Norfolk to Richmond, dated July* 21.

"I have heard from Bermuda as late as the first of the present month by a person who left it at that time. He says there were only about seven hundred marines with some invalids, that no barracks were building or other reparation making to receive a large number of troops, nor was there any talk of an expedition fitting out for our coast; that admiral Cochrane was then there, and in private conversation said there would be peace. I think this information may be depended upon." [*Compiler.*

Volume 6, August 6, 1814, pages 384-385

Our Own Affairs.

Foreign News.—By the arrival of the Com. Decatur at Castine from Rochelle, we have late news from Europe—the parts that relate to us are inserted below.

The accounts in our last number as to the troops about to be sent to America appear fully confirmed. Lord Hill is the commander; the other generals are Picton, Clinton, Barnes, Robinson and Kempt; the flower of Wellington's army is to accompany them.

London, June 4.—The expedition to America is to be increased to 18,000 men.

Volume 6, August 6, 1814, page 385

Leyden, (Holland) June 1. The city of Ghent, and not Gottenburg, is now fixed upon as the place of conference to be opened between the English and American plenipotentiaries. Two of the latter are on the road to Ghent. They say, they have recently been clothed with the most extensive powers on the subject of their mission. *Moniteur, June* 10.

Volume 6, August 6, 1814, page 388

Events of the War—Miscellaneous.

The Creeks, &c.—A tender of the Orpheus frigate is said to have arrived at the *bay of St. Louis*, with information that they had landed 5000 stand of arms and the necessary munitions at Appalatchicola, where the frigate was, with 300 land troops, erecting fortifications &c. Another report makes the quantity of arms much larger. They applied to the Big Warrior for his alliance; he is reported to have said "that he had been so often deceived in their engagements, that he could no longer place reliance in words—that he must have further proofs of their sincerity, before he could place any reliance in their professions or listen in any way to their entreaties." Colonel Hawkins substantiates the report, by advices he had received, that the Indians near the line had been supplied with arms—and those (hostile) between Appalotchicola and Pensacola bay had been sent for and were on their way, nearly exhausted with famine. The colonel was on his way to meet general Jackson at Fort Jackson, on the 1st of August, to hold a great conference with the chiefs of the several hostile tribes, who have submitted. One thousand *Tennessee* militia are expected in the nation—they are excellent negociators with the *Creeks*; and it is said that general *Pinckney* would also make a requisition from Georgia.

The Creeks are so much broken up that we do not apprehend they can be of great service to the enemy in the business of murder; not war—but downright *murder*, which is their warfare. It does not surprise us that the British should excite new assassinations like those at Fort *Mims*—it is their character so to do; but that the *Spaniards* should permit armaments for those purposes to be made in their territory, must raise the indignation of every one. In *that* quarter we can collect a force enough to sweep them into the sea; and if such is to be their *neutrality*, the sooner we are at war with them the better. We are assured that these things will not be suffered.

Promotions. *From the Washington City Gazette.* We are happy to learn that the president of the United States has brevetted the following gentlemen for their gallant conduct at Chippewa, in Upper Canada, on the 4th and 5th of July last. They were pre-eminently conspicuous in the brigade of general Scott, which on that occasion "covered itself with glory."

Major S. Jessup, 24th inf., lieutenant colonel; major J. H. Leavenworth, 8th inf., lieutenant colonel; major J. M'Neal, 11th inf., lieutenant colonel; captain T. Crookes, 9th inf., major; captain Towson, artillery, major; captain T. Harrison, 42d inf., major.

Volume 6, August 6, 1814, pages 398-399

Death of Lieutenant Wilcox.

Extract of a letter from a friend of the late lieutenant Joseph M. Wilcox, who lost his life during the recent Creek war, to general Joseph Wilcox, the father of the deceased, dated

Fort Claiborne,
on the Alabama,
January 19, 1814.

"In the course of last month straggling parties of the hostile savages made frequent incursions down the forks of the Tombigbee and Alabama. Lieutenant Wilcox was detailed with twenty men to oppose their progress and defend fort White. Two days after his taking command there he went in search of the foe; he fell in with 15 or 20, whom he put to flight.

It being positively asserted to lieutenant colonel Russel, commanding, that a body of 400 or 500 savages were on the river Cahaba, he ordered all the disposable force at this post to hold themselves in readiness to march on the first instant for their town. Accordingly we marched, and on the 2d encamped at a place called the Cross Roads; at which point we were joined by lieutenant Wilcox and his command. On the 4th following we re-commenced our march, the third regiment and the militia amounting to 500 men. Agreeably to previous arrangements, captain Dinkins of our regiment with two boat loads of provisions and sixty men, were dispatched up the Alabama, with orders to form a junction with us, at or below the town. Expecting to meet the boats, and the trail we had to travel precluded the possibility of waggon carriage, we were furnished with only a few pack-horses, and were ordered to draw rations only to include the 9th, which we were obliged to carry on our backs. The wretched guide we had positively asserted that he was acquainted with the course, distance and situation of the town to be attacked—which he said was only 60 miles distant.—At the end of four days marching we felt alarmed that we had not reached the Cahaba. However, we continued our march until the 10th at noon, when we discovered 15 or 20 deserted cabins on a high bluff upon the Cahaba, *as we supposed*, for in fact, we did not know *where* we were. This was our situation on the 10th. We had fasted 24 hours; we were 120 instead of 60 miles from any supply, and, we had no account of captain Dinkins or his command. A council of war was convened, and it was determined to return to this post as soon as possible, depending on horse flesh for subsistence. We were very apprehensive for the safety of captain Dinkins and how to communicate with him was difficult to advise; colonel Russell, fully aware of the determined resolution and patriotism of lieutenant Wilcox, proposed to him to take a small canoe and three picked men, and descend the Alabama, with orders to captain Dinkins to return to fort Claiborne, it being obvious that he could not ascend the river in season. At this time we were ignorant of the course, current or distance, from where we were to the mouth of the Cahaba; but judged it to be only 15 miles. Accordingly lieutenant Wilcox started in his canoe with three at 11 o'clock in the night of the 10th. After rowing about ten miles the canoe upset, and all the ammunition got wet, except a few cartridges which some of the men had in their pockets; and one musket was lost. Not deterred by this accident, he righted the canoe, and proceeded down the river, every moment expecting to meet captain Dinkins and reach the Alabama. After rowing all night and the day following without intermission, at four o'clock, P. M., they came in sight of an indian town on the right bank of the Cahaba. In an instant the whole town was in motion; the number of the indians they estimated to be 150. Half an hour after passing the town they found themselves at the mouth of the river, making the distance run 120 instead of 15 miles, as we supposed. The savages pursued them; but such was the swiftness of their motion in the canoe, that only two could head them. These two fired but missed them. After rowing nine miles down the Alabama they met three canoes, it being then dark, they hailed without effect. They continued rowing all that night and the next day until twelve o'clock, when they halted on the east side of the river for half an hour. Here he made four equal parts of the scanty allowance he had for *himself* and distributed among his little crew.

Again he started and continued without interruption until four o'clock P. M., the 12th, when they met two indian canoes, having six savages in one and four in the other. This was fearful odds indeed. As soon as the savages discovered them, they gave the war whoop and put on shore on different sides. The lieutenant and his men landed twelve or fifteen rods above them under cover of the night. At dusk the savages came up to where the lieutenant and his party lay, when they made a furious attack. The little band defended themselves with the utmost bravery until they beat off the savages with the loss of two of them killed—but they carried with them the lieutenant's canoe. He resolved to take the cane brake until moon light; they travelled this dismal swamp until twelve o'clock A. M., when they found themselves on the river bank two miles above the spot where they fought the Indians. There they constructed a can raft, in order to cross the river, with the intention to continue an eastwardly direction towards the Georgia road, and by that means get home. In crossing the river they lost a musket, and their remaining ammunition got wet. They started on the morning of the 15th to make the road, but again concluded to make a wooden raft and float down the river. This being done, they retired into the cane until night. At 3 o'clock P. M., one of the men came down to the beach and discovered a canoe rowing down the river with ten savages. In this critical situation they again resolved to make the Georgia road. Accordingly they travelled that night until the morning of the 14th, and then reached the high lands that border the river bottoms. At this time they had been 3 days with scarcely any sustenance. The day proving cloudy and having no compass, they again abandoned their object and returned to the raft, which they reached at three o'clock on the 15th. As they were preparing to embark on the raft, a canoe hove in sight, rowing up the river with eight savages. These landed and surrounded the lieutenant, his corporal, and one man of his own regiment. One man of the militia having abandoned him on the appearance of the savages upon the 12th. The savages fired and wounded corporal Simpson in the knee—not one of the two muskets nor the rifle the lieutenant carried with him would fire, in consequence of their ammunition having been wet; however they continued defending themselves until their gallant leader was shot thro' the body, and even then, he, though mortally wounded, pursued one of the savages into his cane, knocked him down with his rifle and put him overboard into the river. This was the last the only survivor saw of his brave lieutenant, for at this juncture he crept unperceived into a thick cane brake, expecting very moment to share the fate of his lieutenant and his corporal.

O Fortune, what a capricious, incomprehensible something thou art! How transitory thy favors and how malevolent their distribution! Ten minutes more, and the life of my dear, dear friend would have been preserved—an ornament to his profession—the fond and future hope of his family—a friend to the distressed, and to society an animating and cheerful member! Scarcely was the tragic scene over when captain Dinkins hove in sight. The savages made off so precipitately as to leave their bloody scalping knives and tomahawks behind them.

What a sad spectacle! Before him lay his gallant friend and brother officer weltering in his gore—the brave and faithful corporal beside him—their skulls split with tomahawks. In this condition they lingered ten minutes, when the captain closed their eyes forever.

Their corpses were put on board the barge and brought to this place, where they were interred with all the honor that is due to departed worth and exalted merit."

[Lieutenant Joseph M. Wilcox, was the son of general Joseph Wilcox, a respectable revolutionary officer, formerly of Connecticut, now a citizen of Marietta, Ohio. At the age of 17 years, lieutenant Wilcox was appointed a cadet in the military academy at West Point. At 21 he was appointed a lieutenant in the 3d regiment of the United States infantry. At the age of 23 years, on the 15th January 1814, he died universally lamented by the whole corps to which he was attached. No person under the same circumstances as those which preceded his unfortunate and untimely death, could have exhibited more skill, judgment, activity, or determined courage. Such blood was spilt at Thermopylae.]—*Nat. Int.*

Volume 6, August 20, 1814, page 425

Events of the War—Miscellaneous.

From Florida. *Milledgeville, Aug.* 3. Colonel Melton who has been for some time past stationed in the Creek nation, reached this place last week. His means of information relative to affairs in that quarter have been equally correct and extensive as those of any other person. From every circumstance, he states, there is no doubt that the British have landed a force near or quite 4000 strong, at or in the vicinity of Appalatchicola, where many of the hostile Indians have already assembled.—*Argus.*

Volume 6, August 20, 1814, page 432

Chronicle.

The Pirate, Lafette, of *Barrataria*, was taken on the 9th of July, and is in irons at New Orleans—so says a letter from that city.

—•»)☻ ◉ ☻««•—

NILES' WEEKLY REGISTER.

THE PAST — THE PRESENT — FOR THE FUTURE.

EDITED, PRINTED AND PUBLISHED BY H. NILES, AT $5 PER ANNUM, PAYABLE IN ADVANCE.

Volume 7

(September 3, 1814 - February 25, 1815)

Volume 7, September 10, 1814, page 6

Events of the War.

Extract of a letter from colonel B. Hawkins to the secretary of War, dated.

Creek Agency,
Aug. 16, 1814.

"General Jackson terminated his negociations with the Creeks on the 9th, and left there on the 11th with the regular troops going by water down the Ubama. The line of limits is Coosau river with a reserve of two miles square for Fort Williams, to the falls of the river seven miles above fort Jackson, thence eastwardly to a point 2 miles north of Ofuchshee (a large creek six miles below fort Decatur) thence across Tallapoosa to the mouth of the creek, and up the same ten miles in a direct line thence to Chattohochee, and across it at the first creek two and a half miles below Ckeloyocenna about 68 miles north of the confluence of Chattahochee and Flint, thence to Georgia with an eventful reservation to accommodate the Kinnards."

Volume 7, September 10, 1814, page 9

Events of the War—The Allies.

From a late Jamaica paper.—The Orpheus frigate of 36 guns, captain Pigott, and Shelburne schooner, of 12 guns, lieutenant Hope, lately anchored in the bay of Apalache from Bermuda, and supplied the indians with about ten thousand stand of arms and a quantity of ammunition. Colonel Woodbine, formerly of this island, shortly after joined the indians with about, four hundred men, who had proceeded from George, and the whole amounting to five thousand, marched against the Americans, and from a letter addressed to lieutenant Hope from colonel Woodbine, it was ascertained that an immediate attack was to be made upon fort Mitchell, and, from the want of ammunition, that fortress would undoubtedly become an easy conquest. Numbers of adherents daily flocking to the standard of the indians, and the Americans were in terrible consternation, and removing their property in the greatest haste.

[The the British landed the arms spoken of may be true —but that they had collected a force of five thousand men is false. We have much later accounts of the proceedings of the Creeks than could reach us by way of *Jamaica*. We insert the article chiefly to shew the enemy's good will for a new massacre, as at fort *Mims*.]

Volume 7, September 10, 1814, page 11

Events of the War.

Savannah, Aug. 25. By a gentleman of undoubted veracity who left Havanna on the 7th inst. and arrived at St. Mary's on the 18th—information is received that on or about the 1st inst. two British ships from Europe (the Charon and Hermes) each mounting 24 guns, reported to have on board 400 men, some of whom were marine artillerists, 190 of whom were said to be officers, had arrived at Havanna, under the command of colonel_____, who said he was born at Colerain in Ireland. They applied to the governor of the Island for permission to land at Pensacola; but it was refused—they then applied for permission to land at Havanna for the refreshment of the men until a reinforcement should arrive; this also was refused. The governor is said to have assured the commanding officer that their landing would be repelled within any territory under his command— immediately after which a Spanish vessel was despatched for Pensacola, and it was reported that she conveyed orders for the governor of West Florida to repel the landing of British troops in that province with all the force under his control.

The colonel commanding dined at a public house; he spoke freely of great cruelties committed by the troops under general Jackson during his expedition against the Indians; and seemed exasperated against the Americans. He urged that the country belonged to the Indians—they were the first settlers, and it was his intention to restore it to them. His first stand would be at Colerain in Georgia, and from thence to Savannah. The colonel reported that he expected a reinforcement of 4000 men; that he had on board the two ships 3000 uniforms, epaulets, swords, &c. for officers whom he intended to commission. A gentleman who was on board the *Hermes* read one of the proclamations signed by colonel Woodbine inviting all classes and descriptions of people to the British standard for protection and freedom.

The British brig Childers had conveyed to West Florida a quantity of arms and ammunition, and on her return had called at Havanna—it was well known there are several British vessels that had been employed in that way, and that a large supply of arms and ammunition was deposited in that neighborhood on British account.

Volume 7, September 10, 1814, page 11

Events of the War.

From Pensacola. *Milledgeville, (9) Aug.* 24. We understand that general *Jackson* dispatched a courier to the governor of Pensacola, demanding the surrender of *M'Queen* and *Francis* [who, it was stated, had sought shelter under Spanish authority] and the *reason why* they, and their adherents have received succour and assistance from the subjects of his Catholic Majesty, between whose government, and that of the United States, he conceived there were existing relations of amity and good will. His excellency, it is stated, became highly exasperated at the peremptory manner of the demand; returned an insulting and ambiguous answer—said that he knew nothing of Francis and M'Queen—that Jackson *should hear from him shortly.*

Upon the receipt of this answer, delivered verbally, and which general Jackson, no doubt, supposed to bear something of a threatening appearance, he immediately left Fort Jackson for the purpose of occupying Mobile point—at which post, it is said, he will shortly have a force 5000 to 6000 strong—which, it is supposed, will not only be sufficient for defensive, but if necessary, offensive operations.

The Creeks. We have a variety of rumours and reports of the intrigues and operations of the British with the *Creek Indians.* It is pretty well ascertained that the enemy has landed some men and a considerable quantity of arms at Appalachicola, 130 miles east of Pensacola. Many of the Creeks had taken refuge in the Spanish territory, and it is said they have accepted the supplies. *Jackson,* however, seems prepared to manage the allied forces.

Volume 7, October 1, 1814, pages 40-41

Events of the War.

Copy of a letter from captain Campbell to the secretary of the navy, dated

St. Mary's,
12th September, 1814.

Sir—I beg leave to report the British privateer schooner Fortune of War, captured on the 9th inst. off Sappelo Bar, by gun vessels No. 160, and 151 in company commanded by Thomas M. Pendleton; mounts 2 six pounders with a crew consisting of 35 in number, three weeks from Bermuda, without having made any captures.

She surrendered after receiving two shot from the gun vessel, and having one man killed. Previous to the capture of the privateer, the gun vessels had taken on of her boats and 13 men that had landed on Sappelo.

I have the honor to be, with great respect, sir, your obedient servant,

H. G. CAMPBELL.

The hon. Wm. Jones, secretary of the navy.

Events of the War—Miscellaneous.

From the South. A letter received at Philadelphia from New Orleans, dated August 22, says—An express has just arrived to captain Patterson, informing that the British had arrived at and taken possession of Mobile. It has excited great alarm here.

And the National Intelligencer, of Saturday last, observes—We learn that information reached Nashville, by express, on the 9th inst. that the enemy had landed a body of troops, said to consist of 6000 men, at Pensacola in East Florida. The troops under the command of general Jackson were expected to march in that direction.

Events of the War—Miscellaneous.
From Nashville Whig, Extra,
September 9.

An express arrived here this morning from general Jackson, with the following important information.

————

Head-quarters,
7th military district,
Mobile, August 27, 1814.

Sir—By an express sent from Pensacola as well as from Antonio Callina, a citizen of that place who left there yesterday at 12 o'clock, bringing with him the pass of colonel Nicholas, the British officer commanding there, for his protection, I have received information, which may be implicitly relied on, that three British vessels, the Hermes, Orpheus and Carrian, arrived at Pensacola on the 25th inst. and on yesterday disembarked an immense quantity of arms, ammunition, munitions of war, and provisions—and marched into the Spanish fort between two and three hundred troops. That thirteen sail of the line with a large number of transports are daily expected at that place, with ten thousand troops.

The Havanna papers received there state, that fourteen sail of the line had arrived at Bermuda. It is currently reported in Pensacola, that the emperor of Russia has offered his Britannic majesty 50,000 of his best troops for the conquest of Louisiana, and that this territory will fall a prey to the enemy before the expiration of one month. Sir J. Faubridge and captain Pigot, are the naval commanders. Spain is said by a secret treaty to have ceded Pensacola to Great Britain.

You will immediately perceive the necessity of being on the alert, and taking time by the forelock. I have, therefore to request that you, without delay, cause to be organized, equipped and brought into the field, the whole of the quota of the militia of your state, agreeable to the requisition of the war department of the 4th of July last.

Colonel Robert Butler, my adjutant-general, is now in your state, and has been instructed to make the necessary arrangements for transporting provisioning and bringing to head-quarters these troops, as well as to prescribe their route. You will have them furnished with all the arms within your reach.

Those who cannot be furnished by you, will receive them here; but reliance must not be had on that if to be avoided.

I am, respectfully,

ANDREW JACKSON.

His excellency Willie Blount,
governor of Tennessee.

Copy of a letter from colonel Hawkins, agent for Indian affairs, to his excellency the governor of Georgia, dated

"Creek Agency,
August 23, 1814.

"General Jackson terminated his negociations with the Creeks on the 9th. The line of limits drawn for them is Coosa river, with a reserve of two miles square for Fort Williams, to the falls seven miles above Fort Jackson, thence eastward to a point two miles north of Gakfuskee (a large creek three miles below Autossee on the east side of Talapoosa) thence across Talapoosa to the mouth of the creek, and up the same ten miles in a direct line. Thence to Chat,te,ho,che and across it at the mouth of Summa,cho,co, the first large creek below O,ke,te,joon,ne (about 68 miles north of the confluence of Cat,ta,ho,che) thence ease to Georgia, with an eventual reserve to accommodate the Kinnards.

"We continue to receive daily rumours of hostile appearances at Appalatchicola. Ten British armed vessels off that coast; have maneuvered dexterously by landing and re-embarking their crews, to deceive the Indians in that neighborhood. They furnished considerable munitions of war, and some clothing, and are training the Indians and some ******* for purposes hostile to us.

"We have from a credible Indian source the following from a British naval officer, to the hostile chiefs:

"*The British and other powers had conquered France and seven powers were now united against AMERICA. A little before white frost, you will hear of smoke all around the United States, in the sea ports, and the burning of powder. The War is just beginning.— There will be several armies landing in different places. His king, George, said the seven powers would be able, and were determined to CONQUER AMERICA, and the British would be masters of it. They need not expect to be deceived; the British would fulfil their promises, and NEVER LEAVE THIS LAND AGAIN.*

"The Indians who recently committed a violent outrage below Hartford, were from the banditti assembling under British influence; there were four of them. As I have some confidential people among them, one of whom will probably be here in a week, I expect some interesting details to our present stock, which I shall communicate to you.

I am, respectfully, sir, your obedient servant,

BENJN. HAWKINS.

Governor Early.

Volume 7, October 6, 1814, page 53

From other sources that appear worthy of entire credit, it appears that the Spaniards at Pensacola are more than passive instruments in the hands of the merciless British, to raise the tomahawk in the south. There are many Indians at that place, dressed in British uniforms, and exercised by British officers, &c. Much bloodshed must be expected in that quarter. If the truce and treaty that *Jackson* has lately made with the Creeks, is broken, we shall not probably ever hear of another. How cruel is it in *Englishmen* to bring about the extermination of this race; for exterminated they certainly will be, if they do not cease their murders. They were a happy and contented people, cultivating their *farms* and *manufacturing*, until the *British*, like the devil in *Eden*, tempted them to evil. They have already paid a dreadful penalty for their folly and weakness—but the end is not yet. They still listen to the deceiver. Inhuman *Englishmen!* let the poor savage have peace. Wretched *murderers!* permit us in safety to spare the remnant of the *Creeks*! Monsters, let them return to that progressive state of civilization we fostered with so much charity, justice, and good faith. One lesson of practical christianity, is worth all your regiments of canting "Bible Societies," headed by such men as *George* or *Frederick Guelph*.

Volume 7, October 6, 1814, page 64

Events of the War—Miscellaneous.

Latest from the South. General *Jackson* has laid an embargo on all the ports of the Mississippi, Mobile &c. He is at or near *Mobile*, with 1500 regulars and some militia, number not stated. It is said that the enemy has occupied Mobile Point, which stops the [water] communication with New-Orleans. The state's quota of militia and many volunteers were pouring towards them from patriotic *Tennessee*—a hardy and generous race of freemen. What *Jackson's* immediate designs really are, are unknown to his most confidential officers—but all is life and energy, and we expect some signal event. Preparations have been made for the defence of New-Orleans; the naval force commanded by "pupils of the gallant Porter" assisting. The 7th infantry is cantoned at the navy yard. It is expected that we shall be assisted to drive out the invaders by a large indian force—*Creeks, Cherokees,* and *Choctaws.*

Volume 7, October 15, 1814, page 70

From our Ministers at Ghent.

Highly Important.

The following message was on Monday last sent to both houses of congress, by the president of the United States. The sentiments it excited in both houses were purely national, and almost unanimous.

To the Senate and House of Representatives of the United States,

I lay before congress communications just received from the plenipotentiaries of the United States, charged with negociating peace with Great Britain; showing the conditions on which alone that government is willing to put an end to the war.

The instructions to those plenipotentiaries, disclosing the grounds, on which they were authorised to negociate and conclude a treaty of peace, will be the subject of another communication.

JAMES MADISON.

Washington,
October 10, 1814.

—·»»☺☻☺«««·—

British Attack
Mobile Point

Volume 7, October 15, 1814, pages 78-79

Events of the War—Miscellaneous.

From the south, we have glorious news! See general Jackson's letter below. Of fort Bowyer where this brilliant affair happened, the "National Intelligencer" observes—This little fort, (which was erected in 1812, by lieutenant colonel Bowyer, and consists only of common logs filled in with sand was performed, we learn by a detachment of the 2d regiment, which had not before an opportunity of distinguishing itself in the present war, tho' highly distinguished formerly, for its gallant stand against the savages in covering St. Clair's retreat, where only 16 of its officers survived, and only 4 escaped unhurt. Of these

colonel Sparks and lieutenant colonel Bowyer still remain in the regiment. Lieutenant colonel Bowyer has been recently promoted, and transferred to the Northern frontier. Major Lawrence, who commanded fort Bowyer, is an officer of high promise—a native of Calvert county, Maryland.

It is stated that general Jackson will have under his command, immediately, not less than 12,000 men; part of which is a fine body of regulars—the rest chiefly Kentucky and Tennessee militia, nearly equal to them; and perhaps, for the service required not inferior in real utility. We fear nothing in that quarter. The spirit of the population of the west, with the nature of the country, climate, &c. will probably confine the operations of the *British* forces to the *murdering* of a few men, women and children. 4000 men have been required from *Louisiana,* the number is partly made up of volunteers, 4500 march from Kentucky.

The *British* commanding officer at *Pensacola*—we say commanding at *Pensacola,* a *Spanish* place—is spouting away in great style; and with a force that we do not believe amounts to more than 200 or 300 British and as many Indians, is puffing and blowing beyond any thing that *Bonaparte* has left us samples of in that sort of style. We shall notice him snore at length anon.

An expedition has been fitted out at New-Orleans, supposed against *Barataria* under command of captain Patterson, of the navy. If his means are sufficient, the nest of privates will be destroyed. The people at Orleans have had a meeting, and appointed a committee of defence, &c.

Head-Quarters,
7th Military District,
Mobile,
September 17, 10 A. M.

Sir—I have but a moment to spare to tell you since the departure of my letter of this morning a messenger has returned from fort Bowyer, with the pleasing intelligence that major Lawrence has gallantly repulsed the enemy with great loss, blowing up a vessel of 30 guns. Only four of our men were killed and 5 wounded. The officers bringing the despatches will be here in an hour, when I will be enabled to give you the particulars.

I have the honor to be, very respectfully, your obedient servant.

ANDREW JACKSON,
Maj. gen. Commanding.

The hon. John Armstrong,
secretary of war.

———

*Extract of a letter
received in this city.*

"By a letter just received from general Jackson, he has beaten the British and Indians at Mobile Point, blown up the admiral's ship, and sank one brig. About 20 of their crews saved. The letter I saw.

WM. DONNISON.

Fayettesville, Ten.
Sept. 14, 1814.

Volume 7, October 22, 1814, page 93

Enemy repulsed at Mobile.

Copy of a letter
from major-general Jackson,
to the secretary of war, dated

*H. Q. 7th military district.
Mobile, September* 17.

Sir—With lively emotions of satisfaction, I communicate that success has crowned the gallant efforts of our brave soldiers, in resisting and repulsing a combined British naval and land force, which on the 15th inst., attacked Fort Bowyer, on the point of Mobile.

I enclose a copy of the official report of major Wm. Lawrence, of the 2d infantry, who commanded. In addition to the particulars communicated in his letter, I have learnt that the ship which was destroyed, was the Hermes, of from 24 to 28 guns, captain the honorable Wm. H. Percy, senior officer in the Gulf of Mexico; and the brig so considerably damaged is the Sophie, 18 guns, captain Wm. Lockyer. The other ship was the Carron, of from 24 to 28 guns, captain Spencer, son of earl Spencer; the other brig's name unknown.

On board the Carron, 85 men were killed and wounded; among whom of colonel Nicoll, of the royal marines, who lost an eye by a splinter. The land force consisted of 110 marines, and 200 Creek Indians, under the command of captain Woodbine, of the marines, and about 20 artillerists, with one four and an half inch howitzer, from which they discharged shells and nine pound shot. They re-embarked the piece, and retreated by land towards Pensacola, whence they came.

By the morning report of the 16th, there were present in the fort, fit for duty, officers and men, 158.

The result of this engagement has stamped a character on the war in this quarter highly favorable to the American arms; it is an event from which may be drawn the most favorable augury.

An achievement so glorious in its consequences, should be appreciated by the government; and those concerned are entitled to, and will, doubtless, receive the most gratifying evidence of the approbation of their countrymen.

In the words of major Lawrence "where all behaved so well, it is unnecessary to discriminate." But all being meritorious, I beg leave to annex the names of the officers who were engaged and present; and hope they will, individually, be deemed worthy of distinction.

Major Wm. Lawrence, 2d infantry, commanding; captain Walsh of the artillery, captains Chamberlain, Brownlow, and Bradley of the 2d infantry; captain Sands, deputy comissary of ordnance, lieutenants Villerd, Sturges, Conway, H. Sanders, T. R. Sanders, Brooks, Davis, and C. Sanders, all of the 2nd infantry.

I am confident that your own feelings will lead you to participate in my wishes on the subject. Permit me to suggest the propriety and justice of allowing to this gallant little band the value of the vessel destroyed by them.

I remain, with great respect, your obedient servant,

A. JACKSON,
major general, commanding.

The honorable secretary of war.

Volume 7, October 22, 1814, pages 93-94

Copy of a letter from major Lawrence to major general Jackson, dated

Fort Bowyer,
Sept. 15—12 o'clock
at night.

Sir—After writing the enclosed, I was prevented by the approach of the enemy from sending it by express. At meridian they were under full sail, with an easy and favorable breeze standing directly for the fort, and at 4, P. M., we opened our battery, which was returned from two ships and two brigs, as they approached. The action became general at about 20 minutes past 4, and was continued without intermission on either side until 7, when 1 ship and 2 brigs were compelled to retire. The leading ship, supposed to be the commodore's, mounting 22 thirty-two pound carronades, having anchored nearest our battery, was so much disabled, her cable being cut by our shot, that she drifted on shore, within 600 yards of the battery, and the other vessels having got out of our reach, we kept such a tremendous fire upon her that she was set on fire and abandoned by the few of the crew who survived. At 10 P. M., we had the pleasure of witnessing the explosion of her magazine. The loss of lives on board must have been immense, as we are certain no boats left her except three, which had previously gone to her assistance, and one of these I believe was sunk; in fact, one of her boats was burned along side of her.

The brig that followed her I am certain was much damaged both in hull and rigging. The other two did not approach near enough to be so much injured, but I am confident they did not escape, as a well directed fire was kept on them during the whole time.

During the action a battery of a twelve pounder and a howitzer was opened on our rear without doing any execution, and was silenced by a few shot. Our loss is four privates killed and five wounded.

Towards the close of the action the flag-staff was shot away; but the flag was immediately hoisted on a sponge-staff over the parapet. While the flag was down the enemy kept up their most incessant and tremendous fire; the men were withdrawn from the curtains and N. E. Bastion, as the enemy's own shot completely protected our rear, except the position they had chosen for their battery.

Where all behaved well it is unnecessary to discriminate. Suffice it to say, every officer and man did his duty; the whole behaved with that coolness and intrepidity which is characteristic of the true American, and which could scarcely have been expected from men most whom had never seen an enemy, and were now for the first time exposed for nearly three hours to a force of nearly or quite four guns to one.

We fired during the action between 400 and 500 guns, most of them double shotted, and after the first half hour but few missed an effect.

September 16th,
11 o'clock, A. M.

Upon an examination of our battery this morning, we find upwards of 300 shot and shot holes in the inside of the north and east curtains, and N. E. bastion, of all calibres, from musket ball to 32 pound shot. In the N. E. bastion there were three guns dismounted; one of which, a four pounder, was broken off near the trunnions by a 32 pound shot and another much battered. I regret to say that both the 24 pounders are cracked in such a manner as to render them unfit for service.

I am informed by two deserters from the land force, who have just arrived here, and whom I send for your disposal, that a reinforcement is expected, when they will doubtless endeavor to wipe off the stain of yesterday.

If you will send the Amelia down, we may probably save most or all of the ship's guns, as her wreck is lying in 6 or 7 feet water and some of them are just covered. They will not, however, answer for the fort, as they are too short.

By the deserters, we learn that the ship we have destroyed was the Hermes, but her commander's name they did not recollect. It was the commodore, and doubtless fell on his quarter deck, as we had a raking fire upon it at about two hundred yards distance for some time.

To captain Sands, who will have the honor of handing you this despatch, I refer you for a more particular account of the movements of the enemy than may be contained in my letters; his services both before and during the action were of great importance, and I consider fully justify me in having detained him. Captain Walsh and several men were much burned by the accidental explosion of two or three cartridges. They are not included in the list of wounded heretofore given.

The enemy's fleet this morning at day break were at anchor in the channel about four miles from the fort; shortly after it got under way and stood to sea; after passing the bar they hove too, and boats have been constantly passing between the disabled brig and the others. I presume the former is so much injured as to render it necessary to lighten her.

15 minutes after 1 P. M.—The whole fleet have this moment made sail and are standing to sea.

I have the honor to be, very respectfully, sir, your obedient servant,

WM. LAWRENCE.

Maj. Gen. Andrew Jackson,
com. 7th M. Dist.

Volume 7, October 22, 1814, pages 95-96

Events of the War—Miscellaneous.

Head-quarters,
town of Mobile
September 17, 1814.
Inspector general's office,
7th military district.

General Orders—Our companions in arms have triumphed over the enemy. At 4 o'clock P. M. on the 15th inst. fort Bowyer was attacked, by a superior British naval and land force, and the enemy was repulsed at all points. The naval force consisted of 2 ships from 24 to 28 guns, mounting 24 pound carronades, with three tenders, all under the command of commodore sir W. H. Percy. The land forces of the enemy consisted of one hundred marines, under the command of colonel Nicolls, 300 Indians under the command of captain Woodbine of the British army, and a battery of a 12 pounder and howitzer, under the direction of a British captain of the royal artillery. Our effective force opposed to the enemy was about 120 men, of whom not more than 90 were engaged.

The leading ship called the Hermes, commodore sir W. H. Percy, having approached within the reach of our guns, our battery opened upon her; the guns of which were fired in succession as they could be brought to bear; and at 20 minutes after 4 P. M., the engagement became general. About this time the enemy on shore with colonel Nicolls at the head of the marines, captain Woodbine at the head of their allies the Indians, and the captain of the British royal artillery, with his battery, were put to flight, by two discharges of grape and cannister from a nine pounder. At 5 P. M., the commodore's ship swung head on, to our battery, when we were enabled to rake her so effectually as to silence her guns. Having cut her cable by our shot, she drifted out and grounded stern on, within 600 yards, which again afforded us an opportunity of raking her, and we continued doing so while there was light enough to see that her colors were flying; just about sunset the other vessels cut their cables and stood off with a light breeze, under a tremendous fire from our battery. At a quarter past 7 we discovered the commander's ship to be on fire, and at 10 P. M., her magazine blew up.

We cannot ascertain the precise loss of the enemy, but from deserters, who came in the morning after the battle, we learn that the commander and only 20 men escaped from the Hermes—her crew being originally 170. That 85 were killed and wounded on board the Charon. The loss on board the brigs is unknown, but must have been very great from the circumstance of one of them being infinitely more exposed than the Charon. Our loss was four privates killed and five wounded. During the hottest part of the action our flag staff being shot away, the flag was immediately regained under a heavy fire of grape and cannister, and hoisted on a sponge staff and planted on the parapet.

This achievement of our brothers in arms is dear to us, and calls for, and will have the gratitude of a grateful country! Our arms have triumphed over the enemy. The brave officers, non-commissioned officers and privates under the command of the gallant major Lawrence, have done their duty, and in point of cool and determined courage their conduct cannot be surpassed. There was but one feeling pervading every grade and rank through the whole action, and that was who should be foremost in the race of glory. With them the post of danger was the post of honor.

By command of major general Jackson,

H. HAYNE.
Inspector general and acting adjutant general

Volume 7, October 27, 1814, page 109

Events of the War—Heads of News.

Pensacola. There are many reasons to believe that general Jackson has attacked and we trust carried the nest of mischief in the south, before now. It is notoriously the rallying point of the enemy, and has long since lost all pretentions to the character of a neutral place. Powerful reinforcements from Tennessee must have joined him—2,000 mounted volunteers, under general Coffee, marched from Fayetteville on the 3d instant: He has with him 1,000 Indians.

—»»☉◉☉«««—

British Seek Help Along the Gulf Coast

Volume 7, November 5, 1814, pages 133-135

British Proclamations, &c.

The following proceedings were had by the *honorable* William Henry Percy, a captain in "his majesty's" navy—and lieutenant colonel Nicholls, commanding "his majesty's" forces in the Floridas, before they got their drubbing at Fort Bowyer—which has, perhaps, changed their tone. Their *impudence* is equalled only by their folly.

Though we have laughed heartily at the appeal of the *gallant* colonel to the people of *Kentucky*, &c. and his story of *"French influence"*—the base, villainous and unprincipled application to the celebrated *pirate* Lafitte, for his

alliance—a man who, for about two years past, has been famous for crimes that the *civilized world* wars against—who is supposed to have captured one hundred vessels, of all nations, and certainly murdered the crews of all that he took, for no one has ever escaped him—who was known to the *honorable* captain Percy, "his Britannic majesty's senior officer, &c"—indubitably known, *as such* an outlaw, pirate and murderer—is of a character so infamous and detestable, that, in the strong language of an anonymous writer on another occasion, we would "with trumpet lungs, call upon heaven and earth to punish the offence!"

Gracious Providence!—are such men the *"bulwarks of religion and liberty."*

These fellows have been handsomely beaten by less than 100 men at fort Bowyer, with all their spouting. The poor creature Nicholls, had only about 200 marines, and as many indians, of whom, and to whom, he speaks so pompously!

———

Head quarters, Pensacola,
August 26, 1814.

Order of the day for
the first colonial battalion
of the royal corps of marines.

You are called upon to discharge a duty of the utmost peril. You will have to perform long and tedious marches through wildernesses, swamps and water courses; your enemy from long habit inured to the climate, will have great advantages over you. But remember the 21 years of toil and glory of your country, and resolve, to follow the example of your glorious companions, who have fought and spilt their blood in her service. Be equally faithful and strict in your moral discipline, and this the last and most perfidious of your enemies, will not long maintain themselves before you. A cause so sacred as that which has led you to draw your swords in Europe, will make you unsheath them in America, and I trust you will use them with equal credit and advantage. In Europe your arms were not employed in defence of your country only, but of all those who groaned in the chains of oppression, and in America they are to have the same direction. The people whom you are now to aid and assist have suffered robberies and murders committed on them by the Americans.

The noble Spanish nation has grieved to see her territories insulted; having been robbed and despoiled of a portion of them while she was overwhelmed with distress and held down by the chains which a tyrant had imposed on her glorious struggling for the greatest of all possible blessings (true liberty.) The treacherous Americans, who call themselves free, have attacked her, like assassins, while she was fallen. But the day of retribution is fast approaching. These atrocities will excite horror in the heart of a British soldier, they will stimulate you to avenge them, and you will avenge them like British soldiers. Valor, then, and humanity!

As to the Indians you are to exhibit to them the most exact discipline, being a pattern to those children of nature. You will teach and instruct them, in doing which you will manifest the utmost patience, and you will correct them when they deserve it. But you will regard their affections and *antipathies*, and *never give them just cause of offence*. Sobriety, above all things, should be your greatest care—a single instance of drunkenness may be your ruin, and I declare to you in the most solemn manner that no consideration whatsoever shall induce me to forgive a drunkard. Apprized of this declaration, if any of you break my orders in this respect, he will consider himself the just cause of his own chastisement. Sobriety is your first duty; I ask of you the observance of it among your brethren. Vigilance is our next duty. Nothing is so disgraceful to our army as surprise. Nothing so destructive to our cause.

———

By the honorable William Henry Percy, captain of his majesty's ship Hermes, and senior officer in the gulph of Mexico.

You are hereby requested and directed after having received on board an officer belonging to the first battalion of royal colonial marines, to proceed in his majesty's sloop under your command, without a moment's loss of time for Barataria.

On your arrival at that place, you will communicate with the chief persons there; you will urge them to throw themselves under the protection of Great Britain; and should you find them inclined to pursue such a step, you will hold out to them, that their property shall be secured to them, that they shall be considered British subjects, and at the conclusion of the war, *lands in his majesties colonies in America*, will be allotted to them. In return for these concessions, you will insist on an immediate cessation of hostilities against Spain; and in case they should have any Spanish property not disposed of, that it is to be restored, and that they put their naval force into the hands of the senior officer here, until the commander in chief's pleasure is known. In the event of their not having inclined to act offensively against the United States, you will do all in your power to persuade them to strict neutrality, and still endeavor to put a stop to their hostilities against Spain; should you succeed completely in the object for which you are sent, you will concert such measures for the annoyance of the enemy as you judge best *from circumstances*, having an eye to the junction of their small armed vessels with me, *for the capture of the Mobile, &c.* You will, at all events, yourself, join me with the utmost despatch at this post, with the account of your success.

Given under my hand, on board his majesty's ship Hermes, at Pensacola, this 30th day of August, 1814.

(Signed)   W. H. PERCY, captain.

Nicholas Locker, esq.
Commander of his majesty's ship Sophia.

A true copy from the original in my possession.

WM. C. C. CLAIBORNE.

———

By the honorable William Henry Percy, captain of H.M.S. Hermes, and senior officer of the Gulf of Mexico.

Having understood that some British merchantmen have been detained, taken into, and sold by the inhabitants of Barataria, I have directed captain Lockyer, of H.M. sloop Sophia, to proceed to that place, and to inquire into the circumstance, with positive orders to demand instant restitution, and in

122

case of refusal, to destroy to his utmost, every vessel there, as well as to carry destruction over the whole place, and at the same time to assure him of the co-operation of all H. M. naval force on this station. I trust at the same time that the inhabitants of Barataria consulting their own interest, will not make it necessary to proceed to such extremities.— Hold out at the same time to them, a war instantly destructive to them, and on the other hand, should they be inclined to assist Great Britain, in an unjust and unprovoked war against the United States, the security of their property, the blessings of the British constitution, and should they be inclined to settle on this continent, lands will at the conclusion of the war, be allotted to them, in his majesty's colonies in America. In return for all these concessions, on the part of Great Britain, I expect that the direction of the armed vessels will be put into my hands, (for which they will be remunerated) the instant cessation of hostilities against the Spanish government and the restitution of any undisposed of property of that nation shall be made. Should any inhabitants be inclined to volunteer their services into H. M. Force, either naval or military, for limited service, they will be received, and if any British subject being at Barataria wishes to return to his native country, he will, on joining his majesty's service, receive a free pardon.

Given under my hand, on board his majesty's ship Hermes, Pensacola, the 1st day of Sept. 1814.

(Signed)   W. H. PERCY, Capt. and Senior officer

Monsieur Lafete.

A true copy from the original in my possession.

W. C. C. CLAIBORNE.

———

Head-quarters, Pensacola, August 31st, 1814.

Sir—I have arrived in the Floridas for the purpose of annoying the only enemy Great Britain has in the world. As France and England are now friends, I call on you, with your brave followers, to enter into the service of Great Britain, in which you shall have the rank of *captain*—LANDS will be given to you all in proportion to your respective ranks, on a peace taking place, and I invite you out on the following terms:—your property shall be quartered to you, and your person protected. In return for which I ask you to cease all hostilities against Spain or the allies of Great Britain. Your ships and vessels to be placed under the orders of the commanding officer on this station until the commander in chief's pleasure is known; but I guarantee their fair value to you at all events.

I herewith enclose you a copy of my proclamation to the inhabitants of Louisiana, which will, I trust, point out to you the honorable intentions of my government; you may be a useful assistant to me in forwarding them; therefore if you determine, lose no time; the bearer of this, captain M'Williams, will satisfy you on any other points you may be anxious to learn, as will captain Lockyer of the Sophia, who carries him to you. We have a powerful reinforcement on the way here, and I hope to cut out some other work for the Americans than oppressing the inhabitants of Louisiana. Be expeditious on your resolves and rely upon the veracity of

Your humble servant,

(Signed)   EDWARD NICHOLLS,
Lt. Col. com.
H. B. M. forces in the Floridas.

To Monsieur La Fete,
or the commandant
at Barataria.

———

By lieutenant colonel Edward Nicholls, commanding H. B. M. forces in the Floridas.

Natives of Louisiana, on you the first call is made to assist in liberating from a faithless and imbecile government, your paternal soil. Spaniards, Frenchmen, Italians and British, whether settled or residing for a time in Louisiana, on you also I call to aid me in the just cause. The American usurpation in this country must be abolished, and the lawful owners of the soil put in possession. I am at the head of a large body of Indians, well armed, disciplined, and commanded by British officers. A good train of artillery with every requisite, seconded by the powerful aid of a numerous British and *Spanish squadron of ships and vessels of war*. Be not alarmed, inhabitants of the country, at our approach; the same good faith and disinterestedness, which has distinguished the conduct of Britons in Europe accompanies them here. You will have no fear of litigious taxes imposed on you for the purpose of carrying on an unnatural and unjust war; your property, your laws, the peace and tranquility of your country, will be guaranteed to you by men who will suffer no infringement of theirs; rest assured that these brave men only burn with an ardent desire of satisfaction, for the wrongs they have suffered from the Americans, to join you in liberating these southern frontiers from their yoke, and drive them into the limits formerly prescribed by my sovereign.—The Indians have pledged themselves, in the most solemn manner, not to injure in the slightest degree, their persons or properties, of any but enemies *to their Spanish or English fathers. A flag* over any door whether Spanish, French or British will be a certain protection. Nor dare any Indian put his foot on the threshold thereof, under penalty of death from his own countrymen. Not even an enemy will an Indian put to death, except resisting in arms, and as for injuring helpless women and children the red men by their good conduct and treatment to them, will, if it be possible, make the Americans blush for their more than inhuman conduct, lately on the Escambia, and within a neutral territory.

Inhabitants of Kentucky, you have too long borne with grievous impositions. The whole brunt of the war has fallen on your brave sons; be imposed on no more; but either range yourselves under the standard of your forefathers, or observe a strict neutrality. If you comply with either of these offers; whatever provisions you send down, will be paid for in dollars, and the safety of the persons bringing it, as well as the free navigation of the Mississippi guaranteed to you. Men of Kentucky, let me call to your view, and I trust to your abhorrence, the conduct of those factions, which hurried you into this cruel, unjust and unnatural war, at a time when Great Britain was straining every nerve in defence of her own, and the liberties of the world; when the bravest of her sons were fighting and bleeding in so sacred a cause; when she was spending millions of her treasure in endeavoring to pull down one of the most formidable and dangerous tyrants that ever disgraced the form of man: when groaning Europe was almost in her last gasp, when positions alone shewed an undaunted front, basely did these assassins endeavor to stab her from the rear; she has turned on them, renovated from the bloody, but successful struggle. Europe is happy and free, and she now hastens justly to avenge unprovoked insults. Shew them that you are not collectively unjust, leave that contemptible few to shift for themselves; let those *slaves of the tyrant* send an embassy to Elba, and implore his aid; but let every honest, upright American spurn them with merited contempt. After the experience of 21 years, can you any longer support those brawlers for liberty, who call it freedom, and know not when themselves are free; be no longer their dupes, accept my offer; every thing I have promised in this paper I guarantee to you on the sacred honor of a British officer.

Given under my hand at my head-quarters, Pensacola, this 29th of August, 1814.

(Signed)   EDWARD NICHOLLS

Volume 7, November 19, 1814, page 170

Events of the War—Military.

From the south we have two reports that general *Jackson* has had a second battle with the British, in which he lost 100 men killed and 160 wounded; they losing 400 men killed—but no time, place or other circumstance is mentioned. *It may be true.*

The Seminole Indians have raised the tomahawk—they have received orders from the "bulwark of religion" to strike. They are the most savage tribe in the south. Measures have been taken by the Georgians to chastise them.

Volume 7, November 26, 1814, page 191

Events of the War—Military.

Major general *Pinkney* proceeded to the southward from Savannah, on the 13th inst. and on the same day major general M'Intosh, of the Georgia militia, set out for Fort *Hawkins*.

Volume 7, December 3, 1814, page 206

Events of the War—Miscellaneous.

Amelia Island. A very extensive and profitable trade—an *honest* trade—is carried on between this place and the southern states; and the products of our soil, to a large amount, are there exchanged for the foreign goods required, though the passages are closely watched by the enemy.

Volume 7, December 3, 1814, page 207

Events of the war—Military.

We have a report from New Orleans stating that a new governor had arrived at Pensacola, who had ordered off the British. They have been very quiet on the coast since the drubbing they got at Mobile.

Volume 7, December 10 1814, page 218

Extract of a letter from major-general Andrew Jackson to captain E. Rapier, dated

Head-Quarters,
7th military district.
Mobile,
October 16th, 1814.

Sir—I have just learned that general Coffee, with the volunteers will reach me in a few days. Their patriotism, at this all important crisis has justly entitled them to be hailed as the first of patriots in the union; and will immortalize the state. They have set a fit and proper example to the sister states of the union; and if followed by them will soon make us respectable abroad, the tyrant of England shudder, and obtain for us an honorable peace in a short time.

As soon as general Coffee reaches me I will be in motion, and I trust with the smiles of Heaven to be able to give security to this section of the country in a short time.

——·»»⊖ ⊛ ⊖«««·——

General Jackson Forces British Out of Pensacola

Volume 7, December 17, 1814, page 252

Events of the War.

We have not yet received an official account of the capture of *Pensacola* by general Jackson. It is certain, however, that he has captured that place, and driven off the British. It is also understood that he would immediately retire from the same to Mobile.

Major-general Carroll marched from Nashville on the 23d ult. with 5000 men to reinforce general Jackson, whose force at Pensacola was 6000, and he will probably have at least 15,000 brave men, independent of the local militia.

Volume 7, December 24, 1814, page 269

Events of the War—Miscellaneous.

If the statements in the West India papers are to be believed, the expedition against *New Orleans* will be very formidable. All the force in those islands, together with the troops late in the Chesapeake appear to have been collecting early in last month, and it is thought the whole may amount to from 12,000 to 15,000 men.

Volume 7, December 24, 1814, page 271

Events of the War—Military.

Extract of a letter from major general Jackson to governor Early, dated

Head-quarters, 7th military district,
near Fort Mimms,
November 16, 1814.

"Before this reaches you, information will have been received of my visit to Pensacola.—It was occasioned by the unprecedented conduct of the governor of Pensacola, in harboring, aiding, and countenancing the *British* and their red allies. I entered sword in hand, with about three thousand brave followers, in the face of Spanish batteries, and a British fleet of seven sail, anchored abreast and opposite the town.—The English, by intrigue and base falsehood, induced the Spaniards to abandon the works commanding the harbor, entered them and blew them up; otherwise they would have fallen a sacrifice to their own plans. When this took place, the fleet being at liberty to go out, did so; and I evacuated the town, leaving the Spaniards favorably impressed with our conduct, and disgusted with their British friends. The hostile Indians fled across the bay at our approach; and have, no doubt, lost all confidence in the assurances they have received of British protection.— They have retired, it is believed, towards Apalachicola in great alarm.

"The Seminolies, however, it appears, from information given by colonel Hawkins, are preparing to assume an hostile attitude.—When they hear of the shameful manner in which the Red Sticks were deserted by their allies, they will wish to retract.

The following was in M. S.

General Jackson was opposed by the Spaniards—and several men were lost on both sides in taking the town. The British retreated to their ships, from which they fired at Jackson, but without effect.— They attempted to decoy Jackson into the fort at the time the match was burning; but he cautiously avoided it until the tremendous explosion took effect, and injured none.

5th Dec. in the morning.

Gentlemen who have arrived at Charleston from Havanna report that, "the conduct of the American force under general Jackson, in their late entry into Pensacola, was spoken of in the highest terms by the Spaniards. After general Jackson had evacuated the place, he sent in word to the inhabitants that if any of them had suffered loss of property to let him know it, and he would immediately make their loss good."

Volume 7, December 31, 1814, page 279

Events of the War—Miscellaneous.

New Orleans. The fate of the much-talked of British expedition to New Orleans is probably decided before this time, from the facts stated below. As general Jackson must have been perfectly aware of this expected movement of the enemy, we trust he was fully prepared for it, and we look for the result with confidence and hope. Perhaps, and from the nature of the country and its waters we think it very possible, that New Orleans is destined to the same celebrity as Saratoga and York town.— The commanding general will find a great co-operating power in our gallant naval officers on that station, who are Porter's pupils—capable of attempting any thing that any men have ever performed.

————

*Extract of a letter
from major general M'Intosh
to governor Early,
dated Camp Hope, December 12.*

"Major Dale, arrived at colonel Hawkins' last evening, brings the following intelligence:—*fifty or sixty British vessels had arrived at the Balize* (mouth of the Mississippi.) General Jackson had marched for New Orleans. The infantry from all quarters of his district were marching in the same direction.

"Major Blue of the 39th, with about 1500 or 1600 mounted men, Choctaws, Chicasaws and Creeks, were to march on the first inst. for Apalachicola, in pursuit of the Red Sticks and their allies. Lieutenant Carey of the U. S. Army, and his associates, 3 men and a woman and child, passing on westwardly are missing. They left fort Jackson by water. The woman and child have since been massacred in the streets of Pensacola, having only time to state that she was of this party and that the men were killed.

The Floridas. It is said that the British have negociated an exchange of Trinidad for the Floridas, with *Spain*. As Canada has been acknowledged to be held as a "rod over the back" of the "rebel colonies," we may suppose that by this transfer our enemy intends to hold two "rods" over us, that she may occasionally give our frontier people one of the pious *Sam Johnson's* "whippings," such as "roasting them alive," &c. as that "religious" thing, thought we ought to have received for our "rebellion."

Volume 7, December 31, 1814, pages 281-282

Events of the War—Military.

Copy of a letter from major-general Andrew Jackson, to the governor of Tennessee.

Head quarters, 7th military district,
Tensaw, Nov. 14, 1814.

Sir— On last evening I returned from Pensacola to this place—I reached that post on the evening of the 6th. On my approach, I sent major Pierre with a flag to communicate the object of my visit to the governor of Pensacola. He approached fort St. George, with his flag displayed, and was fired on by the cannon from the fort— he returned and made report thereof to me. I immediately went with the adjutant general and the major with a small escort, and viewed the fort and found it defended by British and Spanish troops. I immediately determined to storm the town, retired and encamped my troops for the night, and made the necessary arrangements to carry my determination into effect the next day.

On the morning of the 7th I marched with the effective regulars of the 3d, 39th, and 44th infantry, part of general Coffee's brigade, the Mississippi dragoons, and part of the West Tennessee regiment, commanded by lieutenant colonel Hammonds (colonel Lowry having deserted and gone home) and part of the Choctaws led by major Blue, of the 39th and major Kennedy of Mississippi territory. Being encamped on the west of the town I calculated they would expect the assault from that quarter, and be prepared to rake me from the fort, and the British armed vessels, seven in number, that lay in the bay. To cherish this idea I sent out part of the mounted men to show themselves on the west whilst I passed in rear of the fort undiscovered to the east of the town. When I appeared within a mile, I was in full view. My pride was never more heightened than viewing the uniform firmness of my troops, and with what undaunted courage they advanced, with a strong fort ready to assail them on the right, 7 British armed vessels on the left, strong blockhouses and batteries of cannon in their front, but they still advanced with unshaken firmness, entered the town, when a battery of two cannon was opened upon the centre column composed of the regulars, with ball and grape, and a shower of musketry from the houses and gardens. The battery was immediately stormed by captain Levall and company, and carried, and the musketry was soon silenced by the steady and well directed fire of the regulars.

The governor met colonels Williamson and Smith, who led the dismounted volunteers, with a flag, begged for mercy , and surrendered the town and fort unconditionally; mercy was granted and protection given to the citizens and their property— and still Spanish treachery kept us out of possession of the fort until 12 o'clock at night.

Never was more cool, determined bravery displayed by any troops; and the Choctaws advanced to the charge with equal bravery. On the morning of the 8th I prepared to march and storm the Barancas, but before I could move tremendous explosions told me that the Barancas, with all its appendages, was blown up. I dispatched a detachment of two hundred men to explore it, who returned in the night with the information that it was blown up, all the combustible parts burnt, the cannon spiked and dismounted, except two: this being the case I determined to withdraw my troops, but before I did I had the pleasure to see the British depart. Colonel Nicholls abandoned the fort on the night of the 6th, and betook himself to his shipping, with his friend captain Woodbine, and their red friends.

The steady firmness of my troops has drawn a just respect from our enemies.— It has convinced the Red Sticks that they have no strong hold or protection, only in the friendship of the United States— the good order and conduct of my troops whilst in Pensacola, has convinced the Spaniards of our friendship, and our prowess, and has drawn from the citizens an expression, that our Choctaws are more civilized than the British.

In great haste, I am respectfully, sir,

ANDREW JACKSON.
Maj. gen. comdg.

Events of the War—Military.

New-Orleans.—The intelligence of an enemy's fleet being off the *Balize*, as stated in our last, must have been premature. We have accounts from New Orleans to the 10th of December, at which time the enemy had not been heard of in that quarter, nor did they seem much to care how soon he came, being amply prepared to receive him. General *Jackson* arrived there about the 2d of that month with a fine body of men. He proceeded down the river a day or two afterwards to inspect the different forts and works, some of which are represented as very powerful; and we are well supplied with block ships, gun boats, rafts, &c. His whole command is estimated at 22,000 men, besides the militia of *Louisiana*—of these about 10,000 were with him on the 2d December, and the *Kentucky* and *Tennessee* boys were pushing on to join him, as were also the *Georgia* troops. The following despatch received at *Milledgeville*, by the governor of Georgia, on the 10th, gives us some information of the enemy.

Milledgeville, Dec. 21.—Yesterday a despatch was received by the governor from general M'Intosh, stating that information had been given by the indians of the arrival at the mouth of the Appalachicola in Florida of a large British fleet, having on board according to the enemy's statement, *fourteen thousand troops*, and a considerable part of them blacks. Seven of the vessels are said to be very large, the remainder of smaller size and loaded with ammunition and presents for the Indians. The British have built a strong fort at Forbe's store, and placed in it a garrison of 300 men. All the Indians have been invited to come to receive presents.— The Red Sticks and many runaway negroes have gone.

If the above news be true, the British evidently intend carrying on an active warfare against this state, and we shall not be surprised if an attempt be made to prevent a junction between our army and that under general Jackson.

The troops at fort Hawkins amounting to about 2500, struck their tents on Monday, and took up the line of march for Mobile, of which place and neighborhood general M'Intosh will have the command, general Jackson intending to remain in the vicinage of New Orleans. Of the route of the army we deem it improper to speak.

[Appalachicola bay may be about 250 miles, south in a direct line from Milledgeville, and about 300 east from the mouth of the Mississippi. The Flint river, which empties into this bay, has a navigation for small vessels or boats a considerable distance into the country inhabited by the Seminoles, the most savage indians of the south, and also the most hostile. It is possible that the "bulwark of religion" may have made his appearance here to give life and spirit to his "dear allies," the savages and negroes and, perhaps, leave a small force, with a full supply of arms and ammunition, for the purpose of murdering women and children on the inland frontiers of Georgia, while with his chief body he proceeds on his grand expedition.]

Pensacola. By a sloop that has arrived at Wilmington, N. C. with a cargo of sugar, and with several passengers from *Havana*, we learn "that great dissatisfaction with king Ferdinand existed there, and that though at first the capture of Pensacola by general Jackson had given a shock in that place which occasioned the stopping of American vessels—yet as soon as they received accounts of the manner in which Pensacola was restored, all difficulties ceased, the vessels were liberated and the Americans treated with great respect."

[*Jackson's* conduct at Pensacola will be approved, we trust, by all men, except the jacobins of his own country, who would convert a *Gabriel* into a *Belzebub*, if he opposed the white, red and black allied savages.]

The British, before they left *Pensacola* committed every excess—"pillage, ravage, destruction and fire marked their progress;" and to cap the whole, they carried off 100 *negroes* belong to their "dear friends" the Spaniards! Letters from thence are filled with eulogiums on the conduct of *Jackson*; they call him the "liberator of Pensacola"—and well might the people of that place declare, that "our *Choctaws* were more civilized than the (*religious*) *English!*"

Events of the War—Miscellaneous.

Fort Bowyer.—The following account of the British disaster at Fort Bowyer, is copied from a Barbadoes paper of Nov. 21— "His majesty's ship Hermes, W. H. Percy, with a gun-brig and four smaller vessels, have recently made an unsuccessful attack upon fort Bowyer, at Mobile, on the gulf of Mexico, east from New Orleans. The Hermes anchored opposite the fort and opened a cannonade, which was returned by the fort, and continued with much activity for several hours, until at length, the cables of the Hermes were shot away, and she drifted in a disabled state, stern on shore, about 700 yards below the fort, and a short time afterwards blew up—and out of 170 on board at the commencement of the contest, captain Percy, with 20 of his crew, only escaped the explosion. The brig and the other four vessels after the disaster, of their commodore, made sail and went out into the gulf with a light breeze. Reinforcements were expected, and the attack was to be renewed.

Events of the War—Miscellaneous.

St. Augustine.—It is stated in a way that, we think, may be fully relied on, that colonel *Woodbine* was at *St. Augustine* early in December last, where he was actually raising a military force, enlisting all red, black and white persons that chose to come forward to the *red cross* of British *humanity*. On the 3d December he is said to have had between 400 and 500 men. Is this the *neutrality* of the Spaniards?

—»»➤ ☉ Ⓞ ☉◄««—

British Activities at Point Petre and St. Mary's

FROM ST. MARY'S, &c.
*From the Savannah Republican
of January* 17.

The following is a copy of a letter from captain Massias to brigadier general Floyd, received last Sunday afternoon by express.

King's Bay,
11th *Jan.*—12 *o'clock.*

Sir—I deem it expedient to apprise you by express, the enemy effected a landing this moment on Cumberland, in two divisions, with nineteen barges. Assisted by two look out boats, and flanked by two gun barges, at first they shewed a disposition towards the bay; but ascertaining we were prepared to receive them, they altered their course and took the Plumb Orchard passage, keeping Cumberland close ahead. The first division effected its landing at Dungenness—the second at the Plumb Orchard.

The officer left in charge of our battery was ordered not to let them approach our side with impunity; which he promptly obeyed.

One of the barges was sent out of line in chase of a boat making a retreat to St. Mary's, but on receiving a shot from an eighteen which came rather near him, he gave up the chase.

3 o'clock, P. M.—(11*th January*.)

Sixteen barges of the largest size, have passed towards Dungeness, and have landed.

I compute his whole force to be about fifteen hundred, *white and black*, their fleet are beating off St. Andrews', at which end they came in.

It was my intention to receive them at Cabin Bluff with riflemen; this could have been done with much advantage, but they were apprized of it, and kept the Plumb Orchard creek.

We are now at the Point, and on the alert, waiting an attack, which I expect momently; in which event I shall do my best.

In the event of a retreat, the assistant deputy quarter-master general has been charged to place a supply of provisions and ammunition at a point selected by myself in our rear.

The men have always two days provisions in advance, ready to march to any point at a moment's warning.

I have the pleasure to anticipate the best of conduct in the officers and men under me: though few, they are well chosen, and discover great eagerness for battle: they behaved well the day we prepared to receive the enemy.

———

Extract of a letter from lieutenant colonel Scott, to the same, (by express) dated

St. Mary's,
12th January, 1815.

Sir—Your orders of the 5th inst. reached me, at this place, whither I had repaired on the first information of a serious attack being intended by the enemy, on the frontiers as well as by sea, having previously issued orders for detachments from the companies within my regiment to march to this place. These detachments have partially arrived, but from the alarms existing on the frontier, I fear much delay will arise before the entire number will arrive at this point.

The alarm guns from the garrison were fired the evening before last, and information soon after reached me of the enemy having entered and anchored in St. Andrews'. Yesterday morning seven large boats advanced up the river, and at 11 o'clock effected a landing at Dungenness, in full view of the garrison at Point Petre; and at 4 P. M. were joined by fifteen barges more. The enemy immediately formed their encampment and pitched their tents. Last night their fires were distinctly seen from this side.

The hostile attitude of the enemy leaves no doubt of an attack being meditated on the garrison and this place.

The alarm in this quarter is great beyond description, in consequence of the very large force of the enemy and the very defenceless state of this place.

Unless reinforcements are forwarded, this country is lost. Agreeably to your orders, I have issued mine to lieutenant colonel Pray, requiring reinforcements from his regiment.

I have the honor to be, sir, your obedient servant.

WM. SCOTT, lieut. col.

P. S. The enemy's force is estimated at 1000.

Volume 7, February 4, 1815, pages 362-364

Events of the War—Miscellaneous.

The Enemy in Possession of
Point Petre and St. Mary's.

Copy of a letter from captain Massias to brigadier general John Floyd, dated

Sweet water Branch,
13th January, 1815.

Sir—The enemy moved against Point Petre this morning at half past seven o'clock, with his whole force, (about fifteen hundred.). His operations were simultaneous. I received information of his approach on my picket, near major Johnson's, with about 800 to a 1000 men and two pieces of artillery; aware of his intentions to place himself in my rear, while he at the same time was advancing in considerable force in front to attack the battery on the St. Mary's, with view to cut off my retreat I made the following disposition of my small but brave force. I ordered captain Stallings to remain at the Point, with about thirty-six effectives, with orders to defend it as long as possible, and if he should be overpowered, to spike the guns, fire the train at the magazine, and retreat to me with the remainder, (about 60 riflemen and infantry.)

I moved against the enemy in the rear, determined to oppose his passage at a narrow defile near major King's, and make good my retreat at all hazards; at about nine o'clock we came up with the defile, near major Johnson's; it is flanked by a marsh on each side, and has a complete cover for riflemen on the right and left, across which the day previous I had caused some large trees to be fallen; and we entered it on one end, the enemy did so on the other. It was my intention to gain the cross roads near major King's, but finding myself stopped, lieutenant Hall, of the 43d infantry, was ordered with a detachment of riflemen, to advance on the enemy's left, and lieutenant Harllee with another detachment, to pass the thicket and endeavored to gain his rear—this order was promptly obeyed. Captain Tatnall, of the 43d infantry, was ordered at the same time to advance in close column and pass the defile; at this moment their bugle sounded, and a brisk fire commenced on both sides. We had already passed some distance, and the enemy had given way twice, when captain Tatnall, who stood near me, received a severe wound which obliged him to fall back. This produced a momentary pause, when the enemy pressed forward, but was received with unequalled firmness. It was at this moment I received unexampled support from serjeant Benson of the 43d infantry, and private Green of the rifle; but our efforts were unavailing, their numbers were too imposing—a thousand to sixty was too much odds; and believing the battery in the hands of the enemy, as but three guns had been fired, it was with reluctance that I ordered a retreat, which I am happy to state was effected in good order. We took a path to Mrs. Gordon's on the North river, at which place I had previously engaged a large boat, in the event of not being able to pass by the bridge near major King's; but the boat was taken away. I had but one resource left, and that was to pass at Miller's Bluff with a paddling canoe. I then sent an order to captain Stallings to retreat by that way, which he promptly obeyed, the enemy followed him close in his rear, and I have the pleasure to state we affected it without the loss of a man. While I lament the necessity of informing you of the loss of the fort at Point Petre, I console myself with a consciousness of having done my best for its preservation, and of being peculiarly fortunate in making good a retreat, always doubtful, and by none believed practicable by myself. The enemy's loss must have been considerable; the defile was covered with blood. An officer of distinction, wearing a pair of gold epaulets, was among the slain—our loss was very inconsiderable, as will appear by the report annexed to this; I have reason to hope that some of those missing will yet join.

I should not do justice to the gentlemen I had the honor to command, did I not say they performed prodigies beyond all reasonable expectation. All were equally brave; but if I may be allowed to discriminate, and to recommend any to your particular attention, it would be captain E. F. Tatnall, 43d infantry; he was conspicuous in every act, and gave me the utmost support.

I cannot but consider my little band highly complimented by the number the enemy thought fit to bring against them.

Very respectfully, your obedient servant,

A. A. MASSIAS,
Capt. C 1st rifle corps U. S.

Return of killed, wounded, prisoners and missing in the action on the 18th January, near Point Petre, (Geo.)

43d infantry—killed none, wounded 1 captain, severely; do. 1 private do.; missing, 4 privates.—Total 6.

Rifle corps—killed, 1 private; wounded, 1 sergeant, prisoner, do. One private, severely; missing, 5 privates—grand total 14.

A. A. MASSIAS,
captain
com. 1st rifle corps U. S. troops.

———

Copy of a letter from
lieutenant colonel Scott
to brigadier general Floyd, dated

"Jefferson,
14th Jan. 1815.

"Dear Sir—Yesterday, the enemy advanced in two divisions against Point Petre, which they carried by storming it. One division landed at major Johnston's, and marched on the rear of the fort—a number of barges made the attack in front. At this time, I was in the town of St. Mary's; the moment I received information of the enemy landing, I assembled the militia (which amounted to ninety men) and marched for King's bay. When I had advanced two miles from St. Mary's, I heard a heavy firing commence in the road leading from King's bay to Point Petre, which convinced me that

131

the enemy had attacked the Point in the rear. I marched out quick step to make an attack on *their* rear. I soon found the firing ceased, which gave me to believe the party of reserve had surrendered—my hope then was to meet a party of reserve to guard their barges. I ordered a few horsemen to reconnoitre their landing. They reported, that their barges were all gone except two, which were adrift. I immediately fell back on St. Mary's; when I got within a mile of the town, I was informed that the enemy were advancing against the town of St. Mary's. I halted my men about a mile from St. Mary's—as I was informed some of the barges were in the North river. I proceeded to town myself. When I arrived, I discovered their barges had got as far as major Moor's causeway, and that major Clark and Mr. Sadler had been appointed by the inhabitants to carry a flag to the enemy to capitulate. The inhabitants appeared much alarmed lest I should make some defence. After getting some refreshments for my detachment, I returned with them. A few minutes after I arrived, a messenger was sent from town, to inform me that a British officer had just landed with a flag, offering the town honorable terms, if they surrendered; and, in case a single gun was fired, the town should be laid in ashes. Knowing my force not sufficient to defend the town, I thought it proper to retire. I had not retired far before I fell in with captain Massias, with the greater part of his command. They retreated by the way of captain Miller's—we are now encamped at Jefferson.

I never experienced so much alarm: The inhabitants are flying in all directions. If we do not get reinforced, there will be scarce a family left in the country: The inhabitants dread colonel Woodbine and his indians, more than the British. Provisions are hard to be got. I shall do every thing in my power to protect the frontier of this part of the county. I have but eighty five men with me. The men, women, and children are all running away. I hope you will contrive some way to reinforce us. I shall never desert this part of the county, while I can raise a man.

While writing a Mr. Brown made his escape from St. Mary's—he informs me, that the enemy are collecting all the horses and saddles about that place. From the best information we could obtain, it appears they intend marching by land to Savannah. I shall endeavor to check their march as much as possible, at every advantageous post. I have not been able to ascertain their numbers. There is still a large force on Cumberland, at Point Petre, and in the town of St. Mary's.

I have the honor to be, your's sincerely,

WILLIAM SCOTT,
lieut. col. com. detachment."

Volume 7, February 4, 1815, pages 363-364

Events of the War—Miscellaneous.

Extract of a letter from lieutenant-colonel Scott to brigadier-general Floyd, dated

Brown's Ferry,
January 18, 1815.

"Sir—I had the honor to receive your's of the 13th inst. by the express, in which you request me to send in my report, which is annexed to this letter. This morning a gentleman arrived here from St. Mary's, who informed me that admiral *Cockburn* had landed in town with an additional force, number unknown. I have since been told that a number of ***** troops had been land since the arrival of the admiral from on board of a bomb brig. The enemy are taking possession of all provisions they can find, and putting them on board their vessels, and are taking in water—they are likewise mounting guns on carriages and training horses, for what purpose I leave you to judge—they have not as yet attempted any fortifications in the town; on the contrary, they have reduced fort Physic; and, it is my opinion, that they will not march by land. I should have wished very much to have made a stand at Crooked River bridge; but captain Massias would not co-operate with me, which was the cause of my falling back to this place yesterday. I have been informed by one of the patriots of Florida that their spies had discovered two indians on the south side of St. Mary's, near Underwood's mills; the indians seeing them, retreated, and were followed until an encampment was discovered with a considerable smoke at different places, when they thought prudent to retire. I have 4 trusty spies out to give me immediate notice of any approaching danger. The distress of the families of this country is beyond description."

Our further advices from the south to the 22d ult. at *Savannah*, at eight o'clock in the evening give us the following facts and reports. A report (on the 19th January) prevailed that colonel Woodbine was coming on in the rear, at the head of 600 indians, and that the settlements on the St. Mary's and Satilla rivers were breaking up in consequence. On the 21st it appeared ascertained that the enemy's force was about 2000 men, part blacks—and it was also stated that the ruffian *Cockburn* had arrived with a reinforcement—and that at St. Mary's they had plundered every body of every thing. [Note: This we should have presumed from the presence of *Cockburn*.] Major-general Pinkney was expected at Savannah about the 23rd. The following articles from the Savannah paper of the 22d is the latest advices we have—and cause us to hope, that, by *stealing* except, no great damage may be done.

Savannah, January 22.—"Here we are, under martial law; not knowing the hour when the British forces may pay us a visit. We have no positive accounts from the southward, however, to warrant a positive conclusion, that they are coming this way. We believe the forces at Cumberland and St. Mary's to be about 6000 men."

Another extract
—same date.

"Martial law was declared to-day. Governor Early has arrived at the lines with 2,000 men. Strong reinforcements are on their way. Our fortifications progress rapidly, and are able to present to sustain and repel the attack of all the British forces said to have arrived."

Another extract
—same date.

"I have only time to say, we are under martial law—the enemy daily expected. Should they have the temerity to approach, I trust we shall give a good account of them—at least, they will not get the place, without a struggle; and that a pretty hard one."

Latest Extract—8 P. M.
"We are in hourly expectation of the arrival of major-general Pinkney, who, we are informed, has ordered on 1500 of the South-Carolina militia: among whom are your country sharp-shooters, who can pick out a squirrel's eye at the distance of one hundred yards. They will match and beat Woodbine's motley crew, even if they have half of the number. A number of your disciplined officers are expected to start from Charleston for this place on the 24th instant."

Volume 7, February 4, 1815, page 364

Events of the War—Military.

It appears by despatches received at Milledgeville, (Georgia) that boats are about to be built to descend the Alabama, to transport general M'Intosh's forces to Mobile, upon which an attack was apprehended. It is probable he will reach the place in time to defend it if the enemy at *New-Orleans* does not get "enough" of the notion of "restoring" the country and makes the attack. Colonel *Hawkins* is at the head of 700 friendly indians to restrain the "Red Sticks" and avenge their murders. He was to leave fort *Mitchell* on an expedition, on the 10th ult.

Volume 7, February 4, 1815, page 368

Events of the War.

We have advices from Savannah to the 24th. It was expected they would evacuate St. Mary's on the 20th, having got all the plunder on board. They are said to have received a good many "allies" there. The barbarians have not *disgraced* themselves—this is impossible—they have only added fresh causes for us to *hate* and *detest* them.

Volume 7, February 11, 1815, page 382

Events of the War—Military.

Savannah, Jan. 28. An official despatch reached town this morning to general Floyd, which states that the enemy evacuated St. Mary's and Point Petre on Tuesday last, after burning the barracks and blowing up the fort at the latter place; and that there is no doubt Savannah is ultimately their object.

A private letter to a gentleman in

this place, from Amelia, states that the enemy evacuated St. Mary's on Tuesday last, after plundering every thing they could lay their hands on—that they intended occupying Cumberland island as their head-quarters—that the incendiary Cockburn commands them—and that they say Savannah is the only place worth holding or taking care of. The writer adds he is assured the impression that the enemy will pay our city a visit is not confined to the ignorant and unthinking. Be vigilant, be watchful.

We will merely observe that for the last four or five days, hundreds of our up country brethren have arrived in this place to aid in its defence. Our city is now garrisoned with numerous troops—our works are completing with spirit and our means increasing daily, which will enable us to defend our rights, and fire sides, our holy sanctuaries, and all that is dear to us.

Major general Pinckney and suite reached our city yesterday morning.

Note: The amount of the enemy's force on the southern coast, appears to have been greatly exaggerated. Major-general Pinckney discharged, on the 29th ult. the whole of the militia this afternoon, by a general order on parade. A draft is to take place of 200 men from the militia of the city, and of 200 more of the country militia in camp—all the rest to go home. This looks well.

Volume 7, February 25, 1815, page 402

Extract from the President's Message.

Washington,
February 18, 1815.

To the senate and House of
representatives of the United States.

I lay before the congress copies of the treaty of peace and amity between the United States and his Britannic majesty, which was signed by the commissioners of both parties at Ghent, on the 24th of December, 1814, and the ratifications of which have been duly exchanged.

While performing this act, I congratulate you, and our constituents, upon an event which is highly honorable to the nation, and terminates with peculiar felicity a campaign signalised by the most brilliant successes.

—»»᛭e⊛e«««—

News of the Treaty at Ghent Reaches the East Coast

Volume 7, February 25, 1815, page 409

Events of the War—Miscellaneous.

Peace.—The news of peace has been received every where with demonstrations of joy. The people felt that their country had triumphed, and were assured, before they knew the terms of the treaty, that our envoys at *Ghent* were not the kind of men to put their hand to a dishonorable instrument.—Most of our cities have been, or about to be, illuminated for the restoration of a blessing which we gave up for a season, I trust, to *secure* its enjoyment. The intelligence has generally been communicated to the British vessels on our coast, and some of them seem already to have left it.

The news of peace was received at Savannah from the British squadron off Amelia Island, on the 11th inst. and at Charleston on the 13th. So that the object of those eastern merchants who despatched expresses with a view to speculations in produce at those places is completely defeated.

Volume 7, February 25, 1815, page 411

Events of the War—Miscellaneous.

Fort Mims. A gentleman belonging to the forces of the United States in the Creek country, thus vents his honest indignation at the allied white and red savages—"We look every day for orders to march and meet the enemy. I am heartily willing as one to spend my last gasp for my country. The ruins of fort Mims, two miles from here, through which I have rode with generals Winchester, Taylor, and other officers, are enough to "harrow up the soul." *The piles of human bones, from aged decrepitude to the infant at the breast, bleached by the rains and winds of Heaven, must arouse a holy rage in every manly bosom.* I expect to see the *hell hounds* of England and their cursed allies in a few days. May the God of Heaven inspire me with an Ajax prayer, or that of Macduff to the manes of a Duncan against Macbeth."

Volume 7, February 25, 1815, page 411

Events of the War—Military.

Extract of a letter from an officer in general M'Intosh's army dated,

"West of Chatahoochie, 8th Jan. 1815.

"The Tom Bigbie is ordered to be navigated, to convey provisions to New Orleans, as bread stuff will be scarce if the communication should be cut off. We have a battalion and all the artificers we could collect building boats at the Tallipoosa, to convey a detachment with two months provisions to Mobile. I hope they will be ready in a few days to receive us. Every nerve is strained to press on our movements. There is no doubt of the British being in the act of taking possession of the Floridas and are establishing posts at the fork of the Chatahuchie and Flint rivers, and at Appalachicola at Forbes' store."

Volume 7, February 25, 1815, page 412

Events of the War.

The Spaniards. By the following letter the reader will find that governor Kendelan has refused peremptorily to allow the British the privilege of landing in East Florida or of carrying on offensive operations in that territory against the frontier of the state of Georgia, and that the Spanish government determine to adhere to the strictest neutrality.

"As soon as you communicated verbally to me the object of your coming to this place, I had the honor of informing you, in the same mode, that I had the strictest orders from my government to observe the most rigid neutrality, and under this supposition, I could not permit you to communicate with the British vessels that might present themselves off this bar; that I would facilitate your going to Providence, and, finally, that you would be pleased to discharge your escort of colored people, who, under the erroneous impression of this province being invaded, you had brought with you

from the Seminoles, for the purpose of guarding you on your route to this place; all which I now repeat to you officially for your information and government, to which I add, by the treaty of peace, made in the year 1783, the two Floridas were ceded by treaty to Spain by Great Britain, with all the rights of sovereignty over the soil which it possessed; and by the treaty of St. Ildefonzo, may with the United States of America, in the year 1785, the northern limits of said province were defined; these are a line beginning on the east bank of the Mississippi, at 31 degrees of latitude, which from said point proceeds to river Chatahoche, and from the fork of this and Flint river by a right line down to the head of St. Mary's, state of Georgia; therefore all the Indians inhabiting the country south of this line, are under the dominion and protection of the Spanish nation, and that part of them living to the eastward of the river Appalacha, are within the limits of the eastern province, under my command. I must therefore distinctly state to you, that I shall consider any landing of English troops within these limits, or any enterprize coming to this province, with any hostile intentions against the United States, as an aggression on the part of Great Britain, and under this impression, shall act in conformity with my duty. On this occasion I have the honor of offering my respects, and request you will have the goodness to inform me of your intentions. God preserve you may years.

I am, &c. Your most obedient,

SEBASTIAN KENDELAN.

To George Woodbine."

NILES' WEEKLY REGISTER.

THE PAST—THE PRESENT—FOR THE FUTURE.

EDITED, PRINTED AND PUBLISHED BY H. NILES, AT $5 PER ANNUM, PAYABLE IN ADVANCE.

Volume 8

(March 4, 1815 - August 26, 1815)

Volume 8, March 11, 1815, page 29

War Events—Military.

Savannah,
January 29th, 1815.

The enemy have evacuated St. Mary's and withdrawn to Cumberland island, after destroying the fort at Point Petre and blowing up the magazine.

Previous to their leaving St. Mary's, they primed the houses with tar, ready to fire them if molested in their retreat.

I regret to inform you, that the new barge Scorpion has fallen into their hands with her equipments, a correct return of which shall be forwarded for your information.

Volume 8, March 11, 1815, page 32

Postscript
National Intelligencer of March 13

Highly Interesting.

To the Editors.—*Fort Stoddart*, Feb. 11. I have only a moment to write, and should not write at all, but that times are become very critical here.

The British seem determined not to leave the Gulf of Mexico, without doing something. Captain Percy, who commanded at the former attack on Mobile Point, was lately at the pass of Christiana, as I am told. He there observed, that they had been deceived in their first attack on fort Bowyer, but that they had now made such arrangements as would humble the Americans.

On Tuesday, 25 vessels anchored off Mobile Point, at the distance of 5 or 6 miles. Two or three appeared to be frigates. The greater part were brigs of war, as was supposed. There were also some large vessels, supposed to be transports. On Wednesday, nine transports were perceived to be landing their troops between the Point and Perdido. The fleet then amounted to 30. A schooner and seven barges entered the bay—the former by way of pass Horn, between Dauphine island and the shore west of the bay. Fort Bowyer at the point, is on the narrow neck of land which stretches out on the east side of the bay, and commands the only channel for large vessels. Some British troops have landed on Dauphine island. On Thursday a heavy firing commenced, it continued a great part of that day, and the day following; and some guns were heard this morning.

We have about 400 men in fort Bowyer, but provisions are extremely scarce there, as well as through the whole of the Mobile country. Our troops in the fort have but about ten days supply. Some was sent down on Wednesday or Thursday, but it is feared it must have fallen into the enemy's hands. I fear our whole army and our whole population will suffer severely. The result on the Point is differently anticipated. I am told, the alarm at Mobile is not so great as it has been on many less occasions.

I confess I have my fears, though, as I never was at fort Bowyer, I cannot judge satisfactorily. The faithful and vigilant collector of Mobile has come up with his books and papers, and other public records.

I am, gentlemen, yours, &c.

P. S. I enclose a letter received this moment, from colonel S. Smith, formerly a senator from Ohio.

*Mobile,
February 10, at night,
half past seven.*

My dear friend—Our little town is in arms, and 1200 militia and indians are under orders to embark with the first fair wind, to assist in the defence of the Point, which is attacked, and has been closely invested, with the most tremendous cannonade for 54 hours. Our ears are stunned with the report of an unceasing fire. The wind is ahead—our force cannot get there in time—the general says I must remain with him. I did want to go with Blue, so says passion—judgment says we are too late. All our town is in bustle—I write this in haste, and with the candle in one hand.

Yours, whether in life or death. Adieu,

JOHN SMITH.

Volume 8, March 11, 1815, page 32

Reported Battle.

Savannah, March 2. We have seen several gentlemen who arrived in town last evening from St. Mary's, and are informed by them that it was asserted there, that on Thursday last a squadron of British barges from Cumberland, containing about 300 seamen and marines, had gone up the St. Mary's river for the purpose of burning Clark's mills—that within a mile of the mills the enemy were met on the banks of the river by 18 or 20 patriots, and as many militia from colonel Scott's camp, who engaged the barges, drove them back, and are said to have killed and wounded upwards of *one hundred* of the enemy. The inhabitants of St. Mary's were much alarmed, fearing that the British would, in consequence of their defeat, burn the town. The commander of the squadron is said to have been killed—on the American side none killed or wounded.

[Letters received in this city yesterday from the southward, confirm the above, and add, that captain Jackson, of the *Lacedemonion* is supposed to be among the killed.]—*Charleston Gazette.*

Volume 8, March 18, 1815, page 42

Military.

Copy of a letter from brigadier general James Winchester to the secretary of war, dated

Mobile, 13th February, 1815.

Sir—On the 8th instant fort Bowyer, on Mobile Point, was invested by the forces of the enemy by land and water.

The roaring of cannon commenced early in the morning, and continued, with short intervals, day and night, until the 11th, when the firing ceased until this morning, or was not heard, owing to a strong N. W. wind. At 9 o'clock this morning, the weather calm, a tremendous firing of artillery was again heard, and continued about one hour, then ceased, or could not be heard on account of the wind. I am uninformed as to the strength of the enemy, but it must be considerable. Near, or quite, 100 sail of vessels, of all sizes, were laying off Dolphin Island within sight of the fort. On this island the enemy has landed a large force, as well as on Mobile Point. I have thrown a detachment across the bay in order to effect a diversion of his forces. I know not the result yet, but have sanguine expectations I shall succeed. The garrison of fort Bowyer is composed of sterling materials, and will only be conquered by an overwhelming force.

Major general M'Intosh has not yet arrived, but is expected in a few days; so is the enemy, for he can penetrate the Pass Heron with small vessels and boats and leave the fort in his rear. I am prepared for him. The troops I have the honor to command are in fine spirits, and full of military ardor.

I have the honor to be, with great respect, sir, your most obedient,

J. WINCHESTER, *Brig. Gen. Com. E Sec. 7th Mil. Dis.*

The honorable secretary of war.

———

The above is the latest information (says the National Intelligencer of Thursday last) we have from the Mobile, and was received last Saturday. We shall not hear from that quarter again probably for several days. The rumor published yesterday, as extracted from a private letter from Savannah,* there is some reason for fear may be true, as the fact of fort Bowyer (not, we think, Mobile) being taken, though it cannot have been taken, as is stated, by surprize; but, if taken, most likely by storm. The overwhelming naval force of the pseudo enemy at that point justifies us in the fears we entertain on the subject. The news of the peace probably reached Mobile about the 1st instant, and not before.

[*Note: Savannah, March 5.—"I have advice from Amelia this evening, of Mobile being taken by the British by surprize. British officers reported at Amelia the arrival of an English frigate at Cumberland from Mobile, with the intelligence. Admiral Cochrane was expected daily with his fleet and troops at Cumberland.]

Volume 8, March 18, 1815, pages 46-47

Major-General Jackson.
From the Richmond Enquirer.

Some notice of the life and character of general Jackson will be desirable at this time to the readers of your columns.—The distinguished post he at present occupies, the honorable manner in which he has brought the Creek war to a termination, the unexampled enthusiasm which he has instilled into his army in defence of the nation—and the confidence which he has every where obtained, through this vast country, has excited much curiosity on the part of the public, to become more intimately acquainted with him. The writer of the Crisis will gratify as far as in his power this anxiety for information concerning a man whose life will constitute, and has constituted already, an important epoch, in the history of our country. General Andrew Jackson was, as I am told, born in North Carolina, where he received a liberal education, and at an early age commenced the practice of the law. He was esteemed eminent in his profession.—His speeches at the bar were always considered nervous and admired for the perspicuity of the style; he was pointed out to me, in Knoxville, as an elegant scholar. In early life he was poor, his industry soon made him rich— generous and brave in his disposition, he was esteemed by all who knew him—and his influence soon became extensive; he was elected a member of the Tennessee convention, and had a large share in the formation of the constitution of that state. On the admission of Tennessee into the union as a sister state, he was elected to the house of representatives, from which he was subsequently transferred by the legislature of Tennessee to the senate of the United States. This last station he occupied until he was appointed a judge of the supreme court of law and equity of Tennessee, which last named office he held for several years. On giving up this appointment which he filled with honor to himself and advantage to his country— he turned his attention to the military art and soon rose to the rank of major- general of militia.—In the capacity of an officer at the head of an army, comment is unnecessary he has appeared and yet appears covered with glory—the laurels with which he has decked his country's standard will bloom for ages. His person remains to be noticed. He is tall, thin and spare, but muscular and hardy, with an eye quick and penetrating.—I have frequently seen general Jackson, such was the impression his appearance made in my mind, that I have said to myself he is a man of iron.—Adversity can make no impression on a bosom braced by such decision and firmness as is visible in his face and manners. Let not the reader conclude from this that he is haughty, distant and imperious—quite the contrary. It is true he sports not with the feelings of others—and no one is permitted to wound his with impunity; but then he is gay, communicative and liberal, and the more you know him, the more you admire and indeed love him. To be a patriot, a soldier and a gentleman, is sufficient to secure the inviolable friendship of this highly distinguished citizen. To the poor he is liberal, to the unfortunate charitable, to the humblest private he is mild and tender, to the base and disaffected to his country stern and unbending and yet just. He is now about fifty-five, but he has a juvenility of appearance that would make him ten years younger. The general is married, but has no children. If in the field and at the head of armies in battles we admire the dauntless soldier; we love the man who at home, and in retirement, is hospitable and friendly, and in this particular the general is pre-eminently conspicuous.

Author of the Crisis.

General Coffee is a native of Nottoway county, Virginia.

Volume 8, March 18, 1815, page 48

Charleston, March 6.—The United States schooner Alligator, sailing master Ashbridge, arrived here on Saturday evening, in three days from Cumberland Island, where she had been with a despatch from major-general Pinckney, announcing to admiral Cockburn the cessation of hostilities.

Admiral Cockburn had received no despatches direct from his government on the subject of peace, and intimated that he should retain his position on Cumberland, until he received official advices of the ratification of the treaty.

By this arrival we have a confirmation of the news from Savannah, of the British having been defeated in a predatory expedition up the river St. Mary's. They acknowledge a loss of about 90 in killed and wounded. One midshipman died of his wounds, and was buried on Wednesday last on Cumberland. The captain of a bomb ship, and the captain of the Primrose brig, were both badly wounded.

Volume 8, March 25, 1815, page 56

The Floridas. A Charleston paper of the 13th instant says—The British troops remained upon Cumberland island, and admiral Cockburn was waiting the arrival of admiral Cochrane, who was daily expected. The Floridas had been actually ceded to Great Britain by Ferdinand VII, but the governor general of Cuba, had refused to deliver them up unless the cortes should also agree to the cession. On admiral Cochrane's arrival it was supposed the British would determine whether to wait further orders on the subject of the Floridas, or take forcible possession of them.

Volume 8, March 25, 1815, page 56

Military.

Surrender of Fort Bowyer.

Copy of a letter from major general Jackson, to the secretary of war, dated

Head-quarters, 7th military district, New Orleans, 24th Feb. 1815.

Sir—The flag vessel, which I sent to the enemy's fleet, returned a few days ago, bringing a letter of assurance from admiral Cochrane, that the American prisoners, taken in the gun-boats, and sent to the Havanna, shall be returned as soon as practicable. The Nymph has been dispatched for them.

Through the same channel, I received the sad intelligence of the surrender of fort Bowyer. I enclose you a copy of colonel Lawrence's letter, and of the articles of capitulation. In consequence of this unfortunate affair, an addition of three hundred and sixty six, has been made to the list of American prisoners. To redeem them and the seamen, I have in conformity with propositions held out by admiral Cochrane, forwarded to the mouth of the Mississippi upwards of 400 British prisoners. Others will be sent to complete the exchange, as soon as they arrive from Natchez, to which place I had found it expedient to order them.

I received a letter from general Winchester, dated on the 16th, stating that major Blue, whom he had ordered to the relief of fort Bowyer, succeeded in carrying one of the enemy's picquets, consisting of 17, but was too late to effect the whole purpose for which he had been detached—the fort having capitulated 24 hours before his arrival.

I learn from the bearer of my late dispatches to the enemy's fleet, who was detained during the operations against fort Bowyer, that his loss on that occasion, by the fire from the garrison, was between twenty and forty.

I have the honor to be, with great respect, your obedient servant,

ANDREW JACKSON,
Major-general commanding,
HON. JAMES MONROE,
sec'y. of war.

Volume 8, April 1, 1815, page 71

The Negroes—A *London* paper has the following extract of a letter from the *Chesapeake*—"The blacks who deserted to us from the Americans, have been drilled at Tangier Island, in this *river*, and formed into a third battalion of marines, and are about to be embarked in the Regulus troop-ship, to assist our expedition in the Floridas, which is destined to act against Louisiana. Major Lewis, royal marines, is to have the command of them, with the temporary rank of lieutenant-colonel, and captain Clements is to be the major. They are a fine body of men, are very tractable, and in all cases where they have been tried, have displayed much bravery."

—·»»)☉◉☉«««·—

Intercepted Documents Show British Involvement

Volume 8, April 8, 1815, pages 101-103

War Events: Or, Things
Incidental to the Late War.

Intercepted Letters.—
From the *Baltimore Patriot.*

[These letters were found on board
the St. Lawrence, at the time of her
surrender to the Chasseur privateer.]

Messrs. Editors, I hand you for
publication extracts from several letters,*
written by British officers on our southern
coast, to their friends employed in the
late expedition against New-Orleans. If
any further testimonials were necessary,
in addition to those which the late war
exhibited, of the lust of plunder which
has so pre-eminently marked the British
officers, these extracts affords them. It
is by no means my intention to condemn
the acquisition by an enemy of such
property, as, in the prosecution of *an
honorable warfare*, the usage of nations
assigns to him; or that he may not
receive, in his march to great deeds, an
impulse from the sentiment, that these
deeds are to be rewarded by the wealth
they acquire; but I mean to express
the strongest indignation against that
predatory system, which has been pursued
by our late enemy, and which inevitably
involved a violation of all those feelings
a magnanimous enemy will always hold
sacred. Impelled by the principle which
these extracts exhibit, we see, in the
train of all their invasions, plunderings,
burnings, rapes, massacres, ransackings
and other equally atrocious enormities,
such as have not been practised since the
days of Gothic barbarity. Perhaps, it may
be said, a peace having now occurred
between us, we ought to throw a veil over
their enormities, and seduously endeavor
to strengthen the bands of amity, by
the kindest offices of charity and good
correspondence. If the British officers
were of that refined and exalted character
which disdains to be behind hand in the
race of good deeds, none would yield
more cheerfully to this sentiment than
myself; but, since the magnanimous
examples furnished by our officers,
during the late war, have, in no degree,
improved their morals, it is due to justice,
to hold them up to the indignation and
contempt of the world.

A READER.

———

*From colonel Malcolm
to rear admiral Malcolm*

Cumberland Island,
5th February, 1815.

"I received you letter of the 5th ult.;
it is written before your last attack on the
place, but I most sincerely hope you will
ultimately succeed. From all accounts
New Orleans is very strong—the enemy
will have gained a great confidence in
themselves from their success. What
a disappointment it will be in England
should you fail—the chance of failure
has not been calculated on, and from the
force employed, it has been made too sure
at first. I have no opinion of either the
Indians or *black new raised corps*; the
former in this country carry on a most
furious war; murder and desolation mark
their track—there is no hope but flying,
or resistance to the last moment of life;
this is what every one says of the Florida
Indians; of course the inhabitants of all
descriptions would fear to come near
you. There is a report here that neither
the 21st or 44th regiments behaved well,
but a report I treat it. I should be sorry to
hear two British regiments slurred in an
attack."

[Note: In this letter of the colonel's
there was a lamentation expressed that his
share of the prize-money, at St. Mary's,
did not exceed *five hundred pounds!*]

———

*From colonel Malcolm
to rear admiral Malcolm,*

Cumberland Island,
11th February, 1815.

"I hope we may hear from you in a
short time, and of your success against
the place you are now before (New-
Orleans)—*It will repay the troops for
all their trouble and fatigues!* I do not
expect, either war or peace, that we will
move from this island this winter; if the

141

war goes on a garrison must be left here in charge of the island."

———

From sir Thomas Cochrane,
of the Surprize frigate,
to captain Pigot,
off New-Orleans, dated

Cumberland Island,
February 12, 1815.

"I came here just two days too late to share in the good things going on. Old Somerville was senior, and ordered the attack on St. Mary's, which Barrie *executed.* The prize-money will be about thirty thousand pounds, *not more.* Had our force been sufficient, the next movement would have been against Savannah, but not mustering above a thousand bayonets, we were content to keep possession of this island, which we are placing in state of defence. Our operations will, I suppose, be shortly put a stop to by our friend *Jemmy Madison,* as peace or war now depends on him— the commissioners at Ghent having signed, and the prince regent ratified, the terms of a peace, and hostilities will cease as soon as he does the same. We hope, in the mean time, better luck will attend you at New Orleans than has hitherto done, and that you will have time to give general Jackson a trimming."

———

From Sir Thomas Cochrane
to Sir Thomas Troubridge,
off New Orleans

N. End, Cumberland Island,
February 12, 1815.

"I hope this will reach head quarters in time for the St. Lawrence, who sails immediately for your part of the world with the news of peace being concluded with his country, but of which I should think you will receive earlier intelligence direct from England. We are in daily expectation of a flag of truce to inform us of Mr. Madison's having ratified the treaty, on his doing which, hostilities will immediately cease. I confess myself by no means sorry for this event. I think we have had quite enough of war for some years to come, although should have wished we had made the Yankees more sensible of our power and ability to punish them, should they again provoke us. *As it is, except the injury done to their trade, we have but little to boast of.* We are all very much grieved to learn the disasters in your quarter. Our loss seems to have been immense; and from the reports we pick up, one is led to believe there was not much prospect of success at the commencement of the attack. We are most particularly unfortunate in our general officers on all occasions. I am afraid general Power and the regiment with him, will not be with you in time to render any service. He was at Bermuda on the 24th ult. at which period the Statira had not arrived.

I came here six weeks ago, and found St. Mary's had been taken two days before my arrival, which, of course, *cuts me out of what has been captured.* Barrie command the party landed; old Somerville was senior officer, the admiral having only arrived the day before me, in consequence of being blown off the coast by strong N. W. gales on his way from the Chesapeake. It was at first supposed, as is usual on all these occasions, that a great deal of money would be made; but if they clear *thirty thousand pounds, it will be as much as they will do.*"

———

From admiral Cockburn,
to captain Evans, dated,

Head quarters,
Cumberland island,
11th February, 1815.

"No general, however, as you now know has come here; you have had them all your way, and though I have learnt by a few hasty lines the unfortunate result of your first endeavors against New Orleans, yet excepting as far as relates to the poor generals and to the gross numbers you lost I know no particulars, not even which of my many friends amongst you are dead or alive, or which have broken bones or whole skins. I trust, however, it will prove that you are amongst the latter, and I hope you will when at leisure favor me with a detailed account of all that has passed in your neighborhood.

We have been more fortunate here *in our small way.* We have taken St. Mary's, a *tolerably rich place,* and with little loss have managed to do much damage to the enemy and we are now in tolerable security upon a large fertile island in Georgia, *though an ugly account of peace being signed (the particulars of which I have sent to sir admiral Cochrane) seems to promise a speedy dismissal to us from this coast.*"

———

From Mr. Swainson,
to lieutenant Douglass,
of H. M. Brig Sophie,

off New-Orleans,
9th Feb. 1815.

"We had some fine fun at St. Mary's; the bombs were at the town and had plenty of plunder. How are you off *for tables*, and *chests of drawers, &c.?*"

———

From J. Gallon, to J. O'Reily, esq.,
on board H. S. Ship Tonnant,
off New-Orleans,

Cumberland island,
9th Feb. 1815.

"We have had fine fun since I saw you, what with the Rappahannock and various other places, we have contrived *to pick up a few trifling things such as mahogany tables, chests of drawers, &c.*

———

From John Miller
to Mr. Thomas Miller,
75 Old Gravel Lane,
St. George's, East London.

H. M. Ship Lacedemonian,
off land,
February 12th, 1815.

"We have lately been employed with the squadron under admiral Cockburn, and have taken Cumberland Island, and the town of St. Mary's from the Yankees. Our troops and sailors, behaved very well, part of the black regiment employed on this service acted with great gallantry. Blacky had *no idea of giving quarters*; and it was with difficulty the officers prevented their putting *the prisoners to death.* The Yankee riflemen fired at our men in ambush. Blacky, on the impulse of the moment, left the ranks and pursued them into the woods, fighting like *heroes.* A poor Yankee, disarmed, begged for mercy. Blacky replied, *"he no come in bush for mercy,"* and immediately shot him dead!!"

———

From J. R. Glover to captain Westful,
of the Anaconda.

Head-quarters,
Cumberland Island,
1st February, 1815.

"We have established our head quarters here, after ransacking St. Mary's, from which we brought property to the amount of *fifty thousand pounds*, and had we two thousand troops, we might yet collect *a good harvest* before peace takes place. My forebodings will not allow me to anticipate either honor or profit to the expedition, of which you form a part, and I much fear the contrary, yet most fervently do I hope my forebodings may prove groundless. The admiral (Cockburn) is as active as ever, and success in general attends his undertakings."

———

From captain Napier
of the Euryalus frigate,
to captain Gordon,
of the Sea-Horse.
Off Cape Henry,

January 24th, 1815.

"Here I am in Lynhaven bay, the clippers sailing every day, and losing them for want of fast sailers. All our prizes are well disposed of. I have had a good deal to do with them, and not many thanks as you may suppose from the agents. I have petitioned the prince regent in behalf of the whole of us, for a good slice of prize money, and I hope to succeed. You, I suppose, will not be displeased at it. Excuse this hasty scrawl, I am in a d—d bad humor, having just returned from an unsuccessful chase."

———

The Infamous Cockburn.—From the documents and facts inserted above, it appears that this great bandit and his gang of thieves "held out to the end" in deeds of deepest rascality. He is a cowardly knave—never has he exposed himself to danger since the war. Like a great tall bully, the hero a brothel, he has blustered and swore most lustily, and sometimes *appeared* willing to fight. Would that the least of the great spirits of our navy had come athwart this Vandal with an equal force!

What will high-minded Englishmen, and the enlightened of all nations, think of the preceding statements? He should be lashed naked through the world with whips of scorpions.

Volume 8, April 8, 1815, page 104

British Impudence.

Savannah, March 23.—The United States vessel, No. 68, John Hulbert commander, left this port for St. Mary's on the 11th inst. A gentleman who was on board writes to his friend in this place from Cumberland, dated March 18, 1815—"On the evening of the 16th we fell in with his majesty's brig of war Erebus, captain Bartholomew, who ordered us to send our boat on board, or he would sink us instantly. We did not comply, and he accordingly fired into us, which damaged our sails and rigging severely. Mr. Hulbert immediately returned the fire and then struck his colors. The British commander afterwards made an apology, and permitted us to proceed. It appears he was yet smarting under the wounds he received up the St. Mary's river, in the expedition against Clark's mills. We had no one hurt on board the gun vessel, but a musket ball was evidently discharged at Mr. Hulbert, as it passed within a few inches of his breast. Although the captain of the Erebus was politely informed by us who and what we were, and that we had despatches for admiral Cockburn—he replied, that "he did not care a d—n for that; we must either send our boat on board, or be sunk." But mark the cowardly John Bull! when he found that we were not to be bullied with impunity, he sent his own boat on board, and denied that he had given orders to fire into us; and even offered, if we thought it would create a difficulty between the two governments, to accompany us to admiral Cockburn, in order to make the necessary explanation. Mr. Hulbert very indignantly informed captain Bartholomew "that he had nothing to do with him or admiral Cockburn but, that he would inform his government about the affair."

We have conversed with one of the gentlemen who was authorised by government to negociate for the negroes and other property which had been taken by the enemy during their stay on Cumberland. He informs us that admiral Cockburn would not give up a single article, except what was taken from off Cumberland island; and that was supposed to be done through courtesy—negroes, &c. that were taken from the other islands, after the treaty of peace was ratified, were not even restored. The enemy evacuated Cumberland island on the 15th inst. and have carried off with them *eight hundred* negroes, a considerable quantity of cotton, &c. stolen since their arrival within our waters. We shall perhaps in a few days be able to lay before our readers the whole correspondence, between the commissioners and admiral Cockburn; and therefore forbear further remarks; Our informant states that Cockburn contradicted the story of the Floridas having been ceded to Great Britain—that he had received no intelligence of the kind.

We are informed that the conduct of the British officers to the commissioners was very insulting and rude. We will not describe the scenes that gentlemen have told us they witnessed on board the fleet while off Cumberland Bar. Modesty forbids us.

Volume 8, April 22, 1815, page 136

There is reason to believe that the patriots of *Florida* are again in considerable force.

Volume 8, April 29, 1815, page 148

War Events—Military.

British Account of an Expedition
up the St. Mary's River

Halifax, March 29. The Americans, in a late account of an expedition up St. Mary's river, having exaggerated our loss, &c. we are happy in giving the following correct statement of the affair:

"On the 23d of February, a flotilla, consisting of seven barges, with seamen and a company of marines, (62) was sent up the river to destroy certain works—this expedition had been, as too frequently is the case, mentioned, and the Americans were apprised of it some days previous to its departure from Cumberland Island. The flotilla had proceeded upwards of 100 miles, and within three quarters of a mile of the spot intended to be attacked, when it was fired upon, from the Florida side, through thick woods, by the patriots, and a number of regular troops and riflemen. The British immediately landed, when a sharp skirmish took place, and in less than twenty minutes the enemy was dislodged—a retreat, however, was deemed necessary, and our little band of heroes had hardly re-embarked and pushed from the shore, when they were attacked by the enemy from positions covered by woods, and when not fifteen yards off, the river being extremely narrow at that place; in about an hour a fire also was opened upon them by a considerable force from the opposite shore; but though attacked upon both sides, and in a river but from 30 to 50 yards wide in most parts of it, the flotilla fought its way through. Our loss on the occasion was but twenty-nine in killed and wounded, of the latter eighteen severely.—Captain Phillott, early in the action received a buckshot above the left knee, and a flesh wound in the right thigh; captain Bartholomew was struck in five different parts of the body, but, though severely wounded, continued in the discharge of his duty; nor would he allow himself to be dressed until every individual wounded was done before him.

"The boats that suffered most were rear admiral Cockburn's from having the flag painted on her bows; and it is surprising how any person in captain Bartholomew's gig escaped, as she was marked, and in the time of the action pulling between the two tires; he giving orders, and removing the surgeon from one boat to another, where the wounded were—most of her crew had balls through their hats, the riflemen aiming at their heads.

There seldom has happened any exploit in which the personal exertions of individuals was so imperiously called for, as in the present. Seldom an occasion where seamen and marines displayed more courage, zeal and ardor for the service, and bore so much fatigue with becoming cheerfulness."

Volume 8, May 20, 1815, page 204

Extract from The Militia.

The following information accompanied the report of the secretary of war to the committee of the senate, respecting the conflicting jurisdiction of the general and state governments over the militia.

———

Defence of the Coast.

It may be said that it is not probable, that the enemy will attempt an invasion of any part of the coast described, with a view to retain it, and less so for the purpose of desolation. It is nevertheless possible, and being so, provision ought to be made against the danger. An unprotected coast may invite attacks which would not otherwise be thought of. It is believed that the arrangement proposed will be adequate, and that none can be advised, to be so, which would prove more economical.

For Savannah and East Florida, special provision must be made. Whether East Florida is left in possession of Spain, or taken immediate possession of by the United States, in either case it menaces the United States with danger to their vital interests. While it is held by Spain, it will be used as a British province, for annoying us in every mode in which it may be made instrumental to that end. The ascendancy which the British government has over the Spanish regency secures to Great Britain that advantage, while the war lasts. We find that at present, the Creek Indians are excited against us, and an asylum afforded to the slaves of the southern states who seek it there. To guard the United States against the attempts of the British government, in that vulnerable quarter, the province remaining in the hands of the Spanish authorities, a force of about 2000 regular troops will be requisite. It will require no more to hold it, should possession be taken by the United States.

The New-Orleans and Natchitoches,

including the Mobile and West Florida, about 2,500 men will be necessary. A local force may be organized in that quarter in aid of it, which it is believed will be adequate to any emergency.

Volume 8, May 20, 1815, page 215

Fort Bowyer has been duly delivered up by the British.

——»»»☌ⓒ☌«««——

British Lingering in Florida

Volume 8, June 10, 1815, pages 261-262

War Events: or Things Incidental to the Late War.

Miscellaneous.

Florida. *Milledgeville, May* 21.— The British have not evacuated Florida. Colonel Nicolls, who commands at Appalachicola, has addressed an insolent letter to the agent for Indian affairs, stating, that according to the treaty of peace *he considers the territories of the Creeks to be as they stood before the war*; and, arrogating to himself the entire control of the Indians, *warns the citizens of the United States from entering the Creek territory, or holding any communication with the inhabitants thereof.* This is evidently done with the view of deterring the commissioners, who are about to enter on the execution of their duty, from running the boundary line as agreed on last summer between general Jackson and the friendly Indian chiefs. Being guilty of a flagrant violation of the late treaty of peace, colonel Nicolls and his *banditti* should be instantly driven off at the point of the bayonet.

A rupture between Great Britain and Spain is spoken of. The British officers at Appalachicola we are told make no secret of the determination of their government to occupy Florida in the course of the ensuing summer—"peaceably if they can—*forcibly*, if they must." Our government, deeply interested in such an event, should look to it in time. If Spain be disposed to part with Florida, the United States ought to possess it, cost what it may. It is essential to our western trade. At all events, if to be avoided, it should not be suffered to pass into the hands of the British.

————

Extract of a letter from colonel Hawkins, agent for Indian affairs, to colonel Nicolls, commanding the British forces in the Floridas.

Creek Agency, 19th March, 1815.

"I have received yours of the 7th, and cannot subscribe to your construction of the voluntary invitation sent by captain Henry to the people of the Creek nation, whose slaves were with you. Your restriction leaves nothing for it to operate on, and he could not have so intended it. You will see in the first article of the treaty of peace that provision is made against carrying away slaves and other private property, such as that in question.

"Being the medium of communication between your superior officers and you on the restoration of peace, as well as the officer of the United States in this quarter charged with their Indian affairs, I must and do protest against your carrying away any negroes belonging to Indians within the United States or citizens thereof, and require that they be so left on your embarkation as that their proper owners may get possession of them."

————

Copy of a letter from colonel Nicolls to colonel Hawkins, dated

"Appalachicola, 28th April.

"Being absent from this post when your letter of the 19th ult. arrived, I take this opportunity to answer it. On the subject of the negroes lately owned by the citizens of the United States or Indians in hostility to the British forces, I have to acquaint you, that, according to orders, I have sent them to the British colonies, where they are received as free settlers and lands given to them. The newspaper you sent me is, I rather think, incorrect; at all events, an American newspaper cannot be authority for a British officer. I herewith enclose you a copy of a part of the 9th article of the treaty of peace relative to the Indians in alliance with us— they have signed and accepted it as an independent people, solemnly protesting to suspend all hostilities against the inhabitants of the United States,— Within these few days I have had a complaint from the Seminoles chief Bow Legs. He states, that a party of American horse have made an incursion into the town, killed one man, wounded another, and stole some of his cattle; also, that they have plundered some of his people on their peaceable way from St. Augustine. May I request of you to enqiure into this affair, and cause justice to be done to the murderer and have the cattle restored. I strictly promise you that for any mischief done by the Creeks under me, I shall do all in my power to punish the delinquents and have the property restored.

"The chiefs here have requested me further to declare to you (that in order to prevent any disagreeable circumstances from happening in future) they have come to a determination not to permit the least intercourse between their people and those of the United States. They have in consequence ordered them to cease all communication directly or indirectly with the territory or citizens of the United States; and they do take this public mode of warning the citizens of the United States from entering their territory or communicating directly or indirectly with the Creek people. They also request that you will understand their territories to be as they stood in the year 1811. In my absence I have directed first lieutenant Wm. Hamley, the head interpreter, to communicate with you on any point relative to the Creeks; and I have given him my most positive orders; that he shall at all times do his best to keep peace and good neighborhood between the Creeks and your citizens.

I am, sir, your very humble servant,

EDWARD NICOLLS,
*Commanding the British forces
in the Floridas.*

We the undersigned, chiefs of the Muscogee nation, declared by his Britannic majesty to be a free and independent people, do in the name of the said nation agree to the 9th article of the treaty of peace between his Britannic majesty and the United States—and we do further declare that we have given most strict and positive orders to all our people, that they desist from hostilities of every kind against the citizens or subjects of the United States.

Given under our hands at the British fort on the Appalachicola, the 2nd day of April, 1815.

HEPOOETH MICCO X.
CAPPACHIMICO X.
HOPOY MECCO T. P.

———

Colonel Hawkins in his reply to the above denies the right of colonel Nicolls or his three Indians to concern with the government of the Creeks.—It is within the knowledge of the agent, we are informed, that one of the chiefs who has signed the acceptance of the terms of peace *never resided in the United States,* and that *neither of the three was ever a member of the national council, or constituted any part of the Creek government.*

Volume 8, June 17, 1815, page 271

War Events—Indian Hostility.

Again has the policy of England, involved the Creek Indians in a quarrel with the United States—and these wretches, who after being supported by our government, when they otherwise must inevitably have starved, are pouring out the cup of their ingratitude on the peaceful citizens of our country. By a gentleman recently from the agency we learn, that they had driven back the commissioners who were proceeding to run the line—driven off the settlers on the Alabama, declared that all travelling through their country by white persons should be put a stop to, and declared that their boundaries should remain as they were in 1811. This resolution of the Indians, we understand, was taken in consequence of a declaration of colonel Nicolls, on the Apalachicola, that the British government would guarantee to the Creek Indians, as their allies, all their possessions as they existed 1811.— *Augusta Mirror, May* 29.

London, April 6.—The honorable captain W. H. Percy and the surviving officers and crew of his majesty's ship Hermes, have been honorably acquitted by a court martial, held on the 18th of January last, on board the Cydnus, in the gulf of Mexico, of all blame in the loss of that ship, which followed the attack of fort Bowyer.

War Events: or Things
Incidental to the Late War.

Major Nicholls.—The following account of the celebrated British major Nicholls is copied from the Aurora:—

This major Nicholls was tried in May, 1812, on thirteen several charges—the first of which was cruelty to a private of marines, by beating him with a bayonet, and inflicting several wounds, one of which was three inches in length, besides several other wounds in the head and contusions on the body, so as to endanger his life.

2. He caused two black seamen, taken from on board an American vessel, of the names of Henry Darraway and Thomas Jones, to be cruelly flogged, without any court martial, and then ordered them to be sent to a desolate rock, and there landed without food or raiment, at an inclement season of the year, so that Jones is believed to have died.

3. Cruelty to a corporal, by beating and knocking out his teeth with a billet of wood.

4. Cruelty to Joseph Rivett, a private, by cruelly beating and jumping on his body.

5. Tyrannical conduct and attempts to influence a court martial in the case of Rivett, and charging the court with acquitting Rivett against evidence.

6. For tyrannically causing Rivett to be tried a second time on the same charges of which he had been before acquitted.

7. Cruelty to Richard Warwell, another marine, whom he so violently beat with a heavy stick, as to oblige him to place himself under the care of a surgeon.

8. Cruelty in inflicting lashes in a private manner and without trial, on a marine, and repeating this cruelty three several times.

9. Cruelty in the same way, to Thomas Robinson, marine.

10. Cruelty in like manner to William Mears, and jumping upon his body.

11. The same cruelty to John M'Glasky, a marine.

12. Cruelty to bombadier Perkins, and reducing him without court martial.

13. Maliciously firing into one of the royal gunboats, and wounding the men therein to the danger of life.

For all these charges he was only reprimanded, in consideration of *his high and gallant services*, though the court said they could not but animadvert in severe terms on the violence he had evinced on those several occasions.

War Events—Indian Affairs.
From the Georgia Journal.

The subjoined correspondence will be read with no small degree of interest. The letter of colonel Nicholls speaks for itself. It not only complains of pretended injuries done the Indians—it not only warns us of the consequences of failing to restore the lands they have voluntarily ceded to us, and to evacuate in due time the forts erected in their nation during the late war; but, menacingly tells us orders have been given the Indians "to put to death without mercy any one molesting them;" they have been abundantly furnished with provision, ammunition and arms, are "impatient for revenge," wait only the signal of attack, and have "a strong hold to retire upon" should a superior force be sent against them. In a word, *it threatens in strong terms a renewal of the Indian war, and an indiscriminate pillage and massacre of our defenceless and extensive frontier.* Particular care is also taken to apprize us of a treaty of alliance *offensive* and *defensive* as well as of commerce and navigation, having been concluded between Great Britain and the Creek Indians. This is a circumstance our government cannot overlook, and will doubtless claim its immediate and serious attention. If colonel Nicholls be authorised to do what he has done, so flagrant an infraction of our rights would warrant an immediate appeal to arms. We are disposed to acquit governor Kindeland of all participation in this nefarious business. His decided opposition last winter to British troops passing through East-Florida for the purpose of invading that quarter of our state, induces us to believe he is ignorant of the game colonel Nicholls has been playing with the indians under the control of the Spanish government. Of this however, we shall be better able to judge on seeing the reply of governor Kindeland to the spirited yet respectful letter of the executive of our state on this interesting subject.

The following is the answer of colonel Hawkins, agent for Indian affairs, to the buccaneering colonel Nicholls, whose insolent letter, warning the citizens of the United States from entering the Creek nation on any pretext, was published in our paper the week before last. [See page 261.]

———

"Creek-agency,
24th March, 1815.

"On the 18th, I had the pleasure to receive your communication of the 28th ultimo. I expected from the tenor of your orders, which I conveyed to you from admirals Cochrane and Cockburn on the 19th of March, that you had left the Floridas 'ere this, with the British troops under your command; and that Spain and the United States would have no more of British interference in the management of their Indian affairs. The newspaper I sent you was one, in which the official acts of our government are published. There could be no motive for falsification— your deeming it incorrect, must have proceeded from a knowledge that your conduct in relation to the negroes was at variance with it. It would have been acceptable in the communication relative to the disposition of "the negroes taken from the citizens of the United States of *Indians* in *hostility to the British*" to have received the number, particularly belonging to the latter. As peace is restored between Great Britain and the United States, I feel a reluctance to put on paper any thing that may have the tendency to tarnish the British character, or that of any officer of its government; but I owe it to the occasion to state the declaration of captain Henry, that *"the English are sent out by their great father and king to restore his Indian people to their lands; and we are desired by him not to take away their negroes, unless they freely give them to us or sell them for money,"* is violated. It is proper also to add, I did not enroll any Indians into the service of the United States, until after the negroes of Marshall, Stedham and Kinnard, three half breeds, were taken from them, by force or stratagem, by British officers. Your restriction of the captain's declaration to negroes belonging to indians friendly to Great Britain, if by that is meant Indians hostile to the United States, is an erroneous one, as there is not one Creek who has negroes so situated.

The Creek chiefs, to use a courtly phrase, have just cause to least to say this is an "unjustifiable aggression." Your having acted by orders, and it being now beyond your control, a remedy must and will be sought for elsewhere.

The documents you enclosed, signed by three chiefs, purporting to be the agreement of the Muscogee nation to the 9th article of the treaty of peace, I shall lay before the chiefs of the nation at a convention soon to be held at Cowetau, and send you the result of their deliberations on it. The result of my reflections with due deference I give you, as on the envelope it purports to be *on his Britannic majesty's service.* It is within my knowledge, one of the chiefs is a Seminole of East-Florida, and has never resided in the United States; and that neither of the three has ever attended the national councils of the Creeks, or are in any way a part of their executive government. If the four witnesses had signed it as principals, and the three chiefs as witnesses, it would have been entitled to equal respect from me.* Could you be serious in communicating such a nullity, with their mock determination "not to permit the least intercourse between their people (meaning the Creek nation) and those of the United States?" &c. As to the territory of the Seminoles it being out of the United States is an affair between them and the government of Spain;

and that of the Creeks is as fixed and guaranteed in their treaty stipulations with the United States. I do not know that any occurrences can happen which will render it necessary for me to communicate with lieutenant William Hambly.—If by doing so, I can render acts of kindness to Indians or others, it would afford me pleasure; but under present impressions the 5th article of the treaty of friendship, limits and navigation between the United States and the king of Spain will govern me in all cases respecting the Indians in the two Floridas.

I am with due regard, sir, your obedient servant,

BENJAMIN HAWKINS.

[*Note: *The witnesses, we believe, were colonel Nicholls, captain woodbine, lieutenant Hambly, and captain Henry*— What a *biting* sarcasm!—Editors Journal.]

On the receipt of the curious epistle from colonel Nicholls alluded to in the above, governor Early transmitted a copy to the governor of East Florida, accompanied by a letter of which an extract follows:

"It has come to my knowledge within a few days past, that a British officer, colonel Nicholls, continues at the British encampment on the river Appalachicola, with the Indians heretofore in hostility against the United States, exercising over them an assumed superintendency, and directing their conduct in relation to our people. As full evidence of this fact, I take the liberty to inclose to your excellency a copy of a letter recently received from that officer by colonel Hawkins, the agent of the United States with the Creek Indians. How does it happen, sir, that a British officer is permitted to reside within the territories of Spain, as an agent of his Britannic majesty with the Indians, and to exercise such powers in relation to the United States? You perceive that he speaks of the "Creeks under him;" that he considers them an independent people—that he has made them say, they "are declared to be independent by his Britannic majesty," and as such have assented to the treaty of peace; and the citizens of the United States are by a fugitive banditti "under him," warned from having any intercourse with the Creek nation, although the great body of that nation reside within the limits of the United States.

"This representation is made to you in the confident belief that you will not after this information suffer the territory of Spain within the province under your command to be used for purposes which in their tendency must be most inimical to us.

We wish for nothing more than to be at peace with the Indians, whether within or without our territory, and if those who have taken refuge in Florida were left to your influence and counsels, we should feel quiet: But we can never rest contented and see a British officer (especially of colonel Nicolls' stamp) acting as their superintendant, civil and military."

The annexed development of the views and intentions of colonel Nicolls in relation to the Creek Indians, was received a few days ago by the executive of this state from the agent for indian affairs.

"British post, Appalachicola river, May 12th, 1815.

"In my letter to you of the 28th ult. I requested you would be so good as to make enquiry into the murder and robberies committed on the Seminoles belonging to the chief called Bow-Legs, at the same time declaring my determination of punishing with the utmost rigor of the law any one of our side who broke it. Of this a melancholy proof has been given in the execution of an Indian of the Atophalga town by Hothly Poya Tustunnuggee, chief of Ocmulgees, who found him driving off a gang of cattle belonging to your citizens, and for which act of justice I have given him double presents and a chiefs' gun, in the open square before the whole of the chiefs, and highly extolled him. These, sir, are the steps I am daily taking to keep the peace with sincerity; but I am sorry to say the same line is not taken on your side, nor have you written to say what steps you are taking or intend to take to secure this mutual good. Since the last complaint from Bow-Legs I have had another from him to say your citizens have again attacked and murdered two of his people—that they had stolen a gang of his cattle, but that he had succeeded in regaining them. I asked him what proof they had of their being killed. They said they had found their bloody clothes in the American camp, which was hastily evacuated on their approach. Now, sir, if these enormities are suffered to be carried on in a christian country, what are you to expect by shewing such an example to the uncultivated native of the woods—(for savage I will not call them—their conduct entitles them to a better epithet.) I have, however, *ordered them to stand on the defensive, and have sent them a large supply of arms and ammunition, and told them to put to death without mercy any one molesting them*; but at all times to be careful and not put a foot over the American line. In the mean time that I should complain to you—that I was convinced you would do your best to curb such infamous conduct.—Also, that those people who did such deeds would, I was convinced, be disowned by the government of the United States, and severely punished. *They have given their consent to await your answer before they take revenge*, but, sir, *they are impatient for it, and well armed as the whole nation now is, and store with ammunition and provisions, having a strong hold to retire upon in case of a superior force appearing, picture to yourself, sir, the miseries that may be suffered by good and innocent citizens on your frontiers, and I am sure you will lend me your best aid in keeping the bad spirits in subjection.* Yesterday in a full assembly of the chiefs, I got them to pass a law for four resolute chiefs to be appointed in different parts of the nation, something in the character of our sheriffs, for the purpose of inflicting condign punishment on such people as broke the law, and I will say this much for them, that I never saw men execute laws better than they do. *I am also desired to say to you by the chiefs, that they do not find that your citizens are evacuating their lands according to the 9th article of the treaty of peace; but that they were fresh provisioning the forts.* This point, sir, I beg of you to look into. They also

request me to inform you, that they have signed a treaty of offensive and defensive alliance with Great Britain, as well as one of commerce and navigation, which as soon as it is ratified at home you shall be made more fully acquainted with.

I am, sir, your very humble servant,

EDWARD NICHOLLS, col.
Commanding H. B. M. Forces
in the Creek Nation.

Addressed

On his B. Majesty's service,

To colonel BENJAMIN HAWKINS, Commanding at Fort Hawkins.

————

REPLY.

Creek Agency,
28th May, 1815.

On the 24th I wrote to you in reply to your's of the 28th ult. and since have had the pleasure to receive yours of the 12th.—I had received from Bow Legs direct, a complaint of an outrage committed "by the people of Georgia, who had gone into East Florida, driven off his cattle and destroyed his property." I have sent this complaint to the governor of Georgia, who will readily co-operate with the officers of the general government, to cause justice to be done the injured, if the complaint is true.— The laws of the United States provide completely for the protection of the Indian rights, and those interested with their execution have the power of doing it. All that is wanted is proof against the transgressors.

The Indians of Aulotchwan, who without provocation murdered and plundered a number of the subjects of Spain at St. Johns, have engendered such a deadly feud between the parties, that it will be long before the descendants of the injured can forget and forgive. Spain, from her internal commotions, has found it convenient to settle a peace between them, and these people, it is probable, are taken for Georgians. The Indians of this Agency, as well as those in the Floridas, have long known they have to apply through their chiefs to me for a redress of their grievances. The government of the Creeks is not an ephemeral one. Its last modification is of more than ten years

151

standing. It was the work and choice of the nation, and has a check on the conduct of the Seminoles.

In 1799, a gentleman arrived where you are from England, who had been an officer on half pay. He came in the Fox sloop of war furnished by the admiral on the Jamaica station, by order of the admiralty, "to facilitate to him a passage to his nation the Creeks." This gentleman, after attempting in various ways with the Seminoles, to usurp the government of the Creeks without success, created himself director general of Muscogee, declared war against Spain, murdered some of her subjects, and took St. Marks. He ordered me, with my assistants in the plan of civilization, out of the Creek Nation.

I communicated his proceedings to the national councils, who had been previously acquainted with him, and who replied to him, "that he had a title among them which he well merited—Cap,pe,tun,nee,lox,au, (the prince of Liars) and no other." This director general of Muscogee, after playing a farce for two years, experienced a tragic scene, which deprived him of his liberty. He was put in irons by order of the council whose government he attempted to usurp, and sent to the governor general of Louisiana to answer for his crimes. His Seminoles chiefs were glad to retire with impunity. After this it was unanimously determined in a national council of distinguished chiefs from every town, and a deputation of Choctaws, Chickasaws, and Cherokees, that the warriors should be classed and held in readiness to execute the orders of the executive council; and that the agent for Indian affairs should have the power of executing the treaty stipulations of the Creeks with their white neighbours. Tookaubatche and Cowetau alternately, as the occasion required, was appointed the permanent seat of their national councils, where national affairs alone could be transacted. They have now two speakers.—When the council meets at Cowetau, Tustunnuggee Hopoie, as speaker for the Lower Creeks, is speaker for the nation; and when they meet at Tookaubatche, Tustunnuggee Thlucco, of the Upper Creeks, is speaker for the nation.—Cowetau is head quarters for the present. The Agent for Indian Affairs can convene the council.

To this council I communicated in your own words the pretensions of your three chiefs. They answer—"We have had colonel Nicholls' communication before us—that Hopoith Micco, Caupuchau Micco and Hopoie Micco are the sovereigns of this nation. We know nothing about them as such. We have often invited them to attend our talks. They never would come forward, and Hopohieth Micco is a hostile Indian. The have nothing to do with our affairs. They reside in the Spanish territory."

After mentioning a solitary effort of yours "to keep the peace," you say "I am sorry to say the same line is not taken on your side, nor have you written to me to say what steps you are taking or intend to take to secure this mutual good." You could not have expected I should communicate with you, when from your orders you were so soon to leave the country. I have communicated to the national council several outrages committed by bandittis from the Seminoles, and other parts, upon the post road and frontiers of Georgia, repeatedly. They have in two instances had the guilty shot, and sent armed parties after others. As late as the 17th April one man was killed and four wounded on the post road. Our waggons twice attacked and one waggoner killed, several horses taken and carried, as reported, to your depot, at the very time the waggons were carrying seed corn for the Indians, and flour for the support of nearly 5000 totally destitute of food.

The measures in operation here to preserve peace is with an efficient force, red and white troops, to pursue, apprehend and punish all violators of the public peace.—The executive council of the Creeks are continually at Cowetau with an assistant agent to take orders with the warriors when the necessity is apparent, and to call on me when the aid of regular troops is necessary. We do not rely on the exertions of any one but ourselves, to preserve peace among the Creeks, and between them and their neighbors of the United States and the Floridas. We examine fairly, spare the innocent and punish the guilty; and in no case suffer revenge to carve for itself.

On an exparte hearing, you have "armed the Seminoles and given orders to put to death without mercy any one molesting them." This is cruelty without example, scalping men, women and children, for troubling or vexing only, and the executioners the judges. To gratify their revenge, the good and innocent citizens on the frontiers are to be the victims of such barbarity.—Suppose a banditti were to commit a violent outrage, such as that of the 17th April, are we to charge it on the unoffending people of the frontiers, and kill them without mercy, if we could not find out the guilty? You have issued the order, provided and issued munitions of war for its execution, prepared and provisioned a strong hold to retire upon, in case of superior force appearing, to protect them in this mode of gratifying their revenge. You will be held responsible and your strong holds will certainly not avail. If you are really on the service of his Britannic majesty, is an act of hostility which will require to be speedily met and speedily crushed. But, sir, I am satisfied you are acting for yourself on some speculative project of your own. The sovereign of Great Britain could not from his love of justice in time of peace, his systematic perseverance in support of legitimate sovereigns, almost to the impoverishing of his own nation, suffer any of his officers to go into a neutral country to disturb its peace.

If the Seminolie Indians have complaints to make, if they will do it through the chiefs of the Creek nation, or direct to me or through an officer of his Catholic majesty as heretofore, I will cause justice to be done. In cases of murder, the guilty if practicable shall be punished; in case of theft restitution shall be made.

The treaties you have made for the Creek nation, with the authority created by yourself for the purpose, must be a novelty. It would surprize me much to see your sovereign ratify such as you have described them to be, with a people such as I know them to be, in the territories of his Catholic majesty.—I shall communicate what has passed on the subject between us to the officers of Spain in my neighborhood, that they may be apprized of what you are doing.

As you may not have recent news from Europe, I send you some news-papers detailing important events there on the 4th of April.

I am, &c.

BENJAMIN HAWKINS,
Agent for Indian affairs.

To colonel Nicolls, commanding
His B. M. Forces, Appalachicola.

Volume 8, July 1, 1815, page 311

War Events.

Col. Nicolls.—It appears that this *great* man has left the Floridas for Bermuda, in the gun-brig Forward, accompanied by captain Woodbine, an indian chief and about *50 slave troops.*

Volume 8, July 8, 1815, pages 334-335

War Events.
From the London Gazette.

Colonial Department.
Downing-street,
April 17, 1815.

A despatch, of which the following is a copy, has been this day received by earl Bathurst, one of his majesty's principal secretaries of state, from major-general sir John Lambert, K. C. B. Commanding on the coast of Louisiana.

Head-Quarters, Isle Dauphine,
Feb. 14, 1815.

My Lord—My despatch dated January 29th, will have informed your lordship of the re-embarkation of this force, which was completed on the 30th; the weather came on so bad on that night, and continued so until the 5th of February, that no communication could be held with the ships at the inner anchorage, a distance of about seventeen miles.

It being agreed between vice-admiral sir Alexander Cochrane and myself that operations should be carried towards Mobile, it was decided that a force should be sent against fort Bowyer, situated on the eastern point of the entrance of the bay, and from every information that could be obtained it was considered a brigade would be sufficient for this object, with a respectable force of artillery. I ordered the 2d brigade, composed of the 4th, 21st and 44th regiments, for this service, together with such means in the engineer and artillery departments, as the chief and commanding officer of the royal artillery might think expedient. The remainder of the force had orders to disembark on the Isle Dauphine, and encamp; and major-general Keane, whom I am truly happy to say has returned to his duty, superintended their arrangement.

The weather being favorable on the 7th for the landing to the eastward of Mobile Point, the ships destined to move on that service, sailed under the command of captain Ricketts, of the Vengeur, but did not arrive in sufficient time that evening to do more than determine the place of disembarkation, which was about three miles from fort Bowyer.

At day-light the next morning the troops got into the boats, and 600 men were landed under lieutenant colonel Debbeig of the 44th, without opposition, who immediately threw out the light companies under lieutenant Bennett, of the 4th regiment, to cover the landing of the brigade. Upon the whole being disembarked, a disposition was made to move on towards the fort, covered by the light companies. The enemy was not seen until about 1000 yards in front of their works; they gradually fell back, and no firing took place, until the whole had retired into the fort, and our advance had pushed on nearly to within three hundred yards. Having reconnoitred the forts with lieutenant-colonels Burgoyne and Dickson, we were decidedly of opinion, that the work was formidable only against an assault; that batteries being once established, it must speedily fall. Every exertion was made by the navy to land provisions, and the necessary equipment of the battering train and engineer stores. We broke ground on the night of the 8th and advanced a firing party to within one hundred yards of the fort during the night. The position of the batteries being decided upon the next day, they were ready to receive their guns on the night of the 10th, and on the morning of the 11th, the fire of a battery of four eighteen pounders on the left, and two 8 inch howitzers on the right, each about one hundred yards distance, two 6-pounders at about three hundred yards, and eight small cohorns advantageously placed on the right, with intervals between of one hundred and two hundred yards, all furnished to keep up an incessant fire

for two days, were prepared to open. Preparatory to commencing, I summoned the fort, allowing the commanding officer half an hour for decision upon such terms as were proposed. Finding he was inclined to consider them, I prolonged the period at his request, and at 3 o'clock the fort was given up to a British guard and British colors hoisted; the terms being signed by major Smith, military secretary, and captain Ricketts, R. N. and finally approved of by the vice-admiral and myself, which I have the honor to enclose. I am happy to say our loss was not very great; and we are indebted for this, in a great measure, to the efficient means attached to this force. Had we been obliged to resort to any other mode of attack, the fall could not have been looked for under such favorable circumstances.

We have certain information of a force having been sent from Mobile, and disembarked about 12 miles off, in the night of the 10th, to attempt its relief; two schooners with provisions and an intercepted letter fell into our hands, taken by captain Price, R. N. stationed in the bay.

I cannot close this despatch without naming to your lordship, again, lieutenant colonels Dickson, royal artillery, and Burgoyne, royal engineers, who displayed their usual zeal and abilities; and lieutenant Bennett, of the 4th, who commanded the light companies and pushed up close to the enemy's works.

Captain honorable R. Spencer, R. N. who had been placed with a detachment of seamen under my orders, greatly facilitated the service in every way by his exertions.

From captain Ricketts, of the R. N. who was charged with the landing and disposition of the naval force, I received every assistance.

(Signed)   JOHN LAMBERT,
Major-general comm'dg.

Earl Bathurst, &c.
Fort Bowyer, February 14, 1815.

War Events.

Milledgeville, June 21.—The following extract of a letter from a gentleman in St. Mary's, to the executive of this state, leaves little doubt of Florida having been secretly transferred by Spain to the British government.

June 10.—"It is proper your excellency should know that on the 7th inst. a brig and transport arrived at Amelia Island, with colonel Nichols, captain Woodbine, an Indian Chief, and his son. They have been asked, if they were prepared to take possession of the province? One of them replied, *they were not yet supplied with money and provisions* for the purpose; *that* was the *sole* cause of delay; the supply was soon expected."

We can now account for the insolence of colonel Nichols, and his attempting to foist himself into the Creek agency for Indian affairs. Information has been received by colonel Hawkins, that the British white force at Appalachicola, which was only 40 or 50, has been somewhat diminished, and their number of ***** troops increased from 60 or 70 to about 300.—*Journal.*

The commissioners appointed by government to mark out in conformity with Jackson's treaty, the future boundaries of the Creek Nation, have postponed doing so till suitable arrangements can be made for that purpose. Not the least objection we are told was made by the Indians to the line being run. Colonel Kershaw passed through town yesterday on his way to his seat in North Carolina. Mr. Barnet has gone to Huntsville, Mississippi Territory, to lay in an adequate supply of provisions. General Sevier did not attend the meeting.—*ib.*

War Events.

Southern Division.—Major general Jackson has issued a general order on taking command of the southern division of the army of the United States. He has divided it into departments, of which Virginia, North Carolina, and the district of Columbia, form No. 6—South Carolina and Georgia, No. 7—Louisiana and the Mississippi territory, No. 8—Tennessee and Kentucky, and the Illinois and Missouri territories, no. 9.

Major general Gaines commands 6 and 7, and major-general Scott 8 and 9; brigadier-general Bissell, at Tehefuncia; colonel Nicholas at Belle Fontaine; brigadier-general Smith at Prairie du Chien; and lieutenant colonel M'Rea at Norfolk.

Three companies of artillery are to be stationed at Norfolk; 1 at Fort Johnson and Hampton, N. C.; 4 at Charleston, S. C.; 6 of infantry, 4th regiment near Charleston; 1 company of artillery at Savannah; 4 of infantry near T.; 6 companies of infantry, 7th regiment at Fort Hawkins; 2 do. At Fort Jackson; 2 do. at Fort Montgomery; 1 of artillery at Mobile; 1 do. at Fort Bowyer; 2 do. at Plaquemine; 3 at New-Orleans; 10 of infantry, 1st regiment to Tehefuncia; 2 of riflemen at Natchitoches; 10 of infantry, 8th regiment at St. Louis; 8 of riflemen at Prairie du Chien.

War Events.

From the Savannah Republican.— The following is the reply of Juan Jose de Estrama, governor of East Florida, to the communication lately made by the executive of this state, respecting the conduct of colonel Nicolls, in attempting to stir up the Creek Indians to hostility against the United States:

St. Augustine,
15th June, 1815.

I had the honor of yesterday receiving your excellency's letter of the 1st instant, directed to my predecessor,* enclosing a copy of colonel Nicolls' letter, which developes British interference in matter that of right are the exclusive concern of my sovereign and the United States. [*Governor Kindelan, who has received some appointment in the island of Cuba.—*Editors of the Georgia Journal.*]

Although my predecessor had given notice some time since to the captain-general (of Cuba) I now repeat it, informing him that colonel Nicolls remains in the British camp on the Apalachicola with the Indians that have been inimical to the United States, exercising over them an assumed superintendancy, as he shows by his letter to colonel Hawkins, agent of the Creek Indians. *I am sure his excellency will take the most prompt and necessary measures to stop such conduct, and of the result you shall be duly advised.*

Supplement to Volume 8, page 155

"Magnanimity."

Extract of a letter dated Charleston, July 5.

The British, agreeably to their usual good faith, still keep up a force in Florida, and it is supposed here that all the gun-boats to the southward will be ordered to the St. Mary's river, as it was before the war. I understand smuggling is going on there at a fine rate, and no doubt will increase, as three of the best Amelia houses intend to remain there. St. Mary's is almost broken up; it will be long before it recovers from the pillage of Cockburn and Barrie, the latter worse, if possible, than the first. They took four blacks from my father-in-law after the peace was known on Cumberland island, and while the American troops were receiving possession of the fort. Cockburn told him he should be paid for them; I suppose like all their other payments for plundered property. The intercepted letters were not expressive of one half of their dirty acts. They did not leave my father a second shirt to his back—took spoons, casters, glasses, &c. and would have robbed his daughter, a girl of sixteen. Barrie himself took a thermometer down, put it in his pocket, and cooly walked off from Mr. Clark's. The black troops behaved better than the white—the latter were stationed in the new Episcopal church; they left neither sash, glass, cushion, doors, nor even the floor or fence—the blacks lived in the Methodist new church, and left it as they found it, even clean. So much for the bulwark, and the world's last hope."

Supplement to Volume 8, pages 181-182

Mobile Point,
September 14, 1813.

Sir—I have information, from a source in which I place every confidence, that the British armed schooner from the Bahamas arrived at Pensacola on the 10th instant, with a large supply of arms, ammunition, clothing and blankets for the Creek Indians—also, that the old Seminola chief Perriman, and his son William, *the latter lately appointed brigadier-general in the British service, are at Pensacola.* They drove into that place two hundred head of fine cattle and sacrificed them at the heretofore unknown price of from one to eight dollars per head. Fifty cows and calves sold for fifty dollars, so anxious they were to get supplies to join the hostile Indians.

I am well acquainted with those chiefs, and know they have great influence with their people.

It appears the arms, &c. were forwarded in consequence of an address sent to the governor of Jamaica, some time since, by the Creek Indians. The schooner is the property of a well-known free-booter, a captain Johnston of the Bahamas, who has made his fortune by preying on the commerce of France, Spain and the United States—I recollect his breaking out of the prison in New-Orleans, in the year 1809.

I hope the arrival of these supplies will give you a short respite, and enable you to prepare for any force the whole confederation can possibly bring against your post. It would astonish you to see the labor, we have performed at this post. We have, literally speaking, levelled mountains and filled up vallies.

I am, sir, respectfully, your obedient servant,

(Signed)　　JOHN BOWYER,
Lieut. col. commanding.

Brig. gen. Claiborne.

NILES' WEEKLY REGISTER.

THE PAST—THE PRESENT—FOR THE FUTURE.

EDITED, PRINTED AND PUBLISHED BY H. NILES, AT $5 PER ANNUM, PAYABLE IN ADVANCE.

Volume 9

(September 2, 1815 - February 24, 1816)

Volume 9, September 16, 1815, pages 42-43

War Events.

We learn from the south, (say the National Intelligencer) that 600 troops are about to march from Fort Hawkins to attend the commissioners in running the boundary line of the Creek nation, which, it is believed, will consume several months. The Georgia Journal states, that this large force is required by the threatened opposition of the hostile Indians, who have taken refuge in Florida. Those Indians who are considered friendly, are not well satisfied with losing the large portion of territory which they ceded by the treaty; but from them, though they murmur, no molestation is apprehended.

Volume 9, October 28, 1815, page 151

Chronicle—The Creek Indians.

There is some reason to believe that the Creek Indians may give a little trouble. They appear dissatisfied with their late treaty. In consequence, 2000 men are called for from Georgia, by major-general Gaines, for whose detachment orders have been issued by the governor of that state. The line, according to the treaty, has not been run in consequence of the death of general Sevier, and the severe and continued illness of colonel *Hawkins*, two of the commissioners.

Volume 9, November 11, 1815, page 187

Chronicle—The Creeks.

A good deal is said about the dissatisfaction and hostility of the Creek Indians. We are cautioned not to give too easy credit to many reports from this quarter. But it appears that some difficulty was seriously apprehended from the measures pursuing by our government and its agents. 800 regular troops are said to be already in the nation, and several other bodies are moving into it, and, with the requisition made by general Gaines on Georgia, it is estimated that the whole force under his command will nearly amount to 4000 men.

Volume 9, November 11, 1815, page 188

Chronicle—Creek Indians.

St. Stephens, Oct. 6.

In order to allay public anxiety which has been for some time on tip-toe, relative to the result of the talk lately held with the Creek Indians at fort Jackson, we have taken considerable pains to get the most authentic information on the subject. By a gentleman of undoubted veracity, immediately through the nation, and who arrived here last evening, we learn that the conference had certainly broken up, without effecting its object. The Big Warrior and his party (who lately fought with the United States) together with the several tribes who had been at war against us, have determined to oppose the running of the line. The Big Warrior stated that in either case destruction to their nation was inevitable—that if they suffered the line to be run, their country would be too limited to subsist by hunting, and that they had as well die by the sword as with famine—that their had been deceived—that his party had been promised pay as regular soldiers of the United States—that their pay had been denied them—and that they felt it right in consequence, to hold possession of their lands. The Indians were moving off from the road, and showed evident signs of dissatisfaction, though no hostilities or depredations have yet been committed.

Volume 9, November 18, 1815, page 202

Chronicle—The Creeks, &c.
From the Georgia Argus,
November 1.

We learn from a gentleman who passed through the Creek Nation last week, that the commissioners are now engaged in running the Indian boundary line, and was informed by colonel Hawkins, (who had so far recovered his health as to attend with the other commissioners) that they would finish in about six weeks. Our informant further states, that the *Indians* had disappeared, and it was not known where they had gone—that the commissioners apprehended no danger of an attack. We fondly hope that they may not, but we have our fears.

We understand that the commissioners progress rapidly in running the line; it was expected that they would reach the Chatahoochie river, by Sunday night last.

We understand that orders have not yet been issued for detaching the militia to Fort Hawkins.

Volume 9, November 25, 1815, page 214

Chronicle—General Jackson
at Lynchburg.

Among those who visited General *Jackson* at Lynchburg, was *Thomas Jefferson*, who partook of a splendid entertainment given to the hero, by the corporation of that town, of which nearly 300 gentlemen were present. The general's lady is with him, to whom, also, due respect was paid by the ladies of the place.

Mr. *Jefferson's* toast, at the dinner-party, was in the following beautiful terms:—"Honor and gratitude to those who have filled the measure of their country's honor."

General *Jackson* toasted Mr. *Monroe* as Secretary at War.

Volume 9, November 25, 1815, pages 214-215

Chronicle—The Floridas.

It seems a matter of certainty that the Floridas have been ceded to Great Britain, and we are sorry for it; for we can see in the possession of them by that power nothing else than a preparation for some new quarrel with the United States. The part that Spain held was barren and unprofitable, and can be of no service to Britain except to form a rallying point for the savages she may enlist against us; which will, probably, lead to the utter extinction of the Creeks. But what does Britain care for that? Havoc is her holiday amusement.

The Creeks. Extract of a letter from a gentleman at the Creek Agency, to his friend in Milledgeville, dated Oct. 27, 1815:

"We have travellers passing daily, and their report is, that the Indians are as friendly as they ever saw them. A Cassetau chief was here to-day. He came for the express purpose of informing Mr. Hawkins, that two Seminole Indians had come up to let them know that it was all peace and friendship throughout their land—that they had been assisting the British till the white people had taken all their land—and had it not been for that, they might have had it yet. They now say they have thrown down their arms, and if the British wish to fight those engaged in running the line, they might do it themselves—that they were tired and sick of war.

—»»☉◉☉«««—

British Contemplate Consequences of Florida War

Volume 9, December 9, 1815, pages 252-253

The Floridas.
From the London Morning Chronicle,
Sept. 21.

It was natural to expect, after a war like that of the peninsula, in which so much British blood and treasure were exhausted, that the subject of indemnities would come on the carpet, as soon as the object was attained and peace established. It was a very difficult matter, however, to settle this point, in consequence of the indefinite terms of the treaty made by Mr. Canning, and the difficulty of treating with Ferdinand and his ministers, who, far from being prepared to give an indemnity, rather thought we had done more harm than good in aiding to liberate the peninsula, and would have been happy if an Englishman had never trod their ground. Hence, by every means in their power, are they now trying to undo what little, social as well as political, improvements we sought to introduce, and it will be no wonder, if in the next edict issued by the inquisition, it be deemed a crime of heretical pravity, for a Spaniard to be heard speaking English. This indemnity question, consequently, has met with great difficulties, as well for the reasons just assigned as because the services to be compensated were performed to the cortes, and it would be very inconsistent, after his past conduct, for Ferdinand to seek to remunerate them, and indeed he only knows of them by hearsay.

Under this state of things it is easy to conceive the great dilemma in which the ministers have been placed, as well as their worthy representatives in Madrid, who have not learned logic enough to undo the syllogisms and other knotty arguments the monastic counsellors of Ferdinand bring forward on this subject. This indemnity question was, however, warmly agitated in Madrid in November last, and the whole weight and influence of England at last wrested from the tenacious Spaniards, it is generally believed, an indemnity, viz. East and West Florida. It is generally supposed that several demands were made before this point was agreed on, viz. a free trade to Spanish America, the cotton trade of Spain, the Island of Puerto Rico, the Spanish part of St. Domingo, Cuba, the Balcares, Canaries and for what we know, the Phillipine Islands. Either of these bonuses, separately, might, perhaps, have satisfied our wishes, but the Spaniards were too wise to let one go; so it would seem as if he had been forced to be content with the Floridas, because Spain could retain them no longer on account of the North Americans and the neighboring revolutions of Mexico. In making this concession, however, it is not clear, whether some valuable principle has not been given up, and whether some condition has not been exacted from us,

opposed to the feelings and wishes of the people of England.—Time will enlighten us on this point a little more, but in Spanish America, we ought to remember, there is at present a general insurrection against tyrannical power, a strong and irresistable impulse of human nature groaning under oppression, a revolution, in short, the most just and interesting in its nature as well as its consequences to the world, to be found in the annals of history.

To suppress this revolution, we know that the inquisition has been armed with the bayonet and the dagger, that religion has been prostituted, and that all the energies of rancor and malice have been set to work. To suppress this revolution also Spain has frequently called upon England under a plea, that in our treaty we *had guaranteed the integrity of the Spanish monarchy*. It would be long and tedious to carry our readers through the various occasions in which Spain has urged England to interfere and decide against her ultramarine provinces. But this treaty has even, by the agents of the latter, been interpreted into the right of demanding the persons of Spanish Americans landing in England. It has hitherto been thought that these remonstrances, on the part of Spain, have been unnoticed, but in our last treaty there is an additional clause, inserted on August 24, 1814, as the 3d additional article whereas the body of the same is signed on 5th July, same year, which has created some alarm. It is as follows:

"His Britannic majesty being anxious that the troubles and disturbances which unfortunately prevail in the dominions of his Catholic majesty in America should cease, and the subjects of these provinces should return to their obedience to their lawful sovereign, engages to take the most effectual measures for preventing his subjects from furnishing arms, ammunition, or any other warlike article to the revolted in America."

To this another circumstance of a more important nature has lately been added, tending to prove that some change has taken place in the policy of England, which in the last parliament was pledged to be strictly, nay, delicately, neutral between Spain and her ultramarine provinces. If so, it is now generally asked, can this be in consequence of the cession of the Floridas to England? Can we have bartered our honor, our national foresight, and integrity, together with our mercantile interests, for this bauble? Let us look for a moment on the real merits of this gift on the part of Spain and what will accrue to us, by being made lords over the Floridas.

We are not aware, that from time to time, long and elaborate memoirs have been presented to government, on the subject of the Florida, since we held possession of that country, so there have also been respecting the cutting of the Isthmus of Panama, and in all probability they have been on a par. They have been represented as Dorados, or the Elysian fields, and commercial avidity has delineated a comparative desert into a magnificent vent for goods. Yet it is a fact, that the soil of West Florida is sandy, and that the climate is unhealthy, as our experience taught us from the year 1763, till we gave it up, which we even seem to have been glad to do. Neither East nor West Florida supply furs, for the game is extinct, nor are there Indians now to hunt or consume goods. West Florida has indeed some advantages of locality, from being the channel to the sea of a large and fertile tract of country extending from the 31 degree to the sources of the Pearl, Alabama, and Chatahoche rivers; but all this belongs to the United States, and hitherto these rivers have scarcely been used. East Florida possesses no harbors; and indeed the population of both is so extremely thin, that, as commercial and agricultural points, they cannot present an advantage worth the expense of keeping them. They have long been a burden to Spain, who had annually to draw from Mexico 151,000 dollars for their expense of administration. Spain, therefore rids herself of a load, for she is sensible that the inhabitants, who endure all the horrors of Spanish legislation, &c. without either protection or benefits, and behold the rise of Louisiana since its cession to the United States, will not be long before they wish to form part of the same confederation. Nay, this dread of progressive liberty has long given umbrage to the cabinet of Madrid; for this they owe an old grudge to the North Americans, as well as for aiding the revolutions of the Mexicans; but as Spain is too feeble to retaliate, she is now glad to get England to do it for her.

Spain, therefore, in making us masters of the Floridas, would give what to her is scarcely worth keeping, and indeed what she cannot keep long; and we seem to think, that what is worth giving, is worth having. But our possession of the above country seems to be founded on the advantages of a military position, and as a future bridle on the United States. On this score it deserves particular attention.

Beaujour, in his sketch of the United States, a work that certainly develops the views and situation of that country better than any other before published, says, "that the Floridas to the south appear sooner or later, destined to be united to the American republic, since they form part of the boundaries delineated by nature." The government as well as the people of the United States have the same idea; and if England takes possession of that country, they are persuaded it is solely for the purpose of being a thorn in their side, to annoy them in time of war, and counter-balance any attack they may wish to make to the north. Mr. Ellicot, who some years back measured the boundary line between Spain and the United States, observed, "that West Florida must be highly important in a commercial point of view, and, if connected with the country north of it, capable of prescribing maritime regulations to the Gulph of Mexico." That is giving to understand, that in the hands of the United States, and as an outlet to the sea for a great part of the Mississippi Territory and Upper Carolina, and connected with a fertile range of country, in a rapid state of progression, it might be made of great consequence; but these advantages could never be realized by Spain or England, as solitary possessions of a strip of sea coast, and shut out from the interior. Besides, it is only when these back countries are settled and cultivated, that these advantages are to be realized; and this is indeed the material reason why the United States are not possessed of them already. Yet their holding them certainly enters into the future views of the United States; and being so near, with the population in their favor, it is evident they can take them whenever they choose. It is, therefore, when we have laid out large sums in barracks, new cities, (for our garrisons can never be put into

Pensacola and Mobile, once the tomb of our countrymen,) and in other necessary objects to make an establishment, that the United States' back-woods-men will sound their bugle, at the first symptoms of war, and all our trouble and expense will be lost.

Whatever then be the consideration we give for the Floridas, it can only be viewed in the light of a bad debt, for which we get what we can; but when we come to consider that this must be the cause of a new war with the United States, sooner or later, if we can get nothing better, would it not be more advisable to dash the sponge over our debt against Spain, than hereafter endanger the Canadas? By the war out of which we have just emerged with the United States, we have given that country a tone of importance greater than it would have attained by thirty year's growth, and certainly its inhabitants will never henceforward endure what they have been in the habits of hitherto bearing. The possession of the Floridas can, consequently, bring upon us nothing but a war, and if obtained by the sacrifice of any principle dear to the feelings of Englishmen, and essential to but trade, disgrace must be the issue. It is then necessary for us to look narrowly into this affair, before the meeting of Parliament, for in it many of the vital interests of this country are implicated. It indeed seems to be the lot of nations, to derive no instruction but from experience, nor, nowadays, do they avail themselves of the past folly of their neighbors. Absorbed as we are in modeling Europe to our wishes, North and South America seem to be entirely neglected, or if thought of, merely to destroy the future prospects a combination of fortunate circumstances has presented. Sufficient gall has already been infused into the minds of the North American people; their manifesto respecting the late war, and particularly some of its detached features, have been rancorous enough; and if we purchase from Spain a country for the purpose of fomenting dissensions in the bordering States, and placing a barrier to the independence of South America, we create a sympathetic feeling throughout, of which our children may experience the fatal consequences.

Volume 9, December 9, 1815, pages 254-255

[Extract from] the President's Message.

Yesterday, at 12 o'clock, the president of the United States transmitted to both houses of congress, the following message, by Mr. Todd, his secretary.

The Indian tribes within, and bordering on our southern frontier, whom a cruel war on their part had compelled us to chastise into peace, have latterly shewn a restlessness, which has called for preparatory measures for repressing it, and for protecting the commissioners engaged in carrying the terms of the peace into execution.

The execution of the act for fixing the military peace establishment, has been attended with difficulties which even now can only be overcome by legislative aid. The selection of officers; the payment and discharge of the troops enlisted for the war; the payment of the retained troops; and their re-union from detached and distant stations; the collection and security of the public property, in the quarter-master, commissary, and ordnance departments; and the constant medical assistance required in hospitals and garrisons, rendered a complete execution of the act impracticable on the first of May, the period more immediately contemplated. As soon, however, as circumstances would permit, and as far as it has been practicable, consistently with the public interests, the reduction of the army has been accomplished; but the appropriations for its pay, and for other branches of the military service, having proved inadequate, the earliest attention to that subject will be necessary; and the expediency of continuing upon the peace establishment, the staff officers who have hitherto been provisionally retained, is also recommended to the consideration of congress.

Volume 9, January 6, 1816, page 317

Legislature of Georgia.

Excerpt from the Governor's communication to the legislature.

Executive Department,
Georgia,
Milledgeville,
8th Nov. 1815.

I have received a requisition from major general Gaines of the United States army, for two thousand militia, to rendezvous at Fort Hawkins. The object of this requisition was, to have an effective force organized and in the field, sufficient as well to protect the commissioners who are engaged in running the boundary line, as our own frontier, from any hostile menaces of the Creek Indians. I am sorry to say, that a compliance with this requisition has been much retarded by the system of electing officers for detachments; And had an immediate pressure been made by the enemy, we might have had reason to regret serious disasters to the commissioners as well as our own frontier.

Whilst on this subject, I will again call the attention of the legislature to the condition of the volunteer infantry and rifle companies. Of the latter in particular, there are many remnants through the state, who in point of fact are complete exempts from the public service. The authority to consolidate them, given by the act of the last session, is inefficient, owing to their dispersed situation.—Both descriptions ought, by law, to be thrown back into the line, and none suffered to remain in the character of volunteers any longer than they shall preserve their full complement of men.

Volume 9, January 27, 1816, page 371

Executive Appointments.
[Extract]

The following appointments, made by the President of the United States, during the recess of congress, have been recently confirmed by the Senate, viz.

William Barnett, of Georgia, *Benjamin Hawkins*, of North Carolina, and *Edmund P. Gaines*, a major general in the service of the United States, commissioners for running the boundary line with the Creek Indians.

Volume 9, February 3, 1816, page 404

Milledgeville, (Geo.) Jan. 10. It appears by an article in the St. Stephen's paper, that the Seminolie Indians have destroyed the British fort at Appalachicola, and taken the negroes who occupied a small fort near that; and were on their way to Pensacola with a view of restoring to their rightful owners, those of them who had run away from the Spaniards, and the citizens on the frontier of the Mississippi territory.

Volume 9, February 17, 1816, page 430

Season in West-Florida.

A West-Florida paper gives the following animated description of the present season of that place: "Since our residence in Louisiana, we do not recollect to have seen so fine a season as this has been since the first of September last. It is now the 21st day of December, and we have not yet had a frost that would kill the cotton plant, nor materially injure the sugar cane. Our gardens are yet green; roses and wild jessamines blooming, and lillies springing; indeed, all nature presents more of a vernal than a winter aspect."

—◦»»}ϴ ☺ ϴ{«««◦—

162

NILES' WEEKLY REGISTER.

THE PAST—THE PRESENT—FOR THE FUTURE.

EDITED, PRINTED AND PUBLISHED BY H. NILES, AT $5 PER ANNUM, PAYABLE IN ADVANCE.

Volume 10

(March 2, 1816 - August 24, 1816)

Volume 10, March 23, 1816, page 64

General *Jackson*, accompanied by several officers of the army, recently left Nashville for Mobile.

Volume 10, March 23, 1816, page 64

The Creeks. In consequence of some late murders committed by the Creek Indians, 600 troops are ordered from Fort Hawkins to the interior of the nation. It is said that some additional military posts will be established among them. They appear much opposed to the running of the new boundary line.

An ambassador from the *Creek Indians* is said to be in London. But it is stated he is not openly received as such. The question is asked—has the late hostile dispositions of the Creeks any connection with this agency?

Volume 10, May 25, 1816, page 216

General Jackson arrived at New-Orleans on the 23d ult. He was received with great enthusiasm. He reviewed the troops stationed there, and finding them in an unhealthy state, had ordered them to the banks of the Alabama river.

Former British Post on Appalachicola Continues to Cause Problems

Volume 10, June 1, 1816, pages 230-231

THE CREEK INDIANS.

Milledgeville,
May 15.

A part of these deluded people have latterly committed several acts of hostility upon us. We did hope that they had learnt prudence by merited chastisement. The letter below from col. Hawkins may be regarded as entirely authentic. 300 men of the 4th U. S. Infantry marched from Charleston for fort Hawkins, on the 20th ult, they will immediately be followed by two companies of artillery these, with the force already in the neighborhood of the savages and the local assistance that may be relied on, we trust, may be sufficient to command the peace, without bloodshed, or otherwise to punish its violators.

We have understood from a source entitled to credit (says a Charleston paper) that the Upper Creeks, with the approbation of the United States' agent and the governor of East Florida, have determined to break up a settlement which has been some time forming among the Seminoles, by runaway negroes, chiefly from this state. They formed no inconsiderable part of colonel Nicholls' motly force on Appalachicola during the late war; and after the British evacuated the territory, the negroes and a few Indians still held possession of the fort, having received arms and ammunition from their allies.

Important.—*The following letter from colonel Hawkins to the executive of this state was received yesterday by express.*

Creek Agency,
10th May, 1816.

I have received two communications from lieutenant colonel Clinch, who commands at Fort Gaines on Chat,to,ho,cho, (about 65 miles below Fort Mitchell) of the 3d and 7th. The first to inform me "the Indians surprised and took two soldiers who had charge of thirty head of cattle near the Fort, and drove off the cattle. They were pursued 45 miles on the trail which leads to St. Marks. I have demanded the soldiers, their horses, cattle and party of Indians of their chiefs." On the 7th, "the spy I sent after the party reported that they had crossed Flint river near Burgess's old place; they had not killed the two men, but understood they intended to do so, if they become too fatigued to travel. That the Seminoles and all the towns near the confluence of Flint and Chattohochee were preparing for war; they had been drinking their war physic and dancing for several days. It was understood they were to divide themselves in two parties, one to go against Hartford, the other to attack Fort Gaines." "This report is confirmed by an Indian arrived last evening direct from the hostiles; three white men you well know, came this morning to inform me "they were of opinion the Seminoles and adherents are preparing to strike a blow some where; and that all the towns who wish to remain friendly, are preparing to remove above the line." That the Seminoles and lower Indians are determined on a war I have not the smallest doubt.

"I feel it my duty to communicate to you, and through you to my fellow-citizens on the frontiers of Georgia, rumors that are in circulation, as a little vigilance on their part, may save the lives of many helpless women and children."

I deem it my duty to make this communication to you, to give the publicity its importance requires, in conformity with the desire of the colonel, and am, very respectfully, your excellency's obed't serv't,

BENJAMIN HAWKINS,
Agent for I. A.

His excel. gov. Mitchell.

Washington City, June 10. There has been in this city, for some days past, a delegation from the Chickasaw nation of Indians, consisting of general *William Colbert,* the great war-chief of the Chickasaws; major *James Colbert,* interpreter of the Chickasaws; *Et-tis-sue, Mingo,* the great orator; Appa-sau-tub-bee, a chief; Chas-tau-ny, and Col-leet-chee, warriors —conducted by Mr. Wigton King.—These chiefs and warriors, with the rest of their nation, took an active part in the late war, against our combined white and red foes in the South, and can boast they never spilled the blood of a white man, except in war; and then have always taken part with the United States. General Colbert has particularly distinguished himself. He, with seven others of his nation, fought with us as long ago as at St. Clair's defeat; and, in the late war, before his nation was ready for the fight, he singly joined the 3d regiment of the U. S. Infantry; after remaining with them nine months, he returned to his nation, collected his warriors, and marched to fort Montgomery on the Alabama, from thence against Pensacola, crossed the Escambia, and pursued the flying hostile Creeks near to Apalachicola, killing many of the enemy, and returning to fort Mongomery with 85 Creek prisoners.

Colonel Benjamin Hawkins, Indian Agent, Passes

Volume 10, June 29, 1816, page 304

Colonel Benjamin Hawkins—the good, the benevolent and venerable Hawkins, agent for Indian affairs, died at his post among the Creeks on the 6th inst. The Indians have indeed lost a "father," and the United States one of their most faithful and respectable agents. It appears he died as he lived—with complacency and firmness.

Volume 10, July 13, 1816, page 334

Chronicle.

The late British post at Appalachicola, within the Spanish territory, still kept up by runaway slaves and hostile Indians, has recently excited considerable attention in western Georgia. It is thought the public good requires that the horde should be broken up— "peaceably if we can—forcibly if we must."

Volume 10, July 20, 1816, page 351

Chronicle.

We much regret to learn that the dwelling house of the late colonel *Hawkins* has been consumed by fire, and in it all his valuable manuscripts. This is a loss to the world. He devoted much of his time to science and literature, and is supposed to have been more conversant with the character and traditions of the Indians than any man that ever lived; and it was hoped much might have been given to us elucidatory of their history.

Volume 10, July 27, 1816, page 368

Milledgeville, July 10. We learn, by gentlemen from the westward, that a party of the Creek warriors, from 500 to 1000 strong, under the gallant chief M'Intosh, contemplated marching early in this month against the hostile Indians in Florida, the Seminoles, and had given assurances that they would capture and destroy the obnoxious fort on Appalachicola bay — most of the hostile Indians were said to be on a visit at Pensacola, where 600 Spanish troops had lately arrived.

———

Certain Indians were suspected of burning the dwelling of the late colonel *Hawkins* — but the family of the deceased have stated the known accident by which it occurred; which was the negligence of a servant.

Volume 10, August 10, 1816, page 400

Amelia Island. It is reported that the Carthagenian privateers propose to take this island from the Spaniards, and make it a depot for their prizes.—The procedure would powerfully aid their cause.

Volume 10, August 24, 1816, page 431

The infamous colonel *Woodbine* has been indicted at Nassau for perjury.

NILES' WEEKLY REGISTER.

THE PAST—THE PRESENT—FOR THE FUTURE.

EDITED, PRINTED AND PUBLISHED BY H. NILES, AT $5 PER ANNUM, PAYABLE IN ADVANCE.

Volume 11

(August 31, 1816 - February 22, 1817)

—»»☉◉☉«««—

Destruction of the British Fort at Appalachicola

Volume 11, August 31, 1816, pages 14-15

Chronicle—Shred of the Late War.

Washington, Georgia. August 16.— Our readers no doubt recollect, that a few weeks back, Major M'Intosh, a chief of the Creek nation marched at the head of 500 Indians, for the purpose of destroying a fort on the bay of Appalachicola, where an abominable host of Indians and negroes had collected, who were in the habit of plundering and committing depredations on all that came in their way. In this fort, it is believed, nearly 1000 negroes had taken refuge from their masters. M'Intosh has succeeded in destroying them, after 2 or 3 days hard fighting. Our informant, a gentleman immediately from Mobile, observes, that the negroes made a sortie on the Indians under M'Intosh, on the second morning of their besieging the fort, when a direful conflict ensued—the tomahawk and scalping knife (so close was the engagement) were the only weapons used, the negroes however, were driven into the fort, and on the following day, co-operating with M'Intosh, an American gun-boat getting a favorable position, succeeded in throwing a hot ball into the fort, which blew it up, when it was taken with little difficulty. A quantity of arms, &c. not injured by the explosion, rewards M'Intosh and his intrepid followers, for their bravery.

Milledgeville, Aug. 14.—It will be seen by the following letter from colonel Clinch to the executive of this state, that the fort on Appalachicola

bay in East Florida, where the ruffian Nicolls commanded a motley force of British, Indians and Negroes during the late war, and which has since been occupied by runaway negroes and hostile indians, was completely destroyed by our troops on the 27th ult. Mr. Hughes, the bearer of colonel Clinch's letter to governor Mitchell, and who accompanied the detachment of our troops on that expedition, states, that the celebrated chief M'Intosh with a considerable number of indians, had reached the fort and commenced an attack upon it, (which had continued several days) before the arrival of colonel Clinch's detachment. The fire was returned by those in the fort, but no injury sustained on either side. While colonel Clinch was erecting a battery to play on the fort, 3 of the gun-boats from New-Orleans arrived below it. In ascending the bay, 7 men who had landed from one of these boats were attacked by the negroes and 6 of them killed; the 7th made his escape by swimming.—The gun-boats having been brought up (by order of colonel Clinch) opposite the fort, commenced firing on it with heavy ordnance. After the proper elevation of the gun had been ascertained by three or four discharges, a *hot shot* was fired, which penetrating one of the three magazines, containing 100 barrels of powder, created a dreadful explosion, which our informant supposes must have killed more than 100—the others were taken prisoners without further resistance.

———

Copy of a letter from Lieutenant Colonel Duncan L. Clinch, to his excellency governor Mitchell, dated

Camp Crawford, 4th Aug. 1816.

"Sir—I have the honor to inform you, that on the 28th ult. the fort on the Apalachicola in East Florida, defended by 100 negroes and Choctaws, and containing 200 women and children, was completely destroyed, I have the honor to enclose you the names of the negroes taken and at present in confinement at this post, who say they belong to citizens of the state of Georgia. I have given the chiefs directions, to have every negro that comes into the nation taken and delivered up to the commanding officer at this post, or at Fort Gaines."

Volume 11, September 14, 1816, pages 37-38

Appalachicola. – The following is an extract of a letter from a gentleman of the first respectability at New Orleans to the editor of Weekly Register, and details a very interesting event with a request that I would use the facts to "make out a narrative in my own language," knowing how zealous I am "for the glory of our gallant little navy," But I have preferred to give it in his own words; lest, in attempting to amend, I might injure the "unvarnished tale."

The gentleman well observes, "had this thing happened during the war, it would have resounded from one end of the continent to the other, to the honor of those concerned in it; for it yields in gallant daring and complete success to no incident that happened in the late contest."

"Ever since the declaration of war, in 1812, the disaffected negroes have been running away to a place called Appalachicola. – I believe, even before the event alluded to took place, a Colonel *Nichols*, of infamous memory, (no doubt you recollect him) met a number of them in the neighborhood of Pensacola, having, with a Captain *Woodbine*, of equal celebrity, after surveying the country, fixed upon a spot on the river just mentioned, as a proper place for a fortification; and to which, from its contiguity to Georgia, the Carolinas, Louisiana and the Mississippi territory, they could rendezvous without much inconvenience. The place was, in consequence, fortified with all due care, and according to the most approved modern method; and the batteries mounted with four long 24 pounders, six long 6's, a four pounder field-piece and a 5 ½ inch howitzer, well stored with all the munitions of war, and considered as almost impregnable from the difficulty of getting battering artillery to bear upon it. After the peace it was given up by the British to the negroes and Indians, as it stood, with all its stores of artillery, arms and ammunition; Colonel Nichols only demanding an oath, that they would never permit a white man, except an *Englishman*, to approach it, or leave it alive. Since then it had become a great nuisance, not only as a harbor for the hostile Indians, but for all the discontented negroes in the country, whose desertions were frequent. In consequence of the hostile attitude lately assumed by some of the Indians, it was found necessary to forward provisions and munitions of war to our army on the head waters of this river, and this could only be done by passing the fort which, it was understood, the negroes would not suffer any vessel to do.

Application was made to the commandant at Pensacola for permission to ascend the river, it being within the Spanish territory: this was granted, and men; two of our gun-vessels, under command of sailing-masters Loomis and Basset, readied the mouth of the river on the 10th of July, with their convoy, two small schooners. On nearing the fort, a boat and a watering party, with a midshipman, Mr. Lufborough, of Georgetown, and four men, were cut off and all murdered but one, who escaped by swimming. This was an act that could not be passed over, and it was determined to destroy the fort, if possible. Our vessels were ordered to co-operate with the army. I am sorry to say they received no support whatever, and that, on the contrary, they were dissuaded from attempting to pass or destroy the fort, as being impracticable from the size of their guns, only 12 pounders and but two of them.

Not disheartened, however, our gallant little band, less than fifty in number, all told, began to warp up, every now and then throwing a shot to ascertain their distance correctly — the negroes firing their large guns, but evidently without skill. As soon as they found their shot reached the village in the rear of the fort, they determined, as they say, to see if they could not make a bon-fire, having previously cleared away their coppers to heat the shot, neither of them having a furnace. It seems somewhat extraordinary, and almost miraculous, but the very first hot shot bred by Mr. *Bassett*, a judicious, cool and very promising officer, who commanded gun-vessel No. 154, entered their principal magazine and blew up the fort! The concussion was felt at Pensacola, a distance of sixty miles. The fort contained about 300 negroes and 20 disaffected Indian warriors with their families — 270 were killed, and the remainder, nearly all mortally wounded; only three escaped unhurt. Both the principal leaders of the negroes and Indians were made prisoners — on examining them, it appeared that one of the unfortunate sailors was made a prisoner, but only to experience a more dreadful death — he was tarred and burnt alive! When this was known, the two chiefs were seized upon by the friendly Indians, who scalped them and executed them on the spot — a terrible, but just act of retributive justice. They fought under the *British Jack*, with the red or bloody flag. In the fort there were nearly 3000 stand of British arms, in fine order, never used or opened; about 500 carbines, between 800 and 1000 pairs of pistols, 500 steel scabbard swords, and an immense quantity of British uniform clothing, amounting in the whole, to about §300,000 worth of property— there was also 500 kegs of powder secured, which had been stored in the village outside the fort.

You will have gathered, probably, from the foregoing, that the two gun-vessels were simply to convoy the provisions, &c. to the army, and co operate, if necessary — You will also have perceived that they received no aid whatever from the land troops, other than that they confined the negroes in the fort, during their getting up with the gun-boats. Colonel Clinch, who, it seems, commanded the troops, had made an agreement with the Indians to give them all the plunder, except the cannon and balls, that they might capture, but surely he had no right to give away that taken by the gallantry of a separate and distinct corps. Yet such is the fact that the Indians have borne off nearly the whole; a remnant only is left.

"The merits of this transaction, as it regards the navy, in a few words, are these: — surmounting the difficulties of a navigation to which they were entire strangers — approaching a fort, whose guns were not only double their own in number, but absolutely twice their caliber, with eight times their force in men; and destroying a fort, that had cost the English so much time and more money to erect, in the space of 15 or 20 minutes from the first shot, without any other aid than their own resources afforded, and without the loss of a single man, the unfortunate capture of the boat before mentioned being excepted.

"It will, among other of its effects, strike terror into the Indians. It was their dernier resort in all desperate cases. From the quantity of arms left in the fort, I am clearly of opinion that they were designed as a continual supply for the Indians, or as a secure depot by the British in any future transactions against us in this quarter.

"They are, however, happily frustrated, and I think, if they should ever have the temerity to visit us again, they will meet with a repulse similar to that of the 8th of January."

Volume 11, October 12, 1816, page 108

Charleston. A letter from Amelia Island to a gentleman in this city, dated 21st instant, states that a great number of Africans, lately brought from the Havana, have been smuggled into Georgia, with the intention of sending them on to the back parts of this state.— Let the constituted authorities look to this.

Volume 11, October 26, 1816, page 142

Mobile, Sept. 13, 1816.—Our Spanish neighbors at Pensacola have been under considerable apprehensions from the patriot fleet from Carthagena. They have been busied for sometime in making preparations for defence. They cannot, however, make any effectual resistance. It is reported, that the inhabitants of the place were lately on the point of presenting a memorial to the governor, praying him to invite down the American troops, as they presumed that the appearance of the flag of the United States would conciliate the enemy, and preserve their property from destruction. The project, however, died away with their fears.

A week ago, the first superior court was held in the county of Monroe, which includes the country surrendered by the Creek Indians to general Jackson. An Indian was tried and condemned for killing a white man; and a white man was brought up to take his trial for killing an Indian woman: but as no conclusive evidence appeared, the trial was postponed. It is not easy, indeed, to convict white men of offences against the Indians, as the laws of the Mississippi territory, like those of many of the states, reject Indian evidence when white men are accused The Indian chiefs sent forward an Indian witness against their countryman, accused of killing a white man: but he attempted to escape on the way, and his Indian conductors put him to death.

Volume 11, December 7, 1816, page 239

The Creeks.—A deputation of eight chiefs and warriors of the Creek nation of Indians, led by general M'Intosh, has arrived at Washington, city, on a visit to the president of the United States. It is understood that they have full power to treat on all matters relating to their nation.

Volume 11, January 11, 1817, page 336

Chronicle.

Georgia. Concurred resolutions were passed at the last session of the legislature, requesting his Excellency the governor to urge the general government "to take the necessary measures for causing the boundary line between the United States and the Spanish dominions adjacent to Georgia, to be ascertained and marked."

Volume 11, January 18, 1817, pages 339-340

Report on Public Lands
in the Senate of the United States
January 9, 1817.

[*Extract*]. The acquisition of Louisiana by the treaty of 1803, has still more increased the irregularity of the frontier boundary, and added to the number of distant and detached settlements.

The evils and inconvenience resulting from the irregular form of the frontier are manifest. While separate settlements, or such as project, with a narrow front, far into the Indian country, are formed, the causes of provocation to hostility with the Indian tribes are multiplied, and at the same time the means of protection and defence proportionally diminished. Where so many assailable fronts are presented to an enemy the expence would be incalculable; and, indeed, no force within the means of government can be adequate to afford complete protection.

The present irregular form of the frontier, deeply indented by tracts of Indian territory, presents an extended boundary on which intercourse is maintained between the citizen and the savage, the effect of which on the moral habits of both is not unworthy of regard. It is an intercourse by which the civilized man cannot be improved, and by which, there is ground to believe, the savage is depraved — not being sufficiently enlightened to receive a favourable impression from the virtues of civilization, while he is exposed to the contagion of its vices.

[*Extract*]. The removal of the Indian tribes from their lands surrounded by and contiguous to our settlements, will give place to a compact population, and give strength to the means of national defence. This, however, can only take place with the voluntary consent of those tribes, and must be effected by negociation and treaty in the usual manner.

The contemplated exchange is no other than a transfer of the Indian *right of possession* from one portion of the public domain to another. This transfer cannot be made without the agreement of a community independent of our laws, hence it only can be effected by a treaty with them.

Resolved, That an appropriation be made by law, to enable the president of the United States to negociate treaties with the Indian tribes; wich treaties shall have, for their object, an exchange of territory owned by any tribe residing east of the Mississippi, for other land west of that river.

———•))}☺☺ ☺《《《•———

NILES' WEEKLY REGISTER.

THE PAST—THE PRESENT—FOR THE FUTURE.

EDITED, PRINTED AND PUBLISHED BY H. NILES, AT $5 PER ANNUM, PAYABLE IN ADVANCE.

Volume 12

(March 1, 1817 - August 23, 1817)

Volume 12, March 8, 1817, pages 23-24

[Extract of letter (translated)]
from Mr. Onis to the secretary of state.

10th February, 1817.

Sir—I have received the official letter which you did me the honor to address to me, under the date of the 25th of last month, stating that notwithstanding the desire the president had to adjust all differences between Spain and the United States on just conditions, and to their mutual convenience, it was seen, with great regret, that a like disposition was not manifested on the part of Spain.

[Extract] You approved an idea so liberal, so generous and so demonstrative of the disposition of the king, my master, to accommodate the United States in whatever might be agreeable to them, if not incompatible with his interests; and, in consequence, you made known to me, that the United States wished to unite to their dominions the two Floridas. As, in the former negociations, the cession of West Florida, to the rio Perdido, was alone spoken of, and as his majesty was ignorant of the new desires of this government, I said to you, that although I did not positively know whether his majesty would deprive himself of East Florida, and of the important port of Pensacola, which was the key of the gulf of Mexico, yet the desire of his majesty to gratify this government was great, and that it was very probable he might agree to do it, provided that, on the part of the United States, there should be offered to him a just equivalent, and one of reciprocal convenience.

———

Copy of a letter from the secretary of state to the chevalier de Onis, dated

Department of State,
February 20, 1817.

Sir—I have had the honor to receive your letter of the 10th instant.

From full consideration of the contents of this letter, it appears that, although you expect instruction at an early date, to negociate and conclude a treaty, for the adjustment of all differences between the United States and Spain, which you manifest a desire to accomplish, you do not consider yourself authorised to do so on any one point, at this time. I will thank you to state whether I have understood correctly the idea which you intend to convey. In case I have, I have only to remark, that although the delay is particularly to be regretted, it is not perceived, that any advantage can be derived from entering into the negociation, before you have received your instructions.

I have the honor to be, &c.
JAMES MONROE.

Volume 12, April 5, 1817, page 96

The sudden and very numerous emigrations into the Alabama country threaten many with absolute starvation, unless they are shortly relieved by supplies from other parts.

Volume 12, April 12, 1817, page 112

Charleston, April 29.—A gentleman of veracity, who arrived this morning in the Southern State, from St. Augustine, informs us that a new governor is daily expected there, who has power and authority from the government of Old Spain, *to sell the Floridas to the Americans.*

The gentleman alluded to, derived this information from the *highest authority* at St. Augustine.

Note. It is rumored, says the Augusta Chronicle of the 29th ult. that the governor of Pensacola has requested general Gaines to take possession of that place, in order to secure it against the contemplated attack of the patriots. It is certain that our brave general and the Don had had an interview; and there is little doubt but a solicitation of the kind has been made, and received, as it should, a prompt but respectful negative.

The paucity of Ferdinand's resources, and his inability to protect his colonies, appear to be daily manifesting themselves—while the patriots, slowly but surely advancing, are reconciling their discordant materials, increasing their numerical force, and giving a more bold and respectable tone to the character of the revolution.

Volume 12, April 12, 1817, page 112

Milledgeville, March 25.—Early in this month two or three murders are reported to have been committed on the borders of Camden county, by the indians. Complaints have been made to the executive of this state, from time to time, during the last six months, of injury sustained by them from the whites; these murders are more likely to be in *retaliation*, agreeable to savage custom of seeking redress. The Seminole indians, we are assured from high authority, have been plundered, and one or two of them murdered, by a banditti (a remnant of the self-stiled patriots) who infest a part of East Florida, adjacent to this state. The atrocities of these miscreants have probably brought on our citizens the horrors of the tomahawk and scalping knife; and a renewal of such scenes may be anticipated, until that nest of thieves shall be broken up. The depredation on the indians being committed in East Florida, the perpetrators when they can be identified, are not amenable to our laws; and the governor of East Florida either has not the means, or wants the disposition to punish them. A small military force at Trader's hill, would, it is believed, give security to that part of the southern frontier, and our government we hope will see the propriety of stationing there, such number of troops as will secure the peaceful citizens against violence from red or white savages.

Volume 12, April 26, 1817, page 143

Chronicle.

In consequence of the alarm existing on the frontiers of Georgia, by the hostility of the neighboring Indians, general *Floyd*, who commands a brigade of militia in that quarter, has been authorised by the governor to adopt such measures for the safety of the people as he may deem necessary.

Volume 12, May 10, 1817, pages 175-176

Chronicle.

Indian hostility.—The late outrages of the southern Indians are attributed to the continued intrigues of the infamous *Woodbine*, now said to be resident at the mouth of Sewanee, where there is a fort and block house. Besides exciting the Indians to murder and robbery, it seems he is carrying on a trade with *Cuba*, in slaves, inveigled from the United States. Government appears to be impressed with some facts of this nature, from the late marching of troops for the Lower Creek country; and if it be true, that *Woodbine* has a fort and is carrying on the operations attributed to him, we hope it may meet the fate of that at Appalachicola. If the Spaniards lose their neutral character, why should we respect it?— if they are unable to control such proceedings, we must do it.

Volume 12, May 24, 1817, page 208

Chronicle.

The Floridas.—There was a report at Paris that the United States had purchased the Floridas of Spain.

——»»»☻ ◉ ☻«««——

British Responsible for War with Southern Indians

Volume 12, May 31, 1817, pages 210-211

The Southern Indians.

We have always considered the conduct of the British regarding the

Southern Indians, as peculiarly cruel and unjust to them and to us—as a wanton waste of human happiness and human life. From the foundation of our government until the massacre at Fort *Mims* in 1813, the best interests of these tribes had been our particular care: men of high and honorable minds had been stationed amongst them to assist them with counsel, and protect their just rights from every encroachment. A *spirit of peace* was zealously cultivated, and much money expended by us to instruct them in agriculture and the arts needful to their prosperity. Instruments were furnished and schools established; and already they had many pretty well-managed farms—the men driving the plough and attending their cattle, and the women were spinning and weaving, &c. The benevolent *Hawkins* was their common father; his whole soul appeared to be embarked in the project of philanthropy, and every administration seconded his beneficent views.

The time seemed to have nearly arrived when they were to have reaped the fruits of an honest care of them—but the spoiler came; the spirit that had destroyed millions on millions of men in the east, entered the yet peaceable plains of the west, and the restless disposition of the indian was excited to raise the tomahawk against his benefactor! The plough was laid aside; the quiet of the forest was disturbed by the war whoop of the savage, allied to *Englishmen*—defenceless settlements were laid waste, and their innocent people destroyed with a degree of ferocity hardly to be paralleled. Hundreds of those who attacked Fort *Mims*, and massacred the garrison, with all the women and children who sought refuge there (some 15 or 20 excepted, who effected their escape while the savages were busy in slaughtering and burning the rest to death) spoke the English language, and had been in constant intercourse with the whites. What was the consequence? The besom of destruction passed over them, and thousands of them were swept from the face of the earth by the war that general *Jackson* and others carried through all parts of their country. Prostrate, they sued for peace—and their life, justly forfeited by crime, was granted to them. They had nothing to expect but extermination—yet they were spared.

Still Great Britain seemed unsatisfied—blood enough had not been shed; and, though she made peace with us, she furnished the savages with the means of continuing war, and sowed the seeds of new contentions. Depots of arms and ammunition were made; and a very strong fort in the *Spanish* territory, well furnished with cannon and every thing needful to its defence, was given to them as a rallying point and place of refuge. The fort at Appalachicola was blown up by one of our gun boats, and its deluded tenants miserably perished. We then hoped the British had left the indians to themselves, and that a remnant might be saved. But the work goes on—the desire to obtain a pack of peltry at any cost of human life, or maintain an ascendancy in these tribes to injure the people of the United States, continues. Several successive Englishmen, under Spanish license or sufferance, with an official or sort of official character, have been with them—exciting hopes that they [the agents] know *cannot* be realized. Where is this business to stop? *It must stop.* Any British agent found among these Indians, within our territory, exciting them to murder, ought to be seized, and tried, and punished, with less pity than is due to a sheep-killing dog—and, if Spain lends her territory to such men to organize hostility in the tribes, Spain must be dispossessed of it. The law of self-preservation requires it. The women and children of our frontier shall not hold themselves dependent on the *mercy* of *British indian agents* for their lives.

We have said that the conduct of the British in regard to the *Southern* indians was peculiarly cruel and unjust. Their conduct was cruel and unjust to all the tribes, in wantonly leading them to war; but they whose consciences may permit them to justify the murders and burnings at the River *Raisin*, &c. will feel much at a loss to palliate the proceedings of the *enemy* in respect to the Creeks. These were led to battle with a moral certainty that they would be beaten. It was true, they might massacre a few harmless individual Americans, but no one could have been fool enough to suppose that they had power to affect the general operations of the war—and their engagement in it was a wanton waste of human life, and a marring of the most benevolent schemes that had been adopted by us to ameliorate their condition.

The Lower Creeks have lately manifested a very unquiet disposition. They have already forgotten that we refused to exterminate them, as we might, when they exterminate our people, as they could. They have again listened to the seducer, and are acting in a way that will go far to reconcile their best friends to their extermination, which, I fervently say, may heaven forbid!—Such have been their proceedings that, we are told, general *Gaines* expects shortly to be compelled to invade their country and "effectually subdue them"—for which purpose it is thought that a few of the Georgia militia will be called out.

The following letter has been published at *Milledgeville*; and is, upon the whole, about as impudent a thing as we ever saw. If the agent spoken of is ever caught within our territory, let him be punished—if within that of Spain he meditates murder and excites war, a *neutral* country ought not to protect him.* *The period of submission has past.* The republic is no longer in leading strings. England will never openly sanction such proceedings, if we openly punish them. British "humanity and philanthropy" towards the indians!!—Who placed the knife in their hands—who paid bounties for the scalps of babes—who permitted the burning of the wounded? My soul freezes with horror when I look over the pages of the *Register* and view the things that have past. But to the letter—if the "agent" arrives and accomplishes the object hinted at—the dissatisfied Creeks will be extinguished. What need of this? There is room enough for them and for us. Let them live and be happy.

[*Note: The Floridas were not *neutral* during the war—all the excesses of the Creeks were put in motion at Pensacola, &c. And the *British* transported arms, &c. through the country unmolested. Every principle of natural and civil law would have justified us in seizing upon these colonies, and it was a grand mistake that we did not do it. It would have added nothing to the cost of the contest, and might have led to a speedy settlement of our differences with Spain.]

———

A. Arbuthnot to the commanding officer at Fort Gaines.

Okolokne River,
3d March, 1817.

"The head chiefs request I will enquire of you, why American settlers are descending the Chatahouchie, driving the poor Indian from his habitation, and taking possession of his home and cultivated fields.

"Without authority, I can claim nothing of you—but a humane and philanthropic principle guiding me, I hope the same will influence you—and if such is really the case, and that the line marked out by the treaty of peace between Great Britain and the United States, respecting the Indian nations, has been infringed by any of the citizens of the latter, you will represent to them their improper conduct, and prevent its continuance.

"I have in my possession a letter received from the governor of New-Providence, addressed to him by H. B. M. Chief secretary of state, informing him of *orders* given to the British ambassador at Washington, *to watch over the interests of the Indian nations*, and see their rights are faithfully attended to and protected agreeably to the treaty of peace made between the British and the Americans.

"I am in hopes that, ere this, there is arrived at New Providence a person from Great Britain with *authority* to act as agent for the Indian nations—and if so it will devolve upon him to see, that the boundary lines, as marked out by the treaty, *are not infringed*."

Volume 12, June 7, 1817, page 237

Foreign Articles—Florida.

We see a letter published from *S. B. Gardenier*, to his brother in Ohio, stating that he had joined the patriot service in East Florida, in May last (1816)—that after a hard fight with a superior party of royalists, he was taken prisoner and sentenced to the mines for life. "The mines in the Floridas (says he) were so full of Americans, that he and his party with about 50 more, were ordered to those in South America." But in crossing the isthmus he made his escape, and swam to an English brig called the Syphax, whose captain treated him generously and put him on board a patriot privateer, who landed him at Savannah.

Volume 12, June 14, 1817, page 250

Foreign Articles—Florida.

The Spanish commandant at Pensacola has refused a passage to the transports with provisions for the U. S. troops stationed on the Conawa, &c. without the payment of an enormous duty—and is said actually to have seized some of their rations. It is intimated that general Gaines will *negociate* a passage for these vessels.

Volume 12, June 21, 1817, page 271

Foreign Articles.

The patriot privateers have lately made some valuable captures off the Havana. It is also believed that they have captured three armed vessels which lately sailed from this port, among them one formerly called the Jacob Jones, of Boston, carrying 22 guns, on board of which it was thought there was a viceroy for Mexico and a bishop. We fear that this report is too good to be true.

Volume 12, June 28, 1817, page 286

Foreign Articles—Florida.

The governor of *Pensacola* has not yet permitted the provisions destined for the U. S. Troops in the interior, to pass. He received 10 per cent from the contractors for permission to land them, and demands 3 per cent more as an export duty.

Volume 12, June 28, 1817, page 287

Chronicle—Indian Warfare.

The indians on the frontiers of Georgia have lately committed many depredations—stealing cattle, horses, &c. and sometimes murdering the people. A small party assembled at Clark's Mills, in Camden county, to pursue a body of them, who came up with the Indians, and killed three of them. The whole frontier is in a state of alarm; and this rencontre may lead to an open rupture.

Volume 12, June 28, 1817, page 287

Chronicle—Woodbine—Again.

St. Stephens, (*Mississippi Territory*) *May* 23.—Our readers will be able to judge when they read in this day's paper, the late talk of the arch villain Woodbine to the Creek Indians, which has been the cause of the late murders committed on our unoffending citizens of the frontier, by the lower Creeks. The Talk alluded to, was handed us for publication by a gentleman of veracity from fort Jackson, who was called on by the Big Warrior to consult and return an answer. He informs us, that every word and deed of the Big Warrior, on this occasion, has been that of a patriot and a true friend to the United States. It is not our wish to implicate the British government in this business, but we would only remark, that it would be well to watch more narrowly, the conduct of some of their agents, or rather that they select men for such important stations of more honesty and truth than colonel Woodbine. [*Halcyon.*

———

Copy of a Talk sent from the British agent in East Florida, to the Big Warrior, head chief of the Creek nation of Indians.

When the English made peace with the Americans, they included the whole of the Indian nations, viz. Creek, Choctaw, Chickasaw, and Cherokee; those nations were guaranteed in the quiet possession of their lands, and the Americans engaged to give up such lands of the Indians as they had taken possession of during the war.

If they have not done so, or if they have been making further encroachments, the chiefs have only to represent their complaints and the aggressions of the Americans, to the governor of New-Providence, who will forward them to England, or get them conveyed to the British minister at Washington, who has orders from the king of England to see that the rights of the nations above mentioned are protected, and the stipulations contained in the treaty, *in their favor*, are faithfully carried into execution. The Americans have no wish to go to war with Great Britain; they will not, therefore, do any thing contrary to the treaty, and what encroachments have been made, must be without the knowledge of the chief of the American government: and so soon as he is informed thereof by the British minister at Washington, he will order the American people who have taken possession of Indian lands, to *draw back* to their own possessions.

The Indian nations are all one great family; they possess lands their great forefathers handed down to them, and they ought to hand them down entire to their children. If they sell their land, what do they receive for it? Nothing that will last—it is wasted away in a few years. Whether, therefore, they sell or give it away, they are robbing their children of the inheritance they had a right to expect. As a great family they ought to live as such with each other: let the four nations join in bonds of brotherly love; let them smoke the pipe of peace; let the cultivation of their lands be their chief object during the spring and summer, and hunting their diversion during winter; and the produce of their labor will be bought by *good* people, who will come and deal with them, when they know there is any thing to be purchased for goods or money.

If the Americans, or other nations, live near them, let them live in friendship with them, and keep up a good understanding; but on no account sell or give away any of their lands.

I recommend this as a friend of humanity and of good order.

A. ARBUTHNOTT.*

Okolokne, March 11, 1817.

[*Alias, the notorious Woodbine.]

———

The head chiefs of the Upper Creek nation, have desired me, Oponey, to get the straight talk for them; what is written in the foregoing, I believe to be the true and straight talk, received from an Englishman, who carried two deputies to New-Providence, and has returned them to Okolokne.

I Oponey, have been sent by you, the head chiefs of the Upper Creek nation, to see the Seminole Indians; I have done so; they live quietly and peaceably, and

wish to do so with all their red Brethren in every part of the nation.

Opoy Hatcho has desired me to see those things; I have done so, and see all quiet, and had the talk I now send you, and shaken hands with the friend who gave it me.

That the friend I have met came over with goods, by desire of the chiefs of the Lower-towns, and is a true friend to the Indians. The various and untrue talks that you send me from time to time, must be made by some person, an enemy to all us Red Brethren, and ought not to be listened to; let me know who they are, and send me an answer as soon as possible, to the present talk.

OPONEY, his x mark.

Written by order of the aforesaid Oponey, the 11th March, 1817.

A. ARBUTHNOTT.
Witness—Aron Moris.

Volume 12, July 5, 1817, page 299

Foreign Articles—The Floridas.

An idea again generally prevails that the United States are about to have the *Floridas* ceded to them. It is an event that we shall hail with pleasure, as, besides their intrinsic value, and the security a possession of them will afford to an extensive frontier—it will prevent the necessity, for *self preservation*, that we might otherwise have, of destroying the poor indians, led by the intrigues of *foreigners* to murder our people, in the mere wantonness of barbarity.

There is a very probable report that Sir Gregor McGregor has taken possession of Amelia island.

Volume 12, July 12, 1817, page 319

Foreign Articles—Florida.

It is now stated that Amelia island was *to be* taken possession of by Sir Gregor McGregor, on the 2nd inst. The Spanish force there does not exceed 50 men. Later accounts assure us that it *is* taken. It will be very advantageous to the patriots.

Volume 12, July 19, 1817, page 334

Foreign Articles—Florida.

We have accounts that may be relied upon (we believe) informing of the capture of *Amelia* island, without opposition, by general McGregor, on the 1st of July. Not a single gun was fired by either party. Hundreds were flocking to his standard, and he was immediately to proceed to St. Augustine, which, it was expected, would also fall into his hands. A naval force co-operates with McGregor.

The Washington City Gazette gives a report that the United States are to have the Floridas for 8 millions of dollars. This sum would be very convenient for Ferdinand— for that which, though of great value to us, is an annual loss to him.

Volume 12, July 19, 1817, pages 335-336

Chronicle—Indian Affairs.

Milledgeville, June 24.—The annexed documents furnish authentic information respecting the present state of our affairs with the Indians below; and, also the particulars of a late successful attack on two of their marauding parties, by a small detachment of volunteer militia. The frequent irruptions of these savages into our territory for some months back have excited very general alarm among the defenceless inhabitants of our southern frontier, many of whom have abandoned their homes and fled to the interior for safety. The executive of Georgia unwilling to rely any longer on the promised assistance of the national government, which has probably been delayed by the peculiar situation of the war department, has issued orders to general Floyd, requiring him to call into service, from any part of his division, a sufficient force to ensure the protection of the frontier settlements exposed to danger and the effectual chastisement of all future marauding parties of Indians. From the late insidious attempts of the Spanish government to stir up the western savages against us, we have a right to attribute the persevering hostility of the Florida Indians to some such improper interference. The artillery company from Charleston, which was stated to have been stopped at Creek Agency, has, we learn, descended Flint river, and arrived at Fort Scott.

———

Extract of a communication from general Floyd, commanding the 1st division of Georgia militia, to the executive of this state, dated.

St. Mary's,
5th June.

"Your letter of the 29th April affords ample proof of your prompt attention to the unsettled and perilous situation of the southern frontier, bordering on the savages — and I yield cheerfully to both inclination and duty in apprizing you of such occurrences in this quarter, as may have a tendency to involve the interest and public welfare of the state.

"A copy of major Bailey's report to me of a late affair with the Indians is forwarded to you. The misconduct of evil disposed persons on both sides, has produced a state of things worse than open war with our red neighbors, which requires a reciprocity of vigorous measures for the restoration of order and tranquility to the respective frontiers.

"I have just received information of a party of Indians having, on the 30th ult. entered the neighborhood, and in open day light took the cattle from Rollinson's pen. Such is the state of alarm, that many families have broken up."

———

Major Bailey's report to general Floyd.

Camden County,
28th May.

"I deem it expedient to inform you, that on the 20th instant I left Trader's Hill, accompanied by twenty four volunteers, in pursuit of cattle lately driven off from this frontier by a party of Indians. We took their trail, and followed it to where the Maccasooka path crosses the Suannah river. When about a mile from the river, on the 22d, between seven and eight o'clock, P. M. we saw the light of a fire, which we made for, and found it to proceed from an Indian camp of from 5 to 8 men, who we had no doubt, were a party fitted out to do mischief, and then

177

on their way for the frontier settlement. We attacked them at 11 o'clock the same evening, killed one man, and wounded others, who were assisted off by their comrades. At this camp, we got three horses and two guns. On the morning of the 23d we fell in with an Indian trail, which we followed a circuitous route, bearing for the big bend of St. Mary's—at 9 o'clock, P. M. of the 24th, we came up with them at a camp on the waters of St. Mary's river, and attacked them at day break the next morning, killed two, and wounded several. There were 12 or 15 in number. Here we got two guns and sixteen horses, two of which belong to our citizens. I am happy to state that not one of our party received any injury."

Extract of a letter from the Agent for Indian affairs to the acting governor of the state, dated the 10th instant.

Last night a runner from low down Flint river brought me a letter containing the following in formation:—"It seems a small parcel of the Uysehee red people who reside on the Chatahoochee river, a tribe that has always been friendly to our government, and never one of them has been known to join the red stick party, were on a hunting excursion near the water of St. Mary's river, when in the night by moonlight a party of white people rushed upon them, killed one man, and wounded the other four badly—drove off all their horses, took their guns, and every thing else they could carry off from the camp. The four wounded men are now lying very bad, about sixty miles below here, not being able to proceed to their town on Chatahoochee. It is not known whether it was done by the white people that reside in the Spanish government, or in our own government.

It is very desirable to ascertain whether the mischief was done by the people of Georgia, or by those of East Florida. If by the latter, retaliation may be averted from our people by a timely representation of that fact to the chiefs of the town to which the injured party belong. The chiefs of the nation are to meet at fort Hawkins the first of next month, which will afford a fair opportunity of making explanation, if in the mean time you can ascertain the aggressors.— *Journal.*

——»»➤☙◉☙◄««——

The Green Cross of Florida flies over Amelia Island

Volume 12, July 26, 1817, page 347

Foreign Articles—Florida.

The capture of Amelia Island, by general M'Gregor, is certain. He landed his men on the 30th of June, in the rear of Fernandina, marched them through the marsh, breast-deep, and entered the town by capitulation, without firing a gun. There were only about 70 Spanish soldiers on Amelia. He was rapidly recruiting his little army, and intended immediately to march for *St. Augustine*, a strong place, and said to be defended by 500 men, where he will probably have warm work. He has with him a ship of 22 guns, and some smaller vessels. *The official capitulation and M'Gregor's proclamations, &c. must be postponed until our next.*

A small military post on St. John's river, called Fort Nicholai, was abandoned by the Spaniards, who escaped in two gun boats, after the capture of Amelia.

Two schooners were captured at Amelia by McGregor, who has already established a court of admiralty there, with a post office, &c. John D. Heath, formerly a member of the bar, at Charleston, is the judge. A newspaper, in the English language, is intended to be printed. One privateer had received a commission at Amelia and sailed on a cruise.

Forty African slave taken at Amelia, were condemned as prize and sold at auction.

Later accounts say that every thing was tranquil at Amelia. General McGregor was sending off troops to St. John's for St. Augustine, which was closely blockaded by a patriot frigate and a sloop of war—they were thought a match for any naval force that Spain has in the western hemisphere.

The governor of St. Augustine, colonel Croppinger, is represented as a brave man, and very popular with the people.

Volume 12, July 26, 1817, pages 347-348

Chronicle—Southern Indians.

A letter is published in the *Savannah Republican*, dated at St. Mary's June 27, from which it appears that the people of Camden County, Georgia, are abandoning their homes for fear of the Indians. The neglect to establish a military post on that frontier is loudly complained of. The Seminole Indians are remarkable for their ferocity.

Volume 12, August 2, 1817, pages 365-366

Foreign Articles—Florida.

Our latest accounts from Amelia anticipate that McGregor will fail in his expedition by delay in executing it. It is said he ought to have marched immediately on St. Augustine, and that all his forces are dissatisfied. Augustine, in the mean time, is said to have been strengthened.

———

Capitulation of the Island of Amelia.

Brigadier-general MacGregor, commander-in-chief of all the forces, both naval and military, destined to effect the independence of the Floridas, duly authorised by the consituted authorities of the republics of Mexico, Buenos Ayres, New-Grenada and Venezuela, offers to Don Francisco Morales, *capitan, del regimients de Cuba,* and commandant, civil and military, of the Island of Amelia, the following terms:

1st, The commandant, civil and military, Don Francisco de Morales, shall forthwith surrender the garrison of the island, with all the arms and munitions of war belonging to the king of Spain.

2dly, All the officers and troops of the garrison shall surrender as prisoners of war, to be sent to Augustine or to the Havana, with their private baggage, which shall be respected.

3dly, The lives and property of all private persons, whether friends or foes to the system of independence, shall be sacred and inviolate; and to those who do not choose to join the standard of independence, six months shall be allowed to sell or otherwise dispose of their property.

4thly, The general also offers to the inhabitants of Amelia, whether friends or foes, who have absented themselves on account of the present circumstances, the privilege of returning to their homes, and enjoying the benefit of the third article of capitulation, and passports will be freely granted to all who wish to depart.

The preceding were agreed to between the commandant Don Morales and the secretary of general MacGregor,

Fernandina, 29th June, 1817.

FRANCISCO MORALES,
JOSEPH DE YRIBARREN.

Attest—Bernard Segin.

Approved,　GREGOR
MACGREGOR.

———

PROCLAMATION:

Gregor MacGregor, brigadier-general of the armies of the United Provinces of New-Grenada and Venezuela, and general-in-chief of the armies for the two Floridas, commissioned by the supreme directors of Mexico, South-America, &c.

To the inhabitants of the Island of Amelia—Your brethren of Mexico, Buenos Ayres, New-Grenda and Venezuela, who are so gloriously engaged in fighting for that inestimable gift which nature has bestowed upon her children, and which all civilized nations have endeavored to secure by social compacts—desirous that all the sons of Columbia should participate in that imprescriptible right—have confided to me the command of the land and naval forces.

Peaceable inhabitants of Amelia, do not apprehend any danger or oppression from the troops which are now in possession of your Island, either for your persons, property or religion; however various the climes in which they may have received their birth, they are nevertheless your brethren and friends. Their first object will be to protect your rights; your property will be held sacred and inviolable; and every thing done to promote your real interests, by co-operating with you in carrying into effect the virtuous desires of our constituents; thereby becoming the instruments for the commencement of a national emancipation. Unite your forces with our's until America shall be placed by her high destinies to that rank among the nations, that the Most High has appointed. A country by its extent and fertility, offering the greatest resources of wealth and happiness.

The moment is important. Let it not escape without having commenced the great work of delivering Columbia from that tyranny which has been exercised in all parts, and which, to continue its power, has kept the people in the most degrading ignorance, depriving them of the advantages resulting from a free intercourse with other nations; and of that prosperity which the arts and sciences produce when under the protection of wholesome laws, which you will be enabled properly to appreciate, only when you will have become a free people.

You who, ill-advised, have abandoned your homes, whatever may have been the place of your birth, your political or religious opinions, return without delay, and resume your wonted occupations. Deprecate the evil counsels your enemies may disseminate among you. Listen to the voice of honor to the promises of a sincere and disinterested friend, and return to the fulfilment of those duties which nature has imposed upon you. He, who will not swear to maintain that independence which has been declared, will be allowed six months to settle his affairs, to sell or remove his property without molestation, and enjoy all the advantages which the laws grant in such, cases.

Friends or enemies of our present system of emancipation, whoever you be, what I say unto you is the language of truth; it is the only language becoming a man of honor, and as such I swear to adhere religiously to the tenor of this proclamation.

Dated at head quarters, Amelia Island, June 30th, 1817.

GREGOR MACGREGOR.

Jph. De Yribarren, *secretary.*

———

Gregor MacGregor, general of brigade to the armies of the United Provinces of New-Grenada and Venezuela, and general in chief of that destined to both the Floridas, with commission from the supreme governments of Mexico and South-America, &c.

Soldiers and Sailors—The 29th of June will be forever memorable in the annals of the independence of South America. On that day, a body of brave men, animated by a noble zeal for the happiness of mankind, advanced within musket shot of the guns of Fernandina, and awed the enemy into immediate capitulation, notwithstanding his very favorable position. This will be an everlasting proof of what the sons of freedom can achieve when fighting, in a great and glorious cause, against a government which has trampled on all the natural and essential rights which descend from God to man. In the name of the independent governments of South-America, which I have the honor to represent, I thank you for this first proof of your ardor and devotion to her cause; and I trust that, impelled by the same noble principles, you will soon be able to free the whole of the Floridas from tyranny and oppression. Then shall I hope to lead you to the continent of South America to gather fresh laurels in freedom's cause. Your names will be transmitted to the latest posterity as the first who formed a solid basis for the emancipation of those delightful and fruitful regions, now in a great part groaning under the oppressive hand of Spanish despotism. The children of South-America will re-echo your names in their songs; your heroic deeds will be handed down to succeeding generations, and will cover yourselves and your latest posterity with a never-fading wreath of glory. The path of honor is now open before you. Let those who distinguish themselves look forward with confidence to promotion and preferment. To perpetuate the memory of your valor, I have decreed, and do decree, a shield

180

of honor, to be worn on the left arm of every individual who has assisted or co-operated in the reduction of the Island of Amelia; this shield will be round, of the diameter of four inches, made of red cloth, with this device, "*Vencedores de Amalia*, 29th of June, de 1817, 7 y 1," surrounded by a wreath of laurel and oak leaves, embroidered in gold for the officers, in yellow silk for the men. The colors of the corps of national artillery, the first squadron of cavalry, and the regiment of Columbia will have the same device embroidered on the right angle of the colors. Long live the conquerors of Amelia!

Dated at head-quarters, San Fernandina, 1st July, 1817, 7 & 1.

GREGOR MACGREGOR.

Jph. De Yribarren, *secretary.*

Volume 12, August 9, 1817, page 376

Foreign Articles—Florida.

A New York paper says that M'Gregor has issued a quantity of scrip, made payable by the delivery of lands in Florida to the holders at the rate of 50 cents per acre, if he should come into possession of it, or to be paid in cash with interest; on which he is said to have raised upwards of 200,000 dollars.

Mr. Hubbard, sheriff of the city and county of New York, we learn by the papers of that place, having most honorably adjusted the affairs of his office, resigned the same, and left the city in a vessel that he himself had fitted out, to join M'Gregor.

Accounts from Amelia island to the 20th ult. inform us that McGregor then remained there organizing and augmenting his forces, and in settling the executive and judicial departments of his conquest. He is said to have conducted himself with great mildness and propriety, and his great object seems at present to be to secure the possession of the island as a rendezvous for the many vessels sailing under the patriot flag. The following is another of his proclamations:

Gregor MacGregor, general of brigade of the armies of the united provinces of New Genada and Venezuela, and general and chief of the army destined against the Floridas, duly commissioned by the supreme governments of Mexico and South America, &c. &c.

Inhabitants of the north and western districts of East Florida!

The evacuation of Fort San Nicholas by the Spanish forces on the fourth of this month, has placed the adjacent territory under the control and protection of the independent government. I lose no time in assuring you of the enjoyment of your civil liberty, the preservation of your rights, and the protection of your property. I would extend to all those peaceful citizens living in or adjoining the waters of the St. Mary's and St. John's rivers, and the islands and country intervening, all the advantages to be derived from the third and fourth articles of the capitulation of the 29th June, on the surrender of this place—a full protection of their lives and property.

Let not a fear of rapine and spoil drive into opposition or disturb the well disposed inhabitants of Florida. Other and more glorious motives impel those who fight in the cause of liberty. Continue to evince your friendly disposition by remaining quietly at your homes, in the exercise of your domestic employments, and such conduct will insure its rewards.—Join not the ranks of our enemies, nor aid them against us, or you will be met in the spirit of hostility, and your persons and property must share their fate. Rely on the assurances of candor and truth—do not compel us to oppose as foes, whom we would embrace as brothers.

Head-quarters, Fernandina, July 12, 1817, 7 and 1.

GREGOR MACGREGOR.

Volume 12, August 16, 1817, pages 397-398

Foreign Articles—Florida.

We have a report that the royalists have attacked McGregor at Amelia with a great deal of spirit. At our last accounts the patriot flag was still flying, and the fighting had ceased. Further particulars unknown.

The ship Margaret left the port of New York on Sunday last, bound to Amelia Island; but was overtaken and carried back by the revenue cutter, Captain Cahoone. The Margaret had on board several persons, who embarked with the intention of joining the patriots under General *MacGregor*—also munitions of war, it is supposed for his troops. The cutter fired several times at the Margaret before she hove too.

A letter from Amelia island dated the 28th July says, "one of our privateers has sent in a prize.— a brig laden with sugar and coffee, and with twenty-six thousand dollars in specie." M'Gregor appears to be waiting for reinforcements. The accounts said to be from the island are contradictory and inconclusive.

Volume 12, August 16, 1817, page 399

Chronicle—Indian Affairs.

We learn from our southern papers, that the assemblage of the Creeks at fort Hawkins, in July, amounted to between fourteen and fifteen hundred; and many were prevented from attending by the inconvenience of leaving their crops at that important period of the season. The conduct of the Indians at this council, it is said, was marked with great propriety and decorum. The principal chiefs dined every day with general Mitchell, the United States' agent, and in the afternoon executed the points which had been previously discussed and decided upon in council.

At this meeting, we are informed that the United States' agent had sufficient influence to prevail on the council to abrogate their ancient law of retaliation, which permitted a murder to be satisfied by taking the life a relation of the murderer, if the principal could not be found; and have thus forbidden the practice of indiscriminate revenue. On this point they have passed a written law. The agent also procured their consent to the cession of a piece of land which shuts them out entirely from a part of our frontier and secures the citizens from the danger of Indian aggressions. The day the United States' Agent left them an unfortunate affair occurred. The Indians having received a considerable sum of money from the United States, some of the younger warriors determined to have a frolic, before they went home. A principal warrior, one who was next in command to M'Intosh, in the service under general Jackson, among others got drunk and killed his own nephew. The chiefs immediately convened, and after ascertaining the fact of the murder, they ordered the perpetrator to be instantly taken and executed, which was done in less than an hour after the murder had been committed.

Indian Speech. — The following speech of Slapecha Barnett, a half breed Creek Indian, was delivered a short time past before a national assembly of the chiefs:—It evinces a pacific disposition which should be cherished by our government. — *Geo. Argus.*

"*My Countrymen*—God made us all, both red and white Americans, to live on one island. Since the Almighty has said we should live together, why did we join the people who came from beyond the salt-water? Why did we join the British? Let us raise our children to the end that God created them. We can live without the red-coats or their help. Let us, then, raise our corn and eat it. When God gave us this land, he said we should rest our bones upon it—so he said to all those to whom he gave land.

"I think there is but one God; and that that God is just—if we walk strict in *this*, he will save us in the *next* world. The cold water which he gave us still runs—so are the paths for the government of the conduct of good men still here. Foolish as I am, my little understanding tells me, when I see these things, that they are God's works.

''When the white people first came among us, the Great Spirit had forbid our mixture—we did mix—and to avoid the pain of separating the husband from his wife, the father from his children, and the brother from his sister, he has continued the course of the mixed blood in our veins. We must remain in this situation, because God is upon the top of us, and directs it to be so. General Washington acquired a war-name above the rest of men—but the mixture of our blood, and the accession of a part of our strength to his, added not a little to it. You all know, my countrymen, who know any thing of the unfortunate history of our country, how slow was his progress when opposed by the strong and undivided arms of our fathers, and how rapid it has been since Whiskey and Calico have divided us.— We are all one people."

Volume 12, August 23, 1817, page 441

Foreign Articles—Florida.

Our latest accounts from MacGregor, at *Amelia*, are vague and unimportant. It is stated that his admiralty judge has already left him. The expedition will probably soon have an end, and amount to nothing. But the reports are so various that we know not what to believe. The battle said to have taken place at Amelia was a mere exercise of the troops.

NILES' WEEKLY REGISTER.

THE PAST—THE PRESENT—FOR THE FUTURE.

EDITED, PRINTED AND PUBLISHED BY H. NILES, AT $5 PER ANNUM, PAYABLE IN ADVANCE.

Volume 13

(August 30, 1817 - February 21, 1818)

Volume 13, September 27, 1817, pages 78-79

Foreign Articles—Florida.

By a gentleman, passenger in the sloop Hermit, arrived yesterday morning from St. Mary's we have received the following intelligence:

On the 4th inst. general M'Gregor resigned the command of the patriot troops stationed on Amelia Island. He stated that his reasons for resigning were, that he had been deceived by the company who were to supply him with the means to carry on the war in Florida. He and his lady had gone on board the privateer General M'Gregor, bound to Baltimore. Colonels Posey and Parker, with a number of officers and men, had abandoned the cause. The force on the island was about forty officers and men. There were lying opposite the island, the Buenos Ayrean privateer brig Morgiana, of 18 guns and about 100 men, the national brig St. Joseph, of 10 guns and 67 men; the privateer General M'Gregor, of 10 guns and 65 men. The Venezuelian privateer schooner Jupiter had arrived on the 9th inst. with a French hermaphrodite brig, a prize, loaded with sugar and coffee.

On the night of the 8th September about 350 Spanish troops, principally negroes, arrived on the island; and on the morning of the 9th attacked the patriots about a mile from the town of Fernandina, but were beaten off with the loss of a major and horse killed, and one taken prisoner. The loss of the patriots was two killed and four wounded. On the night of the 10th, they made another attack, and were again beaten off, without the loss of any on either side.

A small Spanish schooner arrived on the 11th inst. from the coast of Africa, with slaves; not knowing the place was in the hands of the patriots, went in and was taken possession of by the Morgiana.

[So. Pat.

Several very valuable Spanish ships, prizes, have probably arrived at Amelia.

Volume 13, October 4, 1817, page 95

Foreign Articles—Florida.

It is *conjectured* that *M'Gregor* has arrived in the Chesapeake. The report is again revived that the United States have made, or are about to conclude, a treaty with Spain for the purchase of the Floridas. The price is given at five millions of dollars. Whether in this, the claims for spoliations are to be settled or not, is not stated.

On the 13th of September the Spaniards attacked the town of Fernandina, (Amelia) with between 200 and 300 men—after a sharp contest with the bayonet, they were completely defeated, with the loss of several men, killed and wounded. The force of the "patriots" was about 150, all told; they did not suffer much. Many persons from Amelia had retired to St. Mary's. The infamous colonel Woodbine was at the island—for purposes not stated.—Mr. Hubbard, late sheriff of New-York, seems to have much influence and authority. The people of Florida do not appear to have any love for the "patriots," and anxiously look for a transfer to the United States. Several very valuable prizes had lately arrived at Amelia, and the force, afloat, was respectable for its strength.—Com. Aury, with two large privateers, and a prize of great value, had arrived—he proposed a salute with the United States brig *Saranac*, but the request was passed over in silence. What is to be the issue of this little war we cannot guess; and, indeed, feel very indifferent about it. Those who fight for freedom, if to avenge the wrongs, or even to retaliate the grievances of their country, enlist us in their cause at once; but the affair at Amelia, whatever may have been its original design, seems to have degenerated in a mere asylum for privateers, and to be intended as a depot for smuggling into the United States. The *Saranac*, however, will take care that the "republic suffers no detriment."

—»»⊖ⓞ⊖«««—

Conflict with Seminoles Along Georgia Frontier

Volume 13, October 4, 1817, page 96

Chronicle—The Seminoles

General Gaines, who has been ordered by General Jackson to demand the delivery of certain murderers of the Seminoles—having some reason to believe that they may refuse to give them up, has arranged a concentration of his troops at Fort Scott, and requested of the Governor of Georgia a battalion of riflemen and another of light or mounted infantry, ready to assist him, if they should be wanted—to assemble at Fort Hawkins.

Volume 13, October 11, 1817, page 111

Foreign Articles—Florida.

The Mexican flag has been hoisted at Amelia—Com. Aury commander in chief, Hubbard governor. They now, in turn, talk of attacking the Spaniards.

Proclamation.

Fernandina, East Florida, September 20th.—The inhabitants of Amelia are informed, that to-morrow the Mexican flag will be hoisted on the fort, with the usual formalities. They are invited to return as soon as possible to their homes, or send persons in their confidence to take possession of the property existing in the houses, which is held sacred. All persons desirous of recovering their property are invited to send written orders, without which nothing will be allowed to be embarked.

Proclamations for the organization of the place will immediately be issued.

AURY, *commander in chief.*
R. HUBBARD, *governor, &c.*

Volume 13, October 25, 1817, page 143

The Seminole Indians.

It does not appear that these Indians have yet complied with the requisition of General Gaines, respecting certain murderers harbored amongst them. One of the chiefs in answer to the general is reported to have said, that he expected an English agent, who would settle the affair by driving the Americans back. General Gaines has, however, adopted measures to punish them if they do not behave peaceably, and also to restrain any persons from committing unauthorized depredations upon them.

Volume 13, November 1, 1817, pages 157-158

Foreign Articles—Florida.

There were eight large prizes, fully ladened with sugar, coffee, &c. at Amelia. One of them had on board 1000 boxes of *segars* [cigars] that had been made expressly for the use of the "adored" Ferdinand.

The armed vessels there on the 11th instant were—the brig American Libra, of 3 guns; and the San Joseph, of 6 guns, belonging to the government—and the private armed vessels American Congress, of 12 guns; the Morgiania, of 18; and the Republican of 2;—two others were fitting out. McGregor and the infamous Woodbine have arrived at New Providence from Amelia.

Our latest accounts from this island report, that the civil and military authorities are literally at "*daggers points*"—being actually in arms against each other. There is an "American party" and a "French party"—Hubbard, as the civil governor, is the head of the former, and Aury, as commanding the military, of the other. Battle between them was expected—and report adds that Aury, with his fleet, was actually blockading the island. A Com. Champlin was however expected with four sails, and it was supposed would give the preponderance to Hubbard's part.

Note: These particulars are fully confirmed—but the affair at Amelia has lost its interest with us, and seems to be nothing else than a semi-piratical business. We should be glad if the United States force in that quarter was immediately strengthened.

Volume 13, November 1, 1817, page 160

Chronicle.

There was a report in circulation at New-Orleans, of Lord Cochran's arrival off Appalachicola, with a frigate and other armed vessels; and it was said that his lordship meditated an attack on Pensacola.

Volume 13, November 8, 1817, page 175

Foreign Articles—Florida.

Affairs at Amelia remain unsettled. Governor Hubbard died on the 19th ult. after a few days illness. Colonel Irwin appears to succeed him as the head of the "American" party. Prizes continued to arrive—among them were vessels with slaves; but sales of prize goods had not been extensively effected on account of the contentions of parties. Commodore Champlain had not yet arrived. Captain Elton, in the U. S. Brig Saranac, was closely watching the proceedings at Amelia—he had sent five vessels into Savannah for adjudication, and it is reported that he intended to overhaul the Morgiana, of 13 guns, when she left the port.

Volume 13, November 8, 1817, page 176

Chronicle.

The U. S. Brig Saranac has taken possession of a British vessel and sent her to Savannah, which had been captured by a schooner from Amelia island, the conduct of whose officers and crew makes them deserve to be called and treated as pirates.

Volume 13, November 15, 1817, pages 189-191

East Florida.
From the National Intelligencer.

It has fallen within our power to satisfy some of the queries proposed a few days ago by a correspondent in our columns. The subjoined article, of East Florida, is from a source entitled to the highest credit, and as the reader will perceive, from its unadorned matter-of-fact character, was made without any view to publication. Having derived considerable instruction from a perusal of it ourselves we obtained permission, from the friend to whom it was addressed, to make use of it for the information of the public.

The particulars of the state of East Florida, thus obtained, are the most acceptable at this moment when a rumor is abroad, and stated with a confidence almost amounting to certainty, that our government has obtained, or has an assurance of obtaining, by negociation, a cession of that country from Spain.

However reasonable and probable it appears, that Spain should be willing to divest herself of a territory which is not only of no advantage, but an incumbrance to her; and however willing our government might be to obtain on reasonable terms this country, continually infested as it is by wandering tribes of runaways and outlaws, who held the neighboring country in terror of their ruffian violence; and however certain it is that this country must, at no distant day, enure to the United States we are pretty confident the rumor we have alluded to is premature; and, so far from any treaty or compact having been concluded for the cession of that country by Spain to the United States, we are under the impression that no official communications have passed between the two governments on the subject.

———

Memoranda on the geography, population, &c. of East Florida.

With two exceptions, viz Suarez and Fernandez, who have American wives and families, speaking English entirely, all the other inhabitants of East Florida, who live in that portion of country situated between the waters of the river St. Mary's and St. Johns, within forty miles of the sea, are Americans, with a small mixture of British, or French, or German; but all domiciliated citizens of the United States. Beyond that extent the country is either vacant, or occupied by hunting parties of Indians, without settlement on the Atlantic side; chiefly Alachauays under Bowlegs, who now reside near the mouth of Sawanee alias San Juan, on the bay of Apalache; and, together with runaway and plundered negroes, extend along the sea shore and islands down southerly as far as Tampa bay.

After passing the aforesaid settlement on the waters of St. Johns, few inhabitants are found excepting those immediately round Augustine, which they consider as their residence. They are poor people, chiefly Minorciaris or originals from the Balearic Isles, and supply Augustine market with vegetables. Passing on the southward of Augustine, you find several inhabitants and some negroes about Matanzas, but only one cotton plantation; this is 20 miles south.

At Mosquito, which is 60 miles south, you find four or five cotton plantations, and a good many negroes. Two or three more settlements, of little consequence, are about cape Florida. All these southern settlements are chiefly from Providence, Bahamas; but, being exposed to various depredations and uncertainties, they, as well as all the inhabitants of Augustine, two thirds of whom, as well as Fernandez, have English for their mother tongue, eagerly desiring, and would make any sacrifice to obtain security and a protective government.

The number of white families dwelling between the waters of St. Mary's and St. John's, may be somewhere about one hundred and fifty, mustering somewhere about three hundred and sixty militia, divided into three districts, each of which has a captain and lieutenant, &c. elected by the people of their respective districts, together with a judge or justice of the peace, who tries all causes by an arbitration or jury of twelve men. They have the power of punishing in minor cases; but, when they convict, capitally, the prisoner, together with the proceedings, are remitted to St.

Augustine, for approbation and execution. No military commander or other servant of the government, has power to arrest any inhabitant beyond the lines of his garrison, who must be prosecuted and tried by the authorities of his own district.

The inhabitants are not bound to do any military duty, to muster, nor to pay taxes; nor observe any such regulations except as they make for their own defence and self preservation.

The white population of Augustine is not included in the above, and may consist of one thousand; of whom one hundred and fifty may be able to bear arms. Add to this one hundred and fifty white regular troops, and two hundred and fifty black or colored regulars, besides fifty free colored militia.

The inhabitants of Fernandina, I mean free white people, may be about two hundred and fifty, of whom fifty may be able to bear arms.

The white militia of Amelia, who do not muster in any of the above districts, may be about fifteen men. The negro population of the whole island of Amelia I take to be about 500. That of the three regular districts, including the waters of St John are 500. All others out of Augustine are 500. Whole colored country population, exclusive of Indians, runaways, &c. is 1500. Colored women and children, or slaves, in Augustine not included in the above estimate, may be about 500.

All the inhabitants, even the Spaniards, are tired of living without a government, and of all others would prefer that of the United States, as past circumstances plainly prove; among which may be noticed the simultaneous effort of all the people in 1812 to annex the country to the United States, and also the active part they took to drive back the English in 1814, at St. Mary's, where they had one man killed and one wounded, and beat back seventeen boats filled with British troops. Under these circumstances, they think themselves (as far as is consistent with policy) entitled to the protection of the United States, so far as to keep them from being plundered or imposed upon by any foreign banditti who may take advantage of their present helpless condition, until they can gather strength by increasing their population, which they are now endeavoring to accomplish by inviting emigrations from the United States. To accomplish this, the smallest indirect hint given to the commandant of the vessels or troops of the United States at St Mary's would suffice, by showing any symptom of favor to their endeavors for self preservation.

It now remains to show what intrinsic value belongs to this territory, bordered on all sides by the Atlantic, or intersected by navigable waters, connected with those of the United States. First, the timber, which far exceeds in quality any that grows northerly, consists of forests of live oak, cedar, cypress and pine, all of inexhaustible extent. Secondly, may be mentioned the fertile lands, which from the climate derive qualities not elsewhere to be found: amongst which are, a large tract near Augustine and St. John's, called 12 Mile Swamp, containing 14,000 acres; another extending to Mosquito, 60 miles long; another between Bowleg's and Tampa, 60 miles long, supposed to contain some hundred thousand acres. The whole interior above Alatthuwa, for several days ride, is excellent live oak and hickory land. The interior of the country is unexplored by white people, but said to be fertile and healthy, full of pleasant orange groves, and plentifully stocked with wild cattle.

It has been observed that the inhabitants pay no taxes: by this is meant direct taxes. All foreigners arriving at Amelia or Augustine pay duties (agricultural machines or implements of husbandry excepted) but, as there is no custom house or Spanish post on the Main, which has free communication with the United States, by means of the waters and channels of St. Mary's river, these inhabitants consequently go free of duties, as the Spaniards are unable to enforce their collection. Indeed, the present liberty and independent state of the inhabitants arises rather from a want of power in the Spanish government than from any royal order or concession made to those inhabitants. But, from motives of convenience, as well as interest, the people and the Spanish authorities maintain the most friendly understanding, as all title of property, fee simples, and grants of land, in which the government has been very liberal to the people, are derived from that source.

Indeed, the government has manifested an uniform disposition to cultivate a good understanding with the people, by granting them every kind of indulgence. It is supposed by the inhabitants, that great encouragement will now be given by the governor to new settlers; as it plainly appears that the invasion of MacGregor took place in consequence of the paucity of inhabitants, who, therefore, rather than run the risk of defending themselves, remained neuter.

The town of Fernandina is situated on a peninsula or neck of land, the narrowest part of which may be about two hundred and fifty yards, defended by a strong picket and two block houses, which enclose the whole town.

On the side next the harbor, is a fort well picketed, mounting 8 guns, which commands the anchorage, and reach as far as the middle line of the waters or boundary of the United States.

As the inhabitants afraid to indulge too sanguine expectations of coming immediately under the government of the United States, they consider it the wisest plan to increase the number of inhabitants by all possible means, so as to protect themselves by their own force, and confirm their independence; which, by lowering the value of the province as a Spanish colony, would induce that nation to part with it on easier terms. But, as the government of the United States is the ultimate object of the people, they hope that their past conduct has so far merited the good opinion of the United States as to induce that government to go as far towards protecting them in their liberties and properties, as policy and the nature of circumstances will allow.

Before I drop the subject of East Florida, it would be well to mention the Indians, who, taking advantage of the absence of the inhabitants then employed in besieging St. Augustine, came in from the westward and killed and plundered all they met with, taking off the negroes to a large amount, for which outrage they have never made the smallest satisfaction, but persist in retaining all they took, and granting protection to all runaway slaves from the United States or Florida, whose frontier inhabitants are daily falling a sacrifice to their resentment, which seems indiscriminately directed against all the white inhabitants, with whom they never visit nor have friendly intercourse. Their headquarters, at present is about the mouth of Sawanee river called *San Juan de Amajura* in the old charts, into which river vessels are admitted from New-Providence, who supply them with arms and ammunition in exchange for skins, &c. A certain Captain Woodbine has been with them, and was lately; he is a British officer, and acquired their confidence during the war, by commanding at the British fort of Apalachicola under Colonel Nichols.

Previous to the blowing up of this fort a great many runaway negroes, who composed part of the garrison, doubtful of the event of the siege, deserted from it, and after its destruction went to the south east along the shore of Sawanee; where they joined the other banditti under Bowlegs, and now compose part of those negroes who, together with the barbarous Seminolians, have been robbing and murdering the frontier inhabitants both of Georgia and Florida indiscriminately, and are still continuing it. These are the main enemies the people of Florida have to fear, and against them they desire assistance. This is the grand cause which impedes their growth and hinders them from becoming independent. The Indians are incorrigible in their cruelties. They are naturally enemies to a civilized state of society, as it destroys their independence. They resemble wolves, who would rather be exterminated than domesticated.

Volume 13, November 22, 1817, pages 206-207

Foreign Articles—Florida.

Mr. Gual, a very respectable gentleman, sent as a minister to the United States, from Venezuela, it is said, is appointed governor of Amelia.

We have been informed that the port of Amelia is open for importation, free of duty for four months from the 28th October 1817, of arms and munitions of war, and provisions of every kind.

A Charleston paper says—We have received, from our correspondent at St. Mary's the following proclamation:

"Whereas *Bernardo Febreno* has run away from this port, with the pilot boat *American Libre*, belonging to the republic of Venezuela, leaving me on shore, probably to go and commit depredations on the high seas: I hereby in the name of the government of Venezuela, request all the collectors of the customs and the navy officers of the United States, to seize and detain the said pilot boat *American Libre*, and give information of the same to *Line Clemente*, esq. Philadelphia. The said schooner has no commission.

A. G. VILLERET,
*Major general
of the navy of Venezuela.*

Fernandina,
the 1st of November, 1817.

———

*Charleston Courier office—
Nov. 13.*

From St. Mary's Nov. 8—The U. S. gun vessel No. 168, lieutenant M'Call, has arrived here, after a very boisterous passage. Amelia appears to be all in a bustle, and there is constant cannonading there—the place is under martial law. Report says two prizes are off. Annexed you have the last proclamation issued by commodore Aury.

———

Inhabitants of Fernandina.

For days past you have witnessed the scandalous transactions of a faction, composed of men, who existing, and tolerated on this island by our generosity, have solely been engaged in subverting social order. They are mercenaries, traitors or cowards who abandoned the cause of republicanism in the hour of danger, and who either kind by our enemies, or misled by the intrigues of a few aspiring individuals, have attempted to involve us in all the complicated horrors of a civil war. Citizens, we are republicans from principle, our fortunes have been spent, and our lives oft exposed for this most glorious cause. We have come here to plant the tree of liberty, to fester free institutions, and to wage war against the tyrant of Spain, the oppressor of America, and enemy to the rights of man. We are ever ready to pay obedience to the principles of republicanism, but firmly determined never to adhere to the dictates of a faction.

When the heat of passions shall be no more, when public peace and tranquility are restored, we shall see with a lively pleasure the establishment of a provisional government most suitable to our common interest, and to the advancement of our glorious cause.

Americans, Englishmen, Irishmen and Frenchmen, men of all nations, we are freemen; let us forever be united by the love of liberty and hatred to tyranny.

Soldiers and sailors, martial law is declared to be in force for ten days. Let us give to our brethren of the state of the Floridas, proofs of our military discipline, and of our respect for the property of the inhabitants.

Head quarters of Fernandina, November 5th 1817, 8 and 1 of the independence.

Signed, LUIS AURY.

Volume 13, November 22, 1817, page 208

Chronicle—Indian Affairs.

General Gaines' demand on the Seminole Indians, for the delivery of certain murderers, it seems, has been absolutely refused. – They justify themselves on the plea of retaliation. Hostilities were immediately expected to commence. General Gaines was proceeding for Fort Scott, on the Flint River, where he expected to be joined by 600 Creek warriors, and have an entire force of 2500 men, regulars, militia and Indians. The Seminoles are said to be able to bring 1500 warriors into the field. They are the bravest, most robust, and most truly savage of all the southern tribes. – *Woodbine*, probably, laid the foundation of this new speck of war. The state of Georgia has had a military force stationed in Camden County for a considerable time, to protect the people from these Indians.

Volume 13, November 29, 1817, page 216

Legislature of Georgia.

*Communication from
the Late Governor and the President
of the Senate to the Legislature.*
[Excerpt]

Being appointed by the president

of the United States agent for Indian affairs for the Creek nation, and having determined to accept the same, I have this day resigned the executive government of the state to the honorable *William Rabun*, president of the senate. [Excerpt] In contemplating the situation of the Creek Indians of the present day, residing within our limits, I think it will be generally admitted, that their attachment and adherence to the United States during the late war with Great Britain, which not only involved them in all the horrors of civil war, but caused them the loss of nearly all their hunting grounds, entitle them to our protection and regard; and to a full share of the benefits resulting from the benevolent policy of our government. From these considerations, and with this view of the subject, it will not be expected that the execution of the laws regulating the intercourse with those Indians should be relaxed; so far at least as regards the agency to which I have been appointed, it will be understood, that no intercourse with them, which is forbidden by law, or which may have a tendency to defeat or retard their improvement in the arts of civilized life, will be tolerated. At the same time, for every legal object and honest pursuit, every facility in my power will be afforded.

D. B. MITCHELL.

State-house, 4th March, 1817.

Volume 13, November 29, 1817, pages 216-217

Excerpts from
Governor William Rabun's Message.

*Executive department, Georgia,
Milledgeville, 3d November,* 1817.

The late governor Mitchell having accepted the appointment of agent to the Creek nation of Indians, which had been conferred on him by the president of the United States during the last winter, did on the fourth day of March last, resign the office of governor of this state into my hands as president of the senate.

For a considerable time before and since I came into office, the Indians bordering on our south-western frontiers have manifested a hostile disposition, by embodying themselves, plundering from the citizens of Camden county several hundred head of cattle, and on the 24th day of February last, a party made their appearance near Clark's mills, on the St. Mary's, and wantonly murdered a woman and her two children, set their dwelling house on fire and effected their escape with impunity. This distressing intelligence was immediately communicated to this department by major-general Floyd, and several other gentlemen of that neighborhood. Without delay I transmitted an account of the same to the war department, and earnestly pressed the necessity of an adequate force being placed on that exposed frontier by the general government, in order that protection might be afforded to the defenceless inhabitants who were then flying from their homes. I also instructed major-general Floyd to order from his division a sufficient force to repel those lawless intruders, and to inflict suitable chastisement on them whenever they might be found on our borders, until the pleasure of the general government should be known. The acting secretary of war, in reply to my letter, observed, that the subject was referred to major general Jackson, and that the necessary protection might be expected; but, unfortunately for us, it has not been afforded. We have therefore been under the necessity of maintaining a detachment of our militia, on the frontier of Camden county, for several months past, under the direction of major Bailey of that county. Some time in the month of May, while the major and his party was pursuing a large number of cattle, which had been driven off, they fell in with two companies of Indians, and attacked them with great bravery, killed several, wounded others, put them to flight and returned without sustaining any loss. Since that period, I have not received information of any damage done in that quarter by the Indians.

On the 8th of September, I received a communication from major-general Gaines, dated at fort Montgomery on the 20th July, calling for two battalions of our militia, to be held in readiness, to assist him in reducing the Lower Creek or Seminole tribe to order. I immediately caused the requisition to be complied with, and the two battalions have been detailed and organized, and are now waiting further orders.

Volume 13, November 29, 1817, page 221

Foreign Articles—Florida.

We have nothing new from Amelia Island. But learn that the Mexican privateer Superior, captain Jolly, had captured a Spanish vessel from the coast of Africa, with 290 slaves, and also an English schooner from Havanna for Laguira, with a full cargo of stores for general Morillo, among which were 30,000 lbs. of gunpowder. These prizes were ordered for Amelia, *from whence the negroes will certainly be smuggled into the United States, as many others have lately been.* This trade in human flesh is so profitable, that if that island is not taken possession of by the United States, we shall hear of many slave vessels sent in as prizes that had very conveniently laid off the port to be captured, as certain *English* vessels were taken to the eastward, during the late war.

Volume 13, December 6, 1817, pages 236-237

Excerpt of the President's Message to Congress.

This day at 12 o'clock, the president of the United States transmitted to both houses of congress, the following message, by Mr. Joseph Jones Monroe, his secretary—

[Excerpt] In the summer of the present year, an expedition was set on foot against East Florida, by persons claiming to act under the authority of some of the colonies, who took possession of Amelia Island, at the mouth of St. Mary's river, near the boundary of the state of Georgia. As the province lies eastward of the Mississippi, and is bounded by the United States and the ocean on every side, and has been a subject of negociation with the government of Spain, as an indemnity for losses by spoliation, or in exchange for territory, of equal value, westward of the Mississippi, a fact well known to the world, it excited surprize, that any countenance should be given to this measure by any of the colonies. As it would be difficult to reconcile it with the friendly relations existing between the United States and the colonies, a doubt was entertained, whether it had been authorized by them, or any of them. This doubt has gained strength, by the circumstances which have unfolded themselves in the prosecution of the enterprize, which have marked it as a mere private, unauthorized adventure. Projected and commenced with an incompetent force, reliance seems to have been placed on what might be drawn, in defiance of our laws, from within our limits; and of late, as their resources have failed, it has assumed a more marked character of unfriendliness to us, the island being made a channel for the illicit introduction of slaves from Africa into the United States, an asylum for fugitive slaves from the neighboring states, and a port for smuggling of every kind.

A similar establishment was made, at an earlier period, by persons of the same description, in the Gulph of Mexico, at a place called Galveston, within the limits of the United States, as we contend under the cession of Louisiana. This enterprize has been marked in a more signal manner by all the objectionable circumstances which characterized the other, and more particularly by the equipment of privateers, which have annoyed our commerce, and by smuggling. These establishments, if ever sanctioned by any authority whatever, which is not believed, have abused their trust, and forfeited all claim to consideration. A just regard for the rights and interests of the United States required that they should be suppressed, and orders have accordingly been issued to that effect. The imperious considerations which produced this measure will be explained to the parties whom it may, in any degree concern.

Volume 13, December 13, 1817, page 256

Chronicle—Seminole Indians.

General Gaines has made a further requisition of 500 men from Georgia, to be held in readiness to act against the Seminole Indians. The whole detachment is to be commanded by Brigadier General Glascock. In a letter to the governor of Georgia, General Gaines states that his hopes of terminating the disputes with these Indians without a resort to force, has been disappointed. They report their strength at 2700 warriors; the number is thought to be much over rated; but they seem determined to make a stand. The chief seats of this people are in Florida.

Volume 13, December 20, 1817, pages 257-258

Excerpts from the President's Message.

Every one of the quill-driving family of editors seems to feel it his *right* and *duty* to offer some remarks on the annual messages of the president of the United States to congress, on opening the session;—and, as a man may "as well be out of the world as out of the fashion," we, also, shall briefly notice the late very plain and very interesting communication of Mr. *Monroe*.

The message commences by noticing our "profitable and extensive commerce" It has been found fault with for this—as stating that which is not built upon fact. It is very certain that our commerce is *not* flourishing; a very considerable part of our legitimate trade, is in the hands of foreigners; many of our ships are laid up; many are our partially employed, and the business of ship-building has almost ceased in many of our ports. But the president had regard to this commerce "as augmenting our revenue," and in *that* respect it may be called extensive and prosperous. Even in *this*, however, we are of the opinion, and we have *reasons* for it, that our commerce has not been nearly as "profitable" as it ought to have been; and we did hope that the president would have recommended a close revision of all the laws affecting goods paying *ad valorem* duties. Mr. *Sanford's* motion, in senate, on the 8th inst. may supply this omission—but it is a matter of great importance; many times more so than that which relates to the *internal taxes.*— We are extensively swindled through British agents and goods shipped "to order," and must enlarge the number of articles paying specific duties, or adopt a system by which those paying *according to value* shall be inspected and valued for the purpose of assessing the taxes that they ought to pay. Though I have not the best opinion in the world of "*counting-house morality,*" still it would be as uncharitable as it would be unjust to insinuate, that the body of our *regular* merchants and traders have any part or participation in the smugglings complained of.

[Excerpt] To proceed with the

message. We pass over it with entire satisfaction and much profit, until we arrive at that part which relates to the suppression of the establishments at *Galveztown* and *Amelia* island; and here we pause for the purpose of offering our thanks to the president for those proceedings; though, indeed, they appear to bear against the patriots, in the success of whose efforts we are most truly and sincerely interested. We are not familiar with the proceedings that have taken place at Galveztown, but those at Amelia are known to ever body. Whatever may have been the original design of *McGregor* and those who first dispossessed the Spaniards of the island, it is very certain that it now is only a depot for privateers of the worst description, and for smuggling of the most obnoxious character. I know a man who has boasted that he had $25,000 in one of the southern banks, the product of certain slaves captured and sent to Amelia, and there disposed of to citizens of the United States, who introduced them at their own risk into our country. Many have been thus brought in already, and if Amelia had remained in the possession of those who latterly commanded there, many *prize* cargoes of slaves would have been made off the harbor in a few months,—just as some little boats, with two or three men and unarmed, captured some large vessels ladened with British goods, off the eastern coast, in the late war. As a war measure against Spain, we should heartily rejoice to see *every one* of her ships captured by the patriots—nay, I do not know that I would refuse the latter with their prizes (except of slaves) the perfect freedom of our ports. I am almost willing to make an immediate acknowledgment of some of the provinces as free and independent states—yet cannot bring myself to respect the motives or approve of the conduct of the strange mixture of men that recently ruled at Amelia: But we shall, probably, soon see the reasons *in extenso* on which the president acted, and then we can judge more clearly on this subject.

Volume 13, December 20, 1817, page 267

Foreign Articles—Amelia Island.

We are without any interesting particulars from this island, though we have much matter and speculation respecting it. A report is circulated, and with apparent truth, that the "Venezuelian minister" as he is called, after seeing the president's message, forwarded an express to Amelia advising the authorities there of the contemplated hostility, and directing commodore Aury to defend the place to the last, unless attacked by a very superior force in which case he should enter a solemn protest, in the name of the patriot governments, against the proceeding on our part, &c. The Savannah Republican of the 4th inst. intimates that he had made some preparations to defend the place. But he will hardly attempt to resist:—all was confusion and anxiety at Amelia.

Colonel Bankhead, with a sufficient number of United States troops, was at Point Petre on the 6th inst. waiting the arrival of certain United States' vessels, which were instantly expected, to take possession of the island.

On the 19th and 20th of November an election for nine representatives, to form the legislative body of the island was held. Mr. Gaul has 151 votes, the highest number given. On the 27th of the same month Aury issued a proclamation stating the result of the election, and convoking the assembly on 1st day of December.

———

Florida.

It is *again* stated that Spain has authorized a sale of the Floridas to the United States for $6,000,000. This is six million times more than they are worth to Ferdinand, though they will be of great value to us. It is also said, that the British minister has, by order of his government, remonstrated against any purchase of this country being made by us. We hardly suppose this latter report to have any foundation.—Great Britain has no business to interfere, and we think will not have the impudence to do it.

—»»⊖⊚⊖«««—

War Commences with Encounter at Fowltown

Volume 13, December 20, 1817, page 272

Chronicle.

General Gaines, having arrived at the Flint River, sent a friendly message to the Indian chief on the opposite side, which he would not listen to. A small detachment under Major Twiggs then crossed, the Indians fired upon them, and the fire was returned. The Indians left four killed on the field and fled we suffered no loss. The official letter from General Gaines is in type, but we cannot squeeze it in; an industrious congress occupying more space than we expected. But this letter with other neglected matter shall be preserved.

———

The *Savannah Republican*, of the 9th instant, gives a report that *Woodbine* has arrived at Pensacola from New Providence with an expedition fitted out at that place; that he is accompanied by MacGregor, and has enlisted a considerable number of Indians and blacks in his service. We hope it may be the fortune of General Gaines to catch the wretch that has cost us the lives of hundreds of women and children, that he may be tried and punished as a murderer, as he deserves. We cannot believe that he has any authority from the British government for his proceedings since the peace; and whether he has or has not, his infamous career should be stopped.

Volume 13, December 27, 1817, page 296

Chronicle.

Milledgeville, December 2.
The subjoined intelligence of the commencement of hostilities was received by the executive on Thursday last, and immediately issued from this office in an extra sheet, that our frontier citizens, exposed to danger, might be put on their guard against those predatory attacks of the Indians, which seldom

fail to follow such an occurrence. The governor has ordered out the Pulaski troop of cavalry, a company of infantry from Wilkinson, and another from Laurens, for the protection of the frontier below Hartford. Other measures of defence will be adopted, should they prove necessary.

———

Copy of a letter from major general Gaines to the Governor Georgia, dated at Fort Scott, near the confluence of the Flint and Chatahooche rivers.

21st November 1817.

Sir- The first brigade of United States' troops arrived at this place on the 19th instant. I had previously sent an Indian runner to notify the Fowl town chief Ene-he munt-hy, of my arrival, and, with a view to ascertain whether his hostile temper had abated, requested him to visit me. He replied that he had already said to the commanding officer here all he had to say, and that he would not come.

He had warned major Twiggs not to cross, or cut a stick of wood on the east side of Flint river, alleging that the land was his, that he was directed by the powers above and below to protect and defend it, and he should do so. This being the talk referred to, and his town having continued to be hostile ever since the late war, having participated as the friendly Indians assert, in the predatory war carried on for some time past against the Georgia frontier, I yesterday detached two hundred and fifty men (supposed to be about the strength of the town) under the command of major Twiggs, with orders to bring to me the chief and warriors, and, in the event of resistance, to treat them as enemies. The detachment arrived at the town early this morning and were instantly fired upon, but without effect. The fire was briskly returned by the detachment, and the Indians put to flight, with the loss of four warriors slain, and as there is reason to believe, many more wounded.

Among the articles found in the house of the chief, was a British uniform coat (scarlet) with a pair of gold epaulets; and a certificate signed by a British captain of marines, "Robert White, in the absence of colonel Nichols," stating that the chief had always been a true and

195

faithful friend to the British."

The reports of friendly Indians concur in estimating the number of hostile Indians, including the "Red Sticks" and Seminoles, at more than two thousand independent of the blacks at and near Suwanney, within 120 miles of this place, amounting to near four hundred men, and increasing by the addition of every runaway from Georgia able to get to them. The friendly Indians inform me, that the hostile party and blacks have been promised a British force to assist them, from New-Providence. This promise, though made by Nichols and Woodbine, is nevertheless relied on by these deluded wretches, who I have no doubt, will sue for peace as soon as they find their hopes of British aid to be without foundation.

I have called the militia from Fort Hawkins to this place, and have directed colonel Brearly to confer with your excellency upon the subject of an additional battalion for the protection of the frontier from Oakmulgee to St. Mary's.

I have the honor to be, most respectfully, your obedient servant

EDMUND P. GAINES,
Major general commanding.

Later intelligence. We are indebted to the activity of the editor of the "Reflector," a very neat and well conducted paper printed at Milledgeville, Georgia, for many particulars respecting the war with the Indians. We are compelled to make a very brief abstract of the information at present before us.

———

Col. Arbuckle, with 300 men, was attacked about 12 miles from Fort Scott by a party of Indians, who were put to flight with a supposed loss of 8 or 10 killed. He had 1 killed and 2 wounded. Several murders appear to have been committed by the Indians, and a party of 12 men are said to have been cut off from Fort Scott. The effective force at that place was from 80 to 100 men. A body of friendly Creeks, expected to co-operate, was collected at Fort Mitchell, under McIntosh. The Georgia militia was at Fort Hawkins, supposed to be about

220 miles from Fort Scott, which the Indians had appeared in the immediate vicinity of, and fired some shot on the boats that were building on the river. Warm work is expected — murders are numerous, and, by acting in small bodies, they have already done much mischief. They killed a man in the neighborhood of Fort Gaines; the whole country was in a state of alarm. The most unfortunate particulars that have reached us are that General Gaines ascertained that Major Muhlenburg was ascending Apalacha, and dispatched two boats to his assistance, and to collect provisions. One boat commanded by Lieutenant Scott, with 50 men, was attacked 12 miles below Fort Scott, and the whole massacred, except six, who saved themselves by swimming, four of whom were wounded. From the other boat, and another which had been up the river nothing had been heard.

———

Amelia Island.

We have nothing important from Amelia, except to shew that the smuggling of negroes and goods has been extensively checked. A *prize* vessel with 118 slaves, going into Amelia, was captured by the Saranac on the 30th ult. Another with 250 slaves had just got into port. *The trade in flesh was brisk.* Major general Floyd, of Georgia, has, in pursuance of a requisition, at the instance of the United States' authorities, issued orders for the draft of 500 men from that part of his command most contiguous to St. Mary's; in which vicinity it is supposed they are to be employed.

———»»☾ ◉ ☾««———

Documents Related to Amelia Island

Volume 13, January 3, 1818, pages 301-304

Documents related to Amelia Island.
Mr. McIntosh to Mr. Crawford.

The Refuge, near Jefferson,
Camden county (Georgia)
Oct. 30, 1817.

"Dear Sir—The last letter I had

the honor to address to you, was on the ninth of August; shortly after which the public papers announced that you had left Washington on a visit to Georgia. A few weeks after, I thought it not prudent to venture out of my swamp plantation on the Satilla, and since have been very little at St. Mary's. Since general M'Gregor, and the greater part of his officers (some of whom were men of respectable standing in the United States) have left Amelia Island, there has not been so much ingenuity made use of in misrepresenting the conduct and intentions of the invaders of East Florida; and the accounts which are published of them, are for the most part generally correct. The present chief, commodore Aury, got the command very much against the inclinations of sheriff Hubbard and colonel Irwin.—When he arrived at Fernandina, with his squadron of privateers and prizes, they were entirely without money. He declared, "that if he gave them any aid, it must be on the condition of being made commander in chief; and that as general M'Gregor never had any commission whatever, the flag of the republic must be struck, and that of the Mexican hoisted and that Fernandina should be considered as a conquest of the Mexican republic, (under which he was commissioned) without its being necessary that any other part of the province of East Florida should be conquered." Hubbard and Irwin reluctantly agreed to the mortifying condition of resigning the command. They were never friendly with the commodore, and endeavored, but in vain, to gain over by intrigue a part of his men. Their own party considerably increasing shortly after, they were several times on the point of coming to open war with Aury, and his followers; and under the pretence that Aury's force were composed chiefly of brigand negroes. A few days before Mr. Hubbard's death, (who was called governor without having any power) Aury marched to his quarters with a body of armed men, and obliged him to make such concessions as drove him to an act of intemperance, which soon after terminated his existence.

Since the death of this gentleman, there has been little or no disturbance among them. But it would appear as if the suspicions of the Frenchman did not die with Hubbard, as none of his privateers have left Fernandina.

The parties are designated as the American and French, and, I have been assured by individuals belonging to them both, that each are anxiously looking for reinforcements. Aury has a number of Frenchmen, who were, it is said, officers under Bonaparte. They find it their interest as well inclination to support their countryman.

His great dependence, however, is on about one hundred and thirty brigand negroes—a set of desperate bloody dogs.

The American party, which are rather more numerous than the other, consist generally of American, English and Irish sailors; but now have no declared leader. Irwin wants either spirit or popularity to assume that character. For my own part, I believe that in point of morals, patriotism and intentions they are exactly on a par. Aury's blacks, however, make their neighborhood extremely dangerous, to a population like ours; and I fear that if they be not expelled from that place, some unhappy consequences may fall on our country. It is said that they have declared that if they are in danger of being overpowered, they will call to their aid every negro within their reach. Indeed I am told that the language of the slaves in Florida is already such as is extremely alarming.

The patriots at Fernandina had about ten days ago an unexpected and strange reinforcement.—Twenty half pay British officers, by the way of Turk's island, arrived at St. John's river, and mistaking it for Amelia, a colonel and a couple of others were made prisoners by the Spaniards. The others got safe to Fernandina; but finding that general Sir Gregor M'Gregor had abandoned it they determined immediately on doing so too."

————

Extract of a letter from Mr. Clark, collector of St. Mary's to Mr. Crawford.

Collector's office,
St. Mary's, Georgia,
1st November, 1817.

Honorable William H. Crawford,

Sir—I hasten to communicate the following information by letter, received from a gentleman residing on St. John's river, East Florida. The subject in its

197

bearings, presents considerations of the first importance, as to our political relations with Spain.

The following is extracted from the same:

"Pablo river,
St. John's, October 24, 1817.

About sunset a yawl boat arrived at the landing, when seven persons came from her, who requested shelter for the night, and some refreshment, stating that they were half-pay British officers of the army and navy, from the island of St. Thomas, on their way to England, via the United States: that they had mistaken the bar for St. Mary's, that they left the schooner in the offing under that impression, and intended to send her a pilot by the return of the boat. After staying all night, they embarked at daylight, having procured a negro pilot to conduct them inland, to Fernandina.

Colonel M'Donald, in thanking me for the hospitality he had received, said he felt bound as a gentleman to be candid, and accordingly informed me, that they had lately arrived from London at St. Thomas, in the ship Two Friends, with a great number of officers and munitions of war in abundance; that he had with him 30 officers on board the schooner; that he would command in this quarter; that they would have men sufficient, and a profusion of every thing necessary for active operations. They wanted a war with Spain, and that he had power to draw on England for 100,000 pounds sterling; that they would have a fine train of artillery; and that all these supplies were actually on their way or shipping; that a number of gun brigs and sloops would leave England, reported for the East Indies; but were bound directly here, and to South America.—That they were much disappointed at St. Thomas, on hearing M'Gregor had left Amelia island; and that the capture of Amelia was known prior to their leaving England." [*Captain Thomas was at St. Mary's with Cockburn, and lieutenant of the ship that fired on gunboat 168, after then peace.]

These officers have a soldier-like and genteel appearance and all have their commissions; they said "their object in leaving the schooner was to reconnoitre."

They have all since arrived at Fernandina.

I have the honor to remain, &c.
(Signed,)   ARCHD. CLARK.

———

Extract of a letter from
captain John H. Elton, to
the honorable B. W. Crowninshield,
secretary of the navy, dated

U. S. Brig Saranac,
Cumberland Sound,
September 26th, 1817.

"The patriotism of Amelia island appears to be confined to privateering and plundering. General Aury has the command," &c.

———

Extract of a letter from
captain John H. Elton to
the honorable B. W. Crowninshield,
secretary of the navy, dated,

U. S. Brig Saranac,
Cumberland Sound,
October 10, 1817.

"I have detained a felucha, or small schooner that sailed from Fernandina, under a commission granted by general M'Gregor to one John Morrison, for two reasons; first, as a pirate for having captured an English schooner with regular papers, bound from Nassau to Barracoa, called the Brothers; the commission was granted to John Morrison a citizen of the United States, and who, during the cruise, resided at St. Mary's, in Georgia, and the commission was made use of by one Edward Fenner, who likewise captured a Spanish schooner; both are detained for investigation. They have been out some time, and have received provisions from some English and American vessels they say, gratis. The crew consisted of 18, and I suppose they could not carry provisions for ten days. On the 6th instant I detained the schooner Hornet; she was commissioned by general M'Gregor 22d July last, John Smith commander. She cleared out from Philadelphia in August as the Traveller; she received her arms and men in the Delaware bay, near Lewistown. On the 6th or 7th September she, for the first time, assumed the name of the Hornet, went off Cuba, made two prizes the crew mutinied, and in that state was coming in."

198

"Until I get directions how to consider the island of Amelia, and the people bound to that place, it will be impossible to prevent either slaves or goods being smuggled."

"As most of the patriots there are one day an American citizen, and the next at Fernandina, 'tis easy for them and their agents to evade all the vigilance we are possessed of. One small Spanish vessel, a prize to a privateer, got into the port before we could board, with seventeen slaves. I would have taken her out immediately, but I considered it neutral ground, and that it was the wish of government not to infringe—fearful of that error, our boats are generally sent out to board at sea."

---

*Extract of a letter from
captain John H. Elton,
to the secretary of the navy, dated*

United States' brig Saranac,
Cumberland Sound,
Oct. 19, 1817.

"Day before yesterday I sent out to detain a Spanish slave vessel prize to a Mexican privateer; the captain and owner came in to converse with me, and the officer, neglecting to leave any persons in charge, the people from Fernandina went secretly off, and landed all the blacks on the outer part of the island."

---

*Extract of a letter from
captain John H. Elton,
to the secretary of the navy, dated*

United States' brig Saranac,
Cumberland Island,
November 15, 1817.

Sir—On the 9th instant I sent a boat out to board a vessel from sea. The officer had not been informed to take charge of her, until I had thoroughly over hauled her, if she was a slave vessel. He was at Savannah when the instructions were issued. He returned, and reported it was a slave vessel, prize to the Brutus privateer. I despatched a boat to bring her in for examination. The officer, acting sailing master M'Cluny, met her coming in, and, as it was dangerous to heave her to, remained on his oars, and dropt alongside. They pretended to give him a rope; they did not, but passed him; he caught by a boat astern. The prize master threatened to fire on him, if he attempted to board; and, when musketry was fired under his stern, it was returned. The alarm was given by the boat. I unfortunately was on Cumberland Point, where only one gun was mounted, from which we fired two shot to bring her to. The first lieutenant fired three from the brig. Two of the five struck her; but she succeeded in getting into Fernandina. Although irritated at the insult, I did not conceive it correct to attempt force, to have her driven from neutral waters, but proceeded as I thought most correct; and the enclosed correspondence has passed between general Aury and myself. 'Tis true, shot was fired at her when close to Amelia, but the officer assures me she was on the northern part of the channel when he attempted to board. If half the depth of water is allowed us, she was on our side. I have informed you that the channel over the bar was on their side, or to the southard of a direct line drawn between the islands to the sea. I never have been instructed on that head, but I really think they hold the island by too precarious a tenure, to be yet so very tenacious of their rights. A verbal answer was returned, at first, to my application, that they would protect her. Not knowing how the United States wished to view these people, I did not think proper to attempt to destroy the establishment, but sent, out lieutenant commandant E. R. M'Call, to bring back the privateer Jupiter, to remain as a pledge until I heard from government. It has excited considerable feeling, and no other privateers attempted to sail. The slave vessel was brought over last night, but every thing but slaves, and a small quantity of rice, was taken from her, and she appeared in a very filthy state. The prize master was not sent, neither any of the prize crew. I have written for the former—whether he will be sent I cannot vouch. Yet, as retribution could so soon be had, if force was authorized, and wishing not to interrupt harmony, if it is wished by the United States, I have released the privateer Jupiter; and the High Flyer sailed immediately on a cruise.

A prior correspondence took place, as regarded captain Farnham. It was

199

represented to me that he was a citizen, and only went there to trade. It appears he has been in the service of the patriots for some time. The application was, of course, dropped.

I shall send the slave vessel to Savannah for adjudication, and if the prize master is found, shall send him also. He is an old offender, by the name of Austin.

The situation of Amelia is, by no means, a quiet one. Those at present there act very strangely. There has been a French party and an English party—they have been in constant alarm of each. The French party is now trying as many of the English party as possible, and strangely are making a Botany Bay of the United States, as you will perceive by the proclamation enclosed. So much discontent prevails, that I should not be surprised to see them engaged in civil war. The slave vessels that have hitherto entered Fernandina, I have no doubt have smuggled all their slaves to the United States. Small boats are permitted to pass and repass; as they are rowed by slaves, they can smuggle one or two at a time without detection. Another mode of smuggling is, that the law makes no provision how to consider boats of less than five tons. I sent one of that description to the collector. She was filled with provisions and naval stores from Savannah to Amelia—she had no clearance—the law requires none; but from a passenger on board, I had no doubt, in my own mind, it was to fit out a former slave vessel as a privateer. She was released by the collector. Am I to stop arms, ammunition, &c. bound from the United States to Fernandina, if not cleared as such? They term them boxes of merchandize very frequently, and sometimes have more than they clear out.

------

*Extract of a letter from
Thomas Wayne, esq. purser
on board the U. S. Brig Saranac, dated*

St. Mary's river,
September 27, 1817.

Benjamin Homans.

"On our arrival here, we found general M'Gregor in command of Amelia Island. A few days afterwards he decamped, and embarked on board the privateer M'Gregor, formerly the St. Joseph. The command of the island devolved on colonel Irwin, an American, who was, in a few days, attacked by the Spaniards. After an engagement of forty-eight hours, which was all smoke, it terminated without the loss of a single life, and the Spaniards retreated.

"The noted Woodbine, of infamous memory, arrived here from Nassau, with a view, as was said, to join the patriots; but his friend, M'Gregor, having left the cause, he was disappointed and embarked with M'Gregor, who sailed a few days since for Nassau, to commence some new expedition, which, it is generally supposed, will be to the bay of Espirito Santo, or bay of Tambo, in latitude 28 degrees, 15 minutes North, and longitude 76 degrees, 30 minutes, West. This is an extensive bay, and capable of admitting ships of any size, contiguous to which are the finest lands in East Florida, which Woodbine pretends belong to him by virtue of a grant from the Indians. He says, he has surveyed the whole of the Gulf of Mexico, and Tampo bay is the only place into which large ships can enter.

"The patriots of Amelia are a most heterogeneous set, consisting of all countries and languages, except Spanish Americans. Among them may be found, Americans, French, Irish, Scotch, English, Dutch, Germans, Haytians, Petions, &c. all come ostensibly to aid the cause of the patriots of South America; but their real motive is, no doubt, to prey upon whom they can. Should they continue in Amelia Island, the place will become a second Barrataria.

"At this time the government consists of Mons. Aury who is commander in chief of the naval and military forces; and Ruggles Hubbard, formerly high sheriff of New-York, is the civil governor.

"A number of prizes of considerable value, have been brought into Amelia by Aury's squadron.

"It appears to be the anxious wish of the inhabitants, of the opposite side of the river, to be under the American government, as they are not now secure from either party."

------

*Extracts of letters from
Robert M. Harrison, esq.
consul of the United States
at the Island of St. Thomas,
to the secretary of state.*

St. Thomas,
20th April, 1817.

The increasing number of American seamen, whose ill success in the privateers and pirates that infest those seas, induces them to relinquish these unprofitable pursuits, whenever an opportunity offers, and who almost universally swarm to the island to claim my protection and support, so that they daily almost surround my door, renders it again my duty to request instructions from the Department of State. I have not yet extended to such men any more than a partial assistance, though many of them are in the greatest possible distress, considering that the expenditure of such large sums of money might be considered as advancing beyond the bounds of my duty. It is much to be regretted that the disappointment sustained by so great a number of our seamen should not be sufficient to deter others from embarking in such enterprizes."

———

St. Thomas,
30th May, 1817.

"Numbers of American vessels, originally bound to the Spanish main, where their cargoes could have been disposed of to great advantage, have been deterred from a prosecution of their voyage, from a dread of the piratical cruisers that infest those seas, and have been actually obliged to sacrifice their property here, whilst English vessels prosecute the trade in perfect safety, merely from the circumstance of there being a few British vessels of war in the West India seas. The presence of one of our smallest armed vessels would completely awe those marauders, and enable our merchant vessels to prosecute a legal trade in safety. Her presence, (of the Boxer,) in this neighborhood would be attended with the most salutary effects."

———

[Note] We have copied the documents respecting Galvezton and Amelia as *selected* by the editors of the National Intelligencer, with the single addition of the number of private armed vessels lying in the port of New-Orleans, as listed by the collector—and have also compared the *selection* with the body of the documents submitted by the president for ourselves, and agree with the editors of that paper that "nothing is omitted that is material to a correct view of the subject."

In presenting these documents, the National Intelligencer observes— "It may be remarked, in regard to these documents generally, that there are occasions on which information is communicated to a government, a disclosure of which would be prejudicial to the public interest, or to that of individuals who have given it. The president, it will be recollected, communicated, as requested by congress, such documents only as were conceived not improper to be made public; and— though we have no particular information to justify the suggestion— this appears to us to be one of those occasions on which the executive might act unwisely by exposing to the world all the information in its possession."

We decidedly agree with the sentiment contained in the preceding extract, and think that too much has been communicated as to the names of certain *individuals*, who may thereby be excited to acts of outrage against such as communicated the facts, their character being, in some cases, of the very worst description.

Volume 13, January 3, 1818, page 311

Foreign Articles—Florida.

Through the Washington City Gazette we have the report of a committee appointed to frame a plan of a provincial government for the republic of the Floridas. *P. Gaul, V. Pazes,* and *M. Minder* were that committee. The plan is liberal.

Chronicle.

We have a letter from General Gaines to the governor of Georgia giving an account of a little skirmish of Colonel Arbuckle with a party of Indians, in which we had one killed and two wounded – the Indian loss was greater, and they were dispersed; confirming also the report of the massacre of lieut. Scott's party, as mentioned in our last. General Gaines has left the army and arrived at St. Mary's, to be present at the taking of Amelia; so that he doubtless felt confident as to the strength of the troops collected to accomplish the objects in view. The letter shall be preserved.

Florida Affairs.

The injunction of secrecy under which the following resolution and laws were passed, having been long since removed by the enacting authority, it is deemed unnecessary that they should be longer withheld from the public eye. They are now, therefore, published. *Nat. Int.*

———

Resolution.

Taking into view the peculiar situation of Spain, and of her American provinces, and considering the influence which the destiny of the territory adjoining the southern border of the United States may have upon their security, tranquility, and commerce— Therefore,

Resolved, by the Senate and House of Representatives of the United States of America, in Congress assembled, That the United States, under the peculiar circumstances of the existing crisis, cannot, without serious inquietude, see any part of the said territory pass into the hands of any foreign power; and that a due regard to their own safety compels them to provide, under certain contingencies, for the temporary occupation of the said territory; they at the same time declare that the said territory shall, in their hands, remain

subject to future negociation.

J. B. VARNUM,
Speaker of the
House of Representatives, and

GEO. CLINTON,
Vice-President
of the United States, and
President of the Senate.

January 15, 1811— approved,
JAMES MADISON.

———

An act to enable the president of the United States, under certain contingencies, to take possession of the country lying east of the river Perdido, and south of the state of Georgia and the Mississippi territory, and for other purposes.

Be it enacted by the Senate and House of Representatives of the United States of America in Congress, assembled, That the president of the United States be, and he is hereby authorised to take possession of, and occupy, all or any part of the territory lying east of the river Perdido, and south of the state of Georgia and the Mississippi territory, in case an arrangement has been, or shall be, made with the local authority of the said territory, for delivering up the possession of the same, or any part thereof, to the United States, or in the event of an attempt to occupy the said territory, or any part thereof, by any foreign government; and he may for the purpose of taking possession, and occupying, the territory aforesaid, and in order to maintain therein the authority of the United States, employ any part of the army and navy of the United States, which he may deem necessary.

Sec. 2. *Be it further enacted,* That one hundred thousand dollars be appropriated for defraying such expenses as the president may deem necessary for obtaining possession as aforesaid, and the security of the said territory, to be applied under the direction of the president, out of any monies in the treasury not otherwise appropriated.

Sec. 3. Be it further enacted, That in case possession of the territory aforesaid shall be obtained by the United States, as aforesaid, that until other provision be made by congress, the president be, and he is hereby, authorized to establish, within the territory, aforesaid, a temporary government, and the military, civil, and judicial powers thereof shall be vested in such person and persons, and be exercised in such manner, as he may direct, for the protection and maintenance of the inhabitants of the said territory in the full enjoyment of their liberty, property, and religion.

J. B. VARNUM,
Speaker of the
House of Representatives.

GEO. CLINTON,
Vice-President
of the United States, and
President of the Senate.

January 15, 1811— approved,
JAMES MADISON.

————

An act concerning an act to enable the president of the United States, under certain contingencies, to take possession of the country lying east of the river Perdido, and south of the state of Georgia and the Mississippi territory, and for other purposes, and the declaration accompanying the same.

Be it enacted by the Senate and House of Representatives of the United States of America in Congress assembled, That the act, and the act passed during the present session of congress, entitled "an act to enable the president of the United States, to take possession of the country lying east of the river Perdido, and south of the state of Georgia and the Mississippi territory, and for other purposes," and the declaration accompanying the same, be not printed or published until the end of the next session of congress, unless directed by the president of the United States, any law or usage to the contrary notwithstanding.

J. B. VARNUM,
Speaker of the
House of Representatives.

JOHN POPE,
President of the
Senate, pro tempore.

March 3, 1811— approved,
JAMES MADISON.

————

An act authorizing the president of the United States to take possession of a tract of country lying south of the Mississippi territory, and west of the river Perdido.

Be it enacted, by the Senate and House of Representatives of the United States of America in Congress assembled, That the president be, and he is hereby authorized to occupy and hold all that tract of country called West Florida, which lies west of the river Perdido, not now in possession of the United States.

Sec. 2. *And be it further enacted,* That, for the purpose of occupying and holding the country aforesaid, and of affording protection to the inhabitants thereof under the authority of the United States, the president may employ such parts of the military and naval force of the United States as he may deem necessary.

Sec. 3. And be it further enacted, That for defraying the necessary expenses, twenty thousand dollars are hereby appropriated, to be paid out of any monies in the treasury not otherwise appropriated, and to be applied to the purposes aforesaid, under the direction of the president.

H. CLAY,
Speaker of the
House of Representatives.

WM. H. CRAWFORD,
President of the
Senate, pro tempore.

February 12, 1813— approved,
JAMES MADISON.

Details of the Scott Massacre

Volume 13, January 10, 1818, pages 319-320

Indian News—Official.

Copy of a letter from major general Edmund P. Gaines, to governor Rabun of Georgia, (received by express) dated

Head-Quarters, Fort Scott, December 2, 1817.

Sir — I have the honor to acknowledge the receipt of your excellency's letter of the 20th of last month. The detachment of militia, I have no doubt, will arrive in due time to enable me to put an end to the little war in this quarter, in the course of this or the next month.

With a view to ascertain the strength of the hostile Indians in the vicinity of Fowl Town, and to reconnoitre the adjacent country, I, a few days past, detached Lieutenant Colonel Arbuckle, with 300 men. The Lieutenant Colonel reports that a party of Indians had placed themselves in a swamp, out of which about 60 warriors approached him and with a war-whoop commenced a brisk fire upon the detachment. They returned the fire in a spirited manner. It continued not more than 15 or 20 minutes before the Indians were silenced, and forced to retire into the swamp with a loss which Lieutenant Colonel Arbuckle estimates at from 6 to 8 killed, and a much greater number wounded. We had one man killed, and two wounded.

The enemy have since succeeded in an affair in which the real savage character has been fully exhibited. A large party formed an ambuscade on the 30th ultimo, upon the Appalachicola river, a mile below the junction of the Flint and Chattahoochie, attacked one of our detachments in a boat, ascending near shore, and killed, wounded, and took the greater part of the detachment, consisting of 40 men, commanded by Lieutenant R W. Scott. There were also on board the boat, killed or taken, 7 women, the wives of soldiers; six men only escaped, four of whom were wounded. They report that the strength of the current at the point of attack, had obliged the lieutenant to keep his boat near the shore. That the Indians had formed along the bank of the river, and were not discovered until their fire commenced, in the first volley of which, Lieutenant Scott and his most active men fell. The lieutenant and his party had been sent from this place some days before, to assist Major Muhlenburg in ascending the river with three vessels, laden with military supplies, brought from Fort Montgomery and Mobile. The major, it seems, deemed it proper to retain only about 20 men of the party, and in their place put a like number of sick, with the women, and some regimental clothing. The boat thus laden, was unfortunately detached alone for this place. It is due to Major Muhlenburg to observe, that at the time he detached the boat I have reason to believe he was not apprised of any recent acts of hostility having taken place in this quarter. It appears, however, by a letter from Lieutenant Scott, received about the hour in which he was attacked, that he had been warned of the danger which awaited him: I must, therefore, conclude, that he felt it to be his duty to proceed. Whether he had received from Major Muhlenburg a positive order to this effect, I have not yet learned. Upon the receipt of Lieutenant Scott's letter, I had two boats fitted up with covers of plank, port holes, &c. for defence, and detached them under Captain Clinch, with a subaltern officer and 40 men, with an order to secure the movement of Lieutenant Scott, and then to assist Major Muhlenburg. This detachment embarked late in the evening of the 30th ult. and must have passed the scene of action (15 miles below this place) at night and 7 hours after the affair had terminated. I have not yet heard from Captain Clinch. I shall immediately strengthen the detachment under Major Muhlenburg with another boat, secured against the enemy's fire. He will, there, move up safely by keeping near the middle of the river, which, with his vessels and force, is quite practicable. I shall, moreover, take a position, with my principal force, near the junction of the rivers at the line of demarcation between the United States and Spain, and shall attack any force near that place, or that may attempt to intercept our vessels or supplies below.

The wounded men who made their escape, concur in the opinion that they had seen upwards of 500 warriors (supposed to be hostile) at different places on the river below the point of attack: of the force engaged they differ in opinion; but all agree that the number was very considerable, extending about one hundred and fifty yards along the shore, at the edge of a swamp, in a thick wood.

I am assured by the friendly chiefs, that the hostile warriors of the town on the Chattahoochie, have been for sometime past moving off down the river to join the Seminoles. Those now remaining on the river are believed to be well disposed. One of the new settlers there, however, has been recently killed; but it has been already proven, that the perpetrator of this act, together with most of the warriors of this town (High Town), belonged to and have joined the hostile party. The friendly chief in the neighborhood, promptly dispatched a party in pursuit of the offender, who made his escape towards the Mickasukee town. Oniskays, and several other friendly chiefs, have tendered to me their services, with their warriors, to go against the Seminoles. I have promised to give them notice of the time that may be fixed on for my departure, and then to accept of their services.

The enclosed paper contains the substance of what I have said to the chiefs who have visited me; several of whom reside south of the Appalachico's. The chiefs were desirous I should communicate to them my views and wishes. I felt authorized to say but little, and deemed it necessary in what I should say, to counteract the erroneous impressions by which they have been misled by pretended British agents.

I have the honor to be, most respectfully, your obedient servant,

E.P. GAINES.

His Excellency Governor Rabun.

General Gaines has arrived at Fort Hawkins having left Fort Scott the 5th instant. One object in visiting the frontier at the present moment, was probably to hasten the movement of the troops from this state, who took up the line of march at 10 o'clock on Sunday. Success to them! Previous to their departure the subjoined complimentary general order, was issued, and read to them. We understood that General Gaines contemplates visiting the troops at Point Petre, before he returns to the Indian nation. If so, we should presume, that Fort Scott was not only secure against an attack from the savages, but that offensive operations would cease on our part, till he joins the army, when he will put an end to the little war in that quarter.

"Headquarters,
Fort Hawkins, Dec. 14.

"The commanding general is pleased with the military aspect of the detachment of militia, under the command of Brigadier General Glascock. The officers and men appear qualified to meet the enemy, with honor to themselves and benefit to their country. The Major General is happy to learn that they are anxious to take the field, and co-operate with the United States troops against the hostile savages, whose hands are stained with the blood of helpless women and children. The detachment shall be indulged with an early opportunity of such a co-operation for which the United States troops are equally anxious."

A correspondent at St. Stephens informs us that volunteer companies are forming there to join General Gaines. Access to the General is much easier from the westward.

A gentleman from St. Stephens says that he met between that place and Fort Hawkins, 400 waggons, carts and carriages!

[*Reflector.*

Volume 13, January 10, 1818, page 324

Foreign Articles—Florida.

From the *National Intelligencer of January 6.* Despatches received from the commander of the forces of the United States on our southern border,

205

have brought official information of the occupation of Amelia Island on the 24th ult. by the United States' troops under the command of Colonel *Bankhead*, co-operating with the naval force on that station, under the command of Captain *Henley*.

From the same—It has been stated in public prints in a variety of shapes; in some as a positive fact, in others upon a conjecture, that Mr. *Bagot*, the British minister here, had protested against the transfer by Spain of East Florida to the United States. We have taken pains to ascertain the truth of this statement, and are warranted in assuring our readers that it is altogether without foundation.

The privateers Congress and High Flyer arrived at Amelia, after its surrender. *The latter had* 120 *slaves on board*, and was taken possession of by the authority in command at the place. Heaven forbid, that we should regard these smugglers and dealers in men, as "patriots."

[Note: No opposition was made. Colonel Bankhead has established a temporary police for the preservation of order, until civil authority can be introduced. *Aury's* adherents are represented as a wretched set of negroes, smugglers and adventurers.]

——»»ⱺ◉ⱺ«««——

Congress Mulls Over Slavery Problem at Amelia Island

Volume 13, January 17, 1818, pages 335-337

Congress—House of Representatives. Amelia Island.

Mr. *Middleton*, from the committee on so much of the message of the president of the United States as relates to the illicit introduction of slaves from Amelia into the United States, made the following report:

The committee to whom was referred so much of the president's message as relates to the illicit introduction of slaves from Amelia Island, having carefully taken the matter committed to them into consideration, respectfully report:

That having applied to the department of state for information respecting the illicit introduction of slaves into the United States, they were referred by the secretary of state to the documents transmitted to this house by the president's message of the 15th December last, consisting of various extracts of papers on the files of the departments of state, of the treasury, and of the navy, relative to the proceedings of certain persons who took possession of Amelia Island in the summer of the past year, and also relative to a similar establishment previously made at Galvezton near the mouth of the river Trinity.

Upon a full investigation of these papers with a view to the subject committed to them, your committee are of opinion, that it is but too notorious, that numerous infractions of the law prohibiting the importation of slaves into the United States have been perpetrated with impunity upon our southern frontier; and they are further of opinion, that similar infractions would have been repeated with increasing activity, without the timely interposition of the naval force under direction of the executive of our government. In the course of the investigation, your committee have found it difficult to keep separate the special matter given into their charge, from topics of a more general nature, which are necessarily interwoven therewith: they therefore crave the indulgence of the house, while they present some general views, connected with the subject, which have developed themselves in the prosecution of their enquiry.

It would appear from what had been collected from these papers, that numerous violations of outlaws have been latterly committed by a combination of freebooters and smugglers of various nations who located themselves in the first instance upon an uninhabited spot near the mouth of the river Trinity within the jurisdictional limits of the United States, as claimed in virtue of the treaty of cession of Louisiana by France. This association of persons organized a system of plunder upon the high seas, directed chiefly against Spanish property which consisted frequently of slaves from the *coast* of Africa, but their conduct appears not always to have been regulated by a strict regard to the national character of vessels falling into their hands, when specie or other very valuable articles formed any part of the cargo. Their vessels generally sailed under a pretended Mexican flag, although it does not appear that the establishment of Galvezton was sanctioned by or connected with any government. The presumption, too, of any authority ever having been given for such an establishment, is strongly repelled as well by its piratical character, as by its itinerant nature; for the first position, at Galvezton, was abandoned on or about the 5th of April last, for one near Matagorda, upon the Spanish territory; and at a later period this last was abandoned and a transfer made to Amelia Island in East Florida; a post which had been previously seized by persons, who appear to have been equally unauthorized, and who were at the time of the said transfer, upon the point, it is believed, of abandoning their enterprise, from the failure of resources, which they expected to have drawn from within our limits, in defiance of our laws. There exists, on the part of these sea rovers, an organized system of daring enterprize, supported by force of arms; and it is only by a correspondent system of coercion that they can be met and constrained to respect the rights of property and the laws of nations. It is deeply to be regretted that practices of such a character, within our immediate neighborhood, and even within our jurisdictional limits, should have prevailed unchecked for so long a time; more especially, as one of their immediate consequences was to give occasion to the illicit introduction of slaves from the coast of Africa into these United States, and thus to revive a traffic repugnant to humanity and to all sound principles of policy, as well as severely punishable by the laws of the land.

By the 7th section of the act prohibiting the importation of slaves, passed in 1807, the president is fully authorized to employ the naval force to cruise on any part of the coast of the United States, or territories thereof, where he may judge attempts will be made to violate the provisions of that act, in order to seize and bring in for condemnation all vessels contravening its provisions, to be proceeded against according to law.

By the joint resolution of the senate and house of representatives of 15th January, 1811, and the act of the same date, the president is fully empowered to occupy any part of the whole of the territory lying east of the river Perdido, and south of the state of Georgia, in the event of an attempt to occupy the said territory, or any part thereof, by any foreign government or power; and, by the same resolution and act, he may employ any part of the army and navy of the United States, which he may deem necessary, for the purpose of taking possession and occupying the territory aforesaid, and in order to maintain therein the authority of the United States.

Among the avowed projects of the persons who have occupied Amelia Island, was that of making the conquest of East and West Florida, professedly for the purpose of establishing there an independent government; and the vacant lands in those provinces have been, from the origin of this undertaking down to the latest period, held out as lures to the cupidity of adventurers, and as resources for defraying the expenses of the expedition. The greater part of West Florida, being in the actual possession of the United States, this project involved in it designs of direct hostility against them; and as the express object of the resolution and act of 15th January, 1811, was to authorize the president to prevent the province of East Florida from passing into the hands of any foreign power, it became the obvious duty of the president to exercise the authority vested in him by that law. It does not appear that among these itinerant establishers of republics, and distributors of Florida lands, there is a single individual inhabitant of the country where the republic was to be constituted, and whose lands were to be thus bestowed; the project was therefore an attempt to occupy that territory by a foreign power. Where the profession is in such direct opposition to the fact; where the venerable forms, by which a free people constitute frame of government for themselves, are prostituted by a horde of foreign freebooters, for purposes of plunder; if, under color of authority from any of the provinces contending for their independence, the Floridas, or either of them, had been permitted to pass into the lands of such a power, the committee are persuaded it is quite unnecessary to point out to the discernment of the house the pernicious influence which such a destiny of the territories in question must have had upon the security, tranquility, and commerce of this union.

It is a matter of public notoriety, that two of the persons who have successively held the command at Amelia Island, whether authorized themselves by any government or not, have issued commissions for privateers, as in the name of the Venezuelian and Mexican governments, to vessels fitted out in the ports of the United States, and chiefly manned and officered by our own countrymen, for the purpose of capturing the property of nations with which the United States are at peace. One of the objects of the occupation of Amelia Island, it appears, was to possess a convenient resort for privateers of this description, equally reprobated by the laws of nations, which recognize them only under the denomination of pirates, and by several of the treaties of the United States with different European powers, which expressly denominate them as such.* It was against the subjects of Spain, one of the powers with which the United States have entered into stipulations prohibiting their citizens from taking any commission from any power with which she may be at war for arming any ships to act as privateers, that these vessels have been commissioned to cruise; though, as the committee have observed, no flag, not even that of our own country, has proved a protection from them. The immediate tendency of suffering such armaments, in defiance of our laws, would have been to embroil the United States with all the nations whose commerce with our country was suffering under these depredations; and, if not checked by all the means in the power of the government, would have authorized claims from the subjects of foreign governments for indemnities, at the expense of this nation, for captures by our people, in vessels fitted out in our ports, and, as could not fail of being alleged, countenanced by the very neglect of the necessary means for suppressing them. The possession of Amelia Island as a port of refuge for such privateers, and of illicit traffic in the United States of their prizes, winch were frequently, as before stated, slave ships from Africa, was a powerful encouragement and temptation to multiply these violations of our laws, and made it the duty of the government to use all the means in its power to restore the security of our own commerce, and of that of friendly nations upon our coasts, which could in no other way more effectually be done than by taking from this piratical and smuggling combination their place of refuge.

In order, therefore, to give full effect to the intentions of the legislature, and in pursuance of the provisions of the above recited resolution and acts, it became necessary (as it appears to your committee) to suppress all establishments of the hostile nature of those above described, made in our vicinity, the objects of which appear to have been the occupation of the Floridas, the spoliation of peaceful commerce upon and near our coasts by piratical privateers, the clandestine importation of goods, and the illicit introduction of slaves within our limits. Such establishments, if suffered to subsist and strengthen, would probably have rendered nugatory all provisions made by law for the exclusion of prohibited persons. The course pursued on this occasion, will strongly mark the feelings and intentions of our government upon the great question of the slave trade, which is so justly considered by most civilized nations as repugnant to justice and humanity, and which, in our particular case, is not less so to all the dictates of a sound policy.

Your committee anticipate beneficial results from the adoption of these measures by the executive, in the promotion of the security of our southern frontier and its neighboring seas; and in the diminution of the evasions, latterly so frequent, of our revenue and prohibitory laws. The experience of ten years has however evinced the necessity of some new regulations being adopted in order effectually to put a stop to the further introduction of slaves into the United States. In the act of congress prohibiting this importation, the policy of giving the whole forfeiture of vessel and goods to the United States, and no part thereof to the informer, may justly be doubted. This is an oversight which should be remedied. The act does indeed give a part of the personal penalties to the informer, but these penalties are generally only nominal. As the persons engaged in such traffic are usually poor, the omission of the states to pass acts to meet the act of congress and to establish regulations in aid of the same, can only be remedied by congress legislating directly on the subject themselves, as it is clearly within the scope of their constitutional powers to do.

For these purposes your committee beg leave respectfully herewith to report a bill.

Mr. Middleton also reported a bill in addition to the former acts prohibiting the introduction of slaves into the United States; and the bill was twice read and committed.

The report was not read, but ordered to be printed.

[*Note: See the treaty of peace with France, 1778, art. 21st. U. S. Laws, vol. 1, p. 88; with the Netherlands, 1782, art. 19, v. 1, p. 162; with Sweden, 1783, art. 23, vol. 1, p. 190; with Great Britain, 1794, art. 21, v. 1, p. 218; with Prussia, 1785, art. 20, v. 1, p. 238, and 1797, art. 20, p. 256; with Spain, 1795, art. 14, v. 1, p. 270.]

Volume 13, January 24, 1818, pages 346-350

Amelia Island.
Documents accompanying the message of the President to congress, on the 12th instant.

Department of war,
January 12th, 1818.

Sir—I have the honor to transmit copies of the orders which have been given by the acting secretary of war to major Bankhead, in relation to taking possession of Amelia Island, and copies of the communications which have been made to this department by that officer, which embrace all the information in my possession.

I have the honor to be, sir, with the highest respect, your most obedient servant,

J. C. CALHOUN.

*The President
of the United States.*

*U. S. ship John Adams,
off Amelia, Dec. 22, 1817.*

SIR—We have received orders from our government to take possession of Amelia Island and to occupy the post of Fernandina with a part of our force, which will be moved over as soon as it will be convenient for your troops to evacuate it.

To avoid unnecessary delay, we think proper at this time to inform you, in the event of your acquiescence in this demand, that you will be at liberty to depart with the forces under your command, and such property as belongs unquestionably to them will be held sacred.

You are to leave the public property found by general M'Gregor at Fernandina, in the same condition it was taken, and the property of the inhabitants of Amelia Island must be restored to them, where they have been forcibly dispossessed of it, and no depredations on private property from this period will be permitted with impunity.

Should you, contrary to the expectations of the president of the United States, refuse to give us peaceable possession of the island,the consequences of resistance must rest with you.

We have the honor to be, very respectfully, your most obedient servants,

J. D. HENLEY,
Capt. in the navy
and comd. in chief of the naval
forces of the U. S. off Amelia.

JAS. BANKHEAD,
Maj. 1st battalion artillery,
comd. land forces.

General Aury, *commander in chief
of the forces at Fernandina.*

------

*Head-quarters, Fernandina,
Island of Amelia,
Dec. 22d, 1817,
and 8th of the Independence.*

GENTLEMEN—I have had the honor to receive your official letter of this day. The nature of its contents requiring mature deliberation, I have submitted the same to the representatives of the republic, and, as soon as I shall have obtained their opinion, it shall be immediately sent to you.

I can, however, state to you, gentlemen, that no opposition will be made to surrender the island of Amelia, on the part of this government.

I have the honor to remain, with consideration, gentlemen, your obedient and humble servant,

AURY, commander in chief.

Com. J. D. Henley, and major Bankhead. &c. &c. on board the United States' ship John Adams.

[*Here follows the letter from com. Aury, inserted in our last paper, page 339.*]

———

U. S. Ship John Adams, off Amelia Island, Dec. 23d, 1817.

SIR—We have had the honor to receive your communication of 22d inst. and will briefly remark that, as officers in the service of the United States, we are bound to obey the orders emanating from the authorities of our government, without any discussion or animadversion on our part as to the correctness of them. We have been ordered by the president of the United States to take possession of Amelia Island, and, as the president has expressed his solicitude that the effusion of blood may be avoided, if possible, it must be gratifying to us to be informed by you that no resistance will be made to us.

We will again remark that private property will be sacred, and that our orders extend, only to the public property captured by general McGregor at Fernandina.

We propose to land a force to-day, and to hoist the American flag. Under that flag no oppressive or unjust measures will ever be witnessed; and we feel assured that there will be no difficulties in the arrangement made by us.

The squadron will immediately sail into the harbor, when the commanding officer of the land forces will wait on the commander in chief to make the necessary arrangements for the landing of the troops.

We have the honor to be, very respectfully, sir, your most obedient servants,

J. D. HENLEY,
Captain in the navy, and commander in chief of the U. S. Naval forces off Amelia.

JAMES BANKHEAD,
Major 1st battalion of artillery, and commander of the land forces, &c.

General Aury, commander in chief of the forces at Fernandina.

———

Head-quarters, Fernandina, Island of Amelia, Dec. 23d, 1817, and 8th of the independence.

I have had the honor to receive your letter of this date. I am ready to surrender this place to the forces under your command, whenever you may judge proper to come and take possession thereof.

I have the honor to be, very respectfully, your most obedient servant,

AURY,
commander in chief.

J. D. Henley, esq. captain in the navy, &c.

Jas. Bankhead, esq. Major 1st bat. &c.

———

Department of war, 17th July, 1817.

SIR—Circumstances having made it necessary to occupy without delay, Point Petre, and the St. Mary's river, by a military and naval force, I have to request that you will instruct the officer whom, in pursuance of the order issued through the adjutant general, you may detail to take command at Point Petre, to co-operate with the officer commanding the naval force on that station, in such measures as may be deemed necessary for the preservation of the peace and tranquility of that section of the country, which there is reason to apprehend may be disturbed in consequence of the contest between the Spanish royalists and patriots, for the occupation of the adjacent territory. The officer will be instructed to use due vigilance to prevent the violation of the revenue laws of the United States, and in particular to prevent the illicit introduction of slaves into the United

States; and in order to do this the more effectually, he will prohibit all vessels freighted with slaves from entering the river St. Mary's.

I have the honor be, &c

GEO. GRAHAM.

The officer commanding
at Charleston, S. C.

———

Extract of a letter from George Graham, acting secretary of war, to major James Bankhead, Charleston, S. C. Dated Nov. 12th, 1817.

"I am instructed by the president to direct you to repair immediately to Point Petre, with the effective force under your command, leaving only an officer and a few men as a guard at forts Moultrie and Johnson. Captain Wilson has been ordered to repair with his company, now at fort Johnson, North Carolina, to Point Petre, and a detachment of new recruits, under the command of captain Hook, who was on his route to join the 4th infantry, has also been ordered to that place. The troops enumerated above, and those now stationed at Point Petre, will constitute a force of more than two hundred men, of which you will take the command until the arrival of general Gaines. A remittance of five thousand dollars has been made to your battalion quartermaster, whom you will take with you: and you will make requisitions for the necessary supply of provisions, on the contractor's agents. It will be advisable to take from Charleston a supply of salt meat, and a sufficient quantity of flour and hard bread, to serve two hundred and fifty men for thirty days at least."

———

Department of war,
Nov. 12th, 1817.

Sir—It appearing to the satisfaction of the president, that the persons who have lately taken possession of Amelia island have done it without the sanction of any of the Spanish colonies, or of any organized government whatever, and for purposes unfriendly to, and incompatible with, the interests of the United States, he has decided to break up that establishment, and take temporary possession of Amelia island; for this purpose, the troops ordered to assemble at Point Petre, will co-operate with the naval force which has been ordered to St. Mary's, under the command of captain Henly.

It is the anxious wish of the president that this should be accomplished without the effusion of blood; and he confidently hopes, that the force destined for the purpose will be of such an imposing character, as to induce those persons who now have the military occupation of the island, to abandon it without the exercise of force; but if it should be found to be indispensably necessary, force must be used. You will, therefore, immediately on the arrival of captain Henley at St. Mary's, and, in conjunction with him, despatch an officer to demand the abandonment of the island, by those who now exercise authority there, and take such other measures as may be deemed proper to obtain the peaceable possession of it; also for the preservation of the property of those persons who were residents of the island when it was first captured by general M'Gregor. Should you demand for the evacuation of Amelia be complied with, you will then occupy with a part of your force the position of Fernandina, and take care that the cannon and other implements of war which belonged to the port when captured by general M'Gregor, are not taken off.

If peaceable possession of the island, however, cannot be obtained, and should it be the opinion of captain Henley and yourself, that your joint forces are not competent to the prompt and certain reduction of the naval and military forces which may then occupy the harbor and post of Fernandina, you will, in that event, make a requisition on general Floyd, or such other officer as may command that division of the militia of Georgia in which Point Petre is situated, for a force not exceeding five hundred men, to be held in readiness to march at a moment's warning, and await the arrival of general Gaines, who has been ordered to Point Petre, for ulterior measures.

You will take with you from Charleston the necessary military stores, and such heavy cannon as may be required for the reduction of the fort on Amelia island, in the event of resistance.

As no answer had been received to the communication addressed to you from this department on the 17th July last, it becomes necessary that the receipt of this should be acknowledged, and that you also advise this department regularly of your movements.

I have the honor to be, &c.

GEO. GRAHAM.

Major James Bankhead,
commanding at Charleston, S. C.

Fernandina, Amelia Island,
Dec. 24th 1817.

Sir —I have the honor to lay before you the correspondence held with general Aury, the late commander of this place, and to inform you, that the American flag was raised here yesterday afternoon.

Several days will elapse before general Aury can withdraw his followers, but I have taken every measure to ensure tranquility, by ordering all his black soldiers to be embarked on board one of the ships lying in the port, and by not suffering any person to appear in the town with arms, but his officers; and the moment their vessels are prepared to receive the whole of them, they shall depart.

Most of the inhabitants of this place, at this time, are followers of Aury, and those persons who have been drawn here from motives of speculation, who are, I suspect, of that profligate character generally engaged in the violation or evasion of our revenue laws. I shall, therefore, consult with commodore Henley, and will enforce such regulations as may be most likely to preserve order, until I receive orders from government.

Until this place is completely evacuated by this band of negroes and privateersmen, I have deemed it prudent to keep the whole of my force here. On their departure I shall move all but one company to Point Petre.

I have the honor to be, very respectfully, your most obedient servant,

JAMES BANKHEAD,
commanding detachment
U. S. troops.

George Graham, esq.
acting secretary of war.

Fernandina, Amelia Island,
Dec. 27, 1817.

Sir —I had the honor to forward to the war department, on the 24th inst, a copy of the correspondence with general Aury, previous to the landing of the troops under my command; and I herewith send a duplicate of the same.

Some difficulty has arisen from a want of competent authority, to settle the disputed claims of the residents of this place against the late government and the followers of Aury, who do not seem disposed to comply with their engagements.

One or two vessels have arrived here with cargoes, which the owners are desirous to land, and it might be improper to permit it without obtaining security for the duties which the laws of the United States require; and other vessels loaded in this port have met with some delay in clearing for their destination; but the counsel of general Gaines, who arrived here last night, will regulate my conduct, and will, in a great measure, relieve my anxiety.

I have been obliged to exercise my authority, as commanding officer at this place, to preserve order; and I am happy to say, that nothing unpleasant has occurred. I cannot say when general Aury and his party will sail. Their vessels are much out of order and their arrangements to that effect progress but slowly. The morning after I landed, I ordered all the black and French troops to be embarked on board some of their vessels; but the crews of their privateers, and many others of all nations, whom it is difficult to restrain from violence and excess, are still here.

Until I am honored with your instructions, I hope that the course I may pursue may meet the approbation of the president.

General Gaines leaves this for the western frontier of Georgia the day after to morrow.

I have the honor, &c.

JAS. BANKHEAD,
Maj. 1st bat. art.
and command'g this post,

To the hon. the secretary of war.

212

Navy department,
Jan. 13th, 1818.

Sir—I have the honor to enclose, herewith, copies of orders to capt. John H. Elton, and commodore John D. Henley, in relation to Amelia island; also a letter from the latter officer, communicating information of the surrender of that place to the military and naval force of the United States, together with the correspondence which took place on that occasion.

I have the honor to be, with the highest respect, sir, your most obedient servant,

B. W. CROWNINSHIELD.

To the president of the United States.

Navy department,
July 16, 1817.

Sir—Proceed immediately with the United States' brig Saranac under your command to the river St. Mary's in Georgia, and inform the military commander of your arrival, and of the objects specially designated to you in these orders.

The recent occupation of Amelia island by an officer in the service of the Spanish revolutionists, occasions just apprehensions, that from the vicinity to the coast of Georgia, attempts will be made to introduce slaves into the United States, contrary to the existing laws; and further attempts at illicit trade in smuggling goods in violation of our revenue laws.

You are hereby directed to detain and search every vessel, under whatever flag, which may enter the river St. Mary's, or be found hovering upon the coast under suspicious circumstances, and seize every vessel freighted with slaves, or whose doubtful character and situation shall indicate an intention of smuggling.

In the execution of these orders you will take special care not to interrupt or detain any vessels sailing with regular papers, and of a national character, upon a lawful voyage to or from a port or ports of the United States.

The traffic in slaves is intended to be restrained, and, in the performance of this duty, you will exercise your sound judgment in regard to all vessels you may visit.

Communicate frequently to this department, every event connected with this service, and, if it shall be found necessary, a further naval force will be sent, either to strengthen your command, or to relieve you so as to pursue your original destination. If you find it necessary upon your arrival at St Mary's to employ a good pilot well acquainted with the coast, rivers, and inlets, you are authorized to do so.

I am, very respectfully, your obedient servant,

B. W. CROWNINSHIELD.

Captain John H. Elton, commanding
United States' brig Saranac, New York.

Navy department,
Nov. 14, 1817.

SIR—Having been appointed to the command of the United States' ship John Adams, you are hereby ordered, in conformity to the wishes of the president of the United States, to proceed forthwith to the port of St. Mary's, in Georgia, taking with you the United States' brigs Enterprize and Prometheus, and the schooner Lynx, if the two latter have arrived in New York, and are in a state of readiness to accompany you; but you will not procrastinate the departure of the ship John Adams on account of these vessels, as any of them not fully prepared to proceed with you shall be ordered to join you as soon as practicable at St. Mary's, at which place you will find the United States' brig Saranac, captain John H. Elton, and gun-boat No. 168, lieutenant commandant R M'Call, both of which vessels will act under your orders.

The object of the president of the United States in ordering this naval force to the St. Mary's, is to remove from Amelia island the persons who have lately taken possession thereof, and, as it is understood and believed, without authority from the colonies, or any organized government whatever, and to the great annoyance of the United States. It has therefore been determined that these persons shall be removed from that island, and that possession shall be taken for the present, by the land and naval forces of the United States.

On your arrival at St. Mary's, you will consult with the officer commanding the military force, who is instructed to co-operate with you in the performance of this service.

It is hoped that these persons will withdraw without bloodshed; and you will, for this purpose, should your relative rank be superior to that of the commanding officer of the land forces, make known to the chief commanding in Amelia, the determination of the government of the United States to take possession of the island, and if the said chief, and the armed forces under his command, will peaceably quit the island, you will permit them so to do, taking special care that no depredations be committed on the inhabitants, whom it will be your duty to protect from violation or injury, either in their persons or properly.

Should the force, however, now in command of the island, contrary to all expectations, resist and refuse absolutely to give up and abandon the same, you are, in co-operation with the military force of the United States, to proceed and take possession of the island, in the name and by the authority of the United States.

Should you fall in with, on your way to St. Mary's, or find in Amelia, any vessels from the United States, armed and equipped by American citizens, acting as privateers, contrary to the laws of the United States, you will capture such, and send them to Savannah, in Georgia, to be dealt with according to law.

You will detain all prizes, or other vessels, having slaves on board, as the presumption is strong that they are intended to be smuggled into the United States. You will report, from time to time, to this department, the operations of the force under your command.

I am, very respectfully, &c.

B. W. CROWNINSHIELD.

Commodore J. D. Henley.

P. S. These orders are not to be delivered to any person.

———

U. S. Ship John Adams, off Amelia,
Dec. 24, 1817.

SIR—I have the honor to transmit a copy of the correspondence with general Aury, late commander of this place, and to inform you that the American flag was yesterday hoisted at Fernandina, and the Island of Amelia taken possession of by the land forces under major Bankhead, of the United States artillery.

The black troops of general Aury have been embarked on board one of their ships lying in the port, and the remainder of his followers will be sent off the Island, as soon as the necessary arrangements can be made for the purpose. They are now engaged in watering their ships, and in the course of a week I hope to see all of them over the bar.

Most of the respectable inhabitants of this place retired on its capture by M'Gregor, and those now here are principally adventurers who have been attracted by motives of speculation, and, as I suspect and have every reason to believe, been engaged in the violation of our revenue laws, to prevent which in future, such precautions will be taken as are within my power, and which will I presume be adequate to the purpose.

This will be sent by an express to Darien, the mail leaving this place but once a week.

I have the honor to be, &c.

J. D. HENLEY.

Honorable B. W. Crowninshield,
secretary of the navy.

———

U. S. Ship John Adams,
off Amelia,
Dec. 30, 1817.

SIR— Since my arrival here I have been so much engaged that I ave not had one moment to write to my friends. You no doubt, however, have some idea of my situation; and from my official reports know that the American flag is now flying on Amelia island. As there are many novel cases which must present themselves, I should have been better pleased had my instructions been full; but we are now left to act as circumstances may require; and I am fearful that Aury and his followers will give us much trouble before they quit the island. I am sorry to add that the Americans appear to be much worse than any others. Should we be able to get through this business so as to meet the approbation of the department, I shall feel much gratified; but I trust that should I err in any steps that I may take, it will be considered by the president as an error of judgment; for I do assure you that nothing would be so pleasing to me as to have my conduct here approved by the executive. I have endeavored to keep as close to the letter of my instructions as possible, and have avoided every difficulty that I possibly could. I regret very much the difficulty of communicating with the government. We have only one mail per week, and that does not remain in St. Mary's long enough to enable us to answer letters that we may receive by it.

The situation of my ships you are no doubt acquainted with, as I have written several times to the secretary on that subject. I, however, do not wish to leave this place until everything is settled, and the government have established some kind of police for the better government of this place, which I am in hopes will take place ere long. I am fearful that Aury expects that the American government will relinquish Amelia; which impression will retard his departure.

I have the honor to be, &c.

J. D. HENLEY.

Hon. B. W. Crowninshield,
secretary of the navy.

———

"Extract from the capitulation of the Island of Amelia," dated at Fernandina, 29th June, 1817, and signed by "Francisco Morales and Joseph de Yribarren," attested by "Bernardo Segin" and "approved" by "Gregor MacGregor."

"Brigadier General MacGregor, commander in chief of all the forces, both naval and military, destined to effect the independence of the Floridas, and authorized by the constituted authorities of the republics of Mexico, Buenos Ayres, New-Grenada, and Venezuela, offers to Don Francisco Morales, *Capitan del regimiento de Cuba*, and commandant,

civil and military, of the Island of Amelia, the following terms, &c. &c.

———

Extract from a proclamation of Gregor MacGregor, dated head-quarters, Amelia Island, June 30, 1817, and signed "Gregor MacGregor," attested by "Jos. Yribarren, secretary."

"PROCLAMATION.

"Gregor MacGregor, Brigadier General of the armies of the united provinces of New-Grenada and Venezuela, and general in chief of the armies of the two Florida, commissioned by the supreme directors of Mexico, South America," &c. &c.

"In the name of the independent governments of South America, which I have the honor to represent, I thank you for this first proof of your ardor and devotion to her cause, and I trust that, impelled by the same noble principles, you will soon be able to free the whole of the Floridas from tyranny and oppression."

———

Extract of a letter from general Aury to captain J. D. Henley, commanding the United States naval forces off Amelia island and to major James Bankhead, commanding the United States military forces off the same place, dated at "Head-quarters, Fernandina, Island of Amelia, December 22nd, 1817."

"Allow me, gentlemen, to observe to you, that from the moment we took Fernandina by the force of our arms, we entered into full possession of all the rights appertaining to our enemy, and that to this day we have supported these rights at the risk of our lives and fortunes. The boundaries of the Floridas and the United States, having been fairly settled by the treaty of friendship, limits, and navigation, on the twenty seventh of October, one thousand seven hundred and ninety-five, leave us at a loss to ascertain your authority to interfere in our internal concerns."

215

Foreign Articles—Amelia.

It is stated that a Spanish officer had reached Fernandina to ascertain whether the United States had taken possession of the island as friends or enemies; at the same time expressing his satisfaction that the nest was broken up.

Commodore *Aury* has denounced a certain *William P. Moore* as running away from Amelia with a certain prize vessel, of about 70 tons, armed with 5 guns, with an intention to commit depredations on the high seas—saying that he is unauthorised, and requesting that he may be brought to trial as a pirate.

It was expected that Aury, with his fleet, &c. would leave Amelia about the 20th inst. Some of the U. S. troops were embarking to join general Gaines at fort Scott, for which place the general, as before noticed, had departed.

Chronicle—Indian War.

Milledgeville Journal,
January 6, 1818

Accounts from our Southern frontier, state that Major Muhlenburg, who was ascending the Flint River with three vessels, having onboard a detachment of U.S. troops, provision, &c. was attacked 30 miles below Fort Scott by *twelve hundred* Indians and negroes, on the 16th ultimo.

When the express left, which was on the 18th, the firing from both parties continued; at which time Major Muhlenburg had three men killed and thirteen wounded; but there was not the least apprehension of any the vessels being taken that were under his command. The troops so defended themselves in the vessels, from the, enemy, that they were perfectly safe. No man was killed or wounded except when in the act of warping or casting anchor. Capt. M'Intosh, who commanded a post 12 miles from Fort Scott, with 40 men, was attacked on the 15th ult. by between 2 and 300 Indians. Captain M'Intosh defeated them without losing a single man, and has since been relieved. There had also been a skirmish between the friendly and hostile savages, in which the chief of the former was killed, in consequence of which a number of the party under his command are said to have deserted and joined the hostile Indians.

We learn by a sick soldier who has just returned home from the army, that the detachment of militia from this state had reached Flint River and commenced erecting the fortifications directed by General Gaines. He also states, that the Indians had sent deputies to sue for peace on the conditions formerly rejected by them, and that it was believed in camp, that hostilities would cease without the further effusion of blood. We have no late intelligence from the regulars at fort Scott.

Foreign Articles—Florida.

The Georgia Journal speaks very positively to the fact, that Spain will not dispose of the Floridas to the United States except on receiving six millions of dollars for them, and making the *Mississippi* the boundary of her Mexican dominions. It is nonsense to talk of a transfer on such terms. It is further intimated in the same paper, that Spain supports herself in such absurd demands under the assurance that she will not, in any event, have to contend with us single handed relying upon England and France for allies. We cannot *guess* what the former might do, but should be glad to hear that 10,000 French troops were sent to Mexico, Venezuela, &c. They would soon close *Ferdinand's* accounts in those countries.

Many believe that the acts recently published about Florida (see page 315) were then for the first time officially known to the people. The passage of those laws was noticed in the letters of Mr. Monroe to Mr. Foster in 1811, and the position clearly taken that the United States would not permit the Floridas to pass into the hands of any other power, if it could be prevented. See the correspondence in the first volume of the Weekly Register. We are indebted to the National Intelligencer for the recollection of these things.

Amelia Island.

Mr. *Moore*, who was noticed in our last as advertised by commodore Aury as a pirate, &c. is at Charleston, avows his resentment, at Aury's conduct, denies the charges, and stands prepared to vindicate himself.

The following communication appears in the Savannah Republican of the 11th inst.

Mr. M'Intosh observing, that a part of his letter of the 30th October last to Mr. Crawford is published in the National Intelligencer of the 23d ult [see Weekly Register, page 302] among the documents presented to congress by the president, on the affairs of Amelia Island, conceives it a duty incumbent on him, in justice to the feelings of the family, and to the memory of the late sheriff of New York, Mr. Hubbard, to declare, that the information he received, and communicated to Mr. Crawford, of the cause of the death of this gentleman, he has since understood to be incorrect. He hopes, the public journalists, who have published his letter, will insert in their papers, this tribute to truth and humanity.

Volume 13, February 7, 1818, pages 390-391

Indian News—Official.

Copy of a letter from General Mitchell, agent of Indian Affairs, to the governor of Georgia, dated

Creek Agency,
8*th* January, 1818.

Sir – The messenger who was sent below to propose terms of peace to the Seminoles, has returned; and the enclosed is the substance of his report, which I received by express.

The friendly chiefs and warriors are to meet me at this place on the 11*th* instant, and I have great hopes that our differences with the Seminoles can, with their assistance, be adjusted.

I understand that much apprehension prevails about the safety with which travelers can pass through the nation. It is my opinion there is not the least danger in travelling the road from fort Hawkins to the Alabama, by this place and fort Mitchell, but I would not advise travellers to use the road from fort Perry to fort Gaines; or indeed any road as low down as fort Gaines, for the present.

I am, with high respect and esteem, your very obedient servant,

D.B. MITCHELL, agent, I.A.
His excellency, Wm. Rabun,
Governor, &c.

———

Talk of Tustennugee Hopie, and Hopie Haijo, to the agent of Indian affairs for the Creek nation.

FORT MITCHELL,
December 30, 1817.

My friend—The messenger which was sent to the Mickasukies has returned with an answer to our Talk. The Mickasukies say it was not them that began the war. They were sitting down in peace, and the white people came on them in the night and fired on them. The Mickasukies are still sitting down in their town and doing no mischief, and waiting to see if the white people will make peace with them. The people that shot at the boat and killed all the white people, were the old Red Sticks from the Upper towns, them that turned hostilities last war. The man that was sent to the Mickasukies (Hopoie Haijo) with a peace talk, met the Mickasukies at the half way ground coming with a peace talk to us. Mr. Hambley and Mr. Doyle were taken prisoners – Hopoie Haijo saw them. Tustennugee Chapco has gone to relieve them, and carry them to the fort at St. Marks.

I have sent you this little talk now; our meeting that you appointed will soon be, and then every thing will be made strait. We hear that the army has crossed at Hartford. The Cheehaws have received two letters from the army, and they had no-body to read them, and they don't know the contents and wish the army could be stopped until our meeting is over.

(Signed) TUSTENNUGEE HOPOIE.
(Signed) HOPOIE HAIJO.

———

General Mitchell, in a letter to the editors of this paper, dated the 9th inst.

observes "There does not appear to be any thing new in this quarter, except the prospect of peace with the Seminoles." [*Georgia Journal.*]

From the army. An express arrived at the executive office yesterday, with the following despatch from General Gaines:

HEAD-QUARTERS,
Hartford, Georgia,
January 8, 1818.

Sir — I received on my way to this place the 5th inst. from Lieutenant Colonel Arbuckle, reports of the state of his command up to the 21st December by which I learn that the detachment with transports under Major Muhlenburg had been attacked about thirty miles below fort Scott by a force of Indians and blacks, estimated at from 800 to 1200 that the firing had continued from both sides of the river from the 15th to the 19th Dec. and that our loss amounted to 2 killed and 13 wounded, the loss of the enemy not known. The vessels were so fortified with bulwarks as to secure our troops from the enemy's shot, except when carrying out the anchors to warp, or when working with the rigging.

The loss of a vessel is not apprehended; nor will the delay be likely to produce any serious consequences to our troops above their supplies being sufficient for sometime beyond the period at which others I have ordered, and have reason to believe are on the way, are expected to arrive; and which will be taken up the river in keel boats, secured against the enemy's shot.

A small work commanded by Captain M'Intosh, 12 miles above fort Scott, had been attacked and surrounded for several days, by a large party; but although the captain's force amounted to no more than forty, he maintained his work without the loss of a man. The Indians finding themselves unable to make any impression upon the work or garrison, and having suffered from our shot, retired. Captain M'lntosh's command has since been withdrawn.

A friendly chief, Wm. Perryman, having raised a considerable party of warriors on the Chatahochie, for the purpose of protecting the friendly traders below the line, and of aiding our troops, was attacked by the hostile party and is supposed to have fallen, with Messrs. Hambly and Doyle. It is reported, that most of the party were *forced* (perhaps willingly) to join the enemy.

I have received information that a party of Indians entered the settlement near Trader's Hill a few days past, killed a woman, whose name I have not learned, and took off some three or four negroes. (Editors Journal – This does not accord very well with the late pacific professions of the Indians.)

I had previously ordered a detachment of artillery, with two companies of the militia, drawn from Maj. Gen. Floyd's division, to take a post at Trader's Hill, for the defence of that settlement. I have reason to believe the artillery arrived at the hill about the time the murder was committed, and the militia soon after, and that the Indians were pursued.

The residue of the militia taken from Major General Floyd's division (five companies) are ordered to this place, for the purpose of reinforcing General Glascock's command, excepting one company which will be posted near the Big Bend of Ocmulgee.

The detachment under brigadier general Glascock, delayed by rainy weather, bad roads, and want of punctuality in the contractor's department, will not be able to form a junction with the United States troops at Fort Scott before the 24th of the present month; and as a great part of the detachment will probably be disposed to return home soon after the end of the month, there is reason to apprehend the time will be too limited to make such an impression upon the savages, (which one decisive victory would effect) as to put an end to the war; and leave them convinced, that their future safety will depend alone upon the strict observance of peace on their part.

I have therefore to request the favor of your excellency, to furnish an additional detachment of militia, to consist of four battalions of infantry with four companies of riflemen, to assemble at this place on the first of the next month, prepare for a three month's tour of duty, in the service of the United States.

I shall make arrangements for the necessary supplies to be in readiness at this place in due time for arming, equipping, and subsisting the detachment.

I have the honor to be, with high consideration and respect, your obedient servant,

EDMUND P. GAINES,
Maj . gen. com'g

His excel, governor Rabun.

———

[Note: We understand it is the intention of the governor to comply with the above requisition as far as may be in his power. Four companies of riflemen cannot be furnished, because it is believed there are not so many in the state; and there is no likelihood, at this inclement season, of their volunteering. From the defects of our militia laws, with regard to the election of officers, it will be impossible to organize the infantry, and march them to the place of rendezvous by the first of next month.—The troops called for, we are informed, will be taken from Byne's, Bell's (Oglethorpe) and Glascock's brigades. [*Georgia Journal.*

Volume 13, February 7, 1818, page 391

Congress—Senate.

January, 30. A message was received from the president of the United States, communicating to the senate, in compliance with their request of the 22d instant, a report from the secretary of war relative to the manner in which the troops now operating against the Seminole Indians, have been subsisted, whether by contract, or otherwise, and if they have been regularly furnished.

[The report states, that the troops are regularly subsisted by contract; that the forces now operating against the Seminole Indians, are within the district, the contract for which commenced on the 15th of June last; that the department of war, anticipating an increased demand for rations, in that quarter, made early and liberal advances of money to the contractor, to enable him to give prompt obedience to the requisition of the commanding general; that requisitions were made for deposits in advance, under the terms of the contract, at the several posts on the frontier of Georgia, and in the adjacent territories; that, by the last official reports these requisitions were not complied with, and the commandant had detailed officers to supply the deficiency by purchase; that the contractor reports, that he has sent an ample supply of rations to Fort Scott, from New-Orleans, and that they were shipped on the 5th ult.; that this supply is intended to be conveyed up the Apalachicola river, and it is believed may have arrived at its destination before this period, in which event the purchases ordered by the general will cease. Accompanying the report, is a correspondence, shewing the extent of the failure, and the evils apprehended from an anticipated one, and embracing all the information possessed by the war department on the subject.]

The message and report were read and ordered to be printed.

Volume 13, February 7, 1818, page 396

Chronicle—Indian War.

Some official papers relating to the war with the Seminole Indians are inserted in page 390. We have the general order of the governor of Georgia, calling out eight companies of militia, at the requisition of general Gaines, for a tour of three months; and it seems from a Knoxville paper, that general Jackson is taking measures, by direction of the president, to finish this war immediately—calling for 1000 mounted *Tennesseans*. That they, added to Gaines' force, will soon finish it, cannot be doubted.

Volume 13, February 14, 1818, pages 412-413

Indian News.
From the Georgia Journal, Extra.

[Official]

Copy of a letter from Major General Gaines to the governor of this state, received last night by express.

HEAD-QUARTERS,
Hartford, Georgia,
January 23, 1818.

Sir — By a letter just now received from brigadier general Glascock, I am informed, that a party of Indians concealed in the swamp of Cedar creek, 7 miles east of Flint river, yesterday morning, fired upon and killed Mr. Thos. Leigh, assistant waggon master, and Samuel Lofters, of captain Avary's company of Georgia militia. The waggon master had been sent out with a small party of men and a drove of pack-horses, laden with provisions; which, by a prompt and judicious arrangement on the part of Major Heard, were secured, with the residue of the party and horses. General Glascock immediately ordered out a detachment under Major Morgan, in pursuit of the Indians.

By a letter from colonel Arbuckle of the 18th inst. I learn, that the Indians were to assemble near the mouth of Flint river, on the 21st. for the purpose of concerting measures for the destruction of the inhabitants on the Chatahoochie, and the reduction of Fort Scott. The latter they calculate upon starving out. Fort Gaines it was apprehended would be attacked. One of the inhabitants (Mr. "Weaver) had been killed near the fort; a house had been burnt, and some property destroyed.

The detachment and vessels under major Muhlenburg with military stores arrived at Fort Scott without any material loss, other than that mentioned in my last, although incessantly annoyed by a very large force from each shore, from the 15th to the 25th of December. A supply of provision ordered in November last, had not reached the Appalachicola at the date of colonel Arbuckle's letter, 18th inst. The troops were then without meat, but had engaged nearly one month's supply upon the Chattahoochie, part of which left Fort Gaines under a strong guard on the 16th. The supply of flour at Fort Scott is sufficient allowing full rations of that article for the troops there, until the middle of next month; and the arrival of sixty thousand rations from New-Orleans is daily expected; and even should this supply fail, I have not a doubt of having a competent supply sent down the Flint and Chattahoochie, in time to prevent the troops from suffering.

I have been thus particular in communicating to your excellency the state of our supplies, as well as the movements of the enemy, from an impression that a knowledge of these subjects would be acceptable to you, and beneficial to the state over which you preside — as well as from a wish to draw from you free communications of your views and wishes upon whatever relates to the public service, connected with my command.

I have seen in the newspapers, with equal surprize and indignation, the attempts that have been made to lull the public mind into a belief, that the hostile Indians desire peace, and are willing to lay down their arms! Sir, there will be no peace until those Indians are severely chastised.

The chiefs were required to surrender the offenders! It was deliberately resolved in a large council of the Seminoles and "Red Sticks" at Mickasukee, that the offenders should neither be punished nor surrendered.

Some of their chiefs have triumphantly asserted, that we cannot beat them! — that we never have beaten them, except when we had *red people to help us.*" It is not extraordinary they should entertain these opinions they know little or nothing of the strength or resources of our country and whatever information they have derived from their white friends (British officers and traders) could have no tendency to give them favorable impressions towards us. *They must be beaten before we can reasonably calculate upon peace.*

It is well known that seven of our citizens were killed by those Indians in the two years immediately succeeding the late war with England. Their chiefs admitted this, and that among the number was a woman and two children (Mrs. Garrett of this state.)

The principal chief, Chapichimico, in notifying the warriors of the resolution of the chief's in council, added that, "the day never should come when he would give up or punish a red man for killing a white man." These facts have been communicated to me by Indians, and through interpreters who I believe to be men of truth nor have I a doubt but these facts were well known to those philanthropic writers of Peace, who have had the sagacity to discover, that hostilities were commenced by the troops under my command, on the 20th of November last and that we are the aggressors.

It is not an act of war, according to this doctrine, to massacre and scalp seven unoffending persons, among them a woman and her infants! What number then, I would ask, the massacre of which would constitute an act of war? Sir, my own humble impressions upon this subject are, that the wanton massacre of an *infant not yet able to lisp* the enviable declaration of "I am an American citizen" should be as promptly avenged, as if fifty, or fifty thousand citizens had been thus massacred. When reparation is refused by the nation (whether red or white, civilized or savage) to whom the offenders belong the nation itself becomes accountable, and should be chastised for the outrage.

I have little confidence in the expectation of obtaining any considerable aid from the friendly Indians; even should they join me, the loss of their chiefs may induce them to follow the example of the warriors under Perryman, and go over to the enemy; and I owe it to myself and to the public service to apprize you of the existence of a spirit of opposition, lending to counteract my efforts, having recently manifested itself in what is deemed to be the friendly part of the Creek Nation; originating as I have reason to believe, with some evil disposed white persons, actually engaged in smuggling negroes into the United States from East Florida. A considerable number, as I am credibly informed and believe, have been taken to the immediate vicinity of the Creek Agency. It rests with the agent to detect or explain this apparent violation of law. The movement of the troops and the active and general hostility of the Indians near the Florida line will have a strong tendency to render this abominable traffic difficult and perilous; hence I expect to be honored with the ill will of every one engaged in it.

I have the honor to be, very respectfully, your obedient servant,

EDMUND P. GAINES,
Maj.Gen. commanding.

His excellency Wm. Rabun.

———

Office of the Georgia Journal,
Milledgeville, January 30.

An express from General Gaines to the executive, reached here this morning, with the following unpleasant intelligence.

Head-quarters,
Hartford, Georgia,
January 28, 1818.

Sir:— I have just now received a letter from Wm. Harris, esq. of Telfair, containing the painful intelligence of the massacre of Mr. Daniel Dikes and his family, by a party of Indians, on the Satilla, 40 miles from Telfair court house. Mr. Harris adds, that there was reason to apprehend some other families have fallen near the residence of Mr. Dikes. I have ordered a detachment of cavalry to that frontier, to pursue the Indians as far as practicable.

A detachment of colonel Wimberly's regiment of infantry will be sent down the Flint on the Indian side, towards the Big Bend, with orders to reconnoitre the country, and arrest or attack any parties found in that quarter.

I have the honor to be, very respectfully, your obedient servant,

EDMUND P. GAINES,
Major-general commanding.

His excellency Wm. Rabun.

———

Note: General Jackson left Nashville on the 22nd inst. for Fort Scott, to take command of the army against the Seminoles. The 1000 mounted volunteers from Tennessee were to rendezvous at Fayetteville on the 31st ult. The general was accompanied by a handsome company of young men, promptly equipped, as his guard.

Foreign Articles—Florida.

Some of the forces that were under Aury had left Amelia, on the 24th ult. destination unknown. The commodore still remained, but was expected soon to sail in his brig, the Mexican Congress, formerly the Calypso, of Baltimore. He had been arrested and held to answer, by civil process, for several debts.

We see an article from a Jamaica paper on the value of Florida. The attention of the *British* government is invited to it that the *Americans* may be prevented from forming a *durable navy*— saying that all the live oak timber we had collected was destroyed by sir Alexander Cochrane, and that we have only a few scattered trees standing, "sufficient perhaps to build a frigate." This shews "how the wind blows." We have not a very great supply of live oak, but the frames of seven 74's and six frigates are contracted for, from "scattering trees."

The Savannah Republican, speaking of the same article, says— "Our fleet, we know, is not an empty phantom that haunts the terrified imagination of John Bull, but a scourge which the Ruler of all nations has created to punish the tyrant and despoiler of the seas. We are not therefore surprised that he should view its increase with fearful forbodings of the future sorrow it is to occasion him, and that he should adopt every measure calculated to avoid the coming blow. But into the hands of whomsoever the Floridas may fall, our navy will be very little affected by the event. Not to speak of the immense forests of live-oak spread over the coast of Louisiana and that part of West Florida in our possession, enough of that valuable timber may be obtained in Georgia and South Carolina to build a sufficient number of American ships to chase the English fleet from the ocean and capture it in the best defended harbors of the British empire."

Chronicle—Indian War

General Glascock's brigade of Georgia militia, from the delays that attended their organization and march, &c. merely reached the neighborhood where their services were expected to be wanted, and then returned – their tour of duty being out. Thus all the expense of this brigade and the harassing of the people it occasioned, have produced no possible good whatever. Another brigade had been previously called out to replace Glascock's; but it is believed that before it can reach the scene of action its time will also have expired! We have hope that Jackson and his mounted Tennesseans will close this tedious and wasteful little war with the Seminoles; who are committing many murders on the Georgia frontier. It is understood that the pursuit of them will not be limited by the Florida line.

War with the Seminoles – The volunteers from Tennessee will deserve the high character which that state so justly earned during the late war. – They were rushing to the concentration point. – General Jackson has issued a spirited address to them, which we have not time to copy in this sheet. He has proceeded to head quarters, and left them to follow him under Colonel A.P. Hayne, well known to his country, and deserving its confidence. A company of Kentucky volunteers, from Russelville, has marched to join General Jackson.

—•»»੭ ◉ ੭«««•—

NILES' WEEKLY REGISTER.

THE PAST—THE PRESENT—FOR THE FUTURE.

EDITED, PRINTED AND PUBLISHED BY H. NILES, AT $5 PER ANNUM, PAYABLE IN ADVANCE.

Volume 14

(February 28, 1818 - August 22, 1818)

Volume 14, February 28, 1818, page 14

Foreign Articles—Florida.

Aury was at Amelia on the 6th inst. making all possible haste to depart. All was quiet. The U. S. ship Adams, and brig Enterprize were there—the Saranac and Prometheus and schooners Lynx and Tartar were at Savannah. An English brig with eight slaves on board had been seized. There was to be a public sale of sugars to the amount of $17,777, at St. Mary's, for payment of duties to the United States.

Extract of a letter, received in Providence, (R.I.) from Savannah, dated on the 14th ult. from an officer of the American squadron at Amelia Island: — "You will probably wish to know what sent me there; I will inform you, and, by so doing, give an account of ten of the most miserable days of my life. We took the Patriot privateer, commodore Champlin, with the Sarina, Guineaman, her prize; we were ordered on board the privateer, and sailed under convoy of the Prometheus and schooner Lynx. We had with us forty-two slaves, and arrived here after a long and boisterous passage of eleven days; notwithstanding this vessel is an excellent sea-boat, we suffered much; but nothing, when compared to the sufferings of the slaves, which we had no means to prevent; five or six of them dying in a night, of weakness and cold. The Sarina has, probably, lost more slaves than we have; we have now on board only twenty-five — they are all young, not exceeding fifteen years of age; two are now lying dead on board, and there are a number more that will, in all probability, terminate their miserable existence before another sun. Since our arrival here we have got blankets, which have made the slaves a little more comfortable. It is enough to make the stoutest heart sicken, to look at these miserable objects, and think of the brutality of those who are so hardened as to tear these people from their friends and country. The captain of the Guineaman (a Spaniard) is now on board of her, sick of the coast fever, which, in all probability, will terminate his mortal career. The number of slaves taken from the coast was 113."

Volume 14, February 28, 1818, page 15

Chronicle.

Gregor McGregor is said to have gone to Liverpool.

———»»»☙☺☙☙«««———

General Jackson Joins the Fight in Florida

Volume 14, February 28, 1818, page 16

Chronicle.

Nashville, Jan. 31. — This is the day appointed by general Jackson for the concentration of the troops from this county assembled and marched from here two days since—and yesterday about 100 fine looking men passed through this place on their way to Fayetteville, under the command of major Cook, from Robertson county.

The annexed order has been printed by authority of general Jackson for the purpose of being distributed among the troops after their organization.

General Order.

Volunteers of West Tennessee—Once more, after a repose of three years, you are summoned to the field. Your country having again need for your services, has appealed to your patriotism, and you have met it promptly. The cheerfulness with which you have appeared to encounter the hardships and perils of a winter's campaign, affords the highest evidence of what may be expected of you in the hour of conflict and trial.

The savages on your borders, unwilling to be at peace, have once more raised the tomahawk to shed the blood of our citizens, and already they are assembled in considerable force to carry their murderous schemes into execution. Not contented with the liberal policy that has from time to time been shewn them; but yielding themselves victims to foreign seducers, they vainly think to assail and conquer the country that protects them. Stupid mortals! They have forgotten too soon the streams of blood their ill fated policy heretofore cost them. They have forgotten too, that but a short time since, conquered and almost destroyed, they were only preserved by the mildness and humanity of that country which they now oppose. They must now be taught, that however benevolent and humane that country is, she yet has sacred rights to protect, and with impunity will not permit the butchery of her peaceable and unoffending citizens.

Brave Volunteers—The enemy you are going to contend with, you have heretofore met and fought. You have once done it, and can again conquer them. You go not to fight but to be victorious; remember then that the way to prove successful, is not by being inattentive to the first duties of a soldier, but by bearing and executing with cheerfulness the orders of superiors, and being constantly mindful of the obligations you are under to your country and to yourself. Subordination and attention to discipline are all important and indispensable; without them, nothing like system can be preserved, and this being wanted nothing favorable can result. But in you, every confidence is reposed. Your general will not believe that brave men, who have so promptly come forth at the call of their country, will withhold their assent to regulations which can alone assure them safety and success. Hardships and dangers are incident to war, but brave men will bear them without murmuring or complaining. Knowing you to be such, no fears are entertained but that every duty imposed on you will be met with promptness and cheerfulness.

Your general goes before you to open the way and prepare for your reception. Confiding in your diligence and exertions, he will expect your arrival at your destined point, without unnecessary delay—led by colonel Arthur P. Hayne, an officer in whom he has every confidence. This being effected, he will place himself at your head, and with you share the dangers and hardships of the campaign.

ANDREW JACKSON,
Major General commanding.

—•»»ϴ◉ϴ«««•—

Creek Indians Sign Treaty

Volume 14, March 7, 1818, page 26

Treaty with the Creek Indians.

Substance of the treaty made and concluded between D. B. Mitchell, esq. agent for indian affairs, and the Creek nation of indians, at the Creek agency, January 22, 1818.

Art. 1. In consideration of certain sums of money to be paid to the said Creek nation by the government of the United States, as herein after stipulated to cede and forever quit the claim unto the United States, all right, title and interest which the said nation have or claim in or unto the two following tracts of land, situated, lying and being within the following bounds, viz. 1st, beginning at the mouth of Goose-creek, on the Alatamaha river, thence along the line leading to the mounts at the head of the St. Mary's river, to the point where it is intersected by the line run by the commissioners of the United States under the treaty at Fort Jackson; thence along the said last mentioned line to a point where a line bearing the same shall run the nearest and a direct course by the head of a creek called by the indians Al,cas,aca,ho,ke to the Ocmulgee river; thence down the Alatamaha to the first mentioned bounds at the mouth of Goose creek. 2d, beginning at the high shoals of the Appalachie river, and from thence along the line designated in the treaty made at the city of Washington, on the 14th day of November, 1815, the

Ulcoiouchachee, it being the first large branch, a fork of the Ocmulgee above the Seven Islands thence up the eastern bank of the Ulcofouhatchee by the waters edge to where the path leading from the high shoals of the Appalachie to the Shallow Ford on the Chatahochee crosses the same; and from thence along the said path to the Shallow Ford on the Chatahochee river, thence up the Chatahochee river by the water's edge on the eastern side to Suwama Old Town; thence by a direct line to the head of Appalachie, and thence down the same to the first mentioned bounds at the high shoals of Appalachie.

Art. 2. The United States are to pay within the present year, the sum of twenty thousand dollars and ten thousand dollars annually for the term of ten succeeding years without interest, making in the whole eleven payments in course of eleven years, the present year inclusive and the whole sum to be paid, one hundred and twenty thousand dollars.

Art. 3. Agreed on the part of the United States, that in lieu of all former stipulations relating to Blacksmiths, they will furnish the Creek nation for three years with two blacksmiths and two strikers.

Art. 4. The president may cause any line to be run, which may be necessary to designate the boundary of any part of both or either of the tracts of land ceded by this treaty, at such time and in such manner as he may deem proper. And this treaty shall be obligatory in the contracting parties as soon as the same shall be ratified by the government of the United States.

Milledgeville Reflector,
of Feb. 17.

Volume 14, March 7, 1818, pages 31-32

Chronicle—The Creek Indians.

We have a copy of a long and interesting letter of general Mitchell, agent for Indian affairs, who has lately concluded a treaty with the Creeks, see page 26. He speaks of this people as entirely friendly, and wholly disposed to rely upon the justice and protection of the United States, being exceedingly humbled by the late war. That they are anxious for the suppression of the "Red Sticks" now among the Seminoles in Florida, and that

when he informed the warriors assembled at the agency (at least 1500) that there would be no impediment to their crossing the Spanish line, the famous chief McIntosh, addressed them, and the result was an instantaneous and unanimous resolution to take up arms, and act with the troops of the United States. A list of the officers was made out, and the warriors were to meet on the 17th ult. to march for Fort Scott.

General Mitchell vindicates the Creeks from the charges made against them of being disaffected or hostile to the United States. His letter is dated at *Mount Nebo*, Feb. 13.

———

The Seminoles.—A letter from New Orleans, dated January 28th, states that the Seminoles and Creek Indians inhabiting the promontory of East Florida, against whom our forces are marching, are 4000 warriors strong; "that they have destroyed all their towns, placed their women, children, stock and provisions in a fortified camp, situated in the midst of an immense and almost impassable marsh." This account leads us to expect protracted war in that quarter. [*Nat. Int.*

Volume 14, March 21, 1818, page 64

Chronicle—Indian War.

We have not much information as to the progress of the war against the Seminoles, &c. It is understood that general Jackson has prohibited letters from the army giving accounts of the movements of troops, &c. But his forces are probably organized, and something decisive may be expected at an early date.

It seems to be understood that *Woodbine* and *Nichols*, a pair of precious villains, are with the Seminoles, urging them on to murder; they are, probably, the real authors of the war. It is stated that they have two armed schooners, manned with 50 men each, besides 50 negroes trained as cavalry.—It is thought that they shield themselves under the protection of the Spanish line—but that line will not be respected if hostilities are carried on within it. We hope that these wretches may mix in the fight with a much zeal as they have fermented the war, so that Jackson may give a good account of them.

———»»»☉ ◉ ☉«««———

President Monroe Apprises Congress of the Situation in Florida

Volume 14, April 4, 1818, page 100

Congress—Seminole War.

Wednesday, March 25. The following message was received from the president of the United States:

To the senate and house of representatives of the United States.

I now lay before congress all the information in the possession of the executive, respecting the war with the Seminoles, and the measures, which it has been thought proper to adopt, for the safety of our fellow citizens, exposed to their ravages. The enclosed documents shew that the hostilities of this tribe were unprovoked, the offsprings of a spirit, long cherished and often manifested towards the United States, and that, in the present instance, it was extending itself to other tribes, and daily assuming a more serious aspect. As soon as the nature and object of this combination were perceived, the major general commanding the troops of the United States, was ordered to the theatre of action charged with the management of the war, and vested with the powers necessary to give it effect. The season of the year being unfavorable to active operations, and the recesses of the country affording shelter to these savages, in case of retreat, may prevent a prompt termination of the war; but is may be fairly presumed, that it will not be long before this tribe and its associates receives the punishment which they have provoked and justly merited.

As almost the whole of this tribe inhabits the country within the limits of Florida, Spain was bound, by the treaty of 1795, to restrain them from committing hostilities against the United

States. We have seen, with regret, that her government has altogether failed to fulfil this obligation, nor are we aware that it made any effort to that effect. When we consider her utter inability to check, even in the slightest degree, the movements of this tribe, by her very small and incompetent force, in Florida, we are not disposed to ascribe the failure to any other cause. The inability, however, of Spain to maintain her authority over the territory and Indians within her limits, and in consequence to fulfil the treaty, ought not to expose the United States to other and greater injuries. Where the authority of Spain ceases to exist, there the United States have a right to pursue the enemy, on a principle of self defence. In this instance, the right is more complete and obvious, because we shall perform only what Spain was bound to have performed herself. To the high obligations and privileges of this great and sacred right of self defence, will the movement of our troops be strictly confined. Orders have been given to the general in command not to enter Florida, unless it be in pursuit of the enemy, and in that case to respect the Spanish authority wherever it is maintained; and he will be instructed to withdraw his forces from the province, as soon as he shall have reduced that tribe to order, and secured our fellow-citizens in that quarter, by satisfactory arrangements, against its unprovoked and savage hostilities in future.

JAMES MONROE.
Washington, March 25, 1818.

———

"In the documents accompanying the above message," observes the *National Intelligencer*, "we find an official annunciation of those circumstances which have preceded and attended the recent movements of our troops in the south. These official papers vary so little in substance from the unofficial accounts, that we do not think it material to publish them, with the exception of the following documents, which reduce to form and certainty the rumors we have heard concerning the instructions to our military authorities respecting the prosecution of the war"—

Sir—On the receipt of this letter, should the Seminole Indians still refuse to make reparation for their outrages and depredations on the citizens of the United States, it is the wish of the president that you consider yourself at liberty to march across the Florida line, and to attack them with its limits, should it be a Spanish post. In the last event, you will immediately notify this department.

I have the honor to be, &c. &c.

J. C. CALHOUN.

General Edmund P. Gaines,
Fort Scott, Georgia.

———

Extract of a letter from the secretary of war to major general Andrew Jackson, at Nashville, Tennessee, dated December 26th 1817.

You will repair, with as little delay as practicable, to fort Scott, and assume the immediate command of the forces in that quarter of the southern division.

The increasing display of hostile intentions by the Seminole Indians, may render it necessary to concentrate all the contiguous disposable force of your division upon that quarter. The regular force now there is about 800 strong, and 1000 militia of the state of Georgia is called into service. General Gaines estimates the strength of the Indians at 2700. Should you be of opinion that our numbers are too small to beat the enemy, you will call on the executives of the adjacent states for such an additional militia force as you may deem requisite.

———

Further of Amelia Island.

Thursday, March 26.—The following message was received from the president, by Mr. J. J. Monroe, his secretary:

To the house of representatives of the United States.

I transmit to the house of representatives, in compliance with their resolution, of March the 20th, such information not heretofore communicated, as is in the possession of the executive, relating to the occupation of Amelia Island. If any doubt had before existed of the improper conduct of the persons who authorised, and of those who were engaged in the invasion, and previous occupancy of that island; of the unfriendly spirit towards the United States, with which it was commenced and prosecuted and of its injurious effects on their highest interests, particularly by its tendency to compromit them with foreign powers in all the unwarrantable acts of the adventurers, it is presumed that these documents would remove it. It appears by the letter of M. Pazos, agent of commodore Aury, that the project of seizing the Floridas was formed and executed at a time when it was understood that Spain had resolved to cede them to the United States, and to prevent such cession from taking effect. The whole proceeding in every state and in all its circumstances was unlawful.—The commission to general McGregor was granted, at Philadelphia, in a direct violation of a positive law, and all the measures pursued under it, by him, in collecting his force, and directing its movements, were equally unlawful. With the conduct of these persons, I have always been unwilling to connect any of the colonial governments; because I never could believe that they had given the sanction either to the project in its origin, or to the measures which were pursued in the execution of it. These documents confirm the opinion which I have invariably entertained and expressed in their favor.

JAMES MONROE.

Washington, March 26, 1818.

———

List of papers transmitted with the message of the president to the house of representatives, in pursuance of the resolution of the 20th March, in relation to the occupation of Amelia island.

Extract of a letter to a gentleman in the district of Columbia, dated at Baltimore, 30th July, 1817, with an enclosure, being

Copy of a letter from sir Gregor McGregor, to a gentleman in Baltimore, dated Fernandina, 17th July; 1817.

The same to the same, dated in Nassau, New Providence, 25th December, 1817, with an enclosure, being

Extract of a proclamation.

Extract of a letter to the secretary of state, dated 24th December, 1817, with an enclosure, being directions for sailing into Tampa bay.

Extract of a letter from the same to the same, dated 13th January, 1818, with enclosures, being directions for sailing into Tortola; translation of a letter of marque, and of naturalization, granted by sir Gregor McGregor.

Extract of a letter to the same, dated 19th of January, 1818.

Major J. Bankhead and commodore J. D. Henley to the president, dated Fernandina 20th January, 1818.

Don Vincente Pazos to the secretary of state, dated 8th February, 1818.

Don Luis de Aury to the president of the United States, dated Fernandina, 23d December, 1817.

Memorial of don Vincente Pazos to the president of the United States, dated Washington, 7th February, 1818; accompanied with several documents.

The secretary of state to don Vincente Pazos, dated 5th March 1818.

Volume 14, April 4, 1818, page 104

Chronicle—Indian War.

We have a large collection of newspaper articles relating to the war against the Seminoles—the chief things worthy of record are a follows:

General Gaines, descending the Flint river to Fort Scott, had his boat stove, by which, (notwithstanding all the reports about it) we believe only one soldier was drowned—but it seems that the general himself and the little party that was with him, were a long time in the woods, and suffered exceedingly before they reached fort Scott, being also in momentary danger of falling into the hands of the savages.

The Upper Creeks, 1300 strong, under their chief M'Intosh, as general, and 19 captains, have been organized into companies, and mustered into the service of the United States—they are *now*, probably, in the Seminole country, acting under the command of general Jackson.

The Tennessee militia have also reached Fort Scott before this time; and, if other circumstances will permit, we may soon expect to hear that our army has passed the *Florida* line. It seems understood that we shall take possession of this country to preserve its neutral relations. Various detachments of United States troops are moving towards it.

The Seminoles are as subtle as they are savage—and it is feared they will fight only in detachments. Several skirmishes have taken place, by which a few have been killed on both sides. They have murdered a number of the frontier settlers, in the most barbarous manner. We fear that these wretched creatures have fixed the seal to their extermination.

We have a report that a large party of Indians attempted to surprise general Jackson at a point called Hammock, near the Flint river—but were repulsed with the loss of 500 killed and left on the field, among whom were several whites and negroes. The wounded were carried off. Our loss in killed and wounded is said to have amounted to 100. This report has not been confirmed, nor has it reached us by the direct route.

Report on the Spanish Patriots at Amelia Island

Volume 14, April 11, 1818, pages 113-116

Spanish Patriots.

[Presented to Congress on the 10th ult.]

To the senate and house of representatives of the United States in congress assembled.

The memorial of Vincente Pazos, of Peru, deputed agent of the authorities acting in the name of the republics of Venezuela, New Grenada, and Mexico,

Respectfully Represents:

That several duly constituted authorities of the independent government of South America, having met in this free, this enlightened, friendly and neutral country; and being convinced that nothing could tend more to the advancement of the great cause, in which all the friends of freedom, from the bay of San Francisco to Cape Horn, are deeply engaged, than the conquest of Florida, which would cut off the medium of intercourse between the Spanish islands and the United States, and thus paralize the operations of the government of Spain, in the important contiguous islands, hastening thereby the fulfilment of the ardent desires of those islanders for emancipation from the most cruel oppression: these constituted authorities determined upon the attack of Amelia Island, as the most direct mode of obtaining possession of the contemplated object.

Their views were privately made known to many individuals in the United States, who had emigrated to this country in consequence of the bloody scenes of Carthagena and other places of South America; and to many of the disbanded soldiers of the British and other nations whose profession was that of arms. They were invited to repair to Amelia Island, many of them wishing an asylum, and other desirous of assisting in the patriot cause, under promises of satisfaction, proportioned to their grades and merits, but cautiously avoiding whatever might be construed as a violation of the sovereignty of this highly respected republic, and studiously careful to guard against whatever could, in the most remote degree, be considered as infracting the laws of nations. They met at a place of rendezvous, they attacked, they took, they kept possession of the island of Amelia, with only the van guard.—They expected the arrival of those patriots and foreigners who had voluntarily offered to join them; but to the surprise, to the heart-rending regret of all the friends of this great revolution, the volunteers were stopped in their egress from the United States, and many of them were thrown into prison. These measures, totally unexpected, changed at once the whole appearance of our views. Instead of being enabled to take possession of Florida, (intended finally for the United States) we were confined to Amelia island! The chiefs of the expedition were subject to suspicion, many of the men deserted, and but a few were left to sustain the shock of arms, which was daily threatened by the Spanish troops; they remained however, unappalled; they repelled a formidable attack; but being by the disappointments before mentioned, incapable of active operations, the abandonment of the place was contemplated at the time of general Aury's arrival, whose reinforcements enabled the patriots not only to remain masters of the island, waiting for an augmentation of forces for ulterior operations, but they were enabled to fit out several vessels to annoy the Spanish trade.

The great importance and consequence of the capture of Amelia island, as a key to Florida and to the channel of the Bahamas, will be more easily comprehended by a perusal of these intercepted despatches which accompany this memorial, from the minister of the treasury of the island of Cuba to the bloody Morillo, whose supplies were furnished chiefly from that island; and the island derived those supplies from the United States, through the Floridas. The money requisite for the prosecution of the war against the independents, was obtained by loan from the inhabitants of Cuba: but these judging correctly, that if the patriots could take and hold Amelia island, they would proceed to possess themselves of the rest of the Floridas, and finally of Cuba, long ready for revolt, and that in the event of a revolution of these, the money lent to their government would be lost, refused those advances on the faith of government that they had been accustomed to make.

Thus may the government of the United States now see the importance of these primary movements of the patriots, which were attributed to other causes of a confined, a private, and even of a sinister nature, by writers in the public papers of this country, who imputed motives of the most diabolical kind to the chiefs of this expedition — They loaded them with every insulting epithet, and charged the whole with the irregularities that were committed by unprincipled individuals, who had assumed the patriot flags to cover their depredations; thus involving in one common disgrace those who were duly commissioned, and who had acted in conformity to acknowledged laws, with those who had been guilty of this piratical assumption!

The patriots took many Spanish vessels engaged in the slave trade, and carried them into Fernandina. It would be unworthy the dignity of this memorial, to descend to the suspicion that the persons so violent in these charges, were indirectly engaged in this infernal trade; but the opposition appears to have augmented against the patriots, in proportion to the injury done thereto.

These captured slave-ships were taken, like other vessels, because, declaredly belonging to the enemy; but there is no instance of the captors having violated the laws of this country, in attempting the introduction of the captured slaves into the United States; and if any individual had even attempted so irregular a proceeding, he would have been subject to the laws: but his disgrace would surely not be imputed to those who disclaim any such act.

The documents, now in the hands of the executive of this government, give the most ample testimony of the regular attention paid to the laws of the United States by the patriots; and your memorialist was in hopes, that these favorable representations would have produced a very different result to the one experienced.

The unfavorable impression made upon the government of this country, against the persons employed in this enterprise, appeared to be corroborated by facts appertaining solely to those who, totally disconnected with the patriots, had without authority assumed their flag; and partly under the plea of the Floridas having been pledged to this government, the officers thereof were directed to take possession of Amelia Island, which they did in a hostile manner, but which the patriots refused to defend, under the conviction that a government professing friendly sentiments to those who were following its own glorious example, would, upon due consideration of the subject, under proper representations, redress any grievances to which this exertion of power might have subjected their friends the patriots: and under such consoling expectations your memorialist had the honor of addressing the chief magistrate of this respected republic. [*Address in the hands of the executive.] After waiting, however, for a month, (though every day's delay is highly injurious to the great cause in which we are engaged) instead of receiving such satisfaction as the patriots had vainly anticipated, your memorialist has this day received a letter from the honorable John Q Adams (secretary of state of the United States) excluding all hopes of that reparation of the injuries sustained, that was expected from a great and magnanimous people, whose glorious example had fired the bosoms of their brethren of the south; and nothing remains now, in the fulfilment of the duties of your memorialist to the patriots, whom he represents, but to submit to the august assemblies, whom he has the honor now to address, those evidences of injuries so grievous to the cause of liberty and to the progress of the revolution, which involves the happiness of so many millions.

In this exposition of the grievances and sufferings alluded to, your memorialist begs leave to call the attention of the honorable houses to the following:

It must be advanced (and your memorialist hopes it will be admitted) that the capture of Florida would hasten the great events of the revolution: and that, this being accomplished, it was the avowed intention of the patriots to cede that country to the United States, under such circumstances as might be mutually.

It must also be advanced, that they know not of any existing engagement that had been so concluded between this country and Spain, as to subject the attack, in any manner, to the suspicion of an implication of hostility to the pre-engagements or ultimate views of this republic. For the patriots could not suppose a nation, so powerful and the United States, would permit the king of Spain to keep possession of a country, virtually theirs, as a compensation for the extensive spoliations committed on their trade, so long ago: and especially as the governor of Florida is daily disposing of the lands, leaving nothing, finally, but the sovereignty and the sand banks: and more especially, as the law of congress on that subject was passed in the year 1811, which, by the constitution became effectually null in two years: added to which, a nation, of such political forecast as the United States, knowing that the patriots of the south having declared all the American continental possessions of Spain in a state of revolution, could not be expected to leave undecided a question of so much moment as the possession of Florida, if actually theirs, at a time when it was subject to an attack from without, or a revolution from within: and under a conviction that if left to an external attack, it would involve the United States in a contest with the captors, (for Spain had left it almost defenceless,) or, virtually, decoying a force to be idly spent, which might have been efficiently engaged elsewhere, in the great cause.

Under all these circumstances, your memorialist finds it difficult to abstract his mind from a dilemma which presents itself, and which he submits with great deference.

Either the United States did possess Florida, or they did not. If they did, why not occupy the same and display the American flag: which would have prevented the patriots from attempting the conquest of a country that had consummated its wishes. If they did not possess Florida, why have they, *vi et armis*, taken from the patriots a part thereof, which they had fairly, and by force of arms, conquered, and kept against every attack from their only declared enemy? It is in vain to urge that the patriots were considered as pirates; because it is not the usage of

nations to accept from *pirates* terms of capitulation: and your memorialist begs leave to solicit your honorable houses to ponder well upon the sensibility of this nation, when the Danes delivered up to the English minister the vessels captured from that nation by com. Paul Jones, who, because he had been an English subject, was denominated and threatened by them as a pirate; for the Danes had not then acknowledged your independence. This subject was thought worthy, at a subsequent time, of a formal representation thro' your minister, Mr. Jefferson, then at the court of Versailles; and the injury sustained then, was, till within a short period, made a plea against the restoration of even private property, belonging to the subjects of that crown; [*The case of the brig Henscrew, &c.] and so lasting was the impression of that injury, that it has been thought worthy of remembrance until this day.

Even your venerable and respected philosopher, Franklin, though clothed with ministerial dignity, was called a hoary headed *Traitor!*

The situation of those whom your memorialist has the honor to represent, calls for the reminiscene of these circumstances, that your honorable houses may judge, by the feelings of those days, of the impressions which your acts are calculated to stamp upon the minds of the patriots, which are peculiarly alive to every sentiment emanating from so high and so esteemed a source. The patriots have not only been deprived of the captured territory, but of all the warlike store found therein; they have also remained uncompensated for all their expenditures in the erection of barracks and other necessary buildings; they have not only been deprived of the captured vessels, but of their cargoes. [*The documents are in the hands of the executive.]

The validity of these prizes, and of the property taken, has been by request of the Spanish agents, subjected to the courts of admiralty in the United States for adjudication: though those courts can have no competent jurisdiction over property taken by the citizens of another power, from another people, on the high seas: — And yet the court of admiralty of Savannah has lately decided against the schooner Tantativa's being a good prize to the Brutus privateer, commissioned by the Mexican government; also against a brig, prize to the Gen. San Martin, under Buenos Ayres' colours, seized on the coast. The cargo, too, of a brig, prize to the Mexican Congress, wrecked on the coast of North Carolina has been sold by the collector, and the money deposited in his office.

The patriots have not only been precluded from recovering debts to a large amount, due for the legal sales in the United States, of various goods, but their liberties are endangered by the threats of creditors, to whom comparatively small debts are due; and at the time that these threats are made, the sufferers of all these injuries are ordered peremptorily, by the officers of the United States, to quit a territory that has never belonged to this government, who seem, thereby, to have espoused the cause of our enemies, and to have entered into league against us.

All these things, too, are done when the government of this country are acquainted with the reports of the junction of the Russian and Spanish fleets whose destination is declared to be against the patriots; and thus shall we be subjected while waiting for the restoration of our property, to the risk of having our vessels blockaded in port, thereby hazarding their loss with the prize goods, and thus giving advantages to an enemy insatiable in blood; and to whom reconciliation is impossible; an enemy who may become formidable by such unexpected interferences, but whom the patriots would, otherwise, never hesitate to meet boldly.

In repeating these manifold grievances to your honorable houses, your memorialist looks with confidence, for that dignified and sincere support of the great republican cause, in which those whom he represents are so deeply engaged: and he reposes in the bosom of your august assemblies those representations, depending on such a redress of grievances, as shall comport with the honor, dignity and justice of the government of the United States.

VICENTE PAZOS.

City of Washington, March 6, 1816.

[The foregoing is the petition that the house of representatives refused to receive.]

——»»☻☻☻☻«««——

Correspondence from William MacIntosh

Volume 14, April 18, 1818, pages 130-131

Seminole War.

Milledgeville,
March 31.

We have no very recent information from the army under General Jackson. It is understood, however, that they have left Fort Scott and descended the Appalachicola to meet provisions, a large supply of which had arrived from New-Orleans.

Intelligence from the army of friendly Creek warriors, under M'Intosh, has been received down to the 16th. In descending the Chatahochee, M'Intosh, with a large party of his warriors, kept the west side until he finally took and dispersed the hostile Indians of the Hitchetau tribe, who were in arms under their chief, the Red Ground King. A detail of his operations will be found in the subjoined letters.

————

Extract of a letter from Major Daniel Hughes, U.S. factor, to the editors of the Journal, dated

"FORT MITCHELL,
March 24.

"I have particular pleasure in giving you copies of letters received by me from William M'Intosh, general commanding the Creek regiment of Indians, who marched from here on the 26th ultimo, with only six days provisions, for Fort Gaines. – He arrived there on the 5th inst. Where he received six days corn only for his warriors, and then pushed against the enemy. He is highly deserving the character of a warrior. His conduct proves him the decided friend of our government and laws; he is the violent enemy of the hostile party, and they must expect to feel the weight of his arm if they give him battle.

"He has done what he mentions in his letters, while on his march from this post to join General Jackson, and is exclusively entitled to all the merit of his labor and perseverance."

———

Copies of letters from general William M'Intosh, commanding the Creek regiment to Major Daniel Hughes. U. S. factor at Fort Mitchell.

"Uche Old Fields,
March 2.

"Sir — I wish you would inform our agent and our headmen, that since I left Fort Mitchell, the fourth day, at 12 o'clock, I have taken three of our enemies that were firing on the vessels on this river, and one was wounded at the same place when firing on the vessels, I have got them in strings, carrying them to Fort Gaines, and expect to catch some more before I get there. Nothing more, but the creeks are very high; it as much as we can do to travel. I remain your friend,

WM. M'INTOSH
General commanding."

———

"FORT GAINES,
March 6.

"*Major Daniel Hughes*— I wrote you the other day and told that I had taken three prisoners: I carried them to Fort Gaines to the commanding officer, and he told me he would have nothing to do with them, and said to me, you may deal with them by your own laws. We had proof that they were at the destroying of the boat below the fork of Flint River, and one of them was wounded at that time; they were doing mischief to our friends, and I knew what was the law between us and the United States; I did not want them to stand on our land, and I have taken their lives. I have heard where a good many of our enemies are collected, about forty miles from this place, and I am going to push on there to-morrow as fast as I can, until I can get where they are. This is all I have to say to you and our head men and agent, and whatever I do hereafter I will let you know again. Nothing more; all my men are healthy. Your friend,

Gen. WM. M'INTOSH,
Commanding Creek Indians.
"P. S. The commanding officer at

Fort Gaines had taken the Tame King's son a prisoner, and gave him up to me; I heard no harm against him, and have turned him loose again, and now he has joined us."

———

"March 10, 1818.

"My friend, I received your letter on the 9th day of this month; on the Sunday in the evening there was about fourteen of our old enemies came and gave themselves up to us, with their women and children; I sent their women back with some of our people to the Ufaula, and we have taken two of the men along with us as pilots. They told me, that the red ground chief had got a great many of our enemies collected together to fight, and these two men are piloting us to him. About one hour after we took these people, ten more men can into our camp with white flags, and joined us. I send this to you. I am going to-day, and to-morrow about 9 o'clock the fight will be ended with us; if I conquer the red ground chief, I don't expect to meet as many more in number hereafter; you will hear from me as quick as the fight is over with us. Your friend,

WM. M'INTOSH, *General, commanding the Creek Army.*"

———

"CHAUBULLE CREEK,
MARCH 16.

"Sir — I have the honor of writing to you again, as I promised you I would do so. I went down the Creek Chaubulle the 12th day of March, about ten miles above the camp of Couchatee Micco, or red ground chief, and the creek swamp was so bad we could not pass it for the high waters; my men had to leave their clothes and provisions, and swim better than one half of the swamp, about six miles wide; we marched within about two miles of his station, and the next morning we surrounded his place, but he was gone, and we could not follow him till we could get some provisions we had left behind us; I and major Hawkins followed him and overtook his party, and he got away from us with about 30 men. We have taken 53 men and about 180 women and children prisoners, without the fire of a gun; and we killed ten men that broke to try and make their escape. I have not lost a man since I left Fort Mitchell. He would not have got away from us, but he had some cattle on hand that he tried to drive out of our way; so I sent 100 men to take him and his cattle; when they came in sight, he and his party being well mounted on horses, they got away; we got what cattle he had with him.

We are very scarce of provisions, and I have to send the women and children up into our nation. As for the men, I am going to take them to General Jackson. Now there is no danger on the west side of the Chatahoochie river, as this was all the party that was on this side — we have to look for our enemy on the east side of the river now. You will be so good as to inform my head men and agent of this. I send to you, my friend and brother.

GEN. WM M'INTOSH, *commanding the Creek Indians.*"

Volume 14, April 18, 1818, page 136

Chronicle—Seminole War.

For letters from the Creek chief, M'Intosh, see page 130. The Choctaws were collecting their forces to act against the hostiles. Our army, in the whole, will consist of from 4000 to 5000 men, and if the Seminoles can be brought to action, peace will soon be secured. The Spanish line was crossed on the 10th ult. It is intimated that Augustine and Pensacola, may both be so far taken possession of as to prevent supplies reaching the Indians through them. Our troops have suffered excessively for want of provisions. We have some horrid details of murders by them of men, women and children; but happily they are not very numerous, and the time of danger may be considered as having nearly past.

In a skirmish between 34 of the Telfair militia and about 50 or 60 Indians, five of the former and 10 of the latter were killed. The affair was indecisive, being a "drawn battle." This is all the news we have from the theatre of war, since our last, except as referred to above.

Volume 14, April 25, 1818, page 152

Chronicle—Seminole War.

Letters received, dated the 27th ult. state it was expected that in nine days thereafter general *Jackson* would go against the hostile Indians, to hunt them in their holds. He left fort Scott on the 11th March, to meet provisions from New Orleans, and on the 14th met with an abundant supply—with which he proceeded to the Mickasukee towns. His then collected force was 500 regulars, 1000 militia and several Indian commands, amounting to about 1800, in all. McIntosh's brigade of 776 Indians had not then joined, but were expected the next day. A fort had been erected in Florida, on the site of the Anglo-negro fort, destroyed on the Appalachicola, by the gun boats from New Orleans, and colonel Clinch, some time after the conclusion of the war. It is within 60 miles of St. Marks, in the heart of the Spanish territory. Considerable alarm still prevails in some of the frontier counties of Georgia—some houses are said to have been burnt by the Indians in Wayne county, but we do not hear of any lives being lost.

It seems quite understood that general Jackson will not leave Florida until the war is completely finished. A company of regulars, hale and efficient men, left Baltimore on Thursday the 24th inst. to join him. Pushmatahaw, a firm adherent to the United States and a principal chief of the Choctaws, had marched a party to act under him.

Volume 14, May 2, 1818, page 168

Chronicle—Indian War.

It was reported at Savannah, on the 20th ult. that the indians had advanced within 30 miles of *Darien*, committing many ravages. In consequence, certain bodies of militia were directed to march immediately, and 2000 dollars were raised for the encouragement of volunteers.

We have the names of several persons murdered by the indians. They range about in small parties—a favorable method to protract the war, but the certain means of their own destruction in detail.—Many parties are in pursuit of them.

Milledgeville, April 18.—A letter from general Glascock to the editors of the Journal, dated Fort St. Marks, 7th April, states, that on the 1st inst. a skirmish took place between the advance of the army and a portion of the Mickasuka Indians, (most of them fled on the approach of our troops.)

The Tennessee detachment rushed forward, and participated slightly in the action; they had one man killed and four wounded—seven of the enemy were slain; their number of wounded is not known. Colonel Henderson, of Wilkes county, is stated to have killed an Indian chief, the same who is understood to have headed the party that murdered Lee and Lofters, while crossing Cedar creek. The day after the skirmish general Gaines was ordered with one thousand men to scour and lay waste the adjacent country. He did so, but the enemy had disappeared—five negroes were taken by him.

Fowl-Town, Mickasuka, and some others have been destroyed—1000 head of beef cattle, and several thousand bushels of corn have fallen into our hands. General Jackson has taken possession of St. Mark's, a Spanish post on the river of that name—the commander protested against this measure, but did not think proper to oppose its execution with force. The army has marched against the town of Suwanney, distant about thirty miles, and it is expected reached there on Thursday last; but it was not believed that the Indians would make a stand at that or any other place. Some having surrendered themselves prisoners, and the rest have been dispersed—so that the war with them may be considered nearly at an end. The militia from this state, we understand, will be marched to Trader's hill and discharged in a few days. Captain Arburthnot, [*Is not this alias the infamous Woodbine? Ed.] a British officer, was captured at St. Mark's. If we mistake not he was engaged during the contest with Great Britain, in stirring up the Indians to hostility against us, and commandant for some time at the negro fort erected on the Appalachicola, which was subsequently demolished by our troops.

By the hoisting the British flag, several Indians were decoyed on board of some gun-boats that ascended the St. Mark's river the 31st ult. among them

was a chief, and the prophet Francis, both of whom were hanged—the rest were liberated. St. Mark's, when taken, was strongly fortified, had twenty pieces of heavy ordnance mounted, and was garrisoned by about fifty men, who have since embarked for Pensacola. M'Intosh, whose vigilance and enterprise merit commendation, has captured about 100 more prisoners.—*Journal.*

—•»»Θ☺Θ««•—

More Details on Amelia Island

Volume 14, May 2, 1818, pages 169-170

Of Amelia-Island.
From the National Intelligencer.

It is impossible for us at present to find room for all the papers transmitted by the president to congress, together with his message of the 25th of March, respecting Amelia Island.

The most interesting and authentic paper is the following, which is entirely corroborated in all its parts by the less formal papers which detail the history of general McGregor's views and proceedings:

_____

Major Bankhead and captain Henley to the president, dated Fernandina, Amelia Island, January 10, 1818.

Sir—If any additional testimony were necessary to prove that general Aury had no authority to take possession of this island, it may be found in the documents under which he claims the right to have acted as he has done. At his urgent solicitation we have carefully examined these documents, and from them it is evident that he has had no privilege or power granted to him, even from the establishment at Galvezton or Matagorda, but that which he derived from don Manuel de Herrera, who, it appears was sent by the Mexican congress as minister to the United States, but proceeded no further than the city of New Orleans. During his stay at that place, a correspondence was opened between him and Aury, and the plan of an establishment at Galvezton agreed on. They met at that place, and formed a provisional government, of which Aury was made the governor, subject to the confirmation or rejection of the Mexican congress. Before any communication was had with the said congress, it was dissolved and dispersed by the Spanish forces; and Aury, having lost a number of his vessels on the Mexican coast, and unable to maintain his position, either at Galvezlon or Matagorda, sailed for this place; which he had heard was in possession of the forces under general McGregor. On his arrival here, McGregor had abandoned the post, which was then held by Hubbard and Irvine, with the rabble which had been collected from the streets of Charleston, South Carolina, and Savannah. After considerable contention for the supreme power, between Hubbard and his rabble, and Aury and his black followers, the latter, from the influence of the money brought with them, prevailed, and hoisted the Mexican flag.

These facts, we have no doubt, are all known to you, but as our information is derived from the best authority, the documents in the possession of general Aury, we have thought it proper, and have therefore taken the liberty to make this communication directly to you.

We have the honor to be, with sentiments of the highest respect, your most obedient servants.

J. D. HENLEY,
Commanding naval forces off Amelia-Island.
JAS. BANKHEAD,
Major 1st battalion artillery, southern division, commanding U. S. Troops on Amelia Island.

His excellency James Monroe, president of the United States.

———

Among the papers communicated by Mr. Pazos, along with his remonstrance to executive, the following document is the most prominent:

Translation of sir Gregor McGregor's commission.

The deputies of free America, resident in the United States of the north, to their com-patriot, Gregor McGregor, general of brigade in the service of the United provinces of New Grenada and Venezuela, greeting:

Whereas it is highly important to the interests of the people whom we have the honor to represent, that possession should be taken, without loss of time, of East and West Florida, and the blessings of free institutions, and the security of their natural rights, imparted to their inhabitants: In pursuance to our instructions, and in conformity to the desires of our respective governments, we have commissioned brigadier general Gregor M'Gregor, for the purpose of carrying into execution, either wholly or in part, an interprize so interesting to the glorious cause in which we are engaged.

Therefore, taking into consideration your zeal and devotion to the republic, we request you, in the name of our constituents, to proceed on your own responsibility, and that of the above named provinces, to adopt such measures as in your judgment may most effectually tend to procure for our brethren of both the Floridas, East and West, the speedy enjoyment of those great benefits to which they are invited by the advantage of their geographical situation; and for that purpose we authorize you, without departing from the usages and customs of civilized nations in like cases, and the due observance of the laws of the United States, and particularly those regulating their neutrality with foreign powers, to cause vessels to be armed without the limits of their jurisdiction, and provisionally to grant rank to naval and military officers, until the government, to be established by the free will of the said people, can provide in the most suitable mode for the arrangement of their several departments: in the execution of all which, the instructions delivered to you of this date will serve as your guide.

Signed, sealed, and delivered, at the city of Philadelphia, the 31st of March, 1817.

LINO DE CLEMENTE,
Deputy from Venezuela
PEDRO GUAL,
Deputy from New Grenada, and as proxy for

236

F. Zarate, *deputy from Mexico.*

MARTIN THOMSON,
Deputy from Rio de la Plata.

A true copy of the original in my possession, Philadelphia, 15th January, 1818—8th.

LINO DE CLEMENTE.

Here we find three deputies from three provinces, and a proxy for a fourth, constituting, with the United States, an officer with, in fact, almost imperial powers, if he had been able to carry them into execution: The expedition was therefore in its origin, as well as in its progress, in direct violation of our laws.

———

The following is the reply of the secretary of state to the remonstrance of M. Pazos, against the occupation of Amelia.

The secretary of state to don Vicente Pazos.

Washington,
5th March, 1818.

Sir—Your memorial addressed to the president of the United States, and the papers accompanying the same, have been laid before him: and I am directed to inform you, that his views of the transactions at Amelia Island, and the measures he thought proper to take in consequence of them, have been made known to the world by his communications to congress at the commencement of the present session, and by his message of the 13th of January last. He has given full consideration to your memorial and other papers, and perceiving nothing in them exhibiting the proceedings at Amelia Island in a different character from that in which he had before viewed them, he sees no reason for revoking any of the measures which have been taken by his directions in respect to that place, and nothing that requires any other answer to your representations.

I am, sir, your very humble servant,

JOHN QUINCY ADAMS.

———

The following are copies of letters from Don Pedro Gual and General Aury, to Commodore Henley and Colonel Bankhead, on the former leaving the Island of Amelia:

*"Fernandina,
Jan.* 11, 1818.

"Gentlemen—Being on the point of leaving this place for South America, I avail myself of the opportunity to return to you my thanks for your personal kindness to me and my fellow citizens ever since your troops took possession of this Island. Of the misfortune which they have been compelled to endure, it has certainly been of great relief that the execution of the order of your government was confided to so worthy characters as you; the remembrance of your humane personal deportment shall be forever impressed on our minds.

"I must confess to you, I leave with regret the United States of America, for whose prosperity I have constantly made my most ardent vows to heaven—a nation like your's, whose political institutions are calculated to redeem mankind from bondage and servile submission, cannot be too well appreciated; whatever may be the policy of your administration in regard to us, or the situation of our respective countries in the time to come, I shall be always proud to see in the same hemisphere where I am born, a virtuous people of brethren, happy, free and independent.

"As yourselves, gentlemen, it will give me a particular pleasure to attend to your commands, or be useful at any time to you and your friends.

"I remain, gentlemen, with great respect and esteem, your most obedient,

PEDRO GUAL.

To J. D. Henley, esq. &c. &c. &c.
    James Bankhead, esq. &c. &c. &c."

———

*"Fernandina,
March* 1, 1818

"Colonel—Allow me, before leaving Fernandina, to manifest to you my sincere acknowledgments of gratitude for the manner in which you have acted towards me since you took the command at Amelia; it will remain engraven on my mind.

"Should events ever take you to any part of South America, where I should be, or where I could be of any utility to you or your friends, I beg you will freely dispose of me; it will be gratifying to me to have an opportunity of proving the esteem with which I have the honor to remain your obedient servant,

AURY.

To COL. JAMES BANKHEAD, Fernandina"

———

"Fernandina, March 1, 1818

"Commodore—Allow me, before leaving this place, to manifest to you my sincere acknowledgments of gratitude for the manner in which you have acted towards me since your arrival at Amelia; it will remain engraven on my mind.

"Should events ever take you to any part of South America, where I should be, or where I could be of any utility to you, I beg you will freely dispose of me, as well for your friends; it will be gratifying to me to have an opportunity of proving the esteem with which I have the honor to remain your obedient humble servant,

AURY.

To COM. J. D. HENLEY, U. S. Ship John Adams."

Volume 14, May 2, 1818, page 176

Horrible Picture!
From the Savannah Republican.

If there had been no other motive for the suppression of the Amelia expedition, a sufficient reason would be found, in putting a stop to the importation of Africans, and the measure would have done equal honor to the head and heart of our chief magistrate. Have the wise and virtuous of our own country enacted laws, only for the purpose of having them violated? Are abolition societies daily established in the different sections of our republic in mere mockery? Or are we in earnest, in desiring to put an end to this traffic, so odious in the sight of God and man? Are proofs wanting? We refer to the records of Savannah. Will it be credited, that a *regular chain of*

posts is established from the head of St. Mary's river to the upper country, and through the Indian nation, by means of which, these emaciated wretches are hurried and transferred to every part of the country. The woodsmen of the country, bordering on the river St. Mary's, ride, like so many Arabs, loaded with slaves, ready for market. Pursuit is useless, they push through uninhabited parts, known only to themselves; and with a spirit of enterprize, fitted for better purposes, elude all search. If ready for forming a caravan, an Indian alarm is created, that the woods may be less frequented; if pursued in Georgia, they escape into Florida. What will the humane say, when told of the horrors of these miserable Africans? One small schooner of about 60 tons, contained 130 souls; they were almost packed into a small space, between a floor laid over the water casks and the deck—not near three feet—insufficient for them to set upright—and so close that chafing against each other, their bones pierced the skin and became galled and ulcerated by the motion of the vessel—their food, a very stinted allowance, consisted of rotten rice, in a state of fermentation, and so warm as to comfort their frozen hands—numbers died of hunger, cold and misery—while others crawled about, a sort of living anatomies, dragged, naked and shivering, in this (to them) cold climate and season from their "prison house" and hurried off, on long and painful journies, to satisfy the cupidity of unfeeling adventurers. Putting aside the agonies of the body, what tortures of mind have these afflicted sons of Africa not undergone! When these unhappy sufferers were recaptured by the Saranac, the commonest sailors on board, touched with the tenderest sympathy, divided amongst them, their clothes, and every aid that circumstances made possible, was humanely afforded by the officers. What a sight has Fernandina exhibited! "This cradle of liberty," as some would persuade the public—when privateer sailors have led about, and sold their shares of the spoil to the highest bidder. What a specimen of government! What a proof of connection with Mexico and Venezuela—that forbid this traffic in the new government. But has the president been informed of all this? Can we suppose that the public officers have been silent spectators of all these horrors? The partial publication of these reports answer such interrogation—this is but a faint picture of this monstrous trade. All that has been written and said on the subject of barbarity and cruelty, is yet extant, whenever it is tolerated, and man when he made a trade of his fellow, like the hyaena, becomes "the fellest of the fell." This much for humanity's sake—but for the law, it was the duty of the president to prevent its violation by driving from our frontier this horde of marauders, who disregarded and insulted it, and thanks to him—he has done so.

Volume 14, May 9, 1818, pages 189-190

Foreign Articles—The Floridas.

Ferdinand, intending to sell, or expecting to be dispossessed of Florida, is carrying on a high game.

In the Aurora of Monday, a letter is published, dated Madrid, March 17th, 1818, in which it is stated "that since the seizing of Amelia Island by our government, Ferdinand the VIIth has granted to several of his favorites immense tracts of land in the Floridas," and gives the following as a translation of a transcript from the Spanish:

Cession of land made
by his catholic majesty
to the duke of Allagon.

"All the uncultivated land, which has not already been granted in East Florida, and which lies between the banks of the rivers St. Louisa and St. Johns to their entrance in the sea, and the coast of the gulph of Florida and the islands adjacent, within the entrance or mouth of the river Hispuelos, in the 26th deg. of latitude, following its left bank to its source, drawing a line to the lake Macao from thence down by the road of the river St. Johns to the lake Valdes, striking by another line from the northern extremity of this lake, to the source of the Ananina following its right bank to its mouth by the 28 and 25 degrees of latitude, and continuing along the coast of the sea, with all the adjacent islands, to the mouth of the river Hispuelos."

Cession of land made
by his catholic majesty to the
Conde de Pongen Rostro.

"All the uncultivated lands which have not already been granted in Florida, comprized between the river Perdido to the west of the Gulph of Mexico and the rivers Amaruja and St. Johns, from Popa to its outlet in the sea to the eastward; to the northward of the line of demarcation with the United States of America, and to the southward by the Gulph of Mexico, including all the desert islands on the coast."

The letter further states, "the duke of Allagon has despatched, it is said, a Mr. Serna to the United States."

A British editor says the U. S. will get, by acquiring the Floridas, a regular, supply of *pitch! tar! turpentine! masts!* and *ship plank!* besides live oak that, after 100 years exposure, acquires a stony hardness.

It is added also — that in East Florida, "there is one of the best and most secure harbors in America, which will receive from 50 to 100 sail of the line."

——»)»Ө ⊚ Ө«««——

General Jackson's Forces on the Move into Florida

Volume 14, May 9, 1818, page 192

Chronicle—Another Indian Battle.

Copy of a letter from General William McIntosh, commanding the Creek warrior, to D.B. Mitchell, esq. agent for Indian affairs.

Camp, 30 miles from Mickasuka,
(on the way to Sawanee),
13th April, 1818.

Sir—Since I left you I have not sent you a talk of what we have done, and I now send you this.—I heard yesterday of Peter McQueen being near the road we were travelling, and I took my warriors and went and fought him. There seemed to be a considerable number collected there. When we first began to fight them, they were in a bad swamp, and fought us there for about an hour, when they ran and we followed them three miles. They fought us in all about three hours. We killed 37 of them, and took 98 women and children and six men prisoners, and about 700 head of cattle and a number of horses, with a good many hogs and some corn. We lost three killed and had five wounded. Our prisoners tell us that there was 120 warriors from six different towns. From what we saw, I believe there was more than they say, as some of our prisoners say there was 200 of them. Tom Woodward [*Major Woodward, of Baldwin] and Mr. Brown, and your son, our agent, and all the white men that live in our country were with us through the whole fight, and fought well. All my officers fought so well I do not know which is the bravest. They all fought like men and run their enemies. General Jackson waited for us about six miles from where we fought. After the fight I went and joined him, and we are going this morning to fight the negroes together. They are at Sawannee, and we shall be there in four days. There was among the hostiles a woman that was in the boat where our friends the white people were killed on the river below Fort Scott. We gave her to her friends— her husband and father are with General Jackson— Major Kinnard took her himself. This is all I have to tell you. I wish you would send a copy of this to the Big Warrior and Little Prince.

Your friend,

WILLIAM McINTOSH,
Brig. Gen. comm'g C.W.

D.B. Mitchell,
esq. agent L.A.

Volume 14, May 16, 1818, page 208

Chronicle—Indian War.

Mobile, April 21.— The editor of the Mobile Gazette, is under great obligations to Major Perault, of the United States topographical corps, who arrived here last evening from the seat of war, for the following pleasing information:

General Jackson had left Fort Scott, with a few men, and established himself at the place near Appalachicola, where the negro fort formerly stood.

On the 26th March last, he left the latter place for Fort Gadsden, and seven days after reached the Indian town called Missiskauki, with 1,500 militia, 700 regulars, 800 Indians, and a few others, making in the whole about 3,400; on reaching this town, there was but little skirmishing or fighting. A few Indians were killed, and a few of our men. The Indian town was deserted, Jackson burnt it, and killed the cattle.

From the Indian town, Jackson proceeded to the Spanish town of St. Marks, where he summoned the Spanish post to surrender; they surrendered as prisoners, and have arrived at Pensacola.

From St. Marks, Jackson proceeded to Swaney, near which place the Indians, about 2000, in connexion with some negroes, were expected to make a stand.

The Indian chief, and the prophet Francis, had been decoyed on board an American armed vessel, supposing her to be English, and were hung. The infamously celebrated Arbuthnot (*Woodbine*) is in Jackson's possession, and in irons.

Jackson's army is well provided, and in great spirits, and we may daily expect to hear of a decisive blow from that quarter.

Jackson has been joined by the Tennessee volunteers, and has now about 5000 men subject to his command.

—➤»»θ◎θ«««—

Jackson Declares Seminole War Terminated

Volume 14, May 23, 1818, page 218

Indian War.

Latest from the Army.

Milledgeville, May 5. For the following late intelligence from our troops, we are indebted to Mr. Pearre, (one of the editors of the Augusta Chronicle,) an officer of col. Milton's staff, who is direct from the army.

The army left St. Marks on the 9th ult. and on the 10th were joined by a detachment of mounted troops from Tennessee, under the command of colonels Dyer and Williamson, a small detachment of regulars under the command of captain Call, and 1000 warriors under M'Intosh, who had been left at the Mickasukie to scour the country and gather the stock which was left by the Indians in their retreat. On the morning of the 12th, M'Intosh with a part of his warriors, attacked a party of hostile Indians. The engagement continued about two hours with much spirit, when the hostiles retreated, leaving their women, children and property of all kinds to the mercy of the conquerors—sustaining a loss of 37 killed on the field, and two wounded, and a number of prisoners. The number of Indians engaged was differently represented by different prisoners. M'Intosh had three men killed, and several wounded. Kinnard and Timpooche, (or John) Barnett were conspicuous in this action; the latter evinced military talents which would have done credit to a greater man. These Indians belonged to M'Queen's party, and were the same who massacred the crew of Lieut. Scott in the boats last fall, at the mouth of Flint River. The woman who was taken there, and many articles of soldiers' clothing were found in their possession.

On the 17th the army took possession of *Suwanney*,* after a skirmish of about fifteen minutes, in which three negroes were killed, and three taken prisoners. [*The town Suwanney, 107 miles from St. Marks, is said to have been beautifully situated on the river, and supposed to have contained 600 huts—all which were reduced to ashes.—Ed. Reg.] About 2000 bushels of corn, some cattle, and some few articles of provisions, such as rice, potatoes, sugar, salt, &c. were found in the town, and at a store belonging to Arbuthnot, a few miles below. On the next day a scout was sent across the river for the purpose of pursuing the Indians, but they had got too far advanced to be overtaken. The scouts took some property, and found a small quantity of merchandize concealed in the swamp.

On the night of the 18th two Englishmen, who Arbuthnot had employed as clerks and agents, and two negroes, came from a schooner just arrived below from a piratical cruise, up to the town for provisions, &c.

unconscious of our army being there. They were all taken by our centinels, except one negro, who made his escape. The canoe which they came in was secured, and at day light next morning a detachment was sent to take possession of the schooner, on board of which young Arbuthnot commanded. The result of the expedition was not known when our informant departed.

On the 20th, the Georgia troops commenced their march homeward. In the evening of the same day, M'Intosh and the principal part of his warriors also commenced their return march, with directions to destroy Hoponnie's town and all his warriors, and to take possession of all his property of every description, so as effectually to destroy him.

———

*Extract of a letter
from major general Jackson
to governor Rabun, dated*

BOWLEGS TOWN,
SUWANNEY,
20th April, 1818

"Sir — I have reached and destroyed this and the other town in its vicinity, and having captured the principal exciters of the war, I think I may safely say, that the Indian war, for the present, is terminated. This happy circumstance enables me to dispense with the further services of the brigade of Georgia militia, commanded by brigadier gen. Glasscock; and, at their solicitation, I have ordered them directly to Hartford, to be mustered, paid and discharged.

"The last campaign has consisted more of rapid movements and manoeuvering than of hard fighting; but from every occurrence, I have the utmost confidence, that in the event of a hard fought action, every officer and soldier under my command would have sustained the true American character, and have realized the best hopes of their country.

I have the honor to, be very respectfully, your most obedient servant,

ANDREW JACKSON,
Major Gen' l Comd'g"

Army Attack on Friendly Indian Village

EXPEDITION AGAINST THE CHEHAWS.

The official account of this expedition has been received, and will be found below. Respecting its policy, there are various opinions; and with regard to its tragical result, many contradictory statements. It is asserted, and so far as we have heard it expressed, public opinion favors the belief, that the town destroyed was friendly; and some of its warriors are stated to be now with the army under General Jackson.

We are authorized to state, that the executive has been long since convinced, by information derived from respectable sources, of the hostile disposition of the Indians living in the neighborhood of Fort Early, on the Flint River, particularly those under the influence of the chiefs Felemma and Hupauno. To quiet the apprehensions of the frontier, and prevent depredations in future, Capt. Wright of the militia stationed at Hartford, with such volunteers as he could assemble, was directed by the governor to chastise the Indians above named.

Unfortunately, the detachment it is believed was misled, either by the ignorance or design of the guides, and fell on the old Chehaw Town (supposed to be friendly) which was laid in ashes, and many of its wretched inhabitants put to death.

Hartford, (Ga.)
April 25, 1818.

His excellency governor Rabun:

Sir — I have the honor to inform you that agreeable to your orders, I took up the line of march from this place on the 21st instant, with captains Robinson's and Rogers' companies of mounted gunmen, captain Dean's and Child's infantry, together with two detachments under lieutenants Cooper and Jones, captain Thomason acting as adjutant, in all about 270 effective men.

On the night of the 22d, I crossed Flint River and at day break advanced with caution against the Chehaw Town. The advance guard, when within half a mile of the town, took an Indian prisoner, who was attending a drove of cattle, and on examination, found some of them to be the property of a Mr. M'Duffy (who was present) of Telfair county.

The town was attacked between 11 and 12 o'clock, with positive orders not to injure the women, or children, and in the course of two hours, the whole was in flames, -- they made some little resistance but to no purpose.

From the most accurate accounts, 24 warriors were killed, and owing to the doors of some of the houses being inaccessible to our men, and numbers of guns being fired at us through the crevices, they were set fire; in consequence of which, numbers were burnt to death in the houses; in all probability from 40 to 50 was their total loss. Some considerable number of warriors made their escape, by taking to a thick swamp; a very large parcel of powder found in the town was destroyed. It is supposed their chief is among the slain. The town is laid completely desolate, without the loss of a man. We re-crossed the Flint to Fort Early the same evening, making a complete march of 31 miles (exclusive of destroying the town) in 24 hours.

The conduct of the officers and soldiers on this occasion, (as well as on all others) was highly characteristic of the patriotism and bravery of the Georgians in general.

I am, sir, with respect, your most obedient humble serv't,

OBED WRIGHT,
Capt. Geo. Draf. militia, comd'g.

Copy of a letter from judge Strong to the governor, dated,

Hartford,
27th April, 1818.

Sir — On my route to the Telfair and back, immediately on the frontier, I took much pains to ascertain the disposition

242

of the towns below Chehaw, and from a variety of corroborating facts, I have no doubt but that a majority of their warriors are hostile, and have done most of the recent mischief on our borders. A part if not all the Chehaw towns are also hostile, some were painted, and the cattle of different citizens found there, which had been driven off by the Indians. The recent occurrences there, puts their disposition out of the question — there can be no doubt they will do us all the injury they can. As an individual I therefore feel desirous, that ample means should be placed in capt. Wright's, or some other officer's hands, to fight and beat the Indians below Chehaw, and destroy their towns. In haste, from the bench.

Your's respectfully, C B. STRONG.

———

Messrs. Grantlands — I find some people are misled, or under wrong impressions, as to the late expedition to the nation, supposing the town destroyed by Capt. Wright's detachment (acting under the orders of the executive) was actually friendly. As an officer commanding a volunteer corps, on that occasion, I feel it my duty to state, that when the army, or rather the advance, appeared within a half a mile of the town, we found an Indian herding cattle, the most of which appeared to be white people's marks and brands. A Mr. McDuffee, of Telfair, attached to my corps, swore to one cow as the property of his father, and taken from near where the late depredation on the frontier of Telfair was committed. We found in the town a rifle gun, known to be the one taken from a man of the name of Burch, who fell in the before mentioned skirmish. When we determined to attack the town, positive orders were given to spare the women and children, and all such as claimed protection; which was strictly enforced by the officers, so far as was practicable, or within my observation.

My troop was directed to advance on the right of the town, which was done speedily. On our approach and before a man of my company fired a gun, the Indians, from a sink or cave near the path we were in, fired apparently 12 or 15 guns at my men; the bullets were distinctly heard by all, and slightly felt by two or

three of the men. Some of the Indians found in the town were painted; all I saw evinced a disposition to light or escape. We killed 24 warriors, and burnt the town agreeable to orders. A considerable number of new British muskets, carbines, &c. were destroyed; in nearly all the houses there were explosions of gunpowder. The Indian we found herding cattle informed us, that Hopauna resided there and was then in the town. I am not certain whether he was slain or not. In possession of the last Indian killed, who was painted red, was found two letters, one from colonel Milton, the other from major Minton, both addressed to general Gaines, the seals of which were broken.

JACOB ROBINSON.

April 30th, 1818.

———

The following is a copy of the orders issued by the executive to Capt. Wright.

Head quarters, Georgia,
Milledgeville,
April 14, 1818.

General Orders. — The executive having received information through sources which cannot be doubted, that the wanton and cruel murders so frequently committed on the frontier inhabitants of this state, and which are almost daily practised by the savages, ascertained to be the Phelemmes and Hoppones; inhabitants of two small villages of their names, on or near Flint river, who have during the late hostilities endeavored to conceal their blood thirsty and hostile disposition under a cloak of friendship — And the combined regular and militia force under major general Jackson being too far advanced into the heart of the Creek nation to admit of any speedy operations against them from that quarter; the commander in chief of the state deems it expedient for the safety of the frontier inhabitants, and to prevent further depredation by them, that a sufficient military force should be marched immediately against those towns to effect their complete destruction, and for the speedy accomplishment of which, Captain Obed. Wright, commanding as senior officer of the militia stationed on the frontier, will order captains Dean and Childes, who are stationed at different points on the Ocmulgee, to proceed immediately with their respective commands to Hartford or such other place as he shall deem expedient, between that place and Fort Early, with the exception of a small guard placed under the command of a subaltern or non-commissioned officer to defend the posts they now occupy; he is also authorized to receive such companies as may voluntarily join him.

Captain Timothy L. Rogers, commanding a volunteer troop of light dragoons in Jones, and Captain John Permenter, commanding a volunteer company of riflemen in Twiggs county, will join Captain Wright at Hartford — so soon as the respective companies shall have arrived at that place. Captain Wright will proceed with the whole to Fort Early, where he is authorized to call on Captain Bothwell, or the commanding officer of that station, for the whole of his command, except so many as are actually necessary for its immediate protection. The utmost precaution will be necessary to the accomplishment of this important object, and to effect which, it will be necessary that a profound secrecy should be observed, and the expedition be prosecuted with the greatest possible despatch, in order to take the Indians by surprise; as this is the only probable means of obtaining an effectual and decisive victory over an enemy who will not come in contact on equal terms.

By order of the commander in chief,

E. WOOD, secretary.

Volume 14, May 30, 1818, pages 235-236

Indian War.

Milledgeville,
May 12.

Extract of a letter from General Glasscock, commanding the detachment of Georgia militia, lately in service, to the editors of this paper, dated

"HARTFORD,
May 2, 1818.

"I am happy to inform you that my command has safely arrived at this place, having encountered difficulties almost insurmountable. The object of the expedition being accomplished, we were permitted to return via Mickasukie — having no meat on hand it was all important to make a forced march to fort Early; the men were called upon to know whether they were willing to risque themselves upon what corn they had, which amounted to about six days rations; it was determined that they were. We, therefore, on the 20th of April, took up the line of march, and arriving at Mickasukie, a number of our men were almost worn out with fatigue and hunger. Providence it appeared smiled upon us; our pilot, who was an Indian, observing a small trail, pursued it for some distance, and arrived at a hut which had not been discovered on our advance. It contained 50 or 60 bushels of corn; every countenance, which had but a few moments before been marked with despair, was completely brightened; a spirit of animation flashed throughout the line; but it proved only temporary, for when arriving near the ferry, opposite Chehaw, where we expected a plentiful supply of beef, information reached us that the Chehaw village was destroyed, and that it could not be procured. Never were feelings more shocked than they were on the receipt of this news. My adjutant, Major Robison, who was in our advance with a small detachment of men for the purpose of supplying provisions, sent a runner to get the Indians, who from fear were lying out, to come in, assuring them they would receive protection. — Five of them were prevailed upon to do so, and on my arrival at the river, I found them there, and obtained from them 24 head of cattle, but for which many of my command would not have been able to reach fort Early under four or five days, having suffered so materially from hunger.

To say more to you than I have already said on the subject of the friendship of the Indians in the Chehaw town, appears to me almost useless. If ever there was a transaction calculated to blast the reputation of the state and throw a shade of censure on an officer, it is the destruction of that town, and the circumstances relating thereto. I have had an interview with the officer commanding fort Early (captain Rothwell,) and his Lieutenant, Mr. Jones, who was present at the massacre, as well as with some of the Indians, and from what comes within my own knowledge.

244

I have no hesitation in saying it was an unwarrantable act. What, permit me to ask, must be the feeling of every individual when informed, that in passing through that town, we not only obtained a large quantity of supplies for the use of the army, but had to leave some of our sick under the protection of these very people; and that 40 out of about 80 of that particular town, were regularly mustered into the service of the United States, and have been and were rendering important services at the time their property was destroyed, and in all probability some of their nearest relations murdered. In fact, it has been represented, from a source which admits of no doubt, that one of the Indians from fort Scott, who was on furlough, was killed in the affray; major Howard, an Indian whose friendship was never before doubted — an Indian who in the most hazardous time accompanied major Woodward to fort Gaines; he even after the firing and murder commenced, conscious of his friendship, stepped from within his doors in front of the line, with the flag of friendship; it was not respected; a general fire was made; he fell and was bayoneted. If such acts as these be tolerated, security can never be given to our frontiers, unless there be a general extermination. Already has the life of one man been forfeited. Three men who were left at fort Scott sick, obtained a furlough and not being apprised of the destruction of the town, passed through the place. On arriving at the river, one of them, in obtaining a canoe for the purpose of crossing, was killed; the other two immediately returned; one of them only has arrived — it is apprehended the other is lost. On my arrival at fort Early, finding that no express had been sent on, I immediately procured one and have sent it to fort Scott, apprising the commanding officer of that post of the circumstance, and guarding him against suffering his men to come off in such parties; an express has also been sent on to General Jackson and General Gaines." [*Georgia Journal.*]

From the National Intelligencer.

In the anxious hope that there was some mistake in the circumstances of the narration, we have for some days foreborne to lay before our readers the account too fully confirmed, which we now publish, of the unfortunate massacre of a party of friendly Indians, in Georgia, whilest engaged in the peaceable pursuit of their domestic avocations. This horrible incident is of a character to excite the commiseration of the most implacable enemy of the Indian race. It is an outrage on humanity, which cannot be too sincerely lamented, nor too fully atoned.

There is, even for those Indians who take up arms against us, a palliation for their offence—they are misled by foreign artifice; they are under the influence of a religious impulse entitled to pity, though to no more respect than we are willing to allow to all fanaticism. They should be conquered by beneficence rather than by force; and it is always painful to find the last resort unavoidable, as in the present war. It is lamentable indeed, to find, in the progress of the war, the friendly have been confounded with the hostile, and that our fellow beings have been hunted like the buffalo and the deer, and slain with as little remorse and as little discrimination.

In grieving over this incident — in calling upon the government to relieve the surviving sufferers, and bind up the wounds of the broken hearted—far be it from us to pretend to pronounce on the character of it, as deducible from the conduct of the perpetrators. We certainly incline to believe, from the evidence we have seen, that it was one of those unfortunate mistakes, which, during a war, have frequently occurred, on the ocean and on the land, under commanders the most intelligent and skillful. Bodies of the same army have frequently encountered each other, in consequence of mistaking one another for parties of the enemy, and discovered their error only when mutual loss compelled them to desist from the combat. Instances of such accidents are to be found in the greatest battles ever fought, though they more frequently occur in skirmishes, such as those which have characterized the present Indian war; and may be more readily pardoned in the heat of pursuit, to a party of exasperated militia, led by a nominal commander. Let us hope, that the enquiry, which is to be immediately instituted into this transaction, will eventuate in proving that one Indian town was mistaken for another; and that we may have the consolation of finding, that what we know to have been a cruel slaughter of unresisting friends, was not also an act of cold blooded treachery. But, should it prove otherwise, as citizens of the United States we wash our hands of the shame of the transaction: such an act could not stain the character of a people who would view it with unanimous abhorrence.

Volume 14, May 30, 1818, page 239

Chronicle—Indian War.

In page 235, is inserted a letter from general Glascock, of the Georgia militia, respecting the destruction of the Chehaw, town, with some remarks on that melancholy transaction, from the National Intelligencer. A number of the Georgia papers express their feelings on this subject with severest reprehension of the deed; and give to the act some circumstances of barbarism which we did hope could not have happened. We trust that the affair will be most rigidly examined into—*let justice be done.*

We have nothing important from the army since our last. It is expected that the war is at an end, though a body of troops must remain some time in Florida to preserve the peace.

—⟫☺☺☺⟪—

Affair of Arbuthnot and Ambrister

Volume 14, June 6, 1818, pages 246-247

Indian War.

An awful military act has been performed by General *Jackson*. The wretched *Arbuthnot* and *Ambristie*, have paid the forfeit of their crimes. We were mistaken in believing that the former was only another name for *Woodbine* — that unfeeling monster has escaped; he was in Jamaica early in April last, as appears by a letter received in Baltimore. The decisive conduct of the commanding general may divert his attention to some other means of getting a livelihood than

that of exciting the savages to murder the unoffending.

Every body is familiar with the character and conduct of *Arbuthnot* – he was Woodbine's right hand man, or rather a full partner in his schemes of bloody mischief. *Ambristie*, who served as an engineer under Colonel *Nicholls*, was in command of the negro allies. Another account calls this person *Warburton* – see below. These persons, assisted, perhaps, by others yet unknown, uselessly caused the deaths of several thousand human beings – having been the *real* authors, or at least the principal agents and supporters of the late and present wars with the Creeks and Seminoles.

If rigid *justice* ever required the life of man to expiate his offences or prevent a repetition of wrong, the lives of Arbuthnot and Ambristie, or Warburton, were justly forfeited, if their character has been faithfully represented in any of the multitudinous accounts we have received of their proceedings. But this is an abstract principle and its application, in the present case, may cause a difference of opinion as to its propriety to exist, and especially so if the Florida can be considered as a neutral country – if the fact is not proved that they have trespassed on our territory, and there excited those murders which led to the last or caused the present war. We shall, no doubt, soon have a detail of all the facts belonging to them and their adherents – and no man ought to form a definite opinion respecting their execution until he has a view of the whole ground. This is very certain, that the Floridas have never been a *neutral* country since the year 1813 – and we every day find additional reason to regret that, when Spain openly permitted, or suffered, the country to be a depot for British armies and British agents, to operate upon the restless disposition of the savages within our territory, and carry into effect the "holy" scheme of causing the slaves to rise upon and murder their masters and desolate the southern states, as it was determined should happen – we did not fairly take possession of both *Floridas*, and keep it until Spain at least was *willing* and was *able* to fulfill her treaties with us, as to restraining the savages, and of preventing the country from being an asylum for the most unprincipled set of men that ever disgraced the human form – agents of secret murder and indiscriminate death.

The following are extracts from a letter, written by Charles Cassedy, esq. of Tennessee, to his friend in New-York, and published in the newspapers of that city — it notices some of the facts that have a bearing on the case:

1st. In the year 1814 there were landed, from the best information, within the Spanish province of East Florida, twenty-two thousand stand of arms, and three hundred barrels of fixed ammunition, intended for the Creek Indians. Some of these arms bore the Tower-hill stamp — were new, and were brought into the American camp.

2d. When General Jackson invaded Pensacola, the fort called "The Barrankas" was garrisoned by English troops, who, on his advance, evacuated and blew it up, under an apprehension that he would take it by storm, and turn the guns on their ships of war, which lay in the harbor.

3d. It is very possible, and I imagine that Gonzales Murique, who was at that period governor of Pensacola, previously to this invasion, avowed, in a written communication, that he would "supply the Creek Indians with every thing in his power. Whether this letter was the production of English policy operating on Spanish stupidity; or whether it was the offspring of a mercantile house in Pensacola; or whether it was the impotent fulmination of an infatuated adherent to pusillanimous royalty, cannot be well determined — but, in any event, the neutrality of this province was violated, against the interest of the United States, without even a protest against it on the part of Spain— and without even a communication of the fact, to the officer commanding the 7th military district."

He intimates an intention, hereafter to communicate — "How far the same spirit of covert hostility, to the United States, has been evinced from the same sources, since the commencement of the late affair."

———

From the New Orleans Gazette, May 12.

A party of the Tennessee volunteers, amounting to near 50, arrived in this town on Sunday last, from St. Marks. General Jackson had discharged all his militia; and himself, with 1200 regular troops, had taken up his line of march to the west. We shall not pretend to say what is the object of this movement; or why he has ordered a number of cannon to be despatched from Mobile to Fort Montgomery. If his purpose be to reach the Alabama, Pensacola will not be far out of his way, and he may probably halt there in order to pay his respects to the governor and the Indians his guests.

We are informed that the power of the savages is totally broken, their towns burnt, their corn destroyed, their cattle driven off, and their wives and children, to the number of 350, captured and safely lodged in fort Gadsden. Previously to these results, they had, on three or four different occasions presumed to offer a show of resistance, but their efforts were feeble and spiritless, and they were invariably routed without material loss on the part of our army. The Indians only are liable to this imputation of pusillanimity; their sable allies displayed greater resolution. A detachment of these latter, having been attacked in the night, defended themselves with the courage of men who are conscious of guilt, and hopeless of pardon; and fought till near one half of them were killed. They were commanded by a white man, named Warburton, who was formerly an officer of engineers in the British service, and who acted as aid-de-camp to Colonel Nichols, in his unsuccessful attack on Mobile Point in September 1814. His rencontre, with Jackson terminated his career; he was captured, tried by a court martial, condemned and shot.

Arbuthnot, also a white man, the leader of the Indians, who supplied them with weapons and ammunition, who instructed them in the trade of assassination, and counselled them as to the means of extirpating the frontier inhabitants, was hanged on board of a vessel. It is difficult to contemplate the execution of a criminal without feeling a slight degree of commiseration for his fate: few are so depraved as not to possess some one redeeming good quality to excite regret that it is necessary to offer them victims, to avenging justice. But in viewing the end of Arbuthnot and Warburton (Ambrister), the mind can experience no other sensation than complacency that guilt so full, so unexampled as theirs, has received its merited punishment. And indeed what pity do they deserve; who, born and educated in the bosom of civilized society, have identified themselves with cannibals, thirsting after human blood; who could excite, applaud and recompense their deeds of ferocity?

———

From the Louisiana Gazette, May 12.

A number of Tennesseans, who lately were volunteers in Jackson's army in Florida, arrived here on Sunday from the scene of action. From their report the following particulars are derived concerning the movements of the American army.

The accounts, via Mobile, had left General Jackson on his march to attack the Indian encampment at Swancey. It now appears that on the approach of our troops, some skirmishes took place, in which the savages lost some men. The main body of the Indians then retired to St. Augustine for shelter. General Jackson pursued them some distance, when he discovered an encampment defended by 340 negroes; they were attacked immediately, forced, and about 80 killed or wounded. About 300 Indian women and children were also taken by the army in the march.

Gen. Jackson now discharged the Tennessee volunteers, and with the rest of his army took up a line of march for Fort Gadsden.

It was thought by some that the general might pay a visit to Pensacola. The commander of the blacks, an Englishman, who had served as an engineer under Colonel Nichols, was taken, tried by a court martial and shot. Arbuthnot was hung on the 24th of April.

———

Savannah, May 22 — On the 1st inst. Arbuthnot and Ambristie, who were taken at the capture of fort St. Mark's, were tried by a court martial, in pursuance to an order from General Jackson, of which General Gaines was the president. Both were condemned to die. The former

was sentenced to be hung — the latter to be shot. They were executed on the 3rd inst. agreeably to the mandate of the court. It is said that Ambristie died like a soldier — he was cool and firm to the last moment — Arbuthnot was much agitated, and evinced great fear. A man by the name of Cook, one of the accomplices of Arbuthnot and Ambristie, turned evidence against them, and on his testimony they were convicted. The charges and specifications alleged against them were, 1st. for supplying the Indians with arms and munitions of war. 2d. For stirring them up against the whites. 3d. as spies — Ambristie was a lieutenant in the British army and an intelligent, fine looking man. Arbuthnot is an old offender, and has often been advised to desist from exciting the savages against the frontier people of our state. He was the bosom friend of the *famous* Woodbine; who we fervently wish had fallen into the hands of Jackson — for a greater villain curses not the face of the earth. — *Rep.*

———

From the Georgia Journal.

Messrs. Grantlands— It is due to the public, to myself, and to the men I commanded in the late expedition under Captain Wright, to state, that many false reports, relative to the destruction of the Chehaw village, have been put in circulation by wicked and evil disposed persons; and I am sorry to find that there is so great a disposition among the people to credit the gross misrepresentations that have been made. — I suppose the words of many men in the detachment ought to have as much weight as the declarations of perfidious savages, and those concerned with them in trade. The statement made by Captain Robinson, of Laurens, is substantially true; and the assertion of Mr. Pearre, in the "Reflector," that the detachment carried a white flag, and fired into the Indians while the hand of friendship was extended to them, is not so. The detachment never entered the town as friends; and at the time the Indian, who was killed, held out the flag, or colors, they were firing; from the same house at us.

TIMOTHY L. ROGERS.
Jones county, May 15, 1818.

The Chehaw Village

Volume 14, June 13, 1818, pages 267-271

Indian War.

Destruction of the Chehaw Village.

Copy of a letter from D.B. Mitchell, esq, agent for Indian affairs, to governor Rabun, dated Milledgeville, May 6, 1818.

Sir — On the 2d instant I received information that a party of mounted men had attacked and destroyed the Chehaw town on Flint river, and killed many of the inhabitants. From all I could then learn it appeared to be uncertain what troops they were, and under whose command, or by whose order this unwarrantable and barbarous deed had been done; and as the consequences cannot be foreseen which may result, when the justly exasperated warriors of the town return, and find their town and property destroyed; — their unoffending and helpless families killed or driven into the woods to perish, whilst they were fighting their and our enemies, the Seminoles; deemed it best to come to the state and endeavor to procure correct information. I now find that the party had been sent out by your orders, but failed to execute them; and that the attack on Chehaw was unauthorized.

I present the case for the consideration of your excellency, under a confident hope, that as the people of Chehaw were not only friends, but that their conduct during the present war entitle them to our favor and protection, some immediate step will be taken to render that satisfaction which is due for so great an injury.

The extent of their loss in a pecuniary point of view, I am not at this moment prepared to state, but so soon as I return to the agency I will loose no time in having that ascertained; and in the mean time, permit me to suggest the propriety of instituting some legal enquiry into the conduct of the officers engaged in the enterprise.

I have the honor to enclose an extract of a letter received from old Mr. Barnard on this subject, the contents of which is corroborated by a verbal statement of the Wolf Warrior, who came to me directly from the spot.

I leave this early in the morning for the agency, from whence I will address you again upon this subject.

I am, sir, with high consideration and respect your very obedient servant,

D.B. Mitchell, *Agent for I.A.*

P. S. — Since writing the above, I have received a letter from the Little Prince, speaker of the Lower Creeks, upon this subject, a copy of which I also enclose.

———

Copy of a letter from the Little Prince, speaker of the Lower Creeks, to D.B. Mitchell, agent for I.A. dated Fort Mitchell, April 25, 1818.

My great friend — I have got now a talk to send to you. One of our friendly towns, by the name of the Chehaw, has been destroyed. The white people came and killed one of the head men, and five men and a woman, and burnt all their houses. All our young men have gone to war with General Jackson, and there is only a few left to guard the town, and they have come and served us this way. As you are our friend and father, I hope you will try and find out, and get us satisfaction for it. You may depend upon it, that all our young men have gone to war, but a few that are left to guard the town. Men do not get up and do this mischief without there is some one at the head of it, and we want you to try and find them out.

(Signed)

TUSTUNNUGGIE HOPOIE.

———

Copy of a letter from Timothy Barnard, esq. (a white man) residing on Flint River, to D.B. Mitchell, agent for I.A. dated April 30, 1818.

Sir — The Wolf Warrior, the bearer of this, has just arrived here and brings bad news from the Au,mue,culla town (Chehaw.) Nearly all the warriors belonging to that town are now with our armies. Seven days past a company of

249

white people collected and rushed on the town; and as there were but few red people there, and all friendly, just what few were left to guard their town, the rest still with our army, the white people killed every one they could lay their hands on — killed the old chief Tiger king and one other chief; both I have known always to be friendly to our color, ever since I have been in this land. The whole of what are killed is nine men and one poor old woman. They took off what horses there were, the owners of which, some are still living. They took the horses to the fort, which is not far from the town they have destroyed. The chiefs that are still alive, beg that you will get their horses, or any thing else returned. The red people don't know whether it is the regular troops, or Georgia militia that have committed this unwarrantable act. I have wrote you all that I think is necessary — If you see cause to write any thing to me, to inform them of, I will do it with pleasure. If these people do not get some friendly treatment for the damage done them, I am afraid, when their warriors return back from our army, something bad will happen on some of our color. I am very sorry to have to write you on such a horrid piece of business.

I write you in haste, as the bearer is in great hurry to see you.

I remain, sir, your friend, and most ob't serv't.

(Signed) T. BARNARD.

THE GOVERNOR'S REPLY

Executive Department, Georgia Milledgeville, 20th May, 1818.

Sir — I have the honor to acknowledge the receipt of your's of the 6th instant, enclosing a copy of a letter from old Mr. Barnard, and one from the Little Prince, speaker of the Lower Creeks, both on the subject of the late unfortunate attack made by a detachment of Georgia militia under captain Wright, on the Chehaw village, which had previously been supposed to be friendly.

I have examined these communications with the candor their importance required. It is unquestionably your duty, as agent, to attend to the complaints of the red people and cause justice to be done to them as far as your powers will extend.

It will also readily be acknowledged by all, that my duty as governor of the state, requires that I should defend the cause of the whites, as far as that cause can be supported by the great principles of justice. As you have furnished me with the Indian account of this transaction, and assured me of the friendship towards the whites that existed among them prior to the attack— I feel it incumbent on me to explain to you, and through you to the nation over which you preside, the motives by which the officers were actuated, who conducted the enterprise; and the grounds upon which they will attempt to justify the proceeding, or extenuate the guilt that may, in the view of some men, be attached to them. You will readily acknowledge the decided and inveterate hostility of those Indians which belong to the villages under the immediate direction and control of the chiefs Hoponnee and Phelemmee; and that the orders which emanated from this department for their chastisement was both necessary and proper. You are also well apprised, that the order given confined them specially to that object; so far then as respects myself, I feel perfectly justified in the measures I adopted, and which deemed essentially necessary to prevent a repetition of the horrid murders and depredations committed by those Indians on our unprotected frontier. I will now undertake to offer, in behalf of the detachment, the best apology for their conduct that I may be able to furnish, and which I am authorized to state, can be supported by ample proof. When the detachment was on its way to, and had reached the neighborhood of Fort Early they were credibly informed by several persons of veracity, that the celebrated old chief Hoponnee, whose town had all joined the hostile party, had removed and was at that time living in the village upon which the attack was made and was considered as their principal leader, and that a great portion of them was alleged to be under his immediate direction, although part of them might be with M'Intosh.

They therefore considered themselves authorized to attack it as being one of Hoponnee's towns. The result I need not mention, as you have seen the statements made by captains Wright and Robinson, which I am authorized by very respectable testimony to assure you, was substantially true, except as to the number reported to have been killed, which was fortunately incorrect. Now sir, if I have been misinformed, and given a wrong construction to this affair, I should like very much to have more correct information, but if it should be founded in fact, what more can you or the Indians require, than for me to assure you, that I regret the circumstance, and consider it as one of the misfortunes attendant on war, where the innocent frequently suffer in common with the guilty. This unfortunate affair has been shamefully misrepresented, by many of our citizens, whose delicate feelings seem to have forgotten the many wanton outrages that have been committed on our frontier by the Indians, and would even cover the whole state with disgrace, merely because this small detachment have in this instance, mistaken their orders, and carried their resentment to an improper extent.

The experience of all ages have shown, that it is much easier for us to complain of the conduct of others (and especially those in responsible stations) than to correct our own. I have ascertained that the property left by the Indians who were run off from or near Dr. Bird's store, on the Ocmulgee, some time past, is now in the possession of Mr. Richard Smith in the lower end of Twiggs county and will be delivered at any time when proper application shall be made.

You will please assure the red people under your care, that I feel a disposition to maintain peace and friendship with them on liberal terms.

I have the honor to be, respectfully, your obedient servant,

WM. RABUN.

———

Extract of a letter from Major General Jackson to General Glascock

"*Camp, on the line of March, 16 miles in advance of Fort Gadsden, May 7.*
"I cannot adequately express my

feelings on the outrageous and inhuman attack of Captain Wright and party, on the superannuated men and women of the friendly Chehaw village, which you recite. It will be a stigma on the American nation, unless the general government use their endeavors to bring the perpetrators to justice. I have ordered Wright to be arrested; and he shall be tried by a military court. I have written to the governor of Georgia on the subject, expressing my astonishment at his unwarranted interference with my duties.

"I congratulate you on the safe march of your brigade to Fort early, with a hope that the brave Georgians under your command who have encountered the dangers, fatigues, and privations of a long march, in an unfriendly country, may be speedily restored in health, to their families and homes.

"I am now on my march to Pensacola, which place I shall probably have to occupy with an American garrison."

———

Milledgeville, Georgia, May 26. — We have conversed with several officers lately from the army — they state that the two British emissaries captured at St. Marks and Suwannee, Arbuthnot and Ambruster, both accomplices of the notorious Woodbine, have been tried by court martial, of which general Gaines was president, and being found guilty of exciting the late Indian war, were executed on the 27th of last month — the former was hanged and the latter shot — *Journal.*

Arbuthnot had been a captain in the British service, was about 40 years of age, of genteel appearance, and met his fate like a soldier — When the executioner was fixing the rope around his neck, he desired not to be handled so roughly— observed he was a gentleman, and some say, spoke of his death being avenged — his property, he requested should be given to his son. Ambruster was young, not exceeding 25 — at first, he was insolent and contumacious, but as death began to look him in the face, he lost his composure, and died more like a woman than a man.

The evidence against both, we understand, was clear and strong. Letters, advising the enemy of the movements of our army, and how to act, were intercepted. Documents were also found, proving beyond doubt, that a criminal correspondence had been some time kept up, by them and the governor of New Providence, with the Indians and renegade negroes in Florida: But how indignant must every one be, when informed, that the *prophet Francis*, who was hanged a little before, had in his pocket a new commission of brigadier general from the British government, supposed to have been given to him during his late visit to England, whence he had not long returned.(*see note below) As a scrutiny, we are assured, will develope the blackest perfidy towards this country. Great Britain will likely be disposed to let the matter rest where it is.

General Jackson, with a regiment of regulars and the Tennessee volunteers, crossed the Appalachicola bay on the 7th inst. and expected to reach Pensacola, distant 200 miles, last Thursday. He will probably take possession of the place, and leave in it a sufficient garrison for its defence, and for the protection of our adjacent frontier settlements.

A detachment of 350 men has been left at Fort Gadsden, 200 at St. Marks, and about 250 at Fort Scott, under the command of general Gaines, to overawe and effectually subdue the Indians in that quarter; and a naval force has been ordered to cruise on the south side of Florida Point for the purpose of cutting off the supplies, which such of them as have fled to lake Mayance, might otherwise receive from the contiguous British islands.

We are informed that general Jackson speaks of retiring from the military service of the country very soon. The rapid decay of his constitution, occasioned by great bodily fatigue and exposure, is stated to be the cause. The whole army, it is said, have suffered inconceivably — an officer declares he has never seen such emaciated troops. The prosecution of the Seminole war has probably been attended with as many privations to the soldier, and as much expense to the government, as any contest ever was, of no longer duration or greater magnitude.

[Note: *This "prophet Francis" is doubtless the person referred to in the following paragraph from a British paper of December last— see Weekly Register, vol. xii, page 46 —

"The double sound of a trumpet announced the approach of the *PATRIOT Francis*, who fought so gloriously in our cause in America; he was dressed in a most splendid suit of red and gold, and by his side he wore a tomahawk, mounted in gold, *presented to him by the prince regent*".— The wretch it seems, was also the prime mover of the unprovoked and infernal massacre of the garrison, with the women, &c. of fort Mims, *before* the Creek war — a massacre of untold horrors — too horrible, as related to the editor by an eye witness of the scene of action a day or two after the event, to put upon paper! It was he also, who slaughtered Lieutenant Scot and his party, on the Flint River, not long ago. He had been *outlawed* by his *countrymen* for his perfectly *savage* propensities — was a murderer by trade, a favorite at court, and the ally of England!—— [Ed. Reg.]

———

Mobile, May 12. A number of gentlemen of respectability of the army have arrived here from Appalachicola. General Jackson has ended the Seminole war; all their provisions are destroyed as well as cattle driven off. They have fled towards Tamper bay, and must inevitably starve unless relieved by other exertions than their own.

———

Nashville, Tennessee, May 12.

The following is an extract of a letter from Major General Andrew Jackson, to a gentleman In this place, dated

Camp before St. Marks,
9th April, 1818.

On the 26th ult. I marched from fort Gadsden into the heart of the enemy's country. On the first instant I was reinforced by some friendly Indians and 2 battalions of Tennessee volunteers under col. Elliott; arriving within a mile and half of Muckasuky town, I discovered the Indians posted on an advantageous point of land with a large pond in their front, and secured in their rear by woods and swamps. The spy companies, supported by the horse, were ordered forward, and a short and spirited conflict ensued; the Indians soon gave way, and were pursued through their towns. The three succeeding days were employed in scouring their country, burning their towns and in securing their corn and cattle, of which we found a great abundance; upwards of three hundred houses have been consumed. I have to regret the loss of one man killed (Tucker) and four wounded, (from Tennessee;) of the Indians thirty were killed and four were made prisoners: sixty men women and children of the war party have surrendered — The *great war chief* of the Muckasukees is among the slain.

In the Muckasuky town we discovered evidences of hostility for many years; upwards of three hundred scalps were found; about fifty were suspended on a painted war pole on the *square*, fresh, and of every description, from the tender infant to the aged mother.

Apprehending that the enemy might attempt to occupy St. Marks, learning that they were kindly received there, and discovering that it would prove an advantageous depot for my supplies, I marched for, and reached it on the evening of the 6th. On my arrival, several communications passed between myself and the commandant; when to bring matters to a close, delay being evidently designed, I ordered the light company to advance, and take possession, and Captain M'Ever to assume a position in the rear; while general Gaines was instructed to hold his brigade in readiness to act if resistance were attempted: none however was made and the light companies entered, possessed themselves of the fort, pulled down the flag. Captain M'Ever having hoisted English colors on board his boats, Francis, *the prophet*, Hoemolchemucho and two others were decoyed on board, believing him to be the promised and daily expected aid from New Providence, under the command of Woodbine. These have been hung to-day. To-morrow I march for Suwannee, where I hope to put an end to the war. I have not time to do more than give you a faint view of things as they are. I have been forced to encounter many privations; but they have been surmounted.

_____

St. Stephens, (A.T.) May 9.

Governor Bibb returned to this place on Sunday last. An expedition against the hostile Indians having been arranged, a detachment of volunteers marched from Claiborne the day previously. It is understood that the Spanish territory will no longer furnish an asylum to the enemy.

Yesterday the governor received intelligence from major Youngs, who commanded at fort Crawford, that he having organized a force consisting of regulars, militia from camp Montgomery, and Choctaws, proceeded down the Escambia in boats, attacked the hostile Indians on Pensacola bay, within one mile of the town of Pensacola, on the 25th ult. killed nine, wounded twelve or thirteen, and took eight prisoners, with the loss on his part of one man only. Lieutenant Allen commanded the militia. The expedition was so cautiously and properly conducted, that the enemy were not apprised of danger until the attack was made. The day after the governor of Pensacola issued a proclamation, forbidding the inhabitants to sell or give any supplies to the Indians, and informed the chiefs that they should not be protected. He at the same time advised them to surrender and sue for peace.

Major Youngs speaks in high terms of the good conduct of the detachment under his command. It is highly probable, therefore, that the period is not distant when our follow-citizens the frontier may safely repose in their habitations.

Governor Bibb has just received despatches from major Youngs. The hostile Indians have sued for peace through the governor of Pensacola. They are to report themselves in a few days at Durant's Bluff, from whence they will be conducted to fort Crawford.

So much for the conviction which the late successful expedition has wrought upon the savages, that they shall not murder our inhabitants, and then find shelter in the Spanish territories.

The war on our frontier has probably now terminated, and it remains only, by proper arrangements, to secure our citizens from depredations for the future.

We learn that governor Bibb will proceed to Fort Crawford next week.

It is understood that the governor

of Pensacola manifested, in the affair, a disposition to regard the obligations of the treaty of 1795.

Volume 14, June 20, 1818, pages 292-293

Indian War.

Private letters are said to be received saying that on 21ˢᵗ of May, General Jackson took possession of Pensacola; having made certain requisitions which had not been complied with, he carried the fortress by storm.

———

The Chehaw Village.
From Georgia papers.

Extract from the talk of general William M'Intosh, commanding the Creek warriors, on his arrival at Cowets from the late campaign against the hostiles, to major gen. Andrew Jackson dated

Fort Mitchell,
May 5, 1818.

"My friend — When I returned to my town, I heard with regret that my uncle [Howard] and family had been murdered, and that their town was destroyed. If an Indian kills a white man, I will have him punished — if a white man kills an Indian, he ought to be punished. I wish you to find out who has done this murder, and let me know what those Indians have done, that made the white men kill our people."

———

General Jackson's Reply

Headquarters,
division of the south,
May 7th, 1818.

Sir — You will send or deliver personally, as you may deem most advisable, the enclosed talk to Kinnard, with instructions to explain the substance to the Chehaw warriors.* You will proceed hence to Hartford in Georgia, and use your endeavours to arrest and deliver over in irons to the military authority at Fort Hawkins, captain Wright of the Georgia militia, who has been guilty of the outrage against the women and superannuated men of the Chehaw

village. Should Wright have left Hartford you will call upon the governor of Georgia to aid you in his arrest.

To enable you to execute the above order, you are authorized to take in company with you the Tennesseans that went from here lately to Fort Scott, and await, if you think it necessary, the arrival of the Georgians now on march under major Porter. You will direct the officer commanding Fort Hawkins to keep captain Wright in close confinement until the will of the president be known.

The accompanying letters for the secretary of war, and governor of Georgia, you will take charge of until you reach a post office.

ANDREW JACKSON,
major gen'l com'g.
Major John M. Davis,
asst. general.

[*Note: The substance of this talk was, that the Chehaws should not attempt to take any satisfaction themselves, for the outrage committed on them; that their father, the president of the United States, would see them justified, to whom he has reported the circumstance.]

———

Dublin, Georgia.
24th May, 1818.

Sir — I am directed by maj. gen. Andrew Jackson, commanding the division of the south, to arrest you, and conduct you to Fort Hawkins, where you are to remain until the pleasure of the president of the U. S. is known in your case. You will therefore, consider yourself in arrest, and proceed accordingly.

By order — I am
respectfully yours, &c.
JOHN M. DAVIS,
Asst. Ins. gen. U. S. army.
Capt. Obed Wright,
Georgia militia.

———

Milledgeville, June 2.
Major Davis, of the U. S. Army, in compliance with orders from General Jackson, arrested Capt. Obed Wright in

Dublin, a few days ago, for the purpose of carrying him to Fort Hawkins, and securing him until instructions could be received from the president. Whilst in this place, on Thursday last, the prisoner was released from custody by a writ of habeas corpus, before a court called to determine the case. The court after suitable investigation, decided that the orders of gen. Jackson were informal, as they contained no specific charge against the prisoner, who was accordingly released from custody.

We understand Captain Wright has been arrested by order of Gov. Rabun, and is now on parole in this place, waiting the organization of a court martial.

[Note: It appears that gen. Jackson had ordered Captain Wright to be put in irons. It is contended that Captain Wright was not acting under the authority of the United States, but of that of Georgia.

The Chehaw Indians, we are informed, estimate the property lost in the destruction of their town, at eight thousand dollars. The entire Creek nation will meet at Fort Mitchell on the 7th of this month, to take the affair into consideration. An intemperate letter, we learn has been received by the governor from general Jackson, to which a spirited answer has been returned — and a formal demand of Captain Wright's person has been also made, with which we presume the governor will not comply, if at all, till he hears from the president, to whom he has written on the subject.]

Volume 14, June 20, 1818, page 295

Chronicle—Generals Jackson & Scott.

We sincerely regret to see in the public newspapers a notice of a dispute between those distinguished characters, which cannot have any other effect than to fan the flame of discord, and render a just accommodation more difficult. The cause of difference is said to have been this—General Scott to *one* person only, without any intention that it should ever reach general Jackson and without design to injure his reputation, expressed an opinion unfavorable to the well known general order of the latter. The fact it seems was malignantly communicated, which led to an impetuous correspondence between them. A hope however, is entertained that the matter may be amicably adjusted.

Volume 14, June 27, 1818, page 298

Indian War.

We have not much positive intelligence from gen. Jackson's army, or respecting the state of the war with the Seminoles, since our last. It is strongly intimated that gen. Jackson has carried Pensacola, *by storm*, with the loss of a number of men – that despatches have arrived to the Spanish minister, and that several conferences had taken place between the Spanish and British diplomatique corps in consequence, &c. The *National Intelligencer* observes — "We have little doubt of the correctness of the fact of general Jackson having entered Pensacola; and it is equally probable, if he entered at all, it was by assault, as it is not to be supposed the Spanish authorities would have given up so important a post without at least a show of resistance.

The motives of this step general Jackson's despatches will disclose. It is presumed such a measure was not in the contemplation of the government, although it may necessarily have resulted from the discretion vested in the commanding officer to take such lawful steps as the safety of the frontier might appear to require. If the Indians in arms against us led the way to Pensacola, there can be no doubt of gen. Jackson's being justified in following and dislodging them."

Note: We shall soon know the merits of the case — and when we do, it will be soon enough to condemn the "man of Orleans," — if he deserves it.

New Orleans, May 12. — Letters have been received in town to the 1st inst. from Fort Montgomery, which state that a small party of United States troops under the command of Lieutenant Eddy, whilst ascending the Escambia with provisions, were attacked with a sudden and unexpected volley of small arms from a body of Indians, by which one of the soldiers was killed and two severely wounded. As soon as intelligence of this event reached Fort Montgomery, major W. Youngs put himself at the head of a detachment amounting to 74 men, comprehending regulars, militia and Indians, and set off in quest of the enemy. In the vicinity of bayou Texar, he encountered and routed them, with the loss on his side of only one soldier killed. That of the enemy in killed wounded and prisoners, was 30 — the remainder to the number of 87, sued for peace, and they were sent to the interior of the Creek nation. Bayou Texar is not laid down on any map that we are acquainted with. We believe it flows from the east into the bay of Escambia.

Volume 14, July 4, 1818, page 327

Chronicle—Indian war.

We are without official intelligence from general Jackson; it is thought extraordinary that no letter from him has been published for the information of the people, deeply interested in his transactions: but we have reports in so many ways of his having taken Pensacola, that we cannot doubt the fact. It appears that he possessed himself of the town without firing a gun, but that the governor with about three hundred men, retired to the Barancas, (a strong fort situated at the entrance of the harbor) with a determination to defend himself as long as possible: it was, however, surrendered, after, as it is said, a bombardment of three days, by which a few lives were lost. The Spanish officers and the garrison, it is added, were about to embark for Havana. General Jackson, having accomplished this, left Pensacola for his residence in Tennessee. Some accounts intimate that a considerable number of Indians were at Pensacola.

There is a report which appears worthy of confidence, that the governor of Pensacola proposed to surrender the fort, &c upon certain conditions; one of which conditions was, that a certain very noted Seminole chief, who was in the fort, should be transported to the Havana, at the expense of the American government. If this is true, it affords ample proof of the co-operation of the Spaniards with the Indians, and made it the duty of gen. Jackson to act as he has done. But we have not had any suspicion that he went beyond his instructions; though we have been left to guess at what he was about. We may expect details in a week or two.

—•))) ϴ ⓜ ϴ (((•—

American Military in Control of Pensacola

Volume 14, July 11, 1818, pages 334-338

Indian War.

St. Stephen's, June 6. By the politeness of Dr. Bronaugh, one of general Jackson's staff, who reached this place last evening, we are enabled to lay before our readers the following general order. The laws of the United States are in full force at Pensacola – a custom house established, and Captain Gadsden appointed collector.

————

Head quarters, division of the south, Adjutant general's office, Barancas, May 29, 1818.

Fellow soldiers — You were called into the field to punish savages and negroes, who had, in a sanguinary manner, used the tomahawk and scalping knife, upon our helpless citizens on the frontier. You have pursued them to Mikasuky, St. Marks, Suwanney, and lately to this place, through an unexplored wilderness, encountering immense difficulties and privations, which you met with the spirit of American soldiers, without a murmur. Your general anticipated a close of the campaign, on his return to fort Gadsden; and hailed the hour with feelings of gratitude to Heaven, at the prospect of relieving you from your labors, by placing you in quarters and returning you to your homes. But how great was the disappointment, when he heard of the recent murders committed on the Alabama, by a party of the enemy from Pensacola, where they were furnished with provisions and ammunition by a friendly power. Under this state of things, you were marched here, encountering difficulties which you alone can properly appreciate. Meeting on the way the protest of the governor of West Florida, threatening to employ force if we did not immediately evacuate the country; this new and unexpected enemy was soon taught to feel the impotence of his threats. You entered Pensacola without opposition, and the strong fortress of the Barancas could hold out but one day against your determined courage. Your general cannot help admiring the spirit and military zeal manifested, when it was signified that a resort to storming would be necessary, and would do injustice to his own feelings, did he not particularly notice the judgment displayed by his aid-de-camp, captain Gadsden, of engineers, in the selection of the positions for the batteries; and the gallantry of his second aid, captain Call; and captain Young of the topographical engineers, in aiding him to erect the works under the fire of heavy batteries, within 400 yards; as well as the skill and gallantry of Captain Peters, lieutenants Minton and Spencer, in the direction and management of the 9-pounder; and that of lieutenants Sands and Scallan, charged with the management of the howitzer.

Captain M'Keever, of the navy, merits, (as he has on several occasions) my warmest thanks for his zealous co-operation and activity in landing two of his guns, (should an additional battering train have been necessary) and gallantly offering to lay his vessel before the water battery, in the event of storming the upper works; his officers and crew deserve his confidence.

The general assigns to colonel King the command of Pensacola and its dependencies, and that part of the 7th department lying west of the Appalachicola and Chattuhoochie rivers, until otherwise ordered by general Gaines. The colonel will take measures to have the volunteers now at Pensacola relieved, preparatory to their return march. The Tennessee volunteers will be rationed for five days, and will forthwith move for fort Montgomery, where they will receive further orders.

The general in taking leave of colonel King and his command, tenders to the officers and soldiers an affectionate farewell.

By order,

ROBERT BUTLER, adj. gen.

———

Head-quarters, division of the south.
Adjutant general's office,
29 miles west of Pensacola,

May 31, 1818.

Captain M'Girt, of the territory of Alabama, is authorised and instructed to raise a company of volunteer mounted men for the period of six months unless sooner discharged, to consist of two subalterns and sixty privates, to be under his command as captain. As soon as captain M'Girt raises thirty men, he will proceed directly to Perdido, and scour the country between it and Mobile and Pensacola, putting to death every hostile warrior that may be found, preserving the women and children, and delivering them to the commanding officer at Pensacola. The subalterns will be left to raise the balance of the company, and will immediately join him at Pensacola, where the officer commanding will be instructed to regularly muster them into service.

Captain Boyle, of the said territory, is in like manner instructed and authorised to raise a company, and will proceed with captain M'Girt on raising thirty men, to aid in executing the wishes of the major general, leaving his subalterns to raise the balance of his company, who will be instructed to join him at Pensacola, and be mustered into service.

These companies on reaching Pensacola will be furnished with provisions by the commanding officer, and will then proceed to scour the country between Escambia and Appalachicola rivers, destroying any hostiles as above directed, and on their application at forts Gadsden or Scott, provisions will be issued to them by the respective commanding officers. By order,

ROBERT BUTLER,
adjutant general.

———

Head-quarters, division of the south,
Pensacola, May 29th, 1818.

Major general Andrew Jackson has found it necessary to take possession of Pensacola. He has not been prompted to this measure from a wish to extend the territorial limits of the U. States, or from any unfriendly feeling on the part of the American republic to the Spanish government. — The Seminole Indians, inhabiting the territories of Spain, have for more than two years past, visited our frontier settlers with all the horrors of savage massacre — helpless women have been butchered, and the cradle stained with the blood of innocence. These atrocities, it was expected, would have early attracted the attention of the Spanish government, and faithful to existing treaties, speedy measures adopted to their suppression.

The obligation to restrain them was acknowledged; but weakness was alleged with a concession, that so far from being able to control, the Spanish authorities were often compelled from policy or necessity to issue munitions of war to these savages, thus enabling, if not exciting them, to raise the tomahawk against us. The immutable laws of self-defence, therefore, compelled the American government to take possession of such parts of the Floridas in which the Spanish authority could not be maintained. Pensacola was found in this situation, and will be held until Spain can furnish military strength sufficient to enforce existing treaties.

Spanish subjects will be respected; Spanish laws will govern in all cases affecting property and person; a free toleration to all religions guaranteed, and trade alike free to all nations.

Colonel King will assume the command of Pensacola, as military and civil governor.

The Spanish laws, so far as they affect personal rights and property, will be enforced. Colonel King will take possession of the archives of the province, and appoint some confidential individual to preserve them. It is all important that the records of titles and property should be carefully secured. He will cause an inquiry to be made into all the landed property belonging to the king of Spain, and have possession taken of it. The claims of property within the range of gun shot of fort Carlos de Barancas will be scrupulously examined into, and should they prove valid, a rent allowed, but possession in no wise given. This property is necessary to the United States, and under its laws may be held, an equivalent being paid.

The revenue laws of the United States will be established, and Capt. Gadsden is appointed to act as collector, with full powers; nominate such sub-officers as, in his opinion, will be

necessary to the faithful discharge of the trust imposed on him. He will apply to the governor of Pensacola for military aid in all cases where it may be necessary to correct attempts at illicit trade.

(Signed) ANDREW JACKSON,
Major general commanding.

———

The Spanish governor at Pensacola, with his suite and the late garrison of the place arrived at Havanna on the 28th ult. in two cartels. They were received as American vessels, but the government there would not acknowledge, the *truce.* Their arrival caused some bustle and much anxiety; but it was believed that no hostile measures would be adopted.

———

Capitulation of Pensacola.

Proposals which the civil and military commandant of the province of West Florida makes to his excellency Andrew Jackson, general in chief of the American army before the fort St. Charles, Barancas.

1st. The fort of Barancas will be delivered to the troops of the United States under the following conditions.

Approved – with the exceptions made opposite each article, and possession given at one o'clock P.M. this day.

2nd. The garrison of the fort of Barancas will march out to be transported to Havanna, on the day and hour which shall be agreed upon, with all the honors of war, drums beating, and with their arms and baggage. Those in the employ of the royal finance and of the department connected therewith, shall also be transported to the same destination.

Answer — A roster shall be furnished of all the military and civil officers of the garrison of fort Barancas — the troops lo march out as expressed in the article, their arms to be stacked at the foot of the glacis, and left in possession of the American army until the day of embarcation, when they will be returned.

3d. The commandant of the province and the officers of his staff, of the artillery, engineers, the officers and troops, shall carry with them their arms and personal effects, and shall also have the liberty of disposing of their property of every kind, with perfect security to the purchasers.

Answer — All titles of property legally derived from the crown of Spain will be respected.

4th. The garrison shall be embarked for account of the United States. Every person of the military class or of the royal finance, shall receive, during the passage, such rations as are allowed to every grade by the regulations of Spain.

Approved — so far as relates lo the transportation of the garrison and Spanish rations allowed; provided, they do not exceed the American ration, in which case the American ration only will be allowed.

5th. A competent number of vessels shall be furnished for embarking the personal effects, papers and other property belonging to the commandant, officers and others in the royal employ, and particularly the papers of the secretary's office of the government existing in Pensacola, those of the department of the royal finance, and of the civil and military employs. These papers shall not be subjected to any inspection or recognizance under the pledge of their containing nothing foreign to the functions of the said persons.

Approved — an estimate of the necessary transportation to be furnished agreeably to established usage.

6th. The sick, wounded, and all those who are now or may fall sick, previous to the embarkation of the troops for the Havanna, shall be maintained by the government of the United States until cured, and shall have the same privileges us the rest of the garrison: those who are in a situation shall be embarked at the same time with it, and shall be under the care of and attended by the surgeon and other individuals of the Spanish military hospital.

Approved.

7th. The garrison of Pensacola and the prisoners as also those in the employ of the royal finance, shall enjoy the same privileges as the garrison or Barancas, and shall likewise be transported to Havana, uniting the former to the latter, and all shall be lodged in the quarters they previously occupied in Pensacola, until the moment of embarkation for the port of Havanna.

Approved— an estimate of the necessary transportation to be furnished and included in the estimate for the garrison of fort Barancas.

8th. During their permanence the United States will furnish to the king's store keeper, under the requisite documents from the royal officers, such articles as they may stand in need of, or are not in the king's stores, to complete the rations of the troops, dependants, those in the king's employ, and their families, the reimbursement thereof remaining subject to the decision of the governments of Spain and the United States.

Answer — An inventory of the provisions in possession of the Spanish commissary, to be forthwith furnished. The rations allowed subject to the limitations of the 4th article.

9th. The provisions actually existing in the king's store of Pensacola and Barancas, shall be transported to the former in order that they may serve for the said supply of rations.

Approved.

10th. A duplicate inventory shall be formed by the store keeper, and such officer of artillery, as the commandant of this corps may name, and such other as may be appointed by the general of the troops of the United States, of the artillery, powder, military stores and other effects belonging to this department in Pensacola and Barancas.

Approved — Major Peters of the artillery, is appointed on the part of the American government.

11th. Persons and property shall be respected, concessions and sales of land made by the competent authorities shall be valid and guaranteed by the American government, at whatever time they may have been made until the date hereof.

Answer — all titles legally derived from the crown of Spain, prior to this date, guaranteed and respected.

12th. The commandant of engineers shall name an officer, who with another whom the general of the American army may appoint, shall form a duplicate inventory of the number and state of the royal edifices, in the same manner as is stated for the department of artillery.

Approved — Lieut Sands, of the artillery, appointed on the part of the American government.

13th. The military officers and those in the service of all and the several departments, may embark with them their wives, children and slaves, in which number are to be included the families of these classes who may be absent. Those who have properly to dispose of, or affairs to settle, may remain the time necessary for this purpose. The American authority shall afford them every protection during their permanence, and they shall enjoy the same privilege with the rest of the garrison in their embarcation for Havanna on account of the United States.

Inadmissable— so far as it regards transportation being allowed to the families of those officers not present, and servants not attending upon the officers and the families. Those individuals disposed to remain in the Floridas, will be respected and protected, in all civil and personal rights, and if not embracing the transportation allowed at the present period, they must furnish their own at a future period.

14th. The store keeper general shall form an inventory of the small vessels and crafts and of the other effects under his charge in the same way as stated for the department of artillery.

Approved— Lieut. Parkhurst, Q. M. of artillery, appointed on behalf of the American government.

15th. The officers and troops of this

garrison, with their equipage, shall be transported to Pensacola, where they shall remain as already stated until embarked for Havanna.

Approved.

17th. The Alabama chief with his family now in this fort, and who has been reported to major Young, shall be included in this capitulation, and transported to Havanna.

Approved — His name to be entered in an article, and the Spanish government guaranteeing that he never returns to the Floridas.

18th. The catholic religion, its ministers, and the free exercise shall be maintained.

Answer — A free toleration to all religions granted.

19th. The capitulation is made under the confidence that the general of the American troops will comply with his offer of returning integrally this province in the state in which he received it, as stated in his official letter.

Approved — And the restoration made under the conditions expressed in general Jackson's communication to the governor of Pensacola on the 23d May, 1818.

20th. If any doubt should arise as to the meaning of any of the articles of this capitulation, they shall be construed in the manner most favorable to the Spanish garrison.

Answer — The above articles to be interpreted agreeably to their literal and expressed meaning.

21st. The present capitulation shall be signed and exchanged by the general of the American army, and the commandant of this province as soon as possible and at latest by 5 o'clock in the afternoon, each returning their respective original.

Approved.

Fort of St. Charles, Barancas, 28th May, 1818,

7 o'clock in the morning.

(Signed)   Joseph Masot,

(Signed)   Andrew Jackson,
Maj. Gen. Comd'g.

Additional articles which are to have the same force as the primary, and extended in compliance with what has been agreed upon.

1st. The name required of the Alabama chief is Opayhola. The commandant of this province engages in the name of his government, that the said chief shall never return to the Floridas.

Approved.

2nd. If any vessels of war of his catholic majesty destined for this port, should arrive with a supply of provisions or money, they shall be freely admitted, as well as Spanish merchant vessels.

Approved.

St. Charles, Barancas, 28th may, 1818, 5 o'clock P. M.

(Signed)   Joseph Masot,

(Signed)   Andrew Jackson,
Major Gen. Comd'g.

From the National Intelligencer, of Wednesday, last

Despatches were received at the war department yesterday from General Jackson. The bearer, Mr. Hambly, reached the city on Monday night, and would have been here, he informs us, some days earlier, but for detentions on the road arising from the irregularity of the stages on some parts of the line. General Jackson's letters have been forwarded to the president, and their contents of course are unknown to us; but we understand, generally, that they embrace a full account of his proceedings in the south, down to the expulsion of the Spaniards from Pensacola, and *that the facts they disclose form a most ample justification of his conduct in the Spanish territory.*

To the editor of the Mississippi State Gazette.

Sir— As the general impression is, that general Jackson has, on his own responsibility, tried, shot and hung the noted Arbuthnot, and his companion in villany, perhaps a list of the officers composing the general court martial which sentenced them to death, would be gratifying to your readers, particularly as it discovers great prudence in the commanding general by selecting a court so respectable both for rank and intelligence:

Major general Gaines, *President*

Members.

- Colonel King (Regular Army)
- Lieutenant Colonel Arbuckle (Regular Army)
- Major Twiggs (Regular Army)
- Captain Vashan (Regular Army)
- Captain Gadsden (Regular Army)
- Lieutenant Colonel Gibson (Volunteer)
- Lieutenant Colonel Dyer (Volunteer)
- Lieutenant Colonel Williams (Volunteer)
- Lieutenant Colonel Elliot (Volunteer)
- Captain Crittenden (Volunteer)

Lieutenant Vassell, Recorder.

There was a full court of thirteen members, but I have forgotten the names of the others. An officer just from the fort at St. Marks informs me that the papers found in the possession of those exciters of Indian barbarities was proof (positive) of their being the instigators of the Seminole war.

H. C.

From the *Milledgeville Reflector* — The editor is indebted to Isaac Bailey, esq. of Jefferson, Camden county, for the following intelligence, which he received from a gentleman at fort Albert. — "On the 14th inst. a company of white men, about twenty in number, coming from the Alochawa with a large drove of cattle, had a skirmish with a party of hostile Indians, in which one white man (Garret Vinzeant) and five Indians were killed. "

261

The *Nashville Clarion*, of June 16, says — A gentleman immediately from the army states, that general Jackson having obtained full proof that the Spanish authorities at Pensacola had been active in fomenting the Seminole war, had issued ammunition and rations to the hostile Indians, and had made that post a kind of rallying point for them, whilst vessels bearing the American flag, loaded with provisions for his suffering troops, were forbidden to pass up the Escambia, he determined to prevent the renewal of the scenes of carnage and savage barbarity heretofore witnessed on the frontier which were to be expected as soon as the army was disbanded by first removing the Spaniards from the country. With a part of the army he proceeded to effect this object; he was fired on by the garrison, and two of his men killed. He immediately invested the fort, which after a tremendous cannonade surrendered. The general obtained an immense number of field pieces, small arms, and ammunition. He garrisoned the fort, and sent the Spanish governor &c. to Cuba.

The arrival of the American troops at Pensacola was hailed with joy by the inhabitants. Real property rose in three days, three hundred per cent. The time consumed in repairing the works at Pensacola — arranging the government, &c. will delay the return of our fellow citizens to their homes a few days. General Jackson is with the volunteers and will be in Columbia about the 25th inst. where he means to discharge and pay them off. On the 3d inst he was at Fort Montgomery.

From the *Savannah Republican*. The Creek Indians have lately had a meeting, and determined to abide the decision of the general government, relative to the attack upon the Chehaws.

From the same. On the day previous to the attack on Pensacola the governor warned Jackson not to advance, accompanied with a threat that force would be employed against him, if he did not evacuate the province. The general sent word to the governor that he would answer him next morning, still continuing on his march to Pensacola, where he arrived at 9 o'clock next day and took possession of the town without

opposition. On the third day the army reached the vicinity of the Barancas, reconnoitered the country and selected a suitable place for a breast work about 400 yards from the fort, where shortly after night a party of men were set to work. About ten o'clock they were discovered and fired on by the enemy from the fort, which was returned from a howitzer posted in the rear of a hill above the breast work and continued at intervals during the night. At day-light next morning, the Spaniards commenced firing on the breast work with two twenty-four pounders, which did but little injury. At three, a flag was sent from the fort, when the firing ceased on both sides, and articles of capitulation entered into.

New Orleans, June 9. A vessel from Pensacola entered yesterday at the custom house in this city, with a clearance signed "James Gadsden, acting collector of the port of Pensacola."

By this vessel we learn that general Jackson has gone to Tennessee, and left Colonel King in command at Pensacola with 800 men. The Tennessee volunteers form the garrison of the Barancas; the regular troops are stationed in the town. — It is said that the fort of the Barancas, at the time of its surrender, contained provisions for six months; but the garrison revolted and refused to fight, which circumstance accounts for the feeble defence that was made.

Part of the Spanish troops who formed the garrison of the Barancas, have been sent to the Havana. The remainder were to follow them in a vessel which was expected from Mobile.

———

The governor of St. Augustine, apprehensive of being attacked, was preparing to defend himself as well as he could. We have no advice of any movement of the U. S. troops towards that place.

Two agents from the Spanish government are said to have arrived at Amelia Island on the 13th ult. for the purpose of taking possession of lands in Florida, some time since granted by said government to the duke of Alancon.

General Jackson's conduct at

Pensacola has been the same in principle as the rule that general Wayne would have followed in 1794, had the occasion required it, after the battle with the Indians near the British fort on the Miami-of-the-lakes. The British then (as on every other opportunity) had excited the Indians to war against us, and supplied them with arms and ammunition. The Spaniards at Pensacola did the same. The Indians, if defeated, calculated on flying to Fort Miami for refuge — but, Wayne, apprised of the *friendly* arrangement, sent word to the British commander, that if he suffered an Indian to enter the fort as an asylum — he would attack and carry it by storm and put every man of the garrison to death. The Briton felt convinced that Wayne would do what he promised; and the deluded savages found the gates *inhospitably* shut upon them in the time of their need, — contrary to the stipulations which were understood to have been made on the occasion!

Note: The British editors, at home and in Canada, are quite wroth at our proceedings in Florida, to secure us on one side, against murder, and on the other, against smuggling and dealing in human flesh. When we have room we shall amuse our readers with some very pretty extracts on the subject.

—•»»⊖ⓞ⊖«««•—

Enquiry into Jackson's Actions in Spanish Florida

Volume 14, July 25 1818, pages 369-371

Capture of Pensacola, &c.

The Democratic Press of Saturday last contains an able article entitled an "enquiry into the causes, conduct and consequences of the southern war." It is long, and has been already so extensively copied into other papers, that the following brief analysis may suffice for the Register.

1. The constitution expressly authorises the president to use the military force of the nation to repel invasion, or protect the people thereof and their property, without waiting for congress to declare war: the writer says —

"It is a fact, that, altho' the United States have never since their national existence, had the temple of Janus quite shut up, but, like all other rising empires, have been obliged to maintain their elevation as they go, by arms and warlike attitudes, yet the declaration of war against Great Britain in 1812, is the only declaration of war on the record of congress. There was no declaration of war against France in 1798: but acts of congress simply dissolving treaties and authorising reprisals. There was no declaration of war against Tripoli in 1802; nor against Algiers in 1815; but acts of congress providing merely for the protection of American commerce and seamen against the Tripolitans and the Algerines, authorising captures, and other precautionary measures of hostility. There certainly was no act of congress, in 1811, authorising the frigate President to make war on the Little Belt."

He then instances the several wars with the Indians during the administration of President Washington, and observes that no one denied his constitutional authority to employ the public force in offensive operations for the public protection." The Seminoles *had* invaded our territory and murdered and plundered our people and conflagrated their dwellings — and, he says, "to stop repulsion at a degree of latitude, and leave invasion there unmolested to coil up its folds and renew its ravages, is the pretended, and the bloody scruple of a perverted conscience, untrue to its country, incompatible with its constitution, its existence and its history.'"

Hence the war against the Seminoles is made out to be perfectly within the constitutional authority of the president, and the pursuit of them justified as a plain measure of safety.

2. He then considers the war as carried on in the Spanish territory, and briefly alludes to some of the intrigues of the Spaniards with the Indians, as early as 1790, when they interfered to prevent a negociation with the Creeks, through the secretary of East Florida, who came to New York with a large sum of money for the purpose —

"Late similar intrigues need not be recapitulated, they are well known. Spain and England have been the patrons of this new and most atrocious edition of the spirit of the Propaganda: The United States of America have lost not less than twenty thousand of their people, of all ages, sexes and conditions, most barbarously sacrificed to the grim deity of this infernal system; while their benevolent endeavours to reclaim and civilize the savage have been retarded and almost destroyed by his votaries. — Coeval with the existence of the American governments, these intrigues, as they are termed, have never ceased to be prosecuted; they have grown with our growth, till, such is the prodigious mutation of a short time, their reaction upon their authors, places in the grasp of this adolescent republic the lawful means of wresting from the Spanish monarch a province which received its name from a Spaniard whose demise seems to have been the forerunner of the downfall of his great country.

"The relative condition of the Indians and the European nations whose descendants inhabit North America, is somewhat ambiguous and complicated. In the negociations preceding the treaty of Paris in 1763, France endeavored to prevail on England to consider the Indian tribes of America as independent powers, and to treat respecting them accordingly, as sovereignties under the protection of France. But England refused and France abandoned the overture. At the late treaty of Ghent, the English commissioners renewed this proposal, insisting on their right and duty to negociate for the Indian nations as independent powers under their protection. It is unnecessary here to consider this curious point of political philosophy. Spain shall have either alternative of the syllogism, and yet the capture of St. Marks and Pensacola will be justified. All that is asked for is, that Spain shall not take both, or neither, as suits her predicament. If the Indians, inhabiting Florida, are independent of Spain, then Florida, inhabited by those Indians, is not a Spanish but an Indian territory: and of course Spain cannot complain of our arms repelling the Indian invaders beyond the common frontier, to the uttermost recesses of their territories. On the other hand, if the Indians are dependent on Spain, then they are qualified Spanish subjects, the Spaniards are identified in Florida with the Indians: and it has been demonstrated

that as between the Americans and their Indian invaders, lawful repulsion has no territorial bounds."

The case of gen. Wayne and the commander of the British fort on the Miami, in 1794, is then alluded to — Wayne destroyed the houses and corn fields above and below the fort, and burnt some within pistol shot of it; among them the store house and stores of the famous dealer in scalps, the British col. McKee. The British commander of the fort remonstrated; but Wayne disregarded him, and was justified by his government: —

"The English, it is true, were entrenched on ground *de jure* American territory, and only *defacto* commanded by the English. With this difference there is certainly much similarity in the circumstances of that event of the former war and events of the late one.

"This position, decisively occupied, as it is believed to be, may yet be corroborated. — Gen. Jackson has alleged to the world that the Spaniards first furnished the Indians with means of aggression, and afterwards gave them protection when repelled beyond our borders. A chieftain is the subject of one article of the capitulation of Pensacola. This imputation, thus averred, and vouched, will of course be taken as in proof; at least till disproved. It is moreover a notorious fact that Spain, tho' most potent in the faculty of supplying the Indians with implements of warfare, is altogether unable to coerce their tranquility. — If so, may not repulsion be lawfully carried into the arsenals and magazines of our enemies, whence they sally forth for our invasion? The just and unquestionable principle of self defence would stop far short of the attainment of its legitimate objects, unless permitted to go that indispensable length."

The writer proceeds and gives the following view of certain incidents which have so much excited the sympathy of some* — "Having thus cursorily, as was intended at the outset, examined this interesting subject as respects our own constitutional rights, the rights of the Indians, and those of the Spaniards, something remains to be said of the English episode to the grand epic. A narrative of what is understood to be an outline of the circumstances of the cases of Arbuthnot and Ambristie will serve to show, without illustration, that they deserved the unhappy fate inflicted upon them. When the American army arrived at St. Marks, Arbuthnot was there. After taking his measures for surprising the Seminoles, encamped at the Suwannee towns, about ninety miles distant, the indefatigable general led his eager troops by forced marches to the scene of action. But apprised of his approach the savages had escaped, with their immense convoys of horses, cattle and supplies, on which the American commander had reckoned for a refreshment, very much wanted for his exhausted men. By an intercepted letter of Arbuthnot's it appeared that he was the traitor from whom the Indians derived their intelligence of the general's design to surprize them. While the army laid at Suwannee towns, after this disappointment, about eleven o'clock at night four interlopers were challenged by a centinel, attempting to enter the camp; two negroes, an Indian and Ambristie. They fled, when accosted, but were pursued and overtaken. On the return of the army to St. Marks, a general court-martial was organized to try both these culprits, and condemned them to be executed. Certainly with perfect justice, if martial law is of any avail. Indeed the refined code of the modern law of nations will justify their deaths. "The city of Geneva, says Vattel, 1,2- chap. 4. sec. 68. (the whole of these two sections are worth referring to for the sake of the subject generally) after defeating the attempt of the famous Escalada in 1602, hung up the Savoyards whom they had made prisoners, as robbers who had attacked them without cause or declaration of war. Nobody offered to censure the proceeding, which would have been detested in a formal war." The same stern but salutary principles will justify the death of the wretched chief who was taken and hanged, it is believed, on board the vessel in which Ambristie had freighted his supplies for them.

[Note: *It is strange that the sympathies of the people of the United States are so often most excited when an Englishman is the object. Andre, justly punished in the revolutionary war, for voluntarily entering upon a palpably dishonest and ungentlemanly business, is celebrated as an unfortunate victim, and his name is made familiar to our children [almost] as an *innocent* man, by lugubrious tales and odes, one of which newly-made is just now taking its round through the newspapers; whilst that of a better man than ever he was,— young, amiable and beloved, high spirited and devoted to his country, who suffered under the same rigid law that condemned Andre to the scaffold, though his object was intelligence instead of *corruption*, and who was treated with as much harshness as there was of lenity shewn to the Briton, is not recollected by one in ten thousand. But it was this man's misfortune that he was an American! — I allude to the noble Captain Hale, whose case has been noticed several times in this work: [see vol. 11, pages 129 and 159; and vol. XI, 199.] And such is the extent of this lop-sided sympathy, that I shall not be surprized to hear *Arbuthnot* held forth as a "pattern of piety" and "patriotism," when Hart, of Kentucky, murdered at the river Raisin, is generally forgotten. Capt. Hart's mourning widow breathed her last a few days since at Philadelphia. Prostrated by the savage assassination of her gallant husband, this "lovely woman," as she is described to have been, gradually sunk to the grave, another victim of ruthless war. In Dec. last, by the advice of her friends, she sought an effect of climate at New-Orleans, and in June last arrived at New York, pursuing health. The hope of regaining it was abandoned — she was returning to Kentucky to die among her children and friends, when death arrested her journey.]

The following; is the conclusion of the essay —

"In 1791 a well appointed army was routed by Indians, and well nigh exterminated on the ground where now stands the capital of a state, containing five hundred thousand souls. In 1794, the inconsiderable victory of the 20th of August was hailed with raptures; and the defeat of 1792 was imputed to the absolute inability of government, with Washington at its head, to equip a sufficient force for the expedition. In 1813, the major-general commanding the southern department overran the Indian territories, marking the stages of his march by victory after victory. In 1815, this skilful and excellent officer, with means prepared and forwarded from the ruins of Washington, at the distance of 1500 miles, repelled a most formidable invasion from the southern mart of the empire. In 1818, the same commander has traversed the hitherto inaccessible fastnesses of Florida, chasing the frightful foe before him, with a celerity and under circumstances of greater difficulty than have immortalized a celebrated general of antiquity, whose modesty did not prevent his inscribing on his tablets, with not more truth or merit than gen. Jackson may say, *veni, vide, vici.*

Note: Another and opposite view of this subject, is taken by a writer in the *Richmond Enqiurer.* Speaking of the capture of Pensacola he says —

"This is a direct attack on Spain. It is an act of plain and palpable WAR. It must and will be viewed by Spain and the other powers of Europe as a proof that this republic is governed by a grasping and dominant spirit of ambition, which in its anxiety to enlarge our territory, overlooks and despises the claims, and the possessions of other nations. It will be viewed as an act of PERFIDY. It was only a few months since, that our secretary of state declared to the minister of Spain, that we were attached to peace, and that having for thirteen years borne with patience the insults and wrongs heaped on us by Spain, we would still bear the vexatious delays of that nation, until a sense of justice should return to her, rather than resort to war. The declaration was hardly proclaimed to the world, before our military commander makes war, by seizing on one of her provinces, and usurping its government. Does not this conduct look like Italian duplicity? Can high minded Americans reconcile it to themselves? Heretofore in our contests with other nations, it has been our boast that we had justice, and "thrice is he armed, who hath his quarrel just." But we cannot now make this boast. Our major general has placed us entirely in the wrong."

He then speaks of the right of declaring war being in congress alone —does not believe that the president has authorised the conduct of the general, saying —

"I must then believe, until the contrary be shown, that General Jackson has acted without orders. If so, in what situation are we placed? The peace and welfare of this country subject to the control of, and jeopardized by, a self-willed military commander!! The services, great as they were, of the hero of Orleans, are but a poor compensation for the loss of our liberty ! !"

And concludes as follows —

"What, under present circumstances, must be done, to wipe out this stain upon our national character? I see no other alternative than restitution and reparation. The re-delivery of the province to Spain, (unless by a prompt negotiation we can fairly retain it,) and the arrest and cashiering the officer who has done the wrong."

The editor of the Enquirer gives us to understand that his correspondent, whose name he is at liberty to mention, is worthy of "being heard;" and agrees with him that "Pensacola ought to be immediately restored to the Spanish authorities.

Note: The *Washington City Gazette* of last Saturday says —

"An impression has gone abroad, since the president's return on Tuesday last, and the subsequent deliberations of the cabinet on general Jackson's despatches, that Pensacola will continue for the present, to be held in the occupation of the United States troops; that the general's movements in Florida were considered as justifiable by the existing treaties as well as the critical circumstances which led him to attempt the extirpation of an inveterate enemy from our borders; and that affairs in this quarter will probably remain in status quo till the subject is laid before congress, if farther provocation, in the mean time, does not demand more energetic measures to secure frontier tranquillity."

———

In the absence of information, it is perhaps most prudent at least to refrain from a warm discussion of this subject, until due time is allowed to obtain such facts respecting it as will enable the people correctly to "view the whole ground." We do know that Pensacola has been taken possession of *vi et armis*; but *do not* know, fully or officially, the causes upon which the procedure rests.

Volume 14, August 1, 1818, page 377

Capture of Pensacola, &c.

We have copied from the *National Intelligencer* of Monday last, what must be considered as a semi-official exposition of the conduct and views of the executive respecting Pensacola, &c. It does not afford us all the light desired; but it will, probably, be the cause of bringing before the public the whole of the documents and facts connected with the late war against the Seminoles, including those which led to the capture of their depot, Pensacola.

The fact is, that the war, on the part of the Florida Indians has not yet wholly terminated; and Spain is unable, even if she is willing, to afford us the security which we have a right to demand.

Volume 14, August 1, 1818, pages 383-384

Capture of Pensacola, &c.
*From the National Intelligencer
of July 27*

The president of the United States has, we understand, decided, that Pensacola and the other Spanish posts, which have been taken by general Jackson, in the Floridas, shall be restored to the Spanish authority; but with a requisition, that the king of Spain shall, hereafter, keep such a force in those colonies, as shall enable him to execute with fidelity, the fifth article of the treaty between the United States and Spain. That article, so far as it affects this subject is in the following words—

"The two high contracting parties, shall, by all the means in their power, maintain peace and harmony among the several Indian nations who inhabit the country adjacent to the lines and rivers, which, by the preceding articles, form the boundaries of the two Floridas; and the better to obtain this effect, both parties oblige themselves, *expressly, to restrain, by force, all hostilities on the part of the Indian nation living within their boundary; so that Spain will not suffer her Indians to attack the citizens of the United States, nor the Indians inhabiting their territory*; nor will the United States permit those last mentioned Indians to commence hostilities against the subjects of his Catholic Majesty, or his Indians, in any manner whatever."

On the strict execution of this article, on the part of Spain, it is understood that the president rigorously insists; and that it was the failure to fulfill it, which produced the necessity of crossing the Spanish boundary, during the present war with the Seminole Indians.

These tribes occupy the lands on each side of the line between the United States and Florida; much the greater part of them living within the limits of the king of Spain. They are neither citizens of the United States, nor subjects of the king of Spain. They owe no allegiance to the laws of either power. They cannot, therefore, be tried for treason on account of their levying war against either nation, within whose limits they dwell. They are the owners of the soil which they occupy; hold at least a qualified sovereignty over it, and exercise, on all occasions, the right of making war and peace. To this purpose they are sovereign within the country which they possess; to this purpose the country is their country; and that country may and must, of necessity, become the legitimate seat of war, if the war cannot be otherwise terminated.

This consideration becomes the stronger, when it is remembered, that it was owing to the incompetency of Spain to fulfill the stipulation of her treaty with us, by restraining the hostilities of the Seminoles, by force, that the United States were compelled to take up arms in their own defence. Yet such was the delicacy of our government towards Spain, that the first order issued to the general commanding in that quarter, expressly forbade him to cross the Spanish line. This inhibition was repeated by a second order. But as it was apparent that driving the Indians beyond the limits of the United States, was doing nothing effectual to extinguish the war, since, in filling back within the limits of Florida they were still at home, with all the means of incursion and annoyance which they possessed at the commencement of hostilities, a third order was issued, which authorized the American general, if the Indians should present themselves in body, beyond the line, to cross it and attack them. Shortly after issuing this order, a massacre was committed by the Indians, which demonstrated that no alternatives were left for United States, but to leave our frontier exposed to the mercy of the savages, or to carry the war into Florida, and thus to do for Spain, what she confessed herself unable to do for her self, by terminating by force the hostilities of these savages. A fourth order was, therefore, issued, to this effect to the American General; but by the same order he was expressly commanded, if the Indians should take refuge under a Spanish fort, not to attack them in that situation, but to report the case to the department of war. Such has been the delicacy observed by the United States towards Spain; and no subsequent order, it is understood, has been issued to enlarge the authority of the American general.

In attacking the posts of St. Mark and Pensacola, with the fort of Barancas, General Jackson, it is understood, acted on facts, which were, for the first time, brought to his knowledge on the immediate theatre of war; facts which, in his estimation, implicated the Spanish authorities in that quarter, as the instigators and auxiliaries of the war; and he took these measures on his own responsibility, merely. That his operations proceeded from motives of the purest patriotism, and from his conviction, that, in seizing and holding these posts, he was justified from the necessity of the case, and was advancing the best interests of his country, the character of General Jackson forbids a doubt. Of the important facts alleged by him, satisfactory proof, it is understood, has been already furnished to the president, and proof of the other facts is confidently expected. It is difficult to admit the belief that acts, so totally regardless of the amicable relations between Spain and the United States, so directly repugnant to the stipulation of the treaty above quoted, and, in themselves so hostile and even cruel, will be avowed and adopted by the king of Spain. We trust that they were the mere unauthorized acts of his agents. But should they, contrary to all rational expectation, be so avowed and adopted by that sovereign, there can be little doubt that the means of annoying us from that quarter will ere long be taken from him, by the decision of the competent authority, to be restored no more.

In the mean time, as congress only, have the power, under our constitution, of declaring war, and had made no such declaration against Spain, it is understood that the president does not conceive himself authorized to retain the Spanish posts, inasmuch as such retention would be an act of war.

It is on this ground, we understand, that the resolution has been taken to restore the posts, and to demand from the king of Spain the punishment of those officers, whose improper conduct led to their seizure.

The president, no doubt, sees, in common with his countrymen, the great advantages which the United States would derive from the entire possession of the Floridas; but, confessedly great as these advantages would be, he is not willing to gain them, but by the sanction of an act of congress. — To have retained these posts, under present circumstances, would certainly have had the *éclat of* being a *strong measure*: but we hope never to see a president of the United States disposed to be stronger than the constitution of his country; for that is the paladian of interests far more sacred, and of infinitely higher import to the general cause of human liberty, than any acquisition of territory, however vast or advantageous.

Notwithstanding this unexpected collision in the Floridas, we trust that the relations of amity between the two nations will be preserved; nor can we abandon the hope, that their difference may yet be settled, on fair and honorable conditions. We may even indulge the hope, that the incidents which have grown out of the Seminole war, however adverse their tendency may have appeared to be, may contribute essentially to produce that happy result. Spain must see, and has practically confessed, her incompetency to maintain her authority in the Floridas, against the Seminoles and foreign adventurers; and we hope she will see that it may be much wiser for her to cede those provinces at once, than to attempt to hold them on the impossible condition of fulfilling her treaty with us; or, on the condition now brought home to her, by experience, of subjecting herself to perpetual collisions, and eventual losses, which she may now avoid with ease and honor to herself.

Volume 14, August 8, 1818, pages 398-400

General Jackson's Campaign, &c.
From the Franklin Gazette.

Extract from the journal of a gentleman travelling in the southern section of the United States. The Indians, inhabiting the country lying between Georgia and the Mississippi river, could bring into the field about 11,000 warriors,

The Choctaws — 4000

Creeks — 3300

Cherokees — 1400

Chickasaws — 1300

Seminoles — 1000

This force, if embodied and hostile, would be a serious enemy to the United States; fortunately, however, there exists among the different tribes, jealousies and enmities that will prevent such an association ever taking place, and enable the United States, in the event of hostility with either, to employ as active allies, any of the nations. The Creeks were formerly the most warlike, but the severe conflict in the year 1813, diminished their numbers and their spirit; none of them are, however, enemies to be despised; in personal courage they are seldom deficient, but like all regular troops, having no idea of military combinations, or that confidence and reliance upon each, taught by discipline to the formed soldier, and so essential to victory, they will always be defeated unless they are the assailants, or attacked on ground exceedingly advantageous to them.

Their capacity to endure great fatigue, watching, hunger; their personal activity, knowledge of the forest, added to their courage, render them in a close country an exceedingly dangerous foe.

The Seminoles, with whom we waged the last war, inhabit a tract of country, part of which is within the United States, but the larger portion lies beyond the line separating it from Florida, — They were originally a small party of banished outlaws driven from among the upper and. Lower Creeks; who, increasing in number, living in a country exceedingly difficult to penetrate, associated themselves with a band of desperate runaway negroes, and,

instigated by their natural ferocity, and the artifices of British traders, have always manifested a disposition inimical to the United States, have since the year 1813 been notorious for their depredations upon the whites.

In August last it was very well ascertained, that they were the authors of several murders committed upon the white inhabitants of the frontier. A patient endurance of suffering is always regarded by the Indians, as an indication of weakness, and is sure to produce a repetition of the insult or injury. General Gaines demanded that the murderers should be given up, it was answered with taunt and defiance — and let it be remembered, by those who accuse the country of pursuing a barbarous policy towards the people, and endeavour to involve them in wars, that when PEPITICOXY, the principal warrior and leader, was asked why he was thus hostile to the United States, he replied, by acknowledging, *that the government were always ready to do him justice, and to make peace with him, but that war was fine manly exercise in which he wished to practice his young men!!!*

The 7th regiment crossed the Flint River, dispersed the Indians, burnt Fowlstown and returned. — This act of war was premature; the troops we had in the field, so far from being able to subjugate the enemy, were inefficient to meet him in fair conflict. The Indians assembled, attacked a boat ascending the river, captured it, and put to death 40 persons, composing its crew; they advanced up the river, surrounded our troops in fort Scott, and cut off their communication. General Gaines called upon the state of Georgia for 1500 militia, these men unfortunately were detailed but for two months; and before they could approach towards the enemy, that, period expired, and they returned to their homes.

General Gaines made a second call upon Georgia, for 2000 men for six months; they assembled at Hartford; General Jackson was now authorized to accept the services of 2000 Tennessee volunteers, to call out the friendly Indians, and to take the field himself. With his accustomed activity, he rapidly organized these men for service, and giving them orders to concentrate at fort Scott, he proceeded to Hartford, and placing himself at the head of the Georgia militia, moved them towards the same point. General Jackson had in vain endeavoured to procure provisions for his force; and a correct idea may be formed of the intrepid cast of his character, from the circumstance of his starting, with 2000 men on a march of 10 days, through a wilderness, when his only means of subsistence was a daily pint of corn for each man, and when he well knew, that on his arrival at fort Scott he could obtain but a very scanty supply. At fort Scott general Jackson found the regular troops and friendly Indians. The movement of the Tennessee volunteers had not been marked with the same boldness as that of the other troops; apprehensive of a want of provisions, they halted on the route, and had not yet joined. General Jackson advanced into the Indian country, destroyed their villages, and entering Florida took possession of St. Marks. The Indians fled before him, and the Spaniards dared not oppose his progress.

The state of Georgia affords but few of the necessaries for the subsistence of an army, and the face of the country in which General Jackson operated, abounded with invincible impediments to transportation in wheel carriages; great, therefore, were the sufferings of the troops – subsisting upon a pint of corn – marching through swamps and morasses, wading creeks, and sleeping on the wet ground, without shelter – were privations endured from motives of the purest patriotism, and in which the general participated equally with the meanest soldier in his army.

General Jackson was now about to move his troops from Florida, when he discovered that the governor of Pensacola, instead of exerting himself to fulfill the treaty existing between the United States and his king, by which he was bound to protect our citizens from savages within his dominions, had basely violated the Spanish faith, and protected, encouraged and furnished with the means of war, a worthless band, at the same time, laying waste to the frontier of the Alabama territory, and waging a war of destruction against the most lovely and most innocent part of our population. General Jackson considered that this breach of treaty authorized him to take possession of Pensacola, knowing well

that it was the only movement that could afford the effectual protection he was bound to give to every individual within his military command; and although politicians may argue in their closets that general Jackson exceeded his authority, and treated Spain with less respect than she was entitled to, yet the course of conduct he pursued will be justified by every high minded man, having at heart the true honor and glory of his country.— What — was General Jackson coolly to remonstrate, and politely correspond with the despicable representative of an imbecile tyrant, with a pen dipped in the blood of his fellow-citizens; or was he calmly to look on and witness the butchery of his countrymen, while he waited two months to hear from Washington, whether the violators of a treaty, and the protectors of murderers, were or were not to be chastised? The American general was not deterred from protecting the territory of the United States, and punishing those who encouraged the murder of his countrymen, by any flimsy, wire-drawn, sophistical arguments.

The opposition of the Spanish troops was illy calculated to occasion a display of the full devotion of the American army. The governor retired at their approach, and shutting himself up in the Barancas, declared his determination not to surrender. The Barancas is a fortress, situated on the southern cape of the bay of Pensacola; it consists of a heavy water battery on the beach, protected by, and communicating with a regular work on the bluff. Altho' this work cost the king of Spain an immense sum of money, yet the lower battery is entirely inadequate to guard the water communication into the bay, and the upper work cannot sustain an attack from the meanest train of artillery.

The parapet consists of a sand mound, supported by pine pickets and unprotected by glacis; conflagrate these pickets, the sand must fall into the ditch, and there is no impediment to a platoon marching to the centre of the place.

General Jackson cannonaded the fort — the garrison discovering that scaling ladders, and other preparations were making for the assault, hoisted the white flag and surrendered. General Jackson, with extraordinary forbearance, permitted the Indian chief who had sheltered himself in the fort, to accompany the garrison to Havanna.

General Jackson is a more extraordinary person than has ever appeared in our history. Nature has seldom gifted man with a mind so powerful and comprehensive, or with a body better formed for activity, or capable of enduring greater privations, fatigue, and hardships. She has been equally kind to him in the quality of his heart. General Jackson has no ambition, but for the good of his country; it occupies the whole of his views, to the exclusion of all selfish or ignoble considerations. Cradled in the war of the revolution; nurtured amid the conflicts that afterwards took place between the Cherokee Indians and the Tennesseans, being always among a people who regard the application of force not as the *ultima ratio reguun*, but as the first resort of the individuals; and who look upon courage as the greatest of human attributes, his character on this stormy ocean, has acquired an extraordinary cast of vigor – a belief that any thing within the power of man to accomplish, he should never despair of effecting, and a conviction that courage, activity and perseverance can overcome, what, to an ordinary mind, would appear insuperable obstacles. In society, he is kind, frank, unaffected and hospitable, endowed with much natural grace and politeness, without the mechanical gentility and artificial, flimsy polish, to be found in fashionable life.

Among the people of the west, his popularity is unbounded — old and young speak of him with rapture, and at his call, 50,000 of the most efficient warriors on this continent, would rise, armed, and ready for any enemy.

Having entered the military service of his country at a late period in life, General Jackson appears unaware of the necessity of strict discipline and subordination, and being utterly fearless of responsibility himself, and always taught to believe that his personal liability would be a justification of his conduct, he does not sufficiently reflect how intimately the character of the country is associated with his own, now he is an officer; and that altho' he may freely offer his personal sacrifice, yet it places the government in a most delicate situation to accept it.

_____

From the Augusta Chronicle.

We are informed by an officer of the late expedition, who was left at St. Marks, and who was present at the execution of Francis, that he had in possession when captured, a rifle gun, presented to him by the prince regent, and a tortoise snuff-box set in gold, presented to him by the queen of England; and also a commission of brigadier general in the British service. These facts establish beyond doubt, the alliance and influence of England with the Indians under the jurisdiction of Spain. We have long known the influence the British have had in Florida, as well with the Spanish authorities as the Indians – and that though they were nominally Spanish provinces, yet they were really more under the rule and influence of British agents than the cabinet of Spain.

This proceeded as much, and probably much more, from the inability of Ferdinand than from his acquiescence in or connivance at such measures as have been pursued by the agents of British merchants and trading companies, and confirmed by the officers of Spain, particularly in Pensacola. The Spanish officers and soldiery in Florida have been generally worse paid than any other officers in the world. – It is from this cause, that men who were disposed to act honorably and independently, have been compelled to resign their offices and return home, or commence some other course of life to procure a subsistence: and none but those who have submitted to the baser means of subsisting by speculation and bribery, have been able to hold their offices; this gave occasion to a speculator in that country to say, "every Spaniard had his price." – The English agents saw this and made use of it.

It is from these causes that an agent of a British trading company, (and perhaps the government likewise) procured in 1812, from the governor don Masot, permission to offer in his name through the medium of M'Queen and Opehola, a chief of the Tieliga towns, on the Alabama, a reward of nine dollars for each American scalp that should be brought by the Creek Indians to Pensacola. The English companies have found the trade of this section of the country profitable, and the government have been led to believe that they might make the Creek nation of Indians an ally serviceable to themselves and formidable to the frontier settlers of the state of Georgia, Tennessee, and the Mississippi territory; and to effect this object they have spared neither pains nor expense – the latter from evidences that have come within our knowledge, we think may be moderately estimated at 100,000 dollars a year for the last seven years, and the necessities of the Spanish officers afforded them a ready and open door to effect this purpose.

Many of the officers and soldiers at Augustine have as much as fourteen years pay due them, and those at St. Marks, had some fifteen, some nineteen. When that post was taken possession of by General Jackson, those of Pensacola had been but little better paid, except by the British.

It is from these causes that the British have had such an unbounded influence in the Spanish territories of Florida, and from the ease with which they could place the responsibility on the Spanish authorities, they have used it in the basest manner to excite the Indians to acts of hostility against us – first, from a persuasion that it was impracticable for us to march an army into the country – secondly, that if we should, they would receive succor from the Spanish fortresses on the coast, and that the Americans were a set of robbers who would plunder and extirpate them if in their power, and whom it was right for them to murder and rob at pleasure.

Sufficient evidences of Indian hostility were found in every village the army visited, after leaving Fort Scott, and of the agents of the British government having furnished them with the means of executing their hostile purpose: and the Spanish authorities at St. Marks, acknowledged having supplied them with arms, ammunition, provision and clothing.

The fact of Arbuthnot and Ambristie having excited them to acts of hostility, and having distributed money, ammunition, provision, arms and uniforms to them, were satisfactorily proved; and the philanthropy of Arbuthnot's heart was strongly pourtrayed in a letter to his son directing him to poison his clerk because he was becoming too popular with the Indians.

From the Savannah Republican.

We have been favored with, and had the perusal of, the trial of Arbuthnot and Ambristie, by a military tribunal, on the 28th of April. It is very long, consisting of upwards of sixty pages. We have not permission to publish it; but we will say, that the charges preferred against them were so completely established as not to "leave a loop to hang a doubt"" as to the justice of the sentence. When the facts connected with the execution of these men shall be spread before the world, they will be satisfactory, and conformable to the law of nations. When the letters from Arbuthnot to Mr. Bagot, and the governors of the Bahamas and Havanna, &c. are laid before the American people, they will then see the "cloven hoof" of British influence as plain as the noon day's sun.

[We hope that our friend, Mr. FELL, will obtain ""permission" to publish a paper so interesting.]

Volume 14, August 8, 1818, page 406

Foreign Articles—The Floridas.

We have a loud report, by way of Havanna, that the Floridas have been ceded to the United States. We fear that it is premature. If we recollect aright, it was only about the 27th of April that the negociations with Spain were removed from Washington city to Madrid — it is *possible*, but rather improbable, that so important a subject could have soon been so decided at the latter, though the report adds, that our minister "was on the eve of sailing," (of leaving the Spanish court we presume,) when the cession took place. The National Intelligencer discredits the report— but it is said to be believed by the royal officers at Havanna.

Volume 14, August 15, 1818, page 416

Surrender of Pensacola.

The Aurora informs us that questions to the following import were submitted by the president to the secretaries of state, treasury and war, to which the answers were attached were returned – the first question, the editor says, was warmly supported in the affirmative by one member: --

"1st. May Pensacola be retained, risking all consequences at home and abroad?

2nd. Shall the captured Spanish posts be restored, and General Jackson put on his trial, before a court martial, for a breach of orders, and un-officer like conduct? – or

3rd. Shall the posts be restored, and the acts of General Jackson disavowed, at the same time justifying his motives?

Answer to the 1st – No: it would be declarative war.

To the 2nd – No: it will not appear that the general has violated the spirit of his orders; nor will his conduct be proved unofficer-like.

To the 3rd – Yes: requiring of the Spanish authorities, garrisons adequate to fulfill the requisitions of the treaty between Spain and the United States."

Volume 14, August 8, 1818, page 416

Captain Wright and the Chehaw Village.

Milledgeville,July 28.

Extract of a letter from a gentleman of the first respectability, to the editors of the Georgia Journal, dated

SAVANNAH, July 14th, 1818.

"A letter received at the office of the district attorney, announces the intention of the president to issue a special commission for the trial of captain Wright for murder. In reply, it has been recommended that the trial be postponed to the regular meeting of the circuit court, in December, at this place. Of the circumstances of this unfortunate affair, I really know nothing — but if captain Wright's crime consist merely in a misapprehension of the point of attack, *I trust the state will take care, that he is not over-whelmed by the imposing formality of this prosecution.*"

———

The law of congress, passed in 1802, to regulate trade and intercourse with the Indian tribes, and to preserve peace on the frontiers, under which Captain Wright is to be tried, enacts, that "if any citizen or other person, shall go into any town, settlement, or territory, belonging to any nation or tribe of Indians, or shall there commit murder, by killing any Indian or Indians, belonging to any nation or tribe of Indians in amity with the United States, such offender, on being thereof convicted, shall suffer death." "And when the offender shall be apprehended, or brought for trial into any of the United States, it shall be lawful for the president of the United States to issue a commission to any one or more judges of the supreme court of the United States, and the judge of the district in which such offender may have been apprehended, or shall have been brought for trial; which judges, or any two of them, shall have the same jurisdiction, in such capital cases, as the circuit court of such district, and shall proceed to trial and judgment in the same manner, as such circuit court might, or could do."

For the immediate attainment of the objects of the general government in relation to Captain Wright, the acting attorney of the United States for the district of Georgia, (Mr. Davies having temporarily left the state for the benefit of his health, which has been considerably impaired by an incessant devotion to business) has written to the Creek agent for Indian affairs, we are informed, requesting him to pursue such steps as will authorise the marshal to take Captain Wright into custody; and the governor has been desired to cause him to be delivered to any judicial officer of this county, whenever he shall be demanded by virtue of a warrant from the proper authority, and to detain him till then under his present military arrest. — [*Journal.*

———

Chehaw Village.

When news first reached us of the unfortunate attack on the friendly Indian village of Chehaw, by a party of militia commanded by captain Obed Wright, we expressed our earnest hope that the government would, as far as in its power lay, redress the injuries inflicted on this hapless people.

We are glad to find we were not disappointed in a firm reliance on the just and humane dispositions of those who administer our government.

We now learn from an authentic source, that upon general Jackson's representation of the unauthorised destruction of the Chehaw village, prompt measures were adopted to relieve the sufferers from their distress. The Indian agent (Gov Mitchell,) was directed to assure them, that ample remuneration for their losses would be made. To effect this object, the sum of 10,000 dollars was transmitted to him six weeks ago, accompanied by instructions, to ascertain as speedily as possible, the extent of the injury, and apply the whole of that sum, if necessary, to the relief of the injured and distressed. From a statement lately made in the Georgia papers, it would appear, that the sum would abundantly remunerate them for all their losses.

The agent was also directed to assure the warriors that measures would be immediately adopted to bring the commander of the expedition to trial under the laws of the United States. A commission has accordingly issued to the judges of the federal court, as the Savannah paper has correctly stated, to hold an extra session for his trial.

[*Nat. Int.*

Volume 14, August 15, 1818, page 422

Foreign Articles—Florida.

The Augusta Chronicle, quotes an extract of a letter, received by a gentleman of that place, from a credible source, stating that the two agents of the duke de Allegon, to whom all the unceded lands in East Florida were ceded, had arrived in St. Augustine and claimed the same; and that his excellency governor Coppinger had already placed them in possession of it! They had opened a land office and intended to sell to any purchasers offering! they had also the privilege of purchasing the Indian title to the celebrated Alochaway territory, and had already taken steps to effect the same.

Volume 14, August 8, 1818, page 424

Chronicle—The Seminoles.

We regret to hear that some straggling parties of Indians have lately committed two or three murders, on the frontiers of Georgia. As the nation has sued for peace, we have reason to believe their depredations have now ceased. — They have suffered much by Jackson's campaign, having lost much of their corn and many cattle.

From the Savannah Museum of July 30. There is a rumor in town, that the greater part of the murders committed on the frontier of Wayne and Camden counties, during the last 12 months, were actually perpetrated by a gang of white desperadoes, who had assumed the dress and appearance of Indians, It is said, that altogether there are eight of these new fangled savages, and that two or three of them have been arrested and sent to Milledgeville. We hope, for the honor of humanity, that this report is not true.

General Jackson has partaken of a public dinner at Nashville, on his return from Florida. The party was very numerous and highly respectable. Among others the following toasts were drank —

Major-General Andrew Jackson — His fame is the offspring of his own merit. While our armies are directed by the energies of his genius, we have nothing to fear from foreign aggression.

Pensacola— Spanish perfidy and Indian barbarity, rendered its capture necessary. May our government never surrender it from the fear of war.

Tennessee volunteers — The signal for their march, is their country's call. They are always victorious — strangers to defeat.

The Kentucky volunteers — They have shewn themselves superior to the influence of prejudice. They are brave, and merit the applause of their country.

Volunteer by gen. Jackson — *Our country*: Though forbearance is her maxim, she should shew foreign nations, that under a pretence of neutrality, her rights are not to be outraged.

Volume 14, August 22, 1818, pages 439-440

Elopement of Captain Wright.

This ill-guided man has violated his parole of honor, and fled.— The following is from the Georgia Journal of the 4th inst.

Captain Wright, of noted memory,

has broken his parole of honor, and absconded. On the 26th ult. (the day previous to his disappearing) he addresses the following note to the governor:

"Sir — On the 28th of May last, I was arrested by order of your excellency. Since that time I have waited in the expectation, that a court martial would be ordered for my trial. No charge has yet been made its appearance against me. I therefore pray that your excellency against me. I therefore pray that your excellency would withdraw the arrest. If you should think proper not to do so, suffer me to call and see you, as I have business of importance.
     (Signed)   OBED WRIGHT.

To this communication, no answer was returned. His fears, we understand, were considerably excited by the premature statement in the Savannah Republican, of the determination of the president of the United States to have him tried before the federal court for murder. Dreading a long and loathsome imprisonment in jail, and probably apprehending from the "hue and cry" which had been raised against him, that his conduct would not be impartially investigated, he took the fatal resolution to flee from justice.

A reward of $500, has been offered by the executive for his apprehension. The deputy marshal and assistant agent for Indian affairs, arrived here on Thursday with a warrant to take him into the custody of the civil authority – but the "bird had flown."

Obed Wright is supposed to be about 30 years of age, 5 feet 11 inches high, slender, trim built, said to be very active, fair complexion, light blue eyes, and light brown hair.

———

A *proclamation*, by his excellency William Rabun, governor and commander in chief of the army and navy of the state of Georgia, and of the militia thereof—

Whereas, captain Obed Wright, late of the Georgia militia, was on the 29th day of May last, arrested and confined by the executive authority of this state, for a violation of orders, in the commission of an outrage on the friendly Indians of the Chehaw village, in order that the determination of the president of the United States with regard to the manner in which he should be tried for said offence should be known: And whereas I have received information, that the said Obed Wright did on the night of the 27th inst. break his said arrest, and abscond from the place of his confinement and probably from this state: I have therefore thought proper to issue this proclamation, hereby offering a reward of five hundred dollars, to any person or persons, who may apprehend the said Obed Wright, and deliver him into the custody of the deputy marshal of the United States, for the district of Georgia, residing at Milledgeville. — And I do moreover, hereby require and command, all officers, civil and military, to be vigilant and attentive, in endeavoring to apprehend and secure the aforesaid Obed Wright, if to be found within this state; and to give all aid and assistance in their power, to any person or persons, who may apprehend him for confinement, in order that he may be brought to trial for the crime of which he is charged.

Given under my hand and the great seal of the state, at the state house in Milledgeville, this thirtieth day of July, in the year of our Lord one thousand eight hundred and eighteen, and of the independence of the United States of America the forty-third.
     WM. RABUN.
By the governor,
AB. HAMMOND, secretary of state.

━━➤➤➤☻◉☻◀◀◀━━

Recommended Reading

- Adams, John Quincy. *Message from The President of the United States, Transmitting, in Pursuance of a Resolution of the House of Representatives, Such Further Information, in Relation to Our Affairs with Spain, as, in His Opinion, is Not Inconsistent With the Public Interest to Divulge.* E. De Kraft. Washington. 1819

- A Lieutenant of the Left Wing. *Sketch of the Seminole War, and Sketches During a Campaign.* Dan J. Dowling. Charleston. 1836.

- Ballentine, George. *Autobiography of an English Soldier in the United States Army. Comprising Observations and Adventures in the States and Mexico.* Stringer & Townsend. New York. 1853.

- Barr, James. *A Correct and Authentic Narrative of the Indian War in Florida, with a Description of Maj. Dade's Massacre, and an Account of the Extreme Suffering for Want of Provisions of the Army—Having Been Obliged to East Horses and Dogs' Flesh, &c. &c.* J. Narine. New York. 1836.

- Campbell, Richard L. *Historical Sketches of Colonial Florida.* The Williams Publishing Co. Cleveland, Ohio. 1892.

- Coe, Charles H. *Red Patriots: The Story of the Seminoles.* The Editor Publishing Company. Cincinnati. 1898.

- Cohen, M. M. (An Officer of the Left Wing). *Notices of Florida and The Campaigns.* Burges & Honour. Charleston, S. C. 1836.

- Eaton, John Henry. *The Life of Major General Andrew Jackson: Comprising a History of the War in the South; from the Commencement of the Creek Campaign to the Termination of Hostilities Before New Orleans. Addenda: Containing a Brief History of the Seminole War, and Cession and Government of Florida.* Third Edition.— Revised and Corrected by the Author. M'Carty & Davis. Philadelphia. 1828.

- Ellicott, Andrew, *The journal of Andrew Ellicott, : late commissioner on behalf of the United States during part of the year 1796, the years 1797, 1798, 1799, and part of the year 1800: for determining the boundary between the United States and the possessions of His Catholic Majesty in America.* William Fry. Philadelphia, 1814.

- Forbes, James Grant. *Sketches, Historical and Topographical, of The Floridas; More Particularly of East Florida.* C. S. Van Winkle. New York. 1821.

- Giddings, Joshua R. *The Exiles of Florida: or, The Crimes committed by Our Government against the Maroons, Who Fled from South Carolina and Other Slave States, Seeking Protection Under Spanish Laws.* Follett, Foster and Company. Columbus, Ohio. 1858.

- Hitchcock, Ethan Allen. *Fifty Years in Camp and Field, Diary of Major-General Ethan Allen Hitchcock,* G.P. Putnam's Sons. New York, 1909.

- Latour, A. LaCarriere. *History Memoir of The War in West Florida and Louisiana in 1814-15, with an Atlas.* John Conrad and Co. Philadelphia. 1816.

- McCall, George A. *Letters From The Frontiers, Written During a Period of Thirty Years' Service in the Army of the United States.* J. B. Lippincott & Co. Philadelphia. 1868.

- Narrator, Anonymous. *Narrative of a Voyage to the Spanish Main, in the Ship "Two Friends;" The occupation of Amelia Island, by M'Gregor, &c.— Sketches of the Province of East Florida; and Anecdotes Illustrative of the Habits and Manners of the Seminole Indians: with an Appendix, Containing a Detail of the Seminole War, and the Execution of Arbuthnot and Ambrister.* (Printed for John Miller, Burlington Arcade, Piccadilly.) W. Wilson. London. 1819.

- Onis, Luis De. *Memoir Upon the Negotiation Between Spain and The United States of America, Which Led to the Treaty of 1819. With a statistical notice of that country. Accompanied with an appendix, containing important documents for the better illustration of the subject.* Fielding Lucas, Jr. Baltimore. 1821.

- Parton, James. *Life of Andrew Jackson: in Three Volumes.* [Vol. 1] [Vol. 2] [Vol. 3] Mason Brothers. New York. 1860.

- Potter, Woodburne (A Late Staff Officer). *The War in Florida: An Exposition of Its Causes, and an Accurate History of the Campaigns of Generals Clinch, Gaines and Scott.* Lewis and Coleman. Baltimore. 1836.

- Senate of the United States. *Proceedings of the Military Court of Inquiry, in the Case of Major General Scott and Major General Gaines.* United States Congress. Washington, D. C. 1837.

- Simmons, William Hayne. *Notices of East Florida, With An Account of the Seminole Nation of Indians, by a Recent Traveller in the Province.* A. E. Miller. Charleston. 1822.

- Sprague, John T. *The Origin, Progress, and Conclusion of the Florida War.* D. Appleton & Company. New York. 1847.

- United States War Department, United States Congress. House. Committee on Indian Affairs. *Treaty with the Florida Indians.* Sub-title: *letter from the Secretary of War, transmitting the information required by a resolution of the House of Representatives, of the 5th ultimo, in relation to the instructions given* to the commissioners for negotiating with the Florida Indians, &c. &c. "February 6, 1826. Read, and referred to the Committee on Indian Affairs." Treaty concluded Sept. 18, 1823. Gales & Seaton. 1826.

- Van Ness, William P. (Aristides). *A Concise Narrative of General Jackson's First Invasion of Florida, and of His Immortal Defence of New-Orleans: With Remarks.* Second Edition—with Additions. E. M. Murden & A. Ming, Jr. New-York. 1827.

- Vignoles, Charles. *Observations Upon The Floridas.* E. Bliss & E. White. New York. 1823.

- Williams, John Lee. *The Territory of Florida: or Sketches of the Topography, Civil and Natural History, of the Country, the Climate, and the Indian Tribes, from the First Discovery to the Present Time, with a Map, Views, &c.* A. T. Goodrich. New York. 1837.

- Williams, John Lee. *A View of West Florida, Embracing Its Geography, Topography, &c. With An Appendix, Treating of Its Antiquities, Land Titles, and Canals, and Containing a Map, Exhibiting a Chart of the Coast, a Plan of Pensacola, and the Entrance of the Harbor.* L. R. Bailey. Philadelphia. 1827

—•·)))⊖ 🔘 ⊖(((·•—

⎯•⫸☻◉☻⫷•⎯

www.ingramcontent.com/pod-product-compliance
Lightning Source LLC
Chambersburg PA
CBHW060009100426
42740CB00010B/1444